I0823890

What Persists

Georgia Review Books ⸎ Edited by Stephen Corey

What Persists

Selected Essays on Poetry from *The Georgia Review*, 1988–2014

JUDITH KITCHEN

The University of Georgia Press *Athens*

Athens, Georgia 30602
www.ugapress.org

Designed by Melissa Bugbee Buchanan
Set in Adobe Garamond Pro
Printed and bound by Sheridan Books

The paper in this book meets the guidelines for permanence and durability of the Committee on Production Guidelines for Book Longevity of the Council on Library Resources.

Most University of Georgia Press titles are available from popular e-book vendors.

Printed in the United States of America

20 19 18 17 16 C 5 4 3 2 1

Library of Congress Cataloging-in-Publication Data
Names: Kitchen, Judith.
Title: What persists : selected essays on poetry from The Georgia Review, 1988-2014 / Judith Kitchen.
Description: Athens : The University of Georgia Press, 2016.
Identifiers: LCCN 2015032703 | ISBN 9780820349312 (hardcover : alk. paper) | ISBN 9780820349305 (ebook)
Subjects: LCSH: Poetry.
Classification: LCC PS3561. I845 A6 2016 | DDC 814/.54—dc23
LC record available at http://lccn.loc.gov/2015032703

What Persists was made possible in part by the generous gifts from the friends, fans, and family of Judith Kitchen.

Mary C. Blew
Nancy Boutilier
Kevin Clark
Jennifer Culkin
David Huddle
Nancy Geyer
Greg Glazner
Kate Carol De Gutes
Rebecca McClanahan
Gerry McFarland
Kent Meyers
Kay Mullen
Scott Nadelson
Ann Whitfield Powers
Lia Purpura
Christine Robbins
Stanley Rubin
Marjorie Sandor
Hilary J. Schaper
Tina Schumann
Kathi R. Shannon
Peggy Shumaker
Joseph Usibelli
Georgia Whitney
And anonymous friends.

Contents

Foreword

And the Kitchen Sink: Judith Kitchen's Vision of American Poetry, 1988–2014

STEPHEN COREY

FIRST WE NEVER THOUGHT it could last so long, and then we came to think it would never end; we were wrong on both counts.

In 1991, *Georgia Review* editor Stanley W. Lindberg announced that Judith Kitchen and Fred Chappell would be regular essay-reviewers of new poetry for the journal, each producing two substantial commentaries per year. Judith's invitation was made on the strength of "Speaking Passions" (Summer 1988)—which leads off this book—and "A Want Ad" (Spring/Summer 1990), both produced during the time when we were "auditioning" replacements for Peter Stitt, who reviewed poetry for the *Review* from 1977–87 before departing to edit a new literary journal, *The Gettysburg Review*.

Fred supplied fine discussions through 1997, at which time he stepped down to give more time to other pursuits. Judith, however, kept going . . . and going . . . and going, even through many years of uncertain health brought on by two potentially fatal conditions. In late October of 2014, from an intensive-care hospital bed in Seattle, Judith made final revisions to "Da Capo al Coda," her study of first books by five promising poets of widely varying ages for our Winter 2014 issue. On 6 November 2014, at the age of exactly seventy-three years and three months—she became in 1945 a "Hiroshima" baby—Judith died at home with her longtime husband Stanley Rubin close at hand. After Judith's death, with Stan's blessing, I added "Da Capo al Coda" to the book because it really does represent her "final" word in more ways than one. Also, to complete the record, I created an Appendix entry for her penultimate essay, "When the River Is Ice" (Summer 2014).

Across twenty-seven years, Judith wrote some fifty lengthy essay-reviews for

The Georgia Review, with the emphasis on *essay*. John Stilgoe, one of the outside readers for this book, called Judith Kitchen "one of the two or three leading poetry critics in the United States and one of the five or so in the English-speaking world." *What Persists* is aptly and accurately titled, because Judith did not dash off journalistic reviews meant to be held in mind only until another round of the same popped up from some other hand a week or a month later. Judith's essaying of American poetry is always mindfully broad-sweeping *and* minutely particular, always so wisely and passionately crafted that it manages to speak engagingly and instructively to both expert and neophyte readers.

The Georgia Review and the literary world have been inevitably diminished by the loss of Judith Kitchen's voice, and I am personally saddened that Judith did not live to see this book come off the presses. I had told her for years that I believed her essay-reviews deserved publication as a body of work, and when *The Georgia Review* and the University of Georgia Press reached an agreement in 2013 for a *Review*-generated book series I knew exactly what the inaugural title should be. In early 2014 Judith herself made the selection of pieces and wrote her introduction, and then at my suggestion she created—beautifully and effectively—the appendix that gives thumbnail sketches of all her other essay-reviews and is, literally, a vital part of the collection.

Judith opened that initiating 1988 study, "Speaking Passions," with a comment from the literary critic Leslie Fiedler about Randall Jarrell (1914–62), widely regarded as one of the great poetry critics of the twentieth century:

> Jarrell is everywhere the man who has *just* read something he loves or hates, sometimes the man baffled by what surprised him into admiration or exacerbated him beyond patience by its ineptitude; but always the man speaking his passion, rather than an embodied institution pronouncing judgment. He is resolutely unsystematic, committed to no methodology or aesthetic theory—responsible only to his own responses, hushed only before the mystery of his own taste.

Judith offered this quote not to compare herself with Jarrell but to try to indicate the kind of poetry discussion she loved and hoped to conduct; I repeat it both to claim that she achieved, again and again, what she hoped *and* to assert that she has been as vital a voice for poetry for her decades as Jarrell was for his.

Author's Preface

WHAT WOULD MAKE ANYONE continue to review poetry for going on three decades? I asked myself this question as I was selecting my own "selected." Two hundred thirty-seven books, or an average of around 9.5 books per year; for every one reviewed, at least three more read; for every book read, at least another three considered. We're into the thousands. My answer seems so simple: I've enjoyed it. From the time I was small, I had a passion for poetry, reciting it as I flew up and down in the swing. In junior high, I had a fierce argument about Frost's "Mending Wall" with my Uncle Willy. In high school, I once "taught" a class on Keats's "Ode on a Grecian Urn" that was, I now suspect, roundly unpopular. In college, I was elated with the close reading that opened the work of Elizabeth Bishop, Robert Lowell, and John Berryman even as it was just being published. When I began writing, I turned to poetry first, and only after that to nonfiction. So my tenure as a reviewer for *The Georgia Review* has been a natural extension of my ongoing interests. Over the years, I've enjoyed thinking about what poetry can do, about what each book I looked at did, or did not, accomplish. I've enjoyed encountering new voices; and I've enjoyed assessing new work by established writers. I've loved writing the introductory material, finding topics, gimmicks, whatever—an umbrella under which the essay-review could help me to see different poets from a new perspective.

Most of all, I've enjoyed the freedom to be who I am, to break all my own rules, to be cantankerous and celebratory in the same review. For this collection, I've selected eighteen, approximately forty percent of my output in the past twenty-five years. These essay-reviews represent the range of my taste. They also reveal a cultural history from the dismantling of the Berlin Wall, through 9/11 and the Iraq War, into today's political climate. They chronicle my personal interests while they also make note of what was happening in contemporary poetry. Cumulatively, they reflect a larger context.

I had always felt that I knew more about poetry than I was able to articulate, and it was Stanley W. Lindberg, then editor of *The Georgia Review*, who gave me the opportunity to learn how to talk about work that excited me. In 1990, I was paired with Fred Chappell, each of us writing two in-depth reviews per year. I read Fred's reviews avidly, wishing I could see what he saw, say what he said. Maybe the most agonizing fun I've ever had were the long phone conversations with Stan as, together, we sorted out my cries that "that was not what I meant at all." We argued over commas, semicolons, word choices, you name it, and at least I was able to reject the word "whomsoever," which I said would never—ever—come out of my mouth. But I was grateful for the chance to learn how to say what was on my mind.

So now, after a quarter century, I look back. Early on, for the Fall 1991 issue, I talked about the act of reviewing itself:

> Essentially there are two kinds of reviews: those that tend to categorize and those that offer a "reading." The former passes down a "verdict." The latter does not attempt to judge in terms of abstract ideas, but rather attempts to show the reader why a particular work is worthy of attention, and to suggest what sort of attention the work demands. In such a reading, often a pattern or shape will emerge as the reviewer attempts to map the contours of the writer's imagination; at the same time, the aim of the review is to open this particular landscape to as many others as may wish to follow. Such a review should open responses rather than close them.

Clearly I was sorting out just who I wanted to be, and I know now that I most definitely wanted to become the latter type of reviewer. I wanted to discover what I was thinking as I wrote, and I wanted to feel my way toward a full sense of what was important in and about the poems. Over time, I learned more and more how to respect the writer's cues. This came about, in part, because of another astute editor at *GR*—Stephen Corey. I have him to thank for the fact that my dictionary is now far more ragged at the edges, and the fact that I have learned the need to clarify just about everything I think I've already said. Over the years, his penetrating questions have made me go back in to make it new again. He has been my staunchest supporter and harshest critic—and every critic (like every poet) needs both.

My generation has lived in a comparatively dull time for poetry. After the great modernist movement, after the confessionals and post-confessionals, just where could poetry take us next? Not surprising that confession devolved to "story," followed by a retreat into new formalism. Not surprising that the line lost some of its power or that experimentation was relatively mild, that we ended up with L=A=N=G=U=A=G=E poetry as our only true "movement." Not surprising that, as theory invaded the academy and the ranks of critics thinned, the two would seem almost interchangeable. As early as the Winter 1997 issue, I had had my fill:

> The cleverness with which many of [the critics] treat the poetry they talk about is terrifying. . . . Such sentences as "The phrases seek a continuum of organic time, always mindful that what is organic is gendered" and "My analysis of metaphoric configurations . . . suggests the subtle but precise permutations of signification that occur through historical markings within metaphoric significance" use scholarly discourse to perpetuate certain assumptions—that the reader already agrees with the statement and that the critic's job is simply to point out the instances where it applies. As with so much of this sort of writing, the style is so dense as to be almost impenetrable. Those reviews functioned . . . as places where the critic could show off a kind of knowledge that helps neither writer nor reader.

Dullness has its advantages. It enables you to see what stands out—and why. It allows for retrospection and prediction. You can see the forest and the trees.

So what do I make of my efforts over the years? I see that over time my reviews became more assured. I also see that the early reviews have a kind of energy I now envy. I realize that my taste in poetry has changed over time. The more I learned about craft, the more I admired poets who were masters at rhythm, or slant rhyme, and forms used so subtly you almost didn't notice, then did. Naturally, my taste in content changed as well. Where before I had been hungry for a poem as expansive as Lowell's "The Quaker Graveyard in Nantucket," now I find myself drawn to quiet lyrics that catch me unawares. I've enjoyed charting my discoveries, and I can only hope that my readings have helped both writer and reader alike.

Throughout, I was encouraged to discuss work by older and younger American poets who were not yet part of the contemporary "canon." In short, I was given free rein, and I took it. I used my personal life and my other interests as background music; I held the poetry I was reading up to that light, to see just what role poetry played. And now, gritted teeth and pulled hair aside, I see that my struggle to "get it right" has paid off with my own oddball brand of criticism. I came at poetry from every possible angle, tackling a little bit of everything, including poets from other countries: Australia, Wales, Ireland, Hungary, Norway, Israel, Jordan. I took the liberty to review novels, essays, novels in verse, prose by poets, anthologies, letters, even volumes of selected poems. I commented on prizes and awards, the academy, readings, quotations, other reviews—all the requisite ephemera that constitute the life of poetry. I revisited the work of Robert Lowell when the *Collected Poems* came out; I revisited Sylvia Plath when she became the topic of a book on women; I introduced reviews by talking about Frost, Pound, Stevens, along with Margaret Anderson's *Little Review*, and I was able to muse about grandchildren, soccer, snow, rain, landscape, spies, politics, science, family anecdotes, my own illness—all in the service of the poems I was reading.

What do these selected essay-reviews say about poetry today? At the very least, they show what a wide range of poetry is being written—by women, men, poets who celebrate their ethnicity, poets who show a fierce individualism, poets whose careers have soared, promising poets whose work has all but disappeared. I see poets whose work I admired suddenly being recognized years later. I even see a resurgence of interest in poets who died over the course of my tenure. I hope to have been a source for some of this renewed enthusiasm. There were several poets I looked at more than once, and I felt it was my obligation to note whether they were changing direction, deepening an aesthetic, or possibly just marking time. Some poets have one great book in them; some have more, and then more. Some continue to write what they have always written well. Some change gear, rev up, move into new territory. And I have had the wonderful opportunity to delve into—and comment on—it all.

How did I make my selections? I had to make sacrifices, including discussions of poets whose work I admire, even revere. In the end, I took the straightforward route and chose to retain the recognizable essay-reviews as opposed to the more eccentric variations. I decided to represent nearly every year with the widest variety of poets I could muster, hoping that time alone would speak for the future health of our nation's poetry. I tried to ring the changes on the specific topics with which I began my reviews, omitting those that seemed to me to be most dated. But I couldn't resist adding an appendix to offer a bit of their flavor and provide information on other books and writers I had found myself discussing. Perhaps readers will find something there.

So thank you, Stephen, for persisting with those persistent questions. You made me think around the edges of my own claims. And thanks also to my husband, Stan Rubin, who was always there to force me past my vagueness into something that resembles insight.

Speaking Passions

On William Stafford's *An Oregon Message*; Heather McHugh's *To The Quick* and *Shades*; Linda Pastan's *The Imperfect Paradise*; Brigit Pegeen Kelly's *To the Place of Trumpets*; and Li-Young Lee's *Rose*.

ON THE BACK COVER of Randall Jarrell's *Poetry and Age*, Leslie Fiedler writes, "Jarrell is everywhere the man who has *just* read something he loves or hates, sometimes the man baffled by what surprised him into admiration or exacerbated him beyond patience by its ineptitude; but always the man speaking his passion, rather than an embodied institution pronouncing judgment. He is resolutely unsystematic, committed to no methodology or aesthetic theory—responsible only to his own responses, hushed only before the mystery of his own taste." This description would jar many contemporary reviewers who try to *be* systematic, who commit themselves to methodology or theory and would love to have the authority of institutions. In fact, contemporary reviewers often act more like theorists; the would-be reviewer sheds his or her passion in favor of a dispassionate academic approach. Fiedler's quote, it seems to me, is a pretty good description of what a reviewer ought to be, but seldom is. The risk of taste is the mark of the reviewer who puts his or her responses on the line, knowing that history may or may not support that position. What matters more is the dialogue he or she enters into (however silent) with other readers—readers not of the *reviewer's* work, but the specific book(s) being discussed. Such a reviewer *assumes* other readers, and other passions.

Each book has its own territory, and that territory deserves to be entered on its own terms. The ideal review does not limit a book by looking only at one aspect or attempting to compare the book with books by other authors. It may, of course, be relevant to compare a new book to an author's earlier books, to look at how the new work extends the vision or moves in new directions. And it may also be informative to place a writer within a larger literary tradition by noting similarities with well-known predecessors. But the reviewer should not necessarily take on the role of the critic or theorist. The reviewer's major job is to chronicle the present tense; it is the task of criticism and theory to reflect on what has already happened and/or what might be about to happen.

The last line of Fiedler on Jarrell reads, "And what unfailing taste he possessed." But Jarrell cared most about reading, and about an idealized interested public who would care about his caring, leaving it to history to characterize his taste (in the form of Leslie Fiedler and others), just as he left it to the readers to enter the world of the poetry he discussed. "Responsible only to his own responses," he demonstrated a love for poetry and a passion for reading. Isn't this what most of us are still looking for?

Over the years, William Stafford has given us such a consistent voice and vision that it is difficult to tell the poems in *An Oregon Message* from the poems that appeared over twenty-five years ago in *West of Your City*. Because of this "mix-and-match" quality, William Stafford should be read in large doses—several books at a time—so that his readers can perceive the vastly larger picture which emerges from the intricately woven tapestry of a lifetime's work. Like Wallace Stevens before him, Stafford has built a "language," an interlocking set of images through which one can enter his imaginative spaces. Unlike Stevens, he uses a seemingly transparent, even commonplace, vocabulary. Words and images are repeated from poem to poem, and book to book. It takes accumulated reading to understand the complexity of his vision. So, if one has to choose a place to begin—and begin one must—Stafford's latest book would be a good choice. *An Oregon Message* is an extension of Stafford's central vision and, at the same time, a return to its roots.

An Oregon Message flagrantly blends the humorous, the nostalgic, and the prophetic. It reveals a more didactic side of Stafford, as though he is less willing to let time do its work for him. The messages are gentle, often playful, but always carry the bite of truth. Its first "message" is found in the form of a prose statement preceding the poems, where Stafford—calling his poems "organically grown"—defends his method against what must be seen as hidden critics. "I must be willingly fallible in order to deserve a place in the realm where miracles happen," he writes. Why should Stafford feel compelled to state this at such a late stage in his career? The answer may lie in the new way this book includes the reader as part of its subject matter, thus asking the reader to be fallible with him.

Beginning with a section entitled "The Book About You," Stafford equates the "I" of the poems with the "You" of the title. His life is your life—or very like it. In this way, he allows you to take on his perspective, and his wit. He begins to have fun. He burns books: "Truth, brittle and faint, burns easily, / its fire as hot as the fire lies make—/ flame doesn't care." He confesses, "I let history happen—sorry." He lets out all the stops in "Thinking About Being Called Simple by a Critic," where he alludes first to William Carlos Williams by opening: "I wanted the plums, but I waited." Then, sitting in the dark, he identifies with his critic, agrees with him, finds his own life "so simple there was no way / back into qualifying my thoughts / with irony or anything like that." This playful side of Stafford dominates the first section of the book, then serves as an undercurrent throughout.

What the critic missed in calling Stafford "simple" is a realization of just how deep he is, how serious he can be. This is a serious book—perhaps Stafford's best since *The Rescued Year*—and it goes back to some of his original material with renewed urgency. It reexamines and reaffirms his moral commitments to pacifism and social justice (as in "Serving with Gideon," which unforgettably examines his own near-complicity with racism). It looks at the past—especially his family—and tries to reconcile the polarities of father (patience) and mother (judgment) that have characterized Stafford's earlier work. It continues his concerns for the land, and for how we will use our technologies. And it affirms that, like the bush from Mongolia whose roots will not relax, "some of us have to be ready." What we must be ready for, Stafford does not make clear, but he does suggest an eventual merging of self with the elements—a transcendence far less rhetorical than Whitman's and far more convincing that Emerson's:

> . . . that river divides more than
> Two sides of your life. The only way
> Is farther, breathing that country, becoming
> Wise in its flavor, a native of the sun.
> ("Looking for Gold")

One of the best poems in the book is "1940"—a poem that recalls his most anthologized poem, "Traveling Through the Dark," in both its content and its formal structures, but most in its shiver of premonition:

> *1940*
>
> It is August. Your father is walking you
> to the train for camp and then the War
> and on out of his life, but you don't know.

Little lights along the path glow under their hoods
and your shoes go brown, brown in the brightness
till the next interval, when they disappear in the shadow.

You know they are down there, by the crunch of stone
and a rustle when they touch a fern. Somewhere above,
cicadas arch their gauze of sound all over town.

Shivers of summer wind follow across the park
and then turn back. You walk on toward
September, the depot, the dark, the light, the dark.

Stafford insists on making this a universal poem. It is *your father* walking *you*. Moving through time and space, this poem reconstructs both a personal and a societal history. Sound reveals what sight cannot, and the "gauze of sound" that is the poem transports poet and reader alike into a place where the only thing you can be certain of is uncertainty: "but you don't know." Is this a moment of hindsight? Or is it a man's continual state as he hovers on the verge of the future? Or is it the writer's trigger for imagination? With characteristic deftness, Stafford allows for each of these—and more.

Stafford's metaphor for the daily practice of writing (where one is most open to uncertainty) is found in "Run Before Dawn":

Most mornings I get away, slip out
the door before light, set forth on the dim, gray
road, letting my feet find a cadence
that softly carries me on.

The poem goes on to describe what he passes, what passes him, what dream he finds himself in. It ends in the solitary vision of the creation of the poem:

These journeys are quiet. They mark my days with
adventure too precious for anyone else to share, little
gems of darkness, the world going by, and my breath, and the road.

For William Stafford, the morning "run" over the blank page is a way of living. He faces himself in mirror after mirror, learning to "own" his own face more. Perhaps this is because, after starting at his eventual death (certainly the largest theme in *A Glass Face in the Rain*, 1982), he has opted for continued life. *An Oregon Message* is filled with quiet joy—there is even a poem called "Why I am Happy." Like the lie detector that proclaims a constant truth, the heart makes its own optimistic sound: "saying 'Now,' saying 'Yes,' / saying, 'Here.'"

What fascinates me most about this book is a blurring of time which demands the participation of the reader. Past, present, and future fuse into a timelessness in which all good things can—and will—happen. Stafford hands these moments to us with a written gesture. Multiple tenses merge to create a link between the poet's personal reflective time and the reader's present; a new "present tense" is established on the page in the act of reading:

> You who come years from now to this brief spell
> of nothing that was mine: the open, slow passing
> of time was a gift going by. I have to put my hand out
> on the mane of the wind, like this, to give it to you.
> ("Little Rooms")

> How who you are made a difference once
> but the wind blew, changing everything
> gradually to here, and it is today.
> ("Figuring Out How It Is")

Stafford's weighted vocabulary hovers on the border of metaphysics. Key words (*dark*, *wind*, *hand*, *listen*, *far*, to name a few) surface over and over, acquiring special meanings that, after successive appearances, start to become clear. One must be careful not to reduce this vocabulary to a simple series of equations or to attempt to harness it into a "system." Still, the poems deepen with this extended, charged usage. The word *listen*, for example, is equated with a receptivity that generates poetry itself, and any aspect of listening carries with it that extra meaning. Thus, the reader discerns just a bit more than a faltering piano in "Practice": "Maybe your stumbling / saves you, and that sound in the night is more than the wind."

Some critics (like the one in this poem) have been calling Stafford "simple" for a long time. It's too bad they haven't taken the time to read the body of work and to see how his interlocking images provide a key for reading the poems on several levels at once. Stafford is a major poet—and he has yet to receive proper critical attention. He is stubbornly simple, but not simplistic. This book is ample evidence that this senior figure, of the generation of Lowell and Berryman, has continued to write remarkable poetry. *An Oregon Message* will surprise any reader who thinks of Stafford as a Northwestern myth-spinner. Despite its title, this is not a book of place, but of imagination. Its language is alive, challenging the reader to enter its many dimensions with mind as well as heart.

Two books with the feel of one—that's what Heather McHugh has produced over the last year. These are distinct volumes, each with its own integrity, yet one flows easily into the next and they inform each other in important ways. Both spring from the same source and from the same desire for explanation. Even their titles tell us this is a matter of life and death.

To the Quick is concerned with motion, with relativity. McHugh's physics go beyond the physical into the realm of the emotional ("Earth / has our own great ranges / of feeling—"). Movement itself causes speculation: " . . . the whole night long on the highway, moved, I'll have // a moon to keep me company, as still / as I am, in the glass, while trees and signs and homes keep racing // toward the past. What's staying / anyway? What's going on? . . ." Everything is slippery, and the only thing more slippery than love is the language we use to speak it. Wordplay is the norm for McHugh, but the puns, the twists, the double-entendres are all used, in the end, to call attention to the change—and to the very way that naming calls something into question:

> We put our signature on everything—we draw the line
> at skin for different, at the heart for dead; but now and then
> the EKG machine goes on
> all by itself. There was a time
> we really sang, forgetting differences, and when we did
> the air itself would seem alive—but then
>
> we fell back into dream; our definitions froze.
> ("What We Call Living")

What's dead, here, is love. But it won't stay dead; it rears its ugly, one-sided head and won't let go. *To the Quick* rages against a particular lover, several perverted aspects of love, and the body that harbors unrequited passions, as well as against memory that fixes love, locking it forever into time and place. And yet . . . if you hold this mirror up to see your breath, there it is—proof that you're alive.

What's really alive here is language—and a quick mind receptive to its contradictions, aware of all its facets, intrigued by how it holds itself together. Chance is as good as rule:

> For a second the word express appears
> in an apposition to the word espresso (that's
> what happy is about) and then
>
> the bus is gone from the coffee-house door.
> Again you're in the luckless world, world
> without fortune, where you swear to do
> something unspeakable
> if one more person mentions consciousness.
> ("Capital")

This is a chance world, where neither love nor life are guaranteed forever. One poem, written in memoriam for poet Mitchell Toney, takes off the veneer of language and asks the question from the heart: "What could we say to you / while you died?" The answer seems to be—nothing. Silence is the only language that can take in death. Words skitter away, dragging their baggage of meaning, and, in the face of death, will not suffice.

Each section of *To the Quick* leads off with delicate poems inspired by (and near-translations of) the French poems of Rilke. At once sensuous and wary, these "after Rilke" poems not only set a tone but also provide a perspective from which McHugh can explore her own world. For example, opening the final section is one of these short poems suggesting how the natural world and the world of love diverge: "The fruit is heavier to bear / than flowers seem to be. / But that's a lover talking, / not a tree." And McHugh's final poem in the book extends this theme, building on an earlier image—a starfish which the poet has returned to the sea rather than send it to an old lover. Reminiscent of Elizabeth Bishop's "The Fish," McHugh's "The Matte Over" gives a careful, detailed description of the starfish before she throws it back to a world "the sighted have no rights to." Unlike Bishop's letting go, however, this is not a joyous act of affirmation, but a resignation.

The second book, *Shades*, pulls away from obsessive love, struggling with the larger issues of grief and self-definition. The first third of the book moves from the fact of the death of a friend to the accompanying crisis of faith. It's hard to question a faith in science, but this book starts with the universe and unravels it down to the atom, leaving question after question in its wake. In the end, a sense of self is what is at stake:

> . . . I can't locate
> my old self, young self, you know who—
> my one-and-only, be-all-end-all,
> my intended and my ex, the one I was
> most smitten with . . .
>
> ("Round Time")

The middle third of the book tries to reconstruct the self—a self built mostly on words, and its knowledge that the words shed meanings as rapidly as they gain them. It is a slippery, wily self that must be wheedled and willed into existence:

> Language wasn't any
> funny money I was playing with,
> no toy surprise, no watch or wooden
> nickel, not
> a nickel nickel either, twice

removed, sign of a sign.
I meant to make
so deep a song

it held no end of love.
("Inflation")

If the poet is honest—and there *is* honesty in this play with words—the old love and rage and rage to love must surface. There is a putting-to-rest in *Shades*, but it is angrier and more knowing than that in *To the Quick*. Intimate knowledge of death is brought to bear on the dying of love.

The play with words that often unlocks the meaning of the world can also be a way of holding the world at bay. *Shades* moves into a new phase in its final third; the poems take a good hard look at this world, piling image upon image without the characteristic sheen of language at play. The poems are fascinating, but the balance is precarious. They are dense, descriptive, as though desperate to prove that the five senses can make a larger sense. If there are shades of meaning, they are discovered in juxtaposition of image or in the flow of idea rather than in the quick mind's skittery relativism:

for now, it's five AM, before the break
of day, before a soul would even think
to subdivide the sun, and mourning doves are casting old
consoling silvers down from trees, and even last night's trash is washed
by cool light in the street. In this cafe, unhurried, one can find
a steadiness of commonplaces to be grateful for: the coffee's
regular (as sure as shit, Maggie would say): the sweetpea
winding back and forth along
the cordwork of a southern window
testifies to minor lights and little luxuries;
the baby has a piece of toast. It's all her own.
("Forecast")

Whereas *To the Quick* plays with language in order to release emotion, *Shades* examines language as the possible source of the problem: "Just think of it / and you surround it with // its opposite." *Shades* opens with a poem "about" (though the poem itself warns that her poems are "not / about about") a plane flight; "20–200 on 747" acknowledges Derridian theory—"Just / whose story is this anyway? Out of my mind // whose words emerge? Is there a self the self // surpasses?" The book ends on another flight where meaning does, in fact, seem possible—seen from the right perspective:

. . . Earth's underlying
nature might be likeness—
likeness everywhere disguised

by wave-length, amplitude and frequency.
(If we go far enough away could we
decipher the design?) . . .
("From 20,000 Feet")

Facts, numbers, the world's natural orderings are all there, only to be incorporated into McHugh's ironic sense of how small we are—and how endless our longings. By using language to capture the many shapes of experience, Heather McHugh has made it possible for us to see more of the world in all its fragmentary wholeness.

For years now, I have counted on Linda Pastan to alert me to the nuances of "common" family life. More than any poet I can think of, she chronicles the subtle insights that distinguish our ordinary moments—what she terms "the whole riptide of daily life." Often she does this by juxtaposing our dailiness against the world of myth, specifically Eve in her earthly Paradise or Penelope as she waits at home for Odysseus. What Pastan learns as she examines the old, timeworn stories is applied to the present moment, often with a surprising twist that leaves the reader reeling.

The Imperfect Paradise is no exception. We encounter ourselves in recognizable events—a daughter leaving home, a husband and wife reestablishing cycles of birth (a grandchild) and death (a parent). Built into each of these moments is a questioning voice, one that will accept the inevitable only after it makes a kind of haphazard, intuitive sense. This is the voice that most intrigues me, a voice that can confront what many of us pretend is not there:

Sometimes I believe
if I had one thing
in some other way
everything would be fine,
and we would be happy
the way families are
whose innocence goes with them
to the grave . . .
("Root Pruning")

So we move another summer closer
to our last summer together—
a time as real and implacable as the sea . . .
("The Ordinary Weather of Summer")

Out of such a confrontation comes an acceptance of what is temporary—and a knowledge of what is important. It is important to learn to live with imperfection, to love the imperfection that the fact of death underscores. Pastan seems to conclude, like Frost, that earth may be all we will know of Paradise—but not until after she has questioned a creator who would inflict on us "the strict contract between love and grief."

Love and grief (and the ways each leads to the other) are at the heart of these poems. The "balancing act" is made clear in a poem in which Pastan envisions a human acrobatic act consisting of her dying mother, herself, her son, and her newborn grandson. For one precarious moment they inhabit the earth simultaneously—and then time moves remorselessly on. The seasons come and go: dogwoods blossom for one impossibly lovely week in spring, snow offers its consolations, and summer points up the ordinary life by its very cessation. With the death of her mother, the poet feels that her "whole childhood is coming apart, / the last stitches / about to be ripped out." She tries on the infinite possibilities of other lives—the one she might have lived in her grandfather's peasant village if he had stubbornly refused to change, the one she glimpses when she sees her mother's face in an old photograph, the one she imagines for the beavers who "mate for life."

On the underside of the ordinary "lived" life is the imagined "other" life. One section, entitled "Rereading *The Odyssey* in Middle Age," gives Pastan a vehicle for looking at aspects of desire, infidelity, and the traditional roles of male and female within marriage. And "middle age" provides a new lens through which to view the old themes, just as "the imperfect paradise" seen through Eve's eyes allows Pastan to imagine familiar events as though for the first time. This shadowy imagined life lends some of its passion to the humdrum and the everyday, providing new insights. Using legend and myth against which to measure her own life has been the hallmark of Pastan's work from *Aspects of Eve* on. Often, she rescues the myth *from* stereotype by seeing it through contemporary eyes:

I think of the uses of "shroud":
how the night can be shrouded in fog
in places like this one, near the sea;
how leaves in summer shroud each mother branch;
and how your husband's father looks at you
with wrinkled lids shrouding

those knowing eyes.
What is faithfulness anyway?
("Rereading *The Odyssey* in Middle Age")

Linda Pastan's sense of history is essentially psychological. Whatever she discovers is examined for an underlying motivation, as though our link with the past were a matter of common psychology. "Bird on Bough," for example, uses its epigraph in order to explore "the bird-on-bough aspect of eternity." Looking at a Chinese painting, Pastan recognizes the universality of an image: the bird is the "same bird" she remembers from her past—not literally, but because it unlocks the "eternity / that is childhood." Art—painting or poem—preserves the moment and connects the centuries, but the equation of childhood and eternity is the more surprising, and human, insight. Similarly, in "At Xian" Pastan contemplates the discovery of 6,000 life-size terra-cotta soldiers buried by a Chinese emperor: "Maybe it's only the numbers / we can't comprehend . . ." Fact becomes the vehicle for psychology—and identification: "though we too might send armies / if we could."

The Imperfect Paradise suffers from some over-organization—five carefully ordered sections, each with its own "theme." Unlike *The Five Stages of Grief*, where Pastan was able to discover patterns in sequences of her poems, here she has imposed an organizing principle that seems to take precedence over the content. Both the "Odyssey" section and the final "Eden" section contain what I would call "fillers"—poems that are either too clever or too slight, or those that rely on the legend for their only meaning. If some of the sharper, more biting poems in these sections (such as "The Son" and "Mother Eve") had been interspersed with the "family" poems, they might have further highlighted the underlying similarities between our lives and the lives that populate ancient legends. As it is, however, they seem to be tied too neatly into their own little packages.

Pastan's major strength lies not in the studied rhythmical flow of idea or argument, but in her nervous lines and her startlingly apt images. Take, for example, her description early in the book of a morning walk on the beach: "Along its rough edges / shells and small birds gather, / the rick-rack of life / in all its stages. . . ." It is "rick-rack" that fuses the natural and the domestic worlds and lets them speak to, and for, each other. Unfortunately, the title poem (a series of six sonnets) does none of this; they are too "perfect":

Which season is the loveliest of all?
Without a pause you smile and answer spring,
Thinking of Eden long before the fall
I see green shrouds enclosing everything . . .

This sounds almost like generic poetry—an impersonal postcard. It disappoints because it's coming from Linda Pastan, who has already proved that she can rip through the surface of language, taking apart the family album and rearranging it into something terrible and true—much like Picasso breaking down the human face, forcing us to recognize its complicated geometric truths.

Although the sonnet form seems to mute the emotional power of Pastan's insights, the finest poem in the collection is a formal poem—a pantoum. I'd go so far as to suggest that form, in this case, allows Pastan entry into a territory that is, for her, new, and perhaps frightening. In "Something About the Trees" she discovers something about herself, about the process of aging and the art of letting go. It's a brilliant poem which builds with the form's repetitions (and her own variations) to an almost agonizing question—"when will I be most myself?" Any poet struggles, in a sense, toward identity, but Pastan found a distinctive voice quite early in her career. Who can blame her for wanting to explore new spaces? I hope her experimentation with form will unlock something essential in her vision, enabling her to be "most herself."

I don't expect to understand everything instantly—I don't even want to—but I do expect to understand *almost* everything eventually. *To the Place of Trumpets* by Brigit Pegeen Kelly, winner of the 1988 Yale Younger Poets Series, is a challenge that tantalizes me with the *possibility* of understanding. Here is a book that is rich in particulars—lush details of sight and sound, magical details of the freed imagination—but I can't quite make out the frame on which they are hung, the structure that shapes the work as a whole. The *why* of these poems often hovers over them, then seems to veer off into the clouds.

Maybe that, then, is the organizing principle of the book: a palpable *not-knowing*. Certainly this is a book of questioned faith, and, in some ways, a substitution for faith. For instance, the Catholic Sundays of childhood are subjected to the scrutiny of the child's honest gaze. Retrieving that child in its innocence is a difficult task, and one that Kelly has mastered beautifully. In "Sundays" we see her watching the broken TV under the dime-store counter: everything is red to the point of blurring, she can't tell Bugs Bunny from Weasel or Elmer Fudd, and even the gun "bangs red." Sam, owner of the broken TV, never looks up, never steps beyond his own boundaries: "You could stand at his door and call / Roses have come! Roses have come! / but he'd only send out the blind dog." In his rigidity, Sam stands for the priest, the church, the whole shebang.

What this child—and later the adult—is able to see is that earth is the right place for love (and death), and that neither is subject to the strictures of dogma. So it is that the rebellion takes place: "No one / had to tell me the graveyard was less / than it seemed, the huge white Christ, / placid as lard above the wooden crosses . . ." ("Mount Angel"). Or "And these angels that the women turn to / are not good either. They are sick of Jesus, / who never stops dying, hanging there white / and large, his shadow blue as pitch . . ." ("Imagining Their Own Hymns"). Once the unthinkable is thought, the poems bloom into wild imaginative escape. The angels in the stained-glass window walk off the job, past the rigid pews and fonts, imagining their own hymns as they fly free—like the worldly birds they resemble.

Flight is a central image in *To the Place of Trumpets*. The sight of hot air balloons is equated to a "visitation" in which the colors become the "sound" of a horn, then many horns and clocks and bells and clappers "and your heart / rising to the silence / in all of them." In "Those Who Wrestle With the Angel For Us," her brother's flight (as a pilot) is seen in near-religious terms; he comes close to death—it brushed him briefly in childhood until he "favored the dark"—and actively courts it, daring the constellations before he returns like the "magician's dove." During flight the soul can swing between doubt and belief, as on the rope dangling over the water in "Above the Quarry"—a stunning poem that seems to play hide-and-seek with death. The poem opens:

> The cocks cry *death death* each morning
> But the death they cry is orange-feathered
> And slathered over with sun—not
>
> The foolish, lame-legged death you creep
> After, looking behind cupboard and stove.

From there, the poem circles the quarry, almost with a hawk's eye, until it reaches a moment of cool ecstasy:

> The wings that rise rise as dark flags
> Toward a sun which is pewter and cold as
> The water pooling in the lowest depths
>
> Of the pit; that hill you must stare into,
> Knowing that if a soul can recognize itself
> In one time, one season, one hour of one day,
>
> Then it can walk as through a mirror
> Past itself, and begin . . .

That beginning, for Kelly, seems to be the construction of a new "religion," one that borrows a vocabulary from the old one but has its own set of symbols.

The real world is populated with dogs, corn rows, orchards, and vineyards—a rural landscape that is as real as the cellars the flooding river dreams of. From that world she also plucks the images that give rise to exaltation—hot air balloon, tulip, bell. One of these exultant moments occurs in "Queen Elizabeth and the Blind Girl *or* Music for the Dead Children," when the deaf bell ringer plays the baptismal bells instead of tolling for the dead. He is able to hear (in his imagined song) an exotic bird shop where macaw or cockatoo or soul will rise with the waxwings that "wake / like a hundred green candles in a field."

Color (most often red) denotes this power of imagination. There are red-hatted hunters, clouds of ruby smoke, the crimson slit of a fish's mouth—all shades from pink to rose to orange to purple, including red cans, red lake, red flame, red-and-white balloon. The poems make their own fiery burst of color. But what is underneath the flash and fanfare and the impassioned doubt? One might surmise that the doubt is motivated by a death—"To the Lost Child" suggests one. But just when detail would clarify, it is withheld. Many of the poems seem to reflect more "sensibility" than "sense". Her language has invited me into her world, but I don't know what to make of it. The individual poems seem complete (though obscure), but they have not been integrated into a larger vision. Instead of feeling as though I have heard just exactly what I need to hear, I feel like an eavesdropper: I've overheard more than enough, but didn't catch the drift of why it was important. I keep wanting more of the hidden narrative.

I am able to pinpoint this frustration because one poem—my personal favorite—follows its own convoluted narrative style into strange and wonderful territory. "The House on Main Street" plays the game of "what if," following the "other" life she might have lived if "we had bought the house on Main Street." From her own house on the hill, she looks down with a telescopic view on the funeral to which she has not been invited, wondering who has died. Twisting back on itself in the way of all good stories unfolding, the poem moves from the house on Main Street to the neighborhood with its shoe-repair shop and Presbyterian church, the fat men who sun themselves on the porch, the dentist's office, and the clotheslines. Woven through this clear-eyed view is the memory of an incident of arson and an unsolved murder—nearly as matter-of-fact as the rest, certainly as much a part of the history of the town. And then the poem builds to a moment when the speaker and her daughter were playing in the cemetery, where memory is caught up in the freedom of childhood and they are suddenly running (present tense), certain they can be

connected with flight, not with the stone angels
  shadowing the frozen
    ground, but with a body
that has truly flown, with a mind
    that makes the sky
its home

This would be a wonderful ending—the moment when the poem takes off—and it seems too bad that it is weighed down with an unnecessary epilogue. What works, in the eighteen six-line stanzas that precede the epilogue, is the fusion of the real and the hypothetical, braided to make a larger "story" out of its separate strands. The balance of lyric and narrative is just right.

This is a promising first book, filled with a language that is both private and transcendent. Like Charles Wright, Kelly creates poems that rely on the reader's ability to cross the stepping stones of association. They are exciting, and I'm curious as to where she will go next. If she wants readers to take on the full range of her vision, she will probably have to find the place where internal impulse and external events coincide—a place she may have already glimpsed in "The Leaving":

. . . inside me was the stillness a bell possesses
just after it has been rung, before the metal
begins to long again for the clapper's stroke.

When a poem raises a lump in the throat time after time, it must either be terribly bad or terribly good. In the case of a young Chinese-American poet, Li-Young Lee, there is very little question as to how good these poems are. It's *how* they are good that is hard to define—a question that Gerald Stern tackles, but does not answer, in his introduction to *Rose*. Stern compares Lee to Keats and Rilke, but I feel he is most like Neruda—the Neruda in love with the sensory experiences of the world, the Neruda of the wide associative leaps that make sense only through feeling. What we have here is a fine lyric voice, singing from the very first lines:

Of wisdom, splendid columns of light
waking sweet foreheads,
I know nothing

but what I've glimpsed in my most hopeful of daydreams.
Of a world without end,
amen,

I know nothing,
but what I sang of once with others,
all of us standing in the vaulted room.
(from "Epistle")

Rose chronicles (though not in any direct narrative) a family exodus from China to Indonesia to America. The figure of the father haunts the book—a father both severe and tender, a father idealized in death and yet made human in living memory. In Stern's words, ". . . the poet's job becomes not to benignly or tenderly forgive him, but to withstand him and comprehend him. . . ." The quest for the father may be the underpinning for these poems, but what shapes them is a sensibility unafraid of risk, exploring its complete range of feeling—even the sentimental.

The vision in *Rose* is both personal and collective. It encompasses a sense of family and generation and connectedness that is almost unknown to contemporary American poets. The history of *Rose* is the history of a culture, and it is Lee's sense of continuation that allows for a poem like "Dreaming of Hair," in which the speaker binds himself imaginatively to the earth, stitched in place by his dead father's hair as it rises from the grave. His father's hair, his brother's, his wife's, the ivy that "ties the cellar door"—all are celebrated, and finally fused, in the dream that can contain more than a lifetime.

Water (and the crossing of water) becomes one of the book's dominant strains (it would be wrong to call anything in this book a "theme"). One poem, "Water," has a visionary quality, moving from the "oldest sound" of the amniotic fluid, the first sound we forget, to the water that will eventually fill his father's lungs in congestive heart failure. As the speaker washes his father's feet, he moves into his father's memories—torture and escape and the journey to America—and then outward to the world and the sound of rain that "outlives us." This poem, in turn, illuminates "Rain Diary" where water has seeped into his father's grave and has roused boyhood memories, leading him to say, "I remember my father of rain." The imagery follows its own convoluted logic with such lines as "I searched the hours, perforated by rain," and "I looked in the billowing curtains, / they were haunted by rain," and "I want to be broken, / to be eaten by the anonymous mouths, / to be eroded like minutes and seconds, / to be reduced to water / and a little light." The poem culminates in a language that is nearly biblical:

Rain falls and does not
break. Neither does it stop,
but just pulls up
the gangplank and is gone.
It stands before me,
beside me, lies down
beneath me. How shall I praise it?
Rain knocks at my door and
I open. No one
is there, and the rain marching in place.

The language is the vehicle for the vision that, in the case of "Rain Diary," ends with "Perhaps it is my father, arriving / on legs of rain, arriving / this dream, the rain, my father."

The visionary aspect of the book is seen best in the long central poem, "Always a Rose," where Lee follows a path of association, allowing the rose to surface in memory and to fill his mouth with its bitter, medicinal taste. He takes it in, transforms it into symbol, then moves in a state of ecstasy to where he can make it wholly his by naming it: "Cup of Blood, Old Wrath, Heart O' Mine, Ancient of Days, / Whorl, World, Word." And then he makes it real again, a flower in a glass of water, taking an impossibly long time to die. "I named you each day you remained: / Scorn, Banish, Grieve, Forgive, Love." Although lines like these might suggest that Lee's poems are preoccupied with abstraction, this is not the case. For all their intensity, they have a sincerity that derives, in part, from a precision of detail. He can move us with simple moments, as when in "Eating Alone" he describes his meal: "White rice steaming, almost done. Sweet green peas / fried in onions. Shrimp braised in sesame / oil and garlic. And my own loneliness. / What more could I, a young man, want." (I think here of Neruda's *Odas Elementales.*)

Rose, which was awarded the Delmore Schwartz prize in 1987, contains only twenty-five poems but many of them extend to three or four pages, sustaining an intricacy of thought and rising, at times, to a joy so close to despair that the two are inextricable:

O weepers, stone
girls weeping stone tears,
will you never recover?
Were it not for the rain, I'd linger
and maybe I'd weep.
But I'll do neither today, while someone

waits for me, and the rain
touches me, touches us
over and over, changes each of us,
shoulders and lips, roses and stones,
my love and the world,
all things which fit well.
("The Weepers")

In an age when poetry is cautious, poems like Lee's move beyond the pale, and it is in the realm where they are most incautious, even excessive, that they reach for greatness. Sensuous and alive, they celebrate innocence and achieve the wisdom that the first poem claims to know nothing of. Of a "world without end"—who knows? But Lee discovers meaning in the world, in the lived experience and in the imaginative connections. Certainly the father's life is not in vain as the poet tenderly soothes his own sons. and even more certainly, the world is not ending as he watches blossom become peach and concludes:

There are days we live
as if death were nowhere
in the background; from joy
to joy to joy, from wing to wing,
from blossom to blossom to
impossible blossom, to sweet impossible blossom.
("From Blossoms")

Auditory Imagination: The Sense of Sound

On Pamela Gross's *Blessed Coming Off Ladders*; Jane Kenyon's *Let Evening Come*; Li-Young Lee's *The City in Which I Love You*; Thomas Lux's *The Drowned River*; and Wayne Dodd's *Echoes of the Unspoken*.

> In a poet, the auditory imagination involves a feeling for syllable and rhythm, a sense of the primitive and its relation to the highly developed, an ear for the echoes behind words.
>
> Denis Donoghue, *Warrenpoint*

IN THE LONG TRADITION of talking about poetry—almost as old as the tradition of composing it—"music" has nearly always been listed (though seldom defined) as one of the qualities that characterizes a poem. When we speak of music in poetry, most of us are referring to a combination of cadence, rhythm, meter, rhyme, alliteration, assonance, patterns of vowels and consonants—and something more. That "something," of course, is ineffable, yet in any language it is what often makes the deepest impression. Although we cannot put extrinsic value on any aspect of sound, we instinctively know when it is working on us. This is not so much an unconscious response to the sound of the poem as it is a semiconscious one. When the ear is captivated, the mind (and sometimes the heart) follows.

Perhaps because the sound of a poem is hard to define, many critics ignore it altogether. All too often, reviewers note only the content of the poem and thus speak of the sense of a book as though its meaning is restricted to what can be summarized. The consequence is to divorce the concept of "sense," with its connotations of logic and intellectual meaning, from the *senses*. Such readings can reiterate themes—as in the monthly plot-sketches that have supplanted poetry reviews in *The New York Times Book Review*—instead of attempting a full assessment of a book's worth. But in poetry, words are not chosen for their meaning alone; indeed, the sounds of a poem, and the patterns of sound within a book of poems, are often the best indication of how to make sense *of* it. These sounds are an embodiment. They speak the poet. It is through them that we come to recognize the individual voice making some kind of specific order out of the possibilities of language.

There are syntactical patterns in spoken English that, with all their regional variations, help to determine the stresses in a sentence. Obviously, this is where the difference between words on the page and words in the (Southern? Western? New England?) poet's own voice becomes evident. Often it is possible to identify syllabic stress on the page, but that does not necessarily reveal the poet's own inflection—the way he or she actually "hears" language.

Both William Carlos Williams and Robert Frost were trying to achieve a kind of music that would approximate the spoken voice of Americans—a music each had recorded in his inner ear. Williams, in the vanguard of Modernism, experimented with his "variable foot" in what we call free verse. Frost, working in an older tradition, merged thought with music in the strictest of metrical forms, striving to capture what he called "the sound of sense"—patterns of thought that could be recognized in patterns of sound. When I look at the distinctive results of these two approaches, I cannot help wondering whether there might not also be a "sense of sound"—a way in which sounds themselves serve as the basis of meaning, where sound gives rise to idea. I suspect there is, for sound speaks to us as the center of meaning in many poems. It tells us how to interpret a passage, how to fit a particular poem into the larger context of the book. Reading for sound is one route toward unraveling meaning.

The music of a poem has a logic of its own. If we attend to its sounds, responding through the ear, we may discover what Denis Donoghue calls the auditory imagination of the poet. The very physicality of sound is a part of the process—we reside in the poem (and therefore, briefly, with the poet), where rhythms of thought and of feeling become one. Of course, poetic music is subjective in writer and reader alike. Not all of us will recognize the same poem as being especially musical—what excites one ear may fall flat on another—but it is our job as readers to listen for the individual music of the poet. As I sifted through the thirty books I was considering for inclusion in this review, I noted which books I picked up a second time, a third. What, I wondered, made one book stand out from the larger pile? Again and again, the answer was *sound.* The sense of sound—the poet's particular auditory imagination—caught my attention, kept my attention, pulled me deeper into the shape of the book. The "echo behind words" had worked its magic—a magic I want to explore here, though I can bring only an echo of that echo to these pages.

Blessed Coming off Ladders by Pamela Gross is a testament to precision of language; she brings to poetry a sharp, scientific eye—and an ear to match. The opening lines resound, filling the ear with internal rhyme and unexpected rhythms:

Birds of the Night Sky / Stars of the Field

We are afraid they will disappear
whether we watch too close or not
at all: the small, pale crumbs
of nervous chatter we've marked this dark
with. Fast as we could scatter
them, we've swept them up again, as if
the invisible flight of widgeons whose frail
toy-duck call trolls the night sky's blind
waters would steal our thoughts.

We are pulled into a density of language that captures the vacillations between light and dark, known and unknown. These lines are typical of this truly slim volume (only twenty-one poems in all), and they give some idea of how a complex of sound and intellect can reveal meaning, much as the "chatter" reveals the presence of unseen birds.

But Pamela Gross knows what those birds are—and names them. She is unflinching as she looks hard at what is usually hidden ("the world is all undersides," she says in "Letting Go"). Her telescopic gaze may take her into the night sky, but it's with the microscope that she is most at home. She peels back layer upon layer—of memory, of experience—until she, like the Darwin of "Variations on Domestication," is imagining "the regression toward / a simpler state, to cast off accretions / of habit, the half-life's stubborn / inch-forward-double-back." Each poem a section on her slide, she gazes intently through the outer layers to discover underlying meaning.

Some of that meaning is more readily available to the ear than to the eye. Owls, as they inhabit the night, know something important:

To hear as the owl hears is mostly
a matter of learning to split
differences. Imbalance
mediates a quest for absolutes,
and even in perfect dark, the strike
is perfect. The tiniest rasp
of leaf on leaf is signal enough
to turn the great dish face toward
the hushed breathing of the mouse.
(from "In Pitch Dark")

. . . He knows
how the soft ones wait without
knowing. How their pulses' muted
hammers tap out the simple code
that halts cold his loose flight's
stumble, renders the snub-nosed bullet
of his body helpless to impulse,
to the dizzy, granite-weighted drop.
(from "What the Owl Knows")

Just as the owl discovers a living world from sound, Gross also hears the inaudible. The owl may triangulate to find a victim, but what, she ponders, determines who will be the victim of cancer? Its shadowy image is everywhere in this book, growing "in pitch dark." But the order of the poems reverses the process, giving us first the grief and then the peeled-back stages of discovery. Initially there is the stark fact of the word *tumor*, which later in the book is seen to "ride burrowed / in the body's deep, / unopened pockets," later still becomes "a knot wedged / how long in the shoulder's mass," and in the final poem becomes merely "a colony of cells." A friend/a would-be lover/an unnamed "you" is slowly dying. Even as the progression of the disease is reversed, the growing impossibility of a full relationship unfolds. There are no miracles, or, if there are, they are small and specific, as in the title poem. But the poem goes on to suggest that love outgrows all barriers. Love, then, is what cannot be pinned down. "What name shall I give you?" Gross asks in the face of a passion restricted by marriage and illness.

If Gross has found an answer, it lies in the naming that calls forth her own brand of music. The harsh, packed consonants that evoke the "anger" of "Splitting Wood" give way to the lush vowels of the penultimate poem. Here she learns something of how "to settle for less" by transforming the experience into song:

Letting Go

In summer, in that hour
when the trees take the light's
leaving, the world is all undersides. Each
of the maples' fat hands palms
gold. We open our own hands, as if
we could receive the glittering,
the fuss, the flutter of the paired warblers flirting
with light, with shadow.
As if we could seize their dapple and splash, the bright play
of these butter yellow pieces of flight
in their spill, retrieve, spill.
We want to shake them loose and set
their perfect coins upon our eyes.

Surrender's hard work is slow.
Inhale reluctant to relinquish its
exhale, so fearing the lung will starve.
The body, captive to its notions of next and beyond,
and the heart riveted
to the first truth of letting go:
That it begins with holding.

Blessed Coming Off Ladders is a first book—and I, for one, am eager for more. But this collection is so tight, so integrated, that it will be a hard act to follow.

Jane Kenyon's is a simpler tune, often as stark as the New England landscape she reflects upon. *Let Evening Come* opens, however, with full-blown song:

A second crop of hay lies cut
and turned. Five gleaming crows
search and peck between the rows.
They make a low, companionable squawk,
and like midwives and undertakers
possess a weird authority.
(from "Three Songs at the End of Summer")

But summer is short in New Hampshire, and most of the book has a more melancholy tone. As a collection, *Let Evening Come* is really about solitude, and Jane

Kenyon's solitary voice is distinctive in its search for what is "simple and good." She finds it in a carefully controlled sense of sound, spilling across deceptively simple lines. Look as "Spring Snow," for example. *A, E, I, O, U*—the vowel sounds cluster like bees, swarming in sequence through stanzas which offer a consonant base shifting from *H* to *M* to *N* to *P*, together forming an alphabet of snow that becomes, in the poet's reverie, a projection of early summer:

A thoughtful snow comes falling . . .
seems to hang in the air before
concluding that it must fall
here. Huge aggregate flakes

alight on the muddy ruts
of March, and the standing
water that thaws by day
and freezes by night.

Venus is content to shine unseen
this evening, having risen serene
above the springs, and false springs.
But I, restless after supper, pace

the long porch while the snow falls,
dodging the clothesline I won't
use until peonies send up red,
plump, irrepressible spears.

This progression of sound becomes a movement of mind, which only leads to further solitude. The poet, anchored to landscape, moves through time. In poem after poem, she discovers in herself the child who waited at home while her brother explored the world—a child who could lie on her back in a field and love the world with a passion "so violent / it was hard to distinguish from pain." Perhaps it is this rediscovered "child" who is happier at home than at a dinner party, more comfortable with the companionship of her dog than of most people, more intimate with the sounds that come to her across water than with the claustrophobic noises of neighbors when she visits her in-laws. Perhaps it is this initial pain that, now, makes the poet hold on to her immediate life with such intensity. In this way, she can claim her brother's larger world as her own.

Kenyon claims this world by rendering it specific. Hers is a quiet landscape, something like the final two minutes of Charles Kuralt's *Sunday Morning* television program—a landscape unsullied by human beings in which one can hear the cry of a bird or can savor the slant of falling flakes. And yet *Let Evening Come* is a decidedly human book, filled with empathy and compassion. In "Father and Son," Kenyon speaks from hindsight, watching a dying neighbor cut his last pile of wood:

> August. My neighbor started cutting wood
> on cool Sabbath afternoons, the blue
> plume of the saw's exhaust wavering over
> his head. At first I didn't mind the noise
> but it came to seem like a species of pain.

As the saw's stutter (au-a-a-aw-au) fills the afternoon, the poet feels the powerlessness of those who cannot change the course of things.

This is a book of middle age, a time when "some power has gone from the sun." The speaker of these poems endures the loss of parents, neighbors, friends; she finds echoes in the lives of Keats and Akhmatova; she grieves quietly, privately. This is not a book that "comes to terms," nor does it conquer its fear—rather, it creates a hiatus, a state of waiting. It does not seem to be seeking answers to anything; it merely wants to catch the world before it is gone. With such titles as "We Let the Boat Drift," "Waiting," and "Now Where?" everything seems to be held in abeyance: "If I lie down / or sit up it's all the same: // the days and nights bear me along. / To strangers I must seem / alive."

But nature will not comply, filling the world with its storms, its onrush of seasons, its "irrepressible" buds. The dog must be walked—he is in tune with the day, whatever the weather, happy to launch himself on the world—while the speaker notes her inability to free *herself* from the leash. She is tied to landscape, to human relationship, to a profound sense of self. Life, not death, is what is at stake here—and life is defined by a rich inner voice that sometimes rises to the level of hymn. The title poem acts as both evensong and invocation:

> Let the light of late afternoon
> shine through chinks in the barn, moving
> up the bales as the sun moves down.
>
> Let the cricket take up chafing
> as a woman takes up her needles
> and her yarn. Let evening come.
>
> Let dew collect on the hoe abandoned
> in long grass. Let the stars appear
> and the moon disclose her silver horn.

Let the fox go back to its sandy den.
Let the wind die down. Let the shed
go black inside. Let evening come.

To the bottle in the ditch, to the scoop
in the oats, to air in the lung
let evening come.

Let it come, as it will, and don't
be afraid. God does not leave us
comfortless, so let evening come.

On this reverent note, Kenyon makes a meaningful distinction between resignation and acceptance. With its steady but evocative refrain the poem plays to the ear and its expectations, gaining momentum even as it becomes increasingly hushed. Kenyon's sound pattern here works with—but is not the same as—the pattern of sense. A reader who attends only to the latter will miss much of the richness in these mature and memorable poems.

Li-Young Lee's second book, *The City in Which I Love You*, is the 1990 Lamont Poetry Selection of The Academy of American Poets. This is a work of remarkable scope—musically as well as thematically—offering a sweeping perspective of history from the viewpoint of the émigré. He speaks for the disenfranchised, but from the particular voice of a late-twentieth-century Chinese-American trying to make sense of both his heritage and his inheritance. Positioning himself as father and son, Chinese and American, exile and citizen, Lee finds himself on the cusp of history; his duty, as he sees it, is to "tell my human / tale, tell it against / the current of that vaster, that / inhuman telling."

The City in Which I Love You picks up where Lee's first book, *Rose*, left off. The opening poem, "Furious Versions," is a long, seven-part account of his family's exile. Fueled with the sense that he is the only one who has lived to tell it, Lee recounts his father's fractured life and the loss of his brother. The effect is more than personal; it is admonitory—as if to warn us that we cannot face the "next nervous one hundred human years" without a knowledge of what his past represents. But whereas the central figure in *Rose* is the father, here the "furious versions" belong to the son—because his "memory's flaw / isn't in retention but organization." This long poem seems to fill in some gaps left by the previous book, but its language is angrier, less elegiac:

It was a tropical night.
It was half a year of sweat and fatal memory.
It was one year of fire
out of the world's diary of fires,
flesh-laced, mid-century fire,
teeth and hair infested,
napalm-dressed and skull-hung fire,
and imminent fire, an elected
fire come to rob me
of my own death, my damp bed
in the noisy earth
my rocking toward a hymn-like night.

Although the story is personal and unique, the poems are declamatory, public even in their intimacy. They have as two of their sources Whitman and the Bible, and they have as their intention a passionate need to synthesize and instruct. They challenge us with their heightened rhetoric, exhibiting the dangers (as well as the glories) of eloquence. Lee's very strengths are his potential weaknesses. The echo of Whitman may need to be muted; even Lee's own tremendous verbal resources may demand modulation in order to achieve their finest realization. One more adjective, one more item in a list, and the poem could tip over into excess.

The ambitious title poem, 166 lines in the middle of the book, marks a turning point where the experience of exile is no longer the speaker's alone. "The City in Which I Love You" is a collage of twentieth-century horror rendered in an onrush of fragments, some evoking the nightly news, others surrealistic nightmare. In a devastated cityscape, the "I" of the poem searches for a "you"—an other. The other is more than a beloved (the epigraph is from the *Song of Songs*); rather, it seems to signify some impossible fulfillment, a connection to humanity through which love might still be possible, and suffering redemptive. Informing the poem is a dense language, thick with urgent rhythms and relentless desire—as though language itself were the other, the body of the beloved.

In the face of the larger history, Lee must discover the meaning of his individual life: "He was not me," "They are not me," "None of them is me." This discovery is central to the book, for the next several poems are rooted in a quiet family life—love poems to a woman who tastes like iron and milk, a child who wants a story, a father whom death has made a giant. "Goodnight" is a lullaby, in slant-rhyme couplets, sung to his son. It moves, ultimately, toward full rhyme:

Where did you, so young, learn

such sacrifice? Now
I no longer hear the apples fall. But how

they go! Incessantly, though
with no noise, no

blunt announcements of their gravity.
See!

There is no bottom to the night, no end
to our descent.

We suffer each other to have each other a while.

The book ends with another long poem, "The Cleaving." Here Lee looks to the present; the immigrant figure is no longer his father, the story no longer only autobiographical. It has become a text. A young man with his own identity and history enters a butcher shop. The butcher is familiar—he could be grandfather, father, brother, nomad, Gobi, Northern, Southern. He is American, a man at work:

He lops the head off, chops
the neck of the duck
into six, slits
the body
open, groin
to breast, and drains
the scalding juices,
then quarters the carcass
with two fast hacks of the cleaver,
old blade that has worn
into the surface of the round
foot-thick chop-block
a scoop that cradles precisely the curved steel.

The language is packed, sound clicking against sound, consonants hacking their own blades, reminiscent of Lowell. The sounds are American—harsh, hurried, energetic—and they carry the reader toward meaning as Lee, self-conscious that this is as much the making of poetry as the telling of tale, comes to terms with the violent wrenchings of his immigrant experience. He savors the taste of meat—a hunger at last satisfied, because it is a hunger that *can* be satisfied. He accepts his varied, though finite, human ties. He finds, in the body of a fish, a shape that complements the shape of his mind: "I take it as text and evidence / of the world's love for me, / and I feel urged to utterance, / urged to read the body of the world, urged / to say it / in human terms, / my reading a kind of eating, my eating / a kind of reading, / my saying a diminishment, my noise / a love-in-answer."

"The Cleaving," is the intellectual flip side of the title poem. In it, Lee accepts his body and its appetites, accepts his inevitable death, eschews the need for transcendence. With its exploration into every nuance of the title, its love of detail, and its journey into the abstract, "The Cleaving" has the feel of a major American poem. It throws aside some of the American traditions he has previously followed: "I would eat these features, eat / the last three of four thousand years, every hair. / And I would eat Emerson, his transparent soul, his / soporific transcendence." Above all, "The Cleaving" predicts change—a change that is necessary if Lee is to grow into other books. It is the birth of self out of personal and global history, a self that is not the sum of its stories but of its experience—assimilated, whole, and wholly alive in a chamber of sound:

> No easy thing, violence.
> One of its names? Change. Change
> resides in the embrace
> of the effaced and the effacer,
> in the covenant of the opened and the opener;
> the axe accomplishes it on the soul's axis.
> What then may I do
> but cleave to what cleaves me.
> I kiss the blade and eat my meat.
> I thank the wielder and receive,
> while terror spirits
> my change, sorrow also.
> The terror the butcher
> scripts in the unhealed
> air, the sorrow of his Shang
> dynasty face,
> African face with slit eyes. He is
> my sister, this
> beautiful Bedouin, this Shulamite,
> keeper of sabbaths, diviner
> of holy texts, this dark

dancer, this Jew, this Asian, this one
with the Cambodian face, Vietnamese face, this Chinese
I daily face,
this immigrant,
this man with my own face.

With its mixture of verbal and visionary imagination, *The City in Which I Love You* is reminiscent of Kinnell's *Book of Nightmares*, maybe even of Eliot's *Waste Land*. The personal nightmare becomes general. Lee's poetry makes us look hard at the world and the place our own "furious versions," at once interconnected and isolated, have in it.

It is especially hard to make music out of the ugly, the angry, the horrific, the comic—and these are, at least in part, what Thomas Lux explores in his latest book, *The Drowned River*. The floodgates are open, and Lux unleashes image after image of violence and cruelty. What is most difficult to take is that we recognize the cruelties; they are the petty ones of our daily lives, and they are everywhere. Lux finds them in rusted back-yard swing sets and seedy motels with cinder blocks the color of "exhausted grave grass," as well as in the more exotic instances of a traveling exhibit of torture instruments, or the use of Haitian cadavers in medical schools because they are so thin "that the organs just beneath the skin, the organs / yield to the blade with amazing ease."

These poems are meant to work "just beneath the skin." They enter the ear, unnerve it, and work themselves into the body—loud, irregular, even cacophonous. For example, the consonants of "Cellar Stairs" make a syncopated, unsettling music:

On a shelf above, tools: shears,
three-pronged weed hacker, ice pick,
poison—rats and bugs—and on the landing
halfway down, a keg of roofing nails
you don't want to fall face first into. . . .

Lux floods us with such images because the world itself is flooded with them—this is a media blitz, nothing left out, tribal warfare in our living rooms. Lux takes on the rough political realities of our time, incorporating facts and figures, forcing us to look back at a catalogue of historical horrors—from Stalin ("Uncle Joe never loved nobody, nobody ever loved Joe") through World War I (phosgene and mustard gas) to the dead (or dying) at Andersonville. The peripheral is made central—and Lux dwells on it. But why does he seem to be drowning in obsession? What is at the heart of this book?

Lux is looking for the meaning of life and death, but somehow, in a book of this power, that feels less like a cliché and more like a necessity. In the end, Lux looks for what is human. In a marvelous poems called "Mr. Pope," Lux shows how the word can grow larger than the personality: "I report your verse, / their raging sense / and tenderness, I report / them breathing, shining black / ink on white paper, intact! / I close the heavy, huge book of your life. / You live outside, above, its pages, / within the human therein created."

At the very center of *The Drowned River* is another testament to humanity. "For My Daughter When She Can Read" examines the week before his daughter's birth and her eventual entry into the world. The speaker of the poem is reading three different books, each a litany of "facts"—dictators, tribes, religions—and at the same time dreaming, not of the infant who was "nothing / then . . . under water but not drowned . . . an abstraction," but of "what we always dream of: ourselves." Speaking directly to his daughter, now achingly real to him, he is aware that her birth was accompanied by simultaneous deaths, that the next day's newspapers chronicled movie reviews, government lies, and bulldozers for sale. How to offer his child more than the daily grinding down? He would wish for her both rage (a necessity) and rapture (another kind of necessity).

The Drowned River is not as cynical as this may suggest. Lux counters an existential despair with an equally desperate humor. And underneath it all is song. A quiet song, born of hope—and born of a new sense of self. We encounter that self in "Still," a poem that moves in three-line stanzas, willfully forcing the tongue to stop, to savor each word, to shut down. As the body holds itself still, Lux gives us what we always knew—our own fundamental loneliness:

> not to move
> one centimeter up or down,
> to all but halt the physical,
>
> to call for whatever you call the opposite.
> To be still, this still—eyelashes
> lowered like bars
>
> across sight, and the prison, the body,
> quiet, holding the prisoner sweetly
> in his cell.

The body is a prison. The body is in danger of drowning in dailiness, in compromise, in facts. The spirit, like the final image of "At Least Let Me Explain," must enter the realm of rain, starlight, snow, "each brave flake / not cold / but alone."

Alone, man is left to find meaning. Against the backdrop of history, the poet offers his cache of words and his fund of dark irony. Is it good luck or bad, Lux asks, to be the child who is "filled with world?" The child has no choice, he "hears a falling through the leaves" and "*knows* a bird falls, and grieves / without knowing why or at what cost." This child, called to words and to concern for the world, must seek (as poet) the meaning of his calling.

In the face of nothingness, or, paradoxically, in the face of too much brutal detail, man looks for God. Lux ponders His existence in his most musical poem, a poem filled with an alliteration that weaves a pattern of sound like a web. At the same time Lux is creating this complex of sound, he is unraveling meaning, as suggested by the title, "Irreconcilabilia":

No matter what you do
you cannot hold it long
or take it back again.

The sky, the barely blue
blank sky, the tight moss-bound
houses of sleep, will call.

No matter how hard you love,
that love will pass, will pass,
your friends imparadized,

gone, lost. The summers blaze,
the years, and what you know
grows dim, hurt by the dark.

No matter child, or wife,
or art. The river bends
and bends again seaward.

The soft lip-click of worms,
a spider's feet across
a leaf: you see, you hear.

No matter blessings, rage,
or rest: the dead stay dead.
You walk, spine alive, you kneel,

> you lay your ear down on
> the ground. Does God live there?
> Does God live anywhere?

So, as the root, the unanswerable question. This is an example of how sound leads us to sense—the repetitions alert the ear to a pattern of thought. No matter. . . . In the end, "you see, you hear," and by extension come to know. The quiet tone of this poem, in contrast to the noise and sting of many others, leads us to understand that Lux is reaching for some equilibrium.

Later Lux stops looking for the "capital G" God and comes to terms with one in lower case that we might not recognize but who is both wonderfully human and remote: one who lets the world unfold before him and is sad when people fear their lives—"those solitudes / so small beside the tundra, polar caps, / Congo River (whose every curve he loves)." Lux raises a song in his praise, knowing that the act is a human necessity, not something any god has asked for:

> He loves what's sane, serene, and fiercely calm,
> which he didn't invent but understands.
> The perfect god—and god, yes, is perfect—
> is impassive, patient, aloof, alert,
> and needs not our praise nor our blame.
> And needs not our praise nor our blame.

Many of Lux's poems vividly capture the odd, demented quality of present-day life, and in dwelling on his more tranquil poems, I have chosen those that underscore, by counterpoint, the need to find some order in the chaos. So I have not done full justice to this sharply original voice. *The Drowned River* demands our best attention, forcing us to examine the space where lack of dissent becomes compliance. In it, Lux has expanded old themes and thrust himself into new territory with challenging wit and a terrifying wisdom.

America has generated poets who, for the most part, are storytellers, perhaps because its own story is still in the making. The lyric voice is rare in American poetry; there are lyric moments in otherwise narrative poems, but the pure lyric is hard to find. Luckily, Wayne Dodd brings to his latest book, *Echoes of the Unspoken*, the music of an intensely sensuous inner voice. The lyric is alive—and well—in this exciting volume.

Echoes of the Unspoken invites some analysis of its method, for how the poems unfold is as interesting as what they say. In fact, how they unfold *is* what they say, or a great part of it. Dodd is continually amazed at the "miracle" of words—the sound of them in the ear, the sight of them on the page. "On the Page" shows words making their presences felt, "the mysterious / shapes and sounds they make // generation after century." "What, Lasting, Comes Toward Us" re-creates this mystery: "these presences // come without warning / from hidden sources into the / hidden mind but the words // when one finds them / come from the mysterious / and universal womb // of necessity, that / sudden shadowing / of wings."

Dodd's interest in the history of language and the power of the word is evident in the way his lines call attention to, and divert attention from, meaning. They display themselves on the page in a nervous movement of short lines and white space. He is willing to end his poems on prepositions, truncated, in midsentence or midthought. In this way, he is able to show us the slippage of meanings and, at the same time, call our attention to sound and syntax. Because Dodd is approximating a presyntactic state, a time before words are locked into their man-made prison, his poems feel more like whisper than speech, more like the undercurrent of thought (with its false starts, its meanderings, its barely felt distinctions) than the logic of rhetoric. If one reads these poems aloud, the tongue twists, the eye moves backwards, trying to reassert a kind of sense. Dodd knows this—rejoices in it—giving the reader more the possibility of meaning than a limited, syntactical choice. In fact, he breaks down Frost's concept of the "sound of sense." If there is sense here, it is sense in the making, a felt sense that occurs long before all the commas are in place. We experience the inner voice, alive to every nuance. Notice the play on the sensory as well as the intellectual, the image as well as the abstraction, in a poem like "Song":

Not only thoughts
and will we are rain

falling through
trees our hair

wet about our faces our arms
rising and falling

the rhythm our
life is

sand and wind
on our backs our legs the long

grass oh *the world*
worlds says Heidegger

white petals light
falls on like pollen

the yellow dusting
of words

on our lips our ears our throats

Any line or pair of lines can serve as example. Where, for instance, does "our / life is" fit—at the end of one phrase or at the beginning of another? "White petals light" moves into the next line so that light falls on the petals, but briefly, the petals themselves *are* light. This the mind apprehends instinctively—but how to express it in words? Dodd offers us some visual possibilities.

If *Echoes of the Unspoken* were only an exercise in destruction, it might excite the theorists—but not the poets. The reason to read this book is to find those insights that sometimes get lost in the syntax of narrative, to feel the junctures where self and world converge, to discover something about the process of being alive without having to make something *of* it.

The "world worlds" in these poems. We watch it come into being, as in "Hylocichla Mustelina": "By this time you can see / through the window the trees // in growing light detaching themselves / one by one from the dark // the forest has all night / been part of." But this world (which we all share) is seen individually. Dodd gives us a private vision—one that is essentially lonely. The presences of others are just that: presences, felt even in their absence. In this nether world of the inner ear, time disappears. The world flashes by as if from the window of a train. You look down, as in "All Night," to find a turtle surfacing through the sky mirrored in the pond—and you realize that your life is like the turtle's and that you might, someday, rise through the sky to surface somewhere, somehow.

The world worlds, and we are only fleetingly a part of it. *Echoes of the Unspoken* is filled with phrases that emphasize brevity: "vanishes," "for a moment," "in an instant," "momentary," "while we're here." The world persists; each night we leave it briefly as we dream. Each morning we wake to it, fresh in sunlight, wordless. These small deaths—and births—are preparation. The music is already there; Dodd relies on the world to sing *for* him. What would, of necessity, be formalized in a more public voice, finds only "echoes" here. The reader listens in, and is privy to another way of being. We live inside his silences, just as we live in our own noisy silences. Yet "no one can / hear the sounds we are making, the small // envelope of air / inside us // around us / vanishing forever."

Dodd attends well to the world—and his own state of being: "We wake / in the same moment // to ourselves / and to things." The convergence of self and world generates the private music that ensues and, in Dodd's words, lets us "see / the music happen." In many ways, this is what Williams was trying to do in the first half of this century. In a visual age, we must *see*, as well as overhear, the lyric. The best way to demonstrate how sound does, somehow, create a sense of its own is to watch it working its way to the surface of Dodd's final poem:

On Any Given Afternoon

As if from windows

framed on the ground the familiar
faces look up

toward the light of birds
above us whistle and trill and yodel

in. The green mat of their hair
at the margins, the dark centers of light
their remembered eyes are

in the earth . . . Their mouths
are closed and yet

words enter us
like song, like presence of Being
itself, all

the lost loved voices singing out
the language of existence, its

deep warp of shadows
across the yard,
the countless

deer that move
invisibly near us

in the dense, syllabic woods

Excellent Excesses

On Stanley Plumly's *Boy on the Step*; William Matthews' *Blues If You Want*; Pamela Stewart's *Infrequent Mysteries*; Albert Goldbarth's *Heaven and Earth: A Cosmology*; and Les Murray's *The Rabbiter's Bounty: Collected Poems*.

Those blessed structures, plot and rhyme—
why are they no help to me now
I want to make
something unimagined, not recalled?

ROBERT LOWELL'S "EPILOGUE," the final poem of his last book, asked a question that continues to plague the generation that follows him. There's an uneasy truce between what is imagined and what is recalled, and many contemporary poets have placed themselves squarely in one camp or the other. As for the "structures," contemporary poets straddle that fence as well. But form itself was never an issue for Lowell; he was interested in what he could do within the limits of form and what the forms enabled him to explore.

I hear the noise of my own voice:
The painter's vision is not a lens,
it trembles to caress the light.
But sometimes everything I write
with the threadbare art of my eye
seems a snapshot,
lurid, rapid, garish, grouped,
heightened from life,

yet paralyzed by fact.
All's misalliance.

Interesting that he should reject the photograph, that he sees "fact" as stifling to the imagination. Ironic that Lowell, who could set the reader's imagination flowing with his specific images, his staccato rhythms, his crackling electric sounds, should find these devices inadequate to reveal his *own* imaginary worlds. Intriguing that, so near the end of his life, Lowell could convey such strong desire for a new kind of vision:

Yet why not say what happened?
Pray for the grace of accuracy
Vermeer gave to the sun's illumination
stealing like the tide across a map
to his girl solid with yearning.

The poem pivots on the question, almost seems to settle for what he has accomplished. After all, the "grace of accuracy" is not easy. It's what we look for in a good essay. It's the mirror embedded in the poem. One right word, one specific image, and the writer has given us something we now realize we knew, but did not know we knew. Yet the quest for accuracy is also the impulse to pin something down, to make language serve the event—but language is elusive. Sometimes it takes another way of seeing to "say what happened."

I once watched a film of Picasso painting. After his first few strokes, the canvas was childlike in its simplicity. Then he added new images, drew over others; the painting became a swirl of color. At one point it seemed so satisfying I wanted to stop him. Couldn't he see it was finished? But he went on, dabbing, stabbing, muddling what had been clear. Soon the painting was murky. He should have known better. Now it was ruined! But . . . he continued blending, adding paint over paint until once again the canvas cleared, came into focus, completely transformed into something that had been, for me, *un*imaginable. Picasso led me past my own internal limits to what he'd sensed inside himself.

Excess is the difference between the painting and the photograph; it is also the difference between the painting and an etching. The paint itself—layered, mixed, with its flecks of cobalt blue, its free and energetic or delicately precise strokes—creates the texture. In poetry, language is the paint. There are some excesses in poetry that, in fact, *are* the poetry. Like Picasso, certain contemporary poets use excess in the best sense of the word; their work demonstrates a kind of ebullient linguistic play that, even as it opens the imagination, leads them closer and closer to accuracy. They demonstrate for us the difference between "excess" and "excessive." Within the space between *more than enough* and *too much*, they define the part of the human experience that can't be captured on the film.

Stanley Plumly's sixth collection, *Boy on the Step*, uses certain excesses as part of its method. The lack of critical attention given to this 1989 book has been a serious oversight, and I am pleased to see that Ecco Press has recently issued it in paperback. The volume's intricate evocation of time and place, its complex emotional landscape, even its deliberate silences, make it worthy of our attention.

As usual, Plumly's emphasis is memory itself—with sharply rendered personal experiences serving to demonstrate the process of recollection. So it is that the opening poem, "Hedgerows," begins with "How many names. Some trouble / or other would take me outside" and ends fifty lines later with "and the dead father." In between, there is no mention of the "trouble" or the "father." Rather, in those fifty lines Plumly tries to pin down what his body remembers. He recreates not a single but a composite memory, an ecstasy of image and adjective. The poet searches in language to capture the specifics of a time and place:

> The haw, the interlocking bramble, the thorn,
> head-high, higher a corridor, black windows.

Plumly's distinctive process is one of qualification: the hedge is, in turn, populated, named, measured, remeasured, and reexamined until it finds its proper metaphor as seen through the eyes of the boy. The reader sees through those same eyes, feels the depths of the night and the "voicelessness" that leads to a fleeting desire for death—a death that turns almost simultaneously to the dream of rebirth. The "I" of the poem imagines returning as the wood of the hedge, becoming the elm in the pail or the wooden bowl set before a "boy" who is lost in the thought of his father. The "I" and the "boy" are syntactically differentiated, yet they are linked by memory and dream so that the speaker can step out of the specific memory to watch another version of himself.

This pattern of qualification toward clarification is Plumly's method of developing the "photograph." It is as though the memory must be reconstructed one step at a time—like a negative coming clear—before he can "print" it in the positive of language. Once time and space have been "fixed," Plumly can perform his linguistic magic: he plays with tenses, superimposes memory on the present (and vice versa), allows everything to converge in the moment of the poem. The "accuracy" is one of specifics (colors, height, precise name of bird or plant) *and* of emotional context: by courting nuance, shading into difference,

Plumly constructs for the reader a musing voice that simply won't stop until it satisfies a need for accuracy.

Repetition, in Plumly's hands, creates another kind of accuracy. Images recur, incidents are repeated. The father and uncles stand on the steps, facing the camera; the great trees topple; the foundry flares; rain becomes silk, becomes glycerine, glitters; snow falls and keeps falling until it is ocean. Meaning emerges from the constant mulling and stirring.

"Against Starlings" uses another kind of excess. In a series of six "sonnets" (each line contains ten syllables with no regular rhythmic pattern), Plumly rivals Stevens's "Thirteen Ways of Looking at a Blackbird." The starlings are seen not only as what they are but also through a series of comparisons, and the litany of birds with which they are not to be confused is a study in natural and literary history. The final lines wrench the poem from its ostensible subject to reveal the linguistic paradox and the philosophical quandary at the heart of the book:

> I wished for one to come into the house,
> and left the window open just enough.
> None ever did. That was another year.
> What is to be feared is emptiness and
> nothing to fill it. I threw a stone or
> I didn't throw a stone is one language—
> the vowel is a small leaf on the tongue

Emptiness thus becomes a theme. In "Cedar Waxwing on Scarlet Firethorn," the perception of the fleeting moment becomes a death wish shared by writer and reader: "our desire to die, / to swallow fire, disappear, be nothing." The three following poems end with "not at all," "lost," and "out of this life," but as the book evolves the fear diminishes. The speaker recognizes and accepts a kind of human solitude, so that "Argument & Song," in which the speaker addresses his mother, ends with the knowledge that "I knew I would need a witness / and would fail, and that any / other loneliness / than this would be impossible." Plumly echoes this awareness in several other poems, but nowhere better than in "Cloud Building":

> it wants to leave
> the body through the mouth and come back slowly,
> pure with patience, shine slowly
> as something else we'll never know
> except alone, like the sentimental
> old, who are full of stories,
> or children, who in solitude have silence.

At the center of *Boy on the Step* are the large questions that sound silly when you put them in words—*What does it mean to have been alive?* and *What is the nature and meaning of death?* In "Toward Umbria," the contradictions are erased:

> The season is ending, fire on the wing,
> or the season is starting endlessly again,
> sedge and woodrush and yellow chamomile,
> anywhere a field is like a wall, lapsed, fallow
> or filled, a stain of wildflowers or a wave
> of light washing over stone, everything in time,
> and all the same—

Plumly's version of death, in which we are "scattered, or poured back into the earth," is one of rebirth, renewal. The dead become a part of everything, just as memory is part of the present, just as the present calls up the past ("It comes in the least / disguise . . . "). The impulse is toward a rediscovered anonymity. Yet, deep as that impulse may be, Plumly also honors essence of the individual life. It is not *a* father he remembers in "Above Barnesville," but *his* father, a man who "would not climb the ladder so loved by believers." From his father's denial, Plumly fashions a kind of faith: "For that I love him, and find him safe / in the least of things alive—dust on the road, wind at its back."

The title poem restates this tenet: "None of us dies entirely—some of us, all / of us sometimes come back sapling, seedling, cell . . ." "Boy on the Step" is a series of fourteen more "sonnets" (this time each line contains eleven syllables) in which private memory plays a specific role. The speaker, as observer, becomes the "immortal" child in whom memory resides. In a replay of scenes from his life, the speaker reconnects the fragments and finds, if not meaning, solace. The dead fathers and uncles are whole again: the faded photographs will hold them all, poised on the steps, their moment a gift to be inherited by "the children of memory." Plumly places himself squarely on the step, next in line.

A commentator cannot easily capture the feel of Plumly's work, even with extensive quotations; each poem is a matrix of complex sentences and carefully orchestrated lines—a seamless welding of imagery and idea. The poems are particularly hard to excerpt because they are not centered on one key image or event so much as they are *acts* of memory, language, and desire. With only fifty printed pages for its twenty-three poems, *Boy on the Step* is a short book, but this may be part of its strength, since Plumly's poems tend to sound alike, and the book makes up for its length with a density not usually found in contemporary poetry. Plumly's "excess" is twofold: an accumulation of verbal qualifiers coupled with an elaborate layering of memory on memory. The effect is a kind of edifying distance with a passionate center.

William Matthews' *Blues If You Want* is another book that hasn't received the attention it deserves. This is the eighth collection by a poet who has earned respect with his lively wit, his abundant ideas, and his deep intelligence. Matthews, too, uses excess, uses it wisely and always to his best advantage. His is a humorous, playful overdoing—one of constant movement, darting from thought to thought, leaving the reader reeling in his wake.

Blues If You Want looks at things from multiple points of view, always finding yet another angle from which to examine the world. With his quirky sense of humor, his readiness to laugh at himself, and his receptivity to the oddities of language, Matthews builds for us a linguistic world where he can coin a word like "Housecooling" or pair poems with the titles "Every Dog Has a Silver Lining" and "Every Cloud Has Its Day." But humor is merely the medium through which Matthews can make his observations. It allows him to sidle up to the serious—and this new volume is essentially serious.

Opening with two epigraphs about jazz, the book announces that it will explore the similarities (and differences) between music and writing and, by extension, between musician and writer. In the center of the volume, the speaker of "Every Tub," a jazz musician on the road, states the book's aesthetic challenge:

> See,
> the reason I'm a musician is, Language and I,
> we love each other but we never got it on,
> so as the saying goes, we're just good friends . . .

In "Straight Life," the final poem in the book, Matthews creates a companion piece. Here the speaker discovers that "I was with her / when I learned how some things can't be fully / felt until they're said" and concludes that writing and music spring from the same impulse:

> You lay a thin slather on the reed and take
> on a few bars of breath. Emily Dickinson
> wrote of Judge Otis Philips Lord that *Abstinence*
> *from Melody was what made him die.*
> Music's only secret is silence. It's time
> to play, time to tell whatever you know.

For all his playfulness—or perhaps because of it—Matthews does manage to blend the self-consciousness of language with the deep eloquence of the blues.

There is also here, as in all his work, the spontaneity and innovativeness of jazz. "The Blues" captures an adolescent's inarticulate energies ("I had the cunning of my body a few / bars—they were enough—of music"). "Smoke Gets in Your Eyes" begins with an appreciation of the "smoky libidinal murmur / of a jazz crowd" and ends with the smoker's guilty knowledge that he's killing himself. Yet note the sensuous description of lighting a cigarette:

> It's the reverse of music: only a small
> blue slur comes out—parody and rehearsal,
> both, for giving up the ghost. There's a nostril-
> billowing, sulphurous blossom from the match,
> a dismissive waggle of the wrist,
> and the match is out.

Matthews' light touch reverses the force field and we move backwards through the sentence, from the pleasure to its lethal implications to a burgeoning sense that music has a body of its own.

"It Don't' Mean a Thing If It Ain't Got That Swing" explores the language of love. In it, Matthews leaves his lovers undressing ("She's / all detail and all beautiful"; "He hates being so inarticulate. He hates being / so inarticulate") to begin a "myth" in which Language, stolen from the gods by Prometheus, laments her ephemeral state:

> *Oh, I'd give anything*, she cried,
> *if I could be memorable.*
>
> *Anything?*
> intoned the opportunistic devil from
> behind a papier-mâché boulder. *Yes,*
> *anything*, she said, and thus the deal
>
> was struck and writing was invented.
> But to be written down she gave up
> pout, toss, crinkle,
> stamp and shrug, shiver, flout and pucker,
>
> the long, cunning lexicon of the body,
> and thus what we lazily call "form"
> in poetry,
> let's say, is Language's desperate

attempt to wrench from print
the voluble body it gave away
in order to be read.

Returning to the lovers, Matthews gives their murmurs all the power of love. And for himself, "Could I but find the words and lilt . . . " he mutters as he fumbles toward his own lovesong.

The title of the book suggests some complicity with the reader: take these poems, if you so desire, as Matthews' versions of the blues. At least two of them have, for me, the kind of shattering clarity that reaches somehow below, or beyond, language. "Nabokov's Blues" opens the book with an account of a trip to a museum in which Nabokov's collection of butterflies is accentuated by quoted passages from his work. "And there in the center of the room a carillon / of Blues rang mutely out. There must have been / three hundred of them." Nabokov had noted even the altitude at which each specimen was caught. Leaving, the speaker remembers the room, "vast by love of each flickering detail / each genital dusting to nothing, the turn, / like a worm's or caterpillar's, of each phrase." The poem does not stop at this natural ending; with wry self-deprecation, Matthews pushes into the personal territory where the rage is not for order, but for "the love the senses bear for what they do"—with or without a final coherence:

the way
desire burns bluely at its phosphorescent core:
just as you're having what you wanted most,
you want it more and more until that's more
than you, or it, or both of you, can bear.

The darkest Matthews' blues is "Mood Indigo," and it's also the finest poem in the collection. Listen to the music of its opening stanza:

From the porch; from the hayrick where her prickled
brothers hid and chortled and slurped into their young pink
lungs the ash-blond dusty air that lay above the bales . . .

With sound and rhythm, and with a repetitive syntactical construction, Matthews creates a haunting story in which a young girl slowly sinks into what is, if not insanity, a melancholy torpor in which she "kept to her room," only emerging to wander the fields. The narrative element is important, but more important is the sense that "it" was always there—that she was, quite simply, too sensitive to live in the world:

It became her dead pet, her lost love, the baby sister
blue and dead at birth, the chill headwaters of the river

that purled and meandered and ran and ran until
it issued into her, as into a sea, and then she was its
and it was wholly hers . . .

This is the music it hurts to hear. Throughout the volume, Matthews has managed to spin the word "blue" so we can see its many facets. He has touched down, like one of Nabokov's butterflies flitting from subject to subject, on the breakup of a marriage, the moon in Vermont, the theft of a TV and tape deck, the cooking of onions, a red silk blouse. Some of the poems are less successful than others, and the book's publication was perhaps a bit hasty—*Foreseeable Futures* having appeared just two years earlier. But *Blues* definitely presents, as Matthews claims in "Little Blue Nude," a "reverie on what I love, and whom, / and how I manage to hold on to them."

What *we* hold on to in *Blues If You Want* is the accuracy of "the noise of my own voice." That voice contains both wit and wisdom, and in most cases the two depend on each other. The result is a nervous, quick energy which seems to exceed the topic at hand and pulls the reader into the strobe light of an idiosyncratic mind. Neither snapshot nor painting, Matthews' poems are collage—a careful arrangement of the fictive and the factual. Together they make up a sparkling whole.

Pamela Stewart's fourth collection, *Infrequent Mysteries*, is a book of little excesses. More classically feminine, these excesses take the form of near-surrealism: slight oddities of language and perception, often taking the form of two words put together that don't quite fit. The poems are not surreal in the flamboyant style of Dali, but rather with the blurred edges of the later Monet. The distortions become part of the clarity.

In a close and careful examination of the world, Stewart resists even the suggestion of a lens. Hers is the world of dream and daydream as much as it is one of fact. Where two come together, often with seeming contradiction, Stewart tries to fashion a language capable of bridging the gap. For example, "The Canoe in the Forest" begins with the vivid evocation of a child's imagination and then qualifies it with specific detail:

Like a sliver of light adrift in the pine & russet shade
the canoe in the forest

has moved down to the riverbank, into the slow thick
water of a late August afternoon. Or you could say
that my grandfather with his wolf-
haired hands shifted the heavy tarp
& with a few slick tugs that silver eyelid of a boat
slid out, trembling
in the shallows as he stepped in.

But even as Stewart calls up her grandfather, his hands, and the tarp, she cannot help but see the boat as an "eyelid"; the poem is not a recounted incident but a reconstructed scene. In the story he brought back home, her grandfather found a dead man in the river. In the poem, the child conjures dead men everywhere before she comes to terms with statistics ("Still, all canoes with their silvers, reds & greens / keep slipping along rivers, & dark New England lakes") and realizes that some experiences are singular, that only one canoe went sliding "into that celestial chill."

Many of the poems in *Infrequent Mysteries* contain such contraries. There is a clash between the sharp visual images of the real world and the surprising juxtapositions of a nebulous otherworld. This is characterized by the choice of language or image, and the reader learns to accept this as part of the poem's "meaning." "The Edge of Things," for instance, opens with two stanzas that defy narrative logic:

You want to know who sleeps on the other side
of the wall—there's a feeling
of needles in his legs, a silence of orphans.

His name and age are not important. He must
be less than young. Over that tree,
a hawk blesses one of his hands.
You are not sure, right or left. Or do they mean
the print of ash across his mouth?

The poem goes on, however, to articulate what is central to the volume—that "one side of the wall is unbearable softness." Stewart is willing to explore that vulnerability: "You want to know why this someone is sleeping / during the exact moments that you sleep." The body carries with it its dreaming counterpart. Why is that experience any less real?

Like an iron filing, Stewart is drawn to the magnet of dichotomy. The world divides, and Stewart inhabits the division. As in "The Bostonian Reading Amichai," she can claim that "nothing exact / ever called to me." Unlike Amichai, who can "argue / with God how none of it makes sense," Stewart simply tries to accommodate the blurred edges. She sees herself (as in "On Rereading, Yet Again, *Tender Is the Night*") as having an "other life." That life contains the timelessness of childhood reverie, the supreme darkness of childhood fear, the vast spaces between lovers together or apart; it steps into imaginary spaces and feels the pain of the alcoholic mother or the fantasies of a fatherless girl; it imagines itself the bulimic daughter of Fiction—a cold, demanding father.

But the real world intrudes, as "My Other Insomnia" so clearly demonstrates. Remembering that her first boyfriend was Armenian, the speaker tries to come to grips with history:

> What do I really *know* in this violent dawn
> where rooms stay warm if the bills are paid? I'm safe, useless
> against those drenched & foreign blades. So, I remembered John
>
> & our soft, misplaced kisses as I hear the thick
> blue rain outside batter to get in & fill my sleeplessness
> with that cold, other burning from which I'm not immune.

Infrequent Mysteries is haunted by separation over time and space. The poems step in and out of time, mediating between the person then and the person now. In the present, the speaker watches hunters on a "drab December hill." In the past, she hears her parents arguing. The moments are linked by the same knot in her stomach—"Like her, I'm racked by the long / grey silences between." Stewart's naturally associative mind creates connective tissue, as in the final lines of "Naïve Reading":

> I'm in the mirror
> not yet taking sides. But behind me
> something stirs light as summer leaves
>
> or an eyelash of God—your ghosts
> that lick across the world, like fog.

Stewart's voice is strongest when she is most uncertain. Thus, the sixth section of the long title poem captures the very clarity of confusion: "There's a time before anything is sure— / Is birdsong bright / or dark . . . ?" And there is something very sure in the odd images of "Dreams click awake / testing their teeth on the rafters." One of the dangers of this style is that when the words don't surprise, they may fall flat. Phrases like "buttercups insist on yellow" or "hurt was possible to lose" show strain. And there's a precious quality to "fire / pleasures my existence." These moments are rare; they seem to come when the poem is forced—when the internal twilight does not quite equal the external dusk. Otherwise, Stewart's synesthetic images give us a glimpse of that "other" world where mystery is, briefly, understood.

The title poem flits skittishly from dream to desire, from waking observation to philosophical questioning. Moving between its "walls" and "spaces," the impersonal voice of the speaker asserts that "The personal / is a small space, or no space at all, / until something calls from the world outside." Instantly, the voice becomes more personal, owns its own space in a kind of *ars poetica*:

> I hear the sound of rain before it falls, see
> the light-coming-down which becomes
> that sound. How inexact I am
> among the people within these walls.
> Rain comes from a world outside.
>
> This moment I live in the wall
> of my skull where it's raining.
> I want only the dark sound of it—
> that thin pure voice to inhabit me.

Meditations on the inexact are Stewart's strength. She gives us another side of human experience, one that eludes the silver nitrate of the film. Or else she clicks her multiple exposures so that image folds into image, decade into decade, the final print an accumulation of sensory stimuli that tell their own kind of truth.

Albert Goldbarth's latest book is called *Heaven and Earth: A Cosmology*. Its 118 pages cover just about everything imaginable and, in some way, do examine the dynamics of the universe. Working from a dazzling catalogue of facts (from historical oddities to the latest *Guinness Book of Records*), from a lexicon of the latest scientific theories, from a variety of personal experiences, and with an almost excruciating honesty, Goldbarth perfects the parallel arts of synthesis and digression.

These poems must be experienced. Funny, ironic, bitter, hilarious, irreverent, sexy, serious—the list of adjectives could apply, in turn, to almost every poem. To excerpt is to try to exert control over Goldbarth's exhilarating thoughts, yet the effect of the poems is to be nearly *out* of control, or in a carefully controlled chaos, like a roller-coaster ride. Each loop and curve holds a new surprise; the poems reel with a kind of manic energy, step off into space, return again with acerbic accuracy. In fact, Goldbarth's very style *is* excess: poems with excessively long sentences packed with an excess of fact, speculation, and memories—data of all kinds which threaten to bury the reader or leave him far behind. For example, the opening stanza of "A Paean to the Concept" (a title almost guaranteed to put off the reader) is one long language-loving sentence:

> On show tonight, the maestrochef in his puffpastry headgear
> veers a flapjack cunningly through a high arc like a porpoise-breach,
> from right pan into left then back, the flapjack taking on
> the sinuous wiffle a unicellular creature swims with, finally
> taking on unbroken rushing grace of a pour
> of water itself; the chef by now is one with it, is boneless
> background motion, giving just the tilt and rhythm
> of one of those rubber-ball-attached-by-a-rubber-string-to-a-paddle
> champions, in whom we see the current and its banks are of
> a piece.

The wonder of Goldbarth, his magic, is that, despite the frenzy of words and ideas, it all does add up to something. And it does more than add up—it captivates, fascinates, and even informs. Finally, it moves.

Goldbarth's method almost seems intended to fend off revelation, as if his verbosity were a protective gesture, a kind of forced play. Even when these poems take on painful or personal subjects, they act flippant, almost daring you to care more than they do. Yet in the end, most of them are deadly earnest—which is why they need some mitigating humor. "Sentimental," for example, poses the question of sentimentality. It begins with a stereotypical wedding scene, moves through pie and "puppydogs" to "When my father was buried, / the gray snow in the cemetery was the sheet tin. If I said / that?" From there, Goldbarth evokes "Hollywood hack violinists," moves on, circling through blues singers and crippled girls to the true, and finely rendered, sentiment:

> What if I simply put the page down,
> rocked my head in my own folded elbows, forgot
> the rest of it all, and wept? What if I stepped into
> the light of that page, a burnished and uncompromising
> light, and walked back up to his stone a final time,
> just that, no drama, and it was so cold,
> and the air was so brittle, metal buckled
> out song like a bandsaw, and there, from inside me,
> where they'd been lost in shame and sophistry
> all these years now, every last one of my childhood's
> heartwormed puppydogs found its natural voice.

Goldbarth makes demands on the reader. He challenges you to be as deft, as witty, as expansive, and as emotionally large as he is. Readers who consign him to the category of "humor" fail to see that, as in most good comedy, the poems are a way to bear the pain. Goldbarth may make light of the tedium of Hebrew school—"Elijah this. / The Children of Israel that . / And Moses. Moses in the bulrushes, Moses / blahblahblah"—but he never loses sight of his origins. He writes with empathy of the relatives who came to this country in steerage. In "*Mishipasinghan, Lumchipamudana*, etc.," he moves from the Quechua's thousand words for potato to the one (invented?) word—*peynisht*—which can mean only a political prisoner's stunned state of being. He can, in "Another Portrait," respond to Joseph Epstein's question, "What if Lowell's poem 'My Last Afternoon with Uncle Devereux Winslow' were instead entitled 'My Last Afternoon with Uncle Morris Shapiro'?" The resulting poem is humorous, yes, but also human, humane. One poem, appropriately titled "'Too Much,'" ends with the young boy watching his squabbling parents return home through the snow:

> They're giggling with each other, and their breaths
> run ahead like white minks on a leash.

Goldbarth's poems are spun from an encyclopedic mind that engages odd snippets of information as well as the whole of scientific treatises. Anything is fair game, is part of the celestial mush. So, on reading that ninety direct-mail solicitations were sent to Henry David Thoreau in 1988, Goldbarth begins "A Letter":

> At the end of a day that's rubble around me,
> shrimp husks, tufts on a barber's floor, heaped circus doo,
> at the burr tail-end, the tar tail-end,
> the shitty piggy corkscrew tail-end of a day like that,
> when all the dauby, wadded toilet paper staunchings of the
> shaving mistakes
> of a lifetime buzz about this air like ghost wasps,
> and to try to even say a word like *graciousness* or *honor*
> coughs a bile-larded furball up into the throat . . .
> at the end of a day like that, I pick you up,
> Old Chisel-Puss, and head out to the last, thin brothlight
> just to read some random observation you whittled,
> cleansed in lime and ashes, then set on your simple sill
> for the world to do as it will with it, yes,
> Henry David, Old Man Applemash, Hardwood Grainface, you.

For all the tongue-twisting vocabulary, the poems read easily out loud, reminiscent of T. S. Eliot's ability to catch the exact cadences of speech. Naturally iambic, never singsong, the Goldbarth line is, quite simply, fun.

Heaven and Earth is divided into four sections—*Talk*, *Love*, *Others*, and *Physics*. Each section, however, instantly spills into the other categories. No area of knowledge can be isolate; everything connects in one way or another. If cosmology implies a philosophy, Goldbarth's might be simply this: in a universe so vast, we have each other. We step out into "used light" and recycled breath. Our human connections are imperfect but essential, and they are lovely in their frailty:

> come snuggle next to you, and love what there is
> in a living surface, love what it means to be here
> at the end of uncountable miles of lacelike nerve,
> lung-lining, nephron tubule, snaggled delicate
> blood we see fronded through eyes, here
> where our days with each other
> hang by their precious, hang by their pitiful, threads.
> ("The History of Buttons")

Is *Heaven and Earth* "too much"? Maybe. If so, it's too much of a good thing. Individual poems are hard to keep in mind as others keep coming in seemingly infinite permutations, but, as in the Picasso painting, everything eventually comes clear. The book ends on a quiet note, with the final line of "The Sciences Sing a Lullabye" also defining the poetry. "*History says*: here are the blankets, layer on layer, down and down." Reading this cosmology is like looking through both ends of a telescope at once.

Les Murray's excesses are, first of all, "natural": both the landscape he draws on and the language he employs are exotic to the American eye and ear. (Surely, in a land of dingo and kangaroo, jacaranda and broom, drinks called *bikavér*, and place names like Coolongolook and Flying-Fox Cooking Place—surely, in such a land, language must become an obsession?) Spanning twenty-two years and seven previous volumes, *The Rabbiter's Bounty* is a collected volume designed to introduce Murray to us as one of Australia's finest poets. His range is as wide as his continent; the poems encompass landscape, personal memory, science and technology, Australian folklore and history, English and Celtic culture, politics, philosophy, and religion. But for all its varied subjects, *The Rabbiter's Bounty* is grounded in a family farm at Bunyah, in the bush country north of Sydney. That land—and its history—is the center of the compass from which Murray can draw concentric circles, pulling into the net of his poems the aboriginal culture, the immigrant expansion, four generations of family, neighbors, friends, familiar fields, and the distant horizon. In "Thinking About Aboriginal Land Rights, I Visit the Farm I Will Not Inherit," Murray recognizes the inevitable:

> Watching from the barn the seedlight and nearly-all-down
> currents of a spring day, I see the only lines bearing
> consistent strain are the straight ones: fence, house, corner,
> outermost furrows.

As he envisions the way the bush would come back, "unrobbing" the bee trees, everything returning to what it once was, he nevertheless cannot give up his love for the land, his desire to be part of it: "I go into the earth near the feed shed for thousands of years."

There's a recognized tension between the immigrant's hard-won claim and the longer history of the land ("it is the earth / that holds our mark longest, that soil dug never returns / to primal coherence"), and Murray honors both. An early poem, "Noonday Axeman," captures the wordless pleasure of felling a tree with "Axe-fall, echo and silence." Like a refrain, the phrase resounds throughout the poem:

> Axe-fall, echo and silence. Dreaming silence
> Though I myself run to the cities, I will forever
> be coming back here to walk, knee-deep in ferns,
> up and away from this metropolitan century . . .

He returns to his ancestors ("axemen, dairymen, horse-breakers, / now coffined in silence") but carries with him the "dreaming silence" of aborigines. So it is that Murray fashions his own songlines in the poems like "The Buladelah-Taree Holiday Song Cycle," "The Dialectic of Dreams," or "Walking to the Cattle Place" with its fifteen complex sections. The final part of "Walking" is a synthesis, an "old song and an ancient one," which opens with the voice of the cattle:

> Their speech is a sense of place
> night makes remote
> lucerne fields in the dark hills are renamed
> Moorea, Euboea.
>
> That bull invoking Mundubbera, Karuah
> and Speewah, now, Speewah
> is trying his sultanate out in infinite space.

Sleepy, lingually liquescent.
It is a delectation, the matter of rock-salt,
a drawn sparkling mouth

squaremouth, though, for the mother
mourning at the five-bar
gate for her tongue-sculpted, milky one
manhandled to the mad chute, steel-barred,
gone above gears.

One wants to quote poem after poem, just to savor the excellent excess of sound. Murray's poems are English church bells, ringing each change in crisp air. They are also Australian idiom, the language of working men and farmers. Murray has such a meticulous ear and sure sense of form that he can slip easily in and out of intricate slant rhyme, metrical patterns, shifting rhyme schemes, and rhythmic modulations from short spurts to long luxuriant lines. All of English poetic tradition is clearly behind him, but Murray makes it new again with the sheer energy of his Australian speech rhythms and his honest intimacy. In addition, many of the poems contain multiple voices—fragments from letters, overheard conversation, recounted stories, the speaker's own interior voice—and a rough, expansive humor that is characteristically Australian. "Quintets for Robert Morley" celebrates fat people with real verve ("Never trust a lean meritocracy"), and "The Quality of Sprawl" goes on to define, through a series of examples, the gutsy, utilitarian anti-elitism of Australian culture—a matter of spirit more than style:

Sprawl is the quality
of the man who cut down his Rolls-Royce
into a farm utility truck, and sprawl
is what the company lacked when it made repeated efforts
to buy the vehicle back and repair its image.

The success of the poem is that it ends still elaborating what it never quite pins down:

Sprawl leans on things. It is loose-limbed in its mind.
Reprimanded and dismissed
it listens with a grin and one boot up on the rail
of possibility. It may have to leave the Earth.
Being roughly Christian, it scratches the other cheek
and thinks it unlikely. Though people have been shot for sprawl.

Murray treats us not only to the richnesses of language, but also to the buried meanings of individual words. In "Bent Water in the Tasmanian Highlands," the rapids are seen as "The continuous ocean round a planetary stone, braiding uptilts / after swoops, echo-forms, arches built from above and standing / on flourish, clear storeys, translucent honey-glazed clerestories—" In the final year-long cycle of poems, playing with the word "misericord," he moves to breathtaking elegy:

> Grief is nothing you can do, but do,
> worst work for least reward,
> pulling your heart out through your eyes
> with tugs of the misery cord.

The penultimate poem in *The Rabbiter's Bounty* is philosophical and deeply religious, connecting the immediacy of the present to the expanses of geological time. "Aspects of Language and War on the Gloucester Road" begins, "I travel a road cut through time / by bare feet and boots without socks." As the speaker drives to the railroad station, passing his farm, the cemetery, his great-grandmother's Chinese elm, he meditates on war and on the history of the land—its place names, the brief lives of the settlers. With a careful sprinkling of "the old language"(words like *baga waga* and *ba:rung*), a chorus of exterior voices, and a strong narrative thread, time is condensed as Murray fuses all experience into one elemental tongue:

> . . . and under the purple coast of the Mograni
> and its trachyte west wall scaling in the sky
> I will swoop to the valley and Gloucester Rail
> where boys hand-shunted trains to load their cattle
> and walk on the platform, glancing west at that country
> of running creeks, the stormcloud-coloured Barrington,
> the land, in lost Gaelic and Kattangal, of Barandan.

The final lines of "Recourse to the Wilderness" speak for the rest of the poems, evoking both a personal and historical past, a powerfully felt presence in the world:

> Where the spirits of sea-cliffs
> hovered on the plain
> I would remember routines we had invented
> for putting spine into shapeless days: the time
> we passed at a crouching trot down Wynyard Concourse

telling each other in loud mock-Aranda and gestures
what game we were tracking down what haunted gorge,
frivolous games
but they sustained me like water,

they, and the is-ful ah!-nesses of things.

Born in 1938, Les Murray is earning a reputation as one of the most important writers in English today. From the emu to the bulldozer to the powerline, he celebrates everything. Page after page, like a more musical, more comprehensive Elizabeth Bishop, Murray demonstrates his love of precise detail, his curiosity, his embrace of the physical world. "Bounty" is the right word for this beautifully produced book. Don't wait for the paperback. We not only ought to know his work, we *need* to know it.

Robert Lowell's "Epilogue" concludes with a recognition of mortality:

We are poor passing facts,
warned by that to give
each figure in the photograph
his living name.

Like Lowell, the five poets considered here do more than simply "name"—they bring to life their varied worlds with a strength not only visual but cerebral. Their work is intellectually curious, informed, and even, in a way, philosophical. It displays a quality of mind that dares to *risk*, and that may be what so much American poetry lacks at the moment. With our own anti-elitist tradition, we may have devalued the mind and its essential role. These five poets resist stark realism, turgid confessionalism, formulaic "deep" imagery, and ecological cant. In their individual voices, the recalled and the imagined become one.

Skating on Paper

On C. K. Williams' *A Dream of Mind*; W. S. Merwin's *Travels*; Judith Hall's *To Put the Mouth To*; Debora Pope's *Fanatic Heart*; Gerald McCarthy's *Shoetown*; and Anne Carson's *Short Takes*.

"POETRY IN MOTION!"—the announcer bursts forth with the old cliché as soon as the skaters hit the ice. I am instantly defensive. But, resist as I will, the skaters win. Three hours of Brian Boitano, of Mark Mitchell or Lu Chen, of the dancers Klimova and Ponomarenko, then Duchesnays, Torvill and Dean, three hours of the electric Viktor Petrenko and I am convinced that I know the source of the cliché and that, as is often the case, the source resides in what is most true.

The spotlight catches one figure dressed completely in black, including a hooded mask. Faceless, he is all body—tall and fluid. Through the sound system: the odd beat of a drum, an occasional rasp of flute, a tinkle, a shimmer—nothing that could be called a tune. Against this "music," the body jerks into syncopated motion, begins a wide sweep, a truncated spin. The skates resist the ice, making a sound. Shhhkk. And the ice resists the body, stops it mid-movement. Forces it back on itself. The flashing strobe light momentarily illuminates, then conceals, segmenting motion into separate frames. Faceless, the body reveals the way each jump or spin is made up of a specific sequence of individual moves. Watching this, I understand how those moves go together to make a completed figure. I have *felt* the shape of the line.

The faceless figure turns out to have a name—Gary Beacom of Canada. He returns in white pants, turquoise shirt, yellow tie. His face is expressive; the skating is seamless once more. But I'm haunted by the body that is no longer before me, the skeletal shape that revealed the poem. It's Beacom, not Petrenko, who has taken me to the secret of Petrenko's most amazing leap: the presence of a vision. Petrenko knows what he's reaching for; his face relaxes even before he lands, flashes a quick smile. This is choreography: each line by itself displays amazing skill, yet each is essential to the construction of a whole. The poem has been set in motion.

Too much contemporary poetry is pyrotechnics, manner, attitude. It displays skill—even, in bursts, imagination—yet is lacking in any sense of a whole, a sustaining purpose which gives meaning to the skill displayed. This is not a simple matter. I am convinced that it is possible to learn to write a poem in the same way it is possible to learn to skate, by practicing the individual moves over and over. I am also convinced that the result will look like, even act like, a poem. But it will not be a poem until it is impelled by something beyond the desire to have written a poem. I'd name it *yearning* except that a friend's anecdote comes so quickly to mind: *A graduate student said a poem had moved him. "Moved?" said the professor. "That word has no place in our discussion."* But why not refute the professors who refuse to begin the discussion with emotion? Why not look for the poems that embody the need to fly?

Looking over the many books sent to me to consider for this review, I see that they fall essentially into two categories: those where the line is predominant (that is, the line seems to drive the poem and creates the tone or cadence, even the *meaning*) and those where the overall vision seems to determine the line and the way it will function in the poem. Of course the reader cannot know exactly how a poem came into being, but this latter category consists of poems which could be described as those whose shape was felt before the act of articulation began. Some poems, explicitly or implicitly, raise the question of line versus vision; it becomes part of the drama in reading. It's similar to the way a spectator at an ice show can be involved in the moment-to-moment risks the performer takes—will she make it? will he fall?—all the while building toward the hoped-for recognition of a perfectly completed shape. We watch poets bend and extend their lines in interesting ways and we may go with them for the moment, even admire the daring or subtlety, but in the end we need to see that the flashes of brilliance have been in service of something more complex.

At any rate, that's the sort of concern I bring with me as a reader to six new books of poetry. The line is extremely personal to the poet. It orchestrates individual voice, and poets today are feeling quite free to experiment with how best to capture this personal element. I'm going to pay attention not only to the characteristic line of each poet, but to what the line *does*, how it serves the articulation of the larger version.

C. K. Williams has developed a deliberately elongated line (almost every one is over twenty syllables) that is instantly recognizable to readers of contemporary poetry. *A Dream of Mind*, his latest collection, uses that line to serve as its title. Williams' long lines not only launch the narrative, they also allow enough room for a kind of internal equivocation. They flow more easily when read quietly to oneself than when read aloud. The rhythms are the rhythms of thought—actually, of reason—so that the reader is constantly aware of the mind at work, twisting back on itself in order to fix and define what is otherwise ambiguous. In this way, Williams' lines allow him to become so obsessive about getting it right that the poems often unfold as an unending scrutiny of nuance. For example, the fourteen poems of the second section, entitled "Some of the Forms of Jealousy," let the reader know from the beginning what they are all "about." The meaning, therefore, resides in the process, as can be seen by the opening lines of "Signs":

> My friend's wife has a lover; I come to this conclusion—not suspicion,
>   mind, conclusion,
> not a doubt about it, not a hesitation, although how I get there might
>   be hard to track;
> a blink a little out of phase, say, with its sentence, perhaps a word or
>   two too few;
> a certain tenderness of atmosphere, of aura, almost like a pregnancy,
>   with less glow, perhaps,
> but similar complex inward blushes of accomplishment, achievement,
>   pride—during dinner,
> as she passes me a dish of something, as I fork a morsel of it off, as our
>   glances touch.

By the time we reach the end, we've been caught up in the psychology of the poem's persona, worrying away at the minor details that make up the major portion of our lives. And the fun in the reading is to use our own knowledge of human nature, enough to follow the speaker's logic through to its conclusion and simultaneously reserve judgment so that the speaker might be—definitely *could* be—wrong about everything. "Jealousy" is the ostensible subject, but the intricacies of the mind—its ability to deliberate to the point of utter self-consciousness—are what fascinate the reader, and probably the poet as well.

The expansive lines give sustenance to "She, Though," the eleven-page poem that comprises the middle section, by establishing a *spoken* voice—that of someone telling an anecdote, someone maddeningly literal and, at the same time, fascinating in his fanatic precision. The poem opens with the peculiar vagaries of speech, all its qualifications and ambiguities: "Her friend's lover was dying, or not 'friend,' they weren't that yet, if they ever really were; . . ." The reader is able to maintain an interest in the primary "story," but the real interest is in how the speaker reacts to the "she" of the title. In analyzing a particular woman's response to her roommate's tragedy as well as that woman's relationship to her art, he finds himself enmeshed in his own crisis of identity. This poem is indicative of Williams' characteristic achievement. He is able to render something like the full complexity of consciousness—typically that of an observer catching himself in the act of observation.

If the first half of the book calls attention to the mind at work, the sixteen discrete poems of the title section shift the emphasis slightly from the "mind" to the "dream," with varying connotations, including the imaginary, the insubstantial, the illusory, the pensive, and the visionary. Williams uses the mind and its convoluted forays into logic to decipher the meaning of dream, what he terms "ideas of dreams." But the treacherous mind often ends the speculation with a question mark. In dream, where the mind can make "something out of nothing," the shadowy figures or the reincarnated dead are understood only in abstractions. More often than not, those abstractions lead to even more abstruse questions, as in "Light":

> And if this isn't the case, wouldn't the alternative be as bad; that each
>   element of the dream
> would contain its own entailment so that what came next would just do
>   so for no special reason?

"Reason" is at the heart of *A Dream of Mind*, and yet dream resists reason. It leads, so often, to truly unanswerable questions.

The culminating concern of so many of the poems in the title sequence is that of death, of its place in the human order, of what we are to make of it. "Helen," the long final poem that comprises the fifth section, is the account of one man's experience of his wife's final days. As an observer, he is able to *will* an attitude toward death—that he could keep "all the person she had been" inside himself so she would go on living. But the dream cannot hold. Death is recognized for what it is—a singular event—and he must give her over to it, knowing he couldn't retain the illusion. The poem pushes on from this point, though, in a way of human willfulness, to a closure where the speaker feels that he has entered death with her, has bridged the gap of separation. Unfortunately, the last two stanzas ring false. Grief is not identical to death. This reader, at least, is left stymied by something that does not mesh with her experience.

The long lines that allow Williams to explore this particular kind of consciousness also seem to imprison him in their very flexibility. He almost acknowledges this in "The Method" when he states, "I dream a dream of method, comprehending little of the real forces or necessities of dream, / and find myself entangled in the dream, entrapped, already caught in what the dream contrived, / in what it made, of my ambitions, or of what it itself aspired to . . ." Substitute the word "line" for all but the first "dream" and you discover his problem: the line seems to have a life of its own; it dictates tone; it limits the eventual conclusion. In fact, most of Williams' lines end with a period, a semicolon or, at the very least, a comma, thus completing their function before he goes on. Coupled with the abstract nature of the argument itself, Williams' line demarcates what the reader can easily hold intact in the head. One reads to the end of the line, comprehends the fullness of thought, then readies oneself for the next.

Williams' strength is his limitation: his means are so self-conscious that they inevitably become a stance rather than an exploration. Because these lines represent thought chiefly as a verbal process, there are few images on which readers can focus. We are expected to enter the abstract discourse of the poem rather than bring our own worlds with us. The effect is both stimulating and frustrating. There is serious pleasure in matching one's mind to that of the writer, in seeing things through his eyes—or rather, voice. This is especially true for the humorous poems such as "The Vessel" and "Child Psychology." The frustration comes when there is simply too much of what might be a good thing, as though the lines were stamped out by machine, one after the other, all of a kind. In the book as a whole, their aggregate weight seems to drain energy from the individual pieces. It's a bit like eating a very large Caesar salad. At first the palate is pleased by the sharp sensation, the blend of distinctive tastes. But all too soon the flavor is familiar and there's still so much lettuce on the plate.

Williams' poems are at their best when read individually in the *New Yorker*. There, they have wit and energy. Their "vision" is discernable and their line seems more a mark of virtuosity rather than a mere compulsory figure.

W. S. Merwin's most recent book, *Travels*, is permeated by a healthy nostalgia for what has been lost to us—a sense of history, an identification with place, a connection between generations, the old forms in art. Everything is seen as though through the window of a passing train, briefly illuminated and then receding into the world of memory. The preface poem, "Cover Note," appears separately and sets an elegiac tone (whose echo of Baudelaire signals as well a literary nostalgia):

> Hypocrite reader my
> variant my almost
> family we are so

few now it seems as though
we knew each other as
the words between us keep
assuming that we do
I hope I make sense to
you in the shimmer of
our days while the world we
cling to in common is

burning . . .

Merwin searches for a reader, doubting the ability of new generations to "behold our true meaning" and to conjure, from our images the "rushing of // paws in high grass the one / owl hunting along this / spared valley . . ." Many of the subsequent poems reiterate this fear. In a series of poetic biographies or "written lives," Merwin recalls the checkered history of colonization; the cutting of sandalwood from the Hawaiian hillsides; the Plains Indian, Frank Henderson, who held on to his lost traditions through drawings; the Russian-born botanist who traveled the Amazon and whose knowledge of plants saved his life; the stories of countless "forgotten" people. There are two ways to speak for others, the poet claims in "Writing Lives"—one is "to tell the lives of others / using the distance as a lens // and another way / is when there is no distance / so that water / is looking at water."

Interestingly, Merwin's characteristic lack of punctuation and his enjambed lines enable him to speak both ways, sometimes simultaneously. The flow is layered with response, memory, insight—all rendered in a rush of images and commentary tumbling over each other, much like the experience itself. On the other hand, since many of these poems are fairly long narratives, the reader not only becomes aware of the distance between the poet and his subject but also the "doubled" distance between the *reader* and the poet and the poet's subject. Merwin's lines are themselves a distancing factor at times; the constant enjambment and internal fusion can create a kind of stutter, nearly stopping the flow as the reader backs up to reposition himself in a phrase. The result is a kind of artificial removal by which a reader is kept from an easy engagement with the "story" of the poem. For example, the following lines from "Lives of the Artists" demonstrate how the reader must sort through the syntax:

the strange moon the new hunger they had no
words for and he would have years before
the wagons changed him and he came back
to meet Reverend Haury
who always knew

better and made him a bright Indian
teaching with white words but

The lines rush on, but the reader has to struggle to make sense. However, a closer look at this poem (and many of the others) reveals that there is method here. The poems are written in syllabics, each stanza reiterating the patter which shapes its poem. Lines which at first glance seemed slack take on the tension of structure, become part of a greater whole. By noting the pattern, the reader participates in an aesthetic process.

But Merwin's line is most effective in the several short lyric poems clustered near the end of the book. In these, the structure created for the ear and eye provides a framework within which Merwin, almost in counterpoint, constructs the cadence of a voice and a complex syntax which culminates in a powerful sense of loss. The lines (and phrases within the lines) are suspended; their deliberate slippage points both backward, toward the poem's inception, and forward to its conclusion. The poem spins, centered on its images, in a vortex of its own making. There are many such poems in *Travels*, and I love most of them. "On the Old Way" admirably demonstrates what is meant by "lyric time," in which the overlay of present on past creates a simultaneity where *is* and *was* are one in the same:

After twelve years and a death
returning in August to see the end of summer
French skies and stacked roofs the same grays
silent train sliding south through the veiled morning
once more the stuccoed walls the sore
pavilions of the suburbs glimpses
of rivers known from other summers leaves
still green with chestnuts forming for their
only fall out of old dark branches and again
the nude hills come back and the sleepless
night travels along through the day as it
once did over and over for this was the way
almost home almost certain that it was
there almost believing that it could be
everything in spite of everything

The "only" fall of the chestnuts and the transitory life of the poet are set against the permanence of the landscape and the recurrence of the natural cycles. Time is the culprit, or rather, the knowledge of time that forces the poet to acknowledge the "almost" and the "in spite of" that tell him death is irrevocable. Memory surfaces in the words "again" and "come back" and "once." The title of the collection comes into play—the *poem* is a form of travel, a journey into time and place, into a moment so intense it is nearly unbearable.

The intensity of the lyric moment is echoed and expanded in a series of poems where the syllabic structure again is crucial—this time in order to reinforce the interiority and yet allow the poem a further range. So it is that "Kites," for example, can move inexorably from its opening ("No one who did not have to / would stay in the heaving sepia / roar of the unlit depot hour / after hour") to its soaring conclusion ("the kites will be / watching from their own element / as long as the light lasts / neither living as the living know / of it nor dead with the dead / and neither leaving nor promising / the hands that hope for them"). When Merwin adds rhyme, "Search Part" takes on the sheen of formal elegance and "The Day Itself" (the Harvard Phi Beta Kappa Poem for 1989) becomes witty and ironical. "Immortelles" alternately hoards and then relinquishes an emotional energy so that it embodies, in one sustained and convoluted sentence, Merwin's grief at his mother's death and a deep longing for the unchanged world of childhood, the glass flowers that need no water.

This collection fascinates me. Throughout, Merwin holds on to an established habit of line but finds in certain more traditional forms and techniques a renewed sense of what the line is capable of accomplishing. (Some readers will be reminded of the poet's early books, which established him as a master of classical forms.) *Travels* takes shape almost in spite of its unwieldy premises and the crisis of readership at its core. No, the poem does not bring back the fields and farmland or the sweet smell of sandalwood forest. It will not make recompense to the lives lost to history. It will not stop wars or stay death. Merwin, for all his acute awareness of loss, writes not to alter the world but to honor it. Finally, as in "Inheritance"—which can only be termed a sensory *ars poetica*—the poem is like a perfect pear whose true taste can never quite be recalled. It may slip from communal memory, or surface in the future to be savored in other circumstances:

> . . . and now it was always like this
> with our tongues our knowledge and
> these simple remaining pears

In practiced hands the compulsory figures appear effortless. In most of the poems of *Travels*, Merwin has his proportions right. His tightrope lines are tethered to a larger vision.

The third book in which the line becomes my focus of attention is *To Put the Mouth To* by Judith Hall, selected by Richard Howard for the National Poetry

Series. Hall's poems are for the most part formal—a sonnet sequence, variations on the villanelle—and her regular stanzas are not so much units of thought or sense as they are constructions that enable the poem to take shape. Within the stanza, the line calls attention to itself in a number of ways. As well as the expected repetitions of the villanelle, Hall produces variations in which either whole lines or individual phrases are woven through the poem, keeping the ear alert. The process of reading is not so much one of waiting for the sense to complete itself as it is of watching the patterns unfold, listening for the *sound* of completion.

In fact, Hall's line often defines itself *against* traditional expectations. The sonnets both honor and resist iambic pentameter; at times the line turns without regard to syntax or ends abruptly, so that the sense and the meter are not congruent. This is more than the standard variation within an otherwise metrical poem; this is deliberate, disturbing with the intent to disturb. Coping with the lines becomes a part of how the poem is to be read. They cut into each other, fracture the surface like someone who is desperately trying to evade an issue by talking about almost anything else. A good example of these attributes can be found in a portion of the fourth sonnet of the section entitled "Fragments of an Eve: Scraps from her Album":

> And he rubs me on his skin, rubs me under—
> "Wake up," he says. Then I—; then he—; but
> Do I know what I want? His hands under
> My arms, lifting me up? I want—what?
>
> Another dream of his hush upon
> Mine; mine, his? And wake, and what is gone:
> Mouths kissing husks of hush.

The innovative use of the truncated line allows Hall to curb her feelings and, at the same time, to admit the potency of repression. There is innuendo, indecision, suggestion, suspense, and the final resort to the question mark. This is an interior voice stumbling over itself, catching itself before it reveals too much. The poem serves as an exploration of personal psychology such that the hesitations and the quick change of subject form a kind of tangential poem in which what is not said is what the poems is clearly "about."

The material that Judith Hall simultaneously explores and evades is her relationship with her father and how it defines the woman she has become. This is natural subject matter for a first book, here given expression as poetry of sensibility, with all the fascinations and the pitfalls of that mode. She chronicles the young girl's growing awareness of herself as a distinct personality and re-creates some of the conditions under which a girl learns the meanings of adoration and desire. The adult speaker looks back at the child, trying to recapture the wordless nuance and unarticulated messages she received both from her parents and from society at large. "Pictures of an Exhibition" fuses her adult perspective on photography and pornography with the memory of her father taking snapshots. Through this fusion, the child becomes the object of desire. Within this context, her mother's innocent remark ("Your father would do anything for you") takes on sexual connotations, leading to the poem's last line: "Look at me. You cannot see enough."

As the speaker in this book discovers herself more and more as something to be *seen* in order to be desired, she also turns into the observer. She looks inward, examining her own licit and illicit longings, and outward, where she is oddly objectified in the mirror. Hall seems to suggest that females (she calls herself *an* Eve) are taught early the way in which they will eventually be desired—and that they learn the lesson so well it must be exhumed, like a repressed memory. This is probably true for many women and it bears scrutiny, but as the governing theme for an entire collection it wears somewhat thin. The narcissistic impulse here, however, is at least partially counterbalanced by formal concerns, so that Hall's lines (which might otherwise be maddeningly flirtatious in that they promise a confession they never quite deliver) provide much of the aesthetic pleasure. Consider the play of language as she rings the changes in the first two stanzas of "In an Empty Garden":

> Better to fall, better to fall than wait
> To be held in air; wanting to be held,
> Held in words we use when we embrace.
> I wanted to be held in air or fall,
>
> To be held in air. Wanting to be held,
> I fell along the air's slow drawl,
> Wanting to be held in air or fall,
> As the turning of a body turned a voice away.

There is more interest in the way the lines are realigning themselves than in their cumulative "meaning."

For Hall, *what* something (event, memory, nuance) means seems to be secondary to *how* it means and, to this end, her lines serve her well by creating an excitement of their own. Sometimes an individual line is so elliptical or so loaded with punctuation ("Ha ha: : So I spin: Abridged dances:") that the effect is an alteration of what might be termed "reading time." The reader is asked to take apart language in slow motion, peel individual words back through their roots to pure sound, and pare action until it reveals intention. Hall quotes many sources, weaving the words of others through her own until we are made aware of language itself as an actual force. This force takes on an eerie presentiment in "Her Epithalamium" where, even as she describes her wedding, she turns it into a scholarly dissertation:

> Remember "love": "It delights: *Gilouban*;
> *Geliefan*; *beleven*; *believe*. We *believe* in what we *love*,
> Though to *leave* is part of its history."

The book jacket claims that Hall questions "the imprisoning assumptions of the language we've been given as men and as women." Since much of that language is *unspoken*, Hall tries to find a voice for the ways in which we understand the body. Often, she succeeds. Other times, she buys into the very prison she exposes as she lingers over her own "rituals of loveliness." Everything is gold and lavender, marble and ivory, wish and ablution—and although Hall seems to know that these words represent the aesthetic mold into which women have been pressed for centuries, part of her is most alive in the lush rhetoric of seduction.

To Put the Mouth To is a book whose vision must be seen as slight compared to the expertise it demonstrates. These poems are like porcelain vases on too narrow a base. Luckily, Hall points to a new direction in "Again, I Write You About Tomorrow"—a poem engaged with the world as well as self—where her lines are tougher, more integrated:

> You asked me to remember; no.
> It's your turn. I came this far—didn't mean
> To do what I did; didn't know
>
> How much silence held me.

From that "silence," Hall has, so far, found a way to make another interesting kind of silence. What I'm waiting for is silence voiced.

Fanatic Heart by Deborah Pope is also a first book and it, too, contains autobiographical material. The first of the book's three sections consists of seemingly unrelated poems whose focus is on the moment; they relate something of the poet's present life (a night drive, watching her husband rake the lawn, a vacation at the beach, planting bulbs) or her thoughts on the lives of others (a lost boy, a friend whose child has died, a woman who died while mountain climbing).

Although the poems are clearly discrete, the literal *fact* of death in some informs the others, allowing the ordinary moment to take on full intensity. The best example of this is the final stanza of "On the Mountain," where Pope makes the full connection between loss and the kind of concentration that almost recaptures what is gone:

> Even in death you are more vivid
> than any of us, more vivid than this day,
> a high, deep cloudless blue,
> the full light of late October,
> the autumn-turning trees.
> All over the ground, numberless,
> like fallen gingko leaves,
> bright as stones underwater,
> lovely, yellow gingko leaves
> pooling the shade,
> the color of your wind-scattered hair.
> Nothing I know answers for this.

The second section, opening with "Hard Climb Road" in which Pope's present nuclear family drives northward to her grandmother's funeral, moves into a series of poems about childhood. Fortunately, Pope's childhood seems to have been relatively free of trauma and the emphasis is, again, on the rendering of the moment—the lazy dreamtime of long summer days, the crackling of her father's radio as he worked in his lab, her mother's garden. In the third section, which recalls the growth of the family from "Firstborn" through the early years of her children, Pope has again found an informing device—this time, a number of poems about specific paintings. By carefully examining how the painter has treated his subject, Pope sheds light on the way love and motherhood have affected her. These are some of the best poems about motherhood I have encountered. For one thing, they are not romantic ("Late" ends with "I promise to be happy / I promise to be happy," as though she could will emotion into being, all the while knowing that even though she can "hold you all in my eyes," this does not always ensure happiness). For another, they recognize implicitly that children have their own "private paths," and the poems do not so much hold on to the child as give him over to his growing independence. Lisel Mueller's work has acknowledged this aspect of a woman's life but, maybe because so many female writers have been single or childless, this particular slant on motherhood feels refreshing and necessary.

Pope's honest responses to her own children and husband are framed by the poems on art. The last stanza of "Frank Benson, *Portrait of My Daughters*, 1907" shows how the poet's "reading" of a painting focuses her insights:

> *Daughters, Daughters,*
> their father's tints whisper, holding
> a moment more the light, the long
> pause of their century's spring.
> Even then they had gone from his dream,
> the eldest thrusting her fingers
> deep in the bunched petals,
> the middle one turning away,
> and the youngest holding
> her yet loose hair like a rope
> she is poised to cut.

Even from these short quotations it may be possible to examine the way Pope's lines function in the poem. They become interesting after the fact—when the reader has reached the end of the poem and can see how the details they encompass are, or are not, essential. Until then, the lines serve as simple vehicles for image or narrative. It is as if, from the first, Pope knows what she wants her final effect to be.

Taken at random, such lines as "I am afraid," "was a usual day," "slump on a stool," or "like these leaves" offer little in the way of metrical or imagistic indicators. Intrinsically uninteresting, they need connotation in order to carry with them even a modicum of life. This kind of line is tricky; it can easily become slack or clichéd or, worse, extraneous. To give Pope credit, most of her lines are secured in place by imagistic necessity. Her verbs, though, sometimes veer toward the precious ("the south wind treading the lawn," "morning light haloes our children"). I prefer the moments when she presents the "thing" not as the subject of her sentence, but as the object of her thought, as in part three of "Salter Path":

> The ocean empties each effort
> to think, the monotony
> of its crude maneuver,
> its stupid return and spill.

Fanatic Heart is a book filled with color. I take from my reading the impression of a painting—life as still life, kept still by the interpretive mind that holds the whole intact and fills in the strokes until it all comes clear. But there is a danger. Once that has happened, what would bring us back for more? There are few poems here that carry with them the kind of mystery or insight that calls for subsequent readings. "What We Meant to Say" is mysterious, but I'm inclined to think it's basically confused by all the overlapping pronouns.

The poem from which the title is taken, however, is one to which I would return again and again. "Photograph of a Woman Homesteader, Montana, 1870" demonstrates beautifully how a poem of vision can build its momentum. Pope begins by describing the photograph, assuming that the "girlish" hat must have been carried on the woman's lap a thousand miles "in a wagon that wouldn't take / another ax or bit." But mere description does not suffice, and this poem relies on an insight that simultaneously reveals something about the woman in the photograph and something about the woman looking at it. The poem is a reenactment of that moment of seeing—an insight finally fixed in language. The second stanza moves from observation to speculation so that the external object of Pope's gaze and the internal plumbing of her heart coincide:

> If she has gone mad from famine
> or blizzard, insects or prairie fire,
> delivering herself over and over,
> cords cut, a child lost, days
> before the doctor came, going
> months without hearing her nearest
> neighbor, thinking nothing is so loud
> as this hush, what of that.
> There is something fanatic
> in every heart. The direction
> she has come from is gone.

Typically, when a poem's lines are governed by a controlling vision, the poem closes down on a moment of insight. This poem doesn't quite do that. Rather, it displays its insight as an opening up to larger mysteries. The last three lines (with their enjambment and the full caesura) add immeasurably to the poem's effectiveness. The slight suspension after "fanatic" leaves room for readerly speculation before the phrase is completed in its own surprising way. The word "direction" points both ways, as though the direction were in the heart as well as on the map. And the enigmatic final line works on many levels; both terribly true and presently false, it suggests the full power of the elusive. The poem ends on the flat "what of that" of someone acknowledging that we cannot redeem the past. And yet this pioneer woman lives on the page as much as in the photograph, a testament to the potential in what is overall a skillful first book.

Gerald McCarthy's *Shoetown* won the 1992 Cloverdale Prize for Poetry, an award given to a first-time-published poet from North America or Ireland. "Shoetown" refers to Endicott, New York, where the author grew up, a small, blue-collar city perched on the Susquehanna River and home of Endicott & Johnson shoes. The book opens with the flux of the river. In "Susquehanna," the speaker reenters the town after driving all night and rediscovers not only familiar geography but also memory, clinging to the surface like morning mist:

Shadow, the greenkeep,
leans out over his mower
and calls my name.

I lift the steel pin,
push open the wire gate.
The tractor jerks ahead,
a clumsy moth shredding sunlight
into its canvas wings.

These early lines give a taste of what's to come—memory surfacing in present tense, accurate in the way that only memory can be, full of sound (long *e*, surge of *l*, stammer of *p*) and metaphor. From this point on, the tenses shift easily from present to past to present, and the reader, too, is caught in the act of remembering. Memory is as precise as the humpback Dodge, a "blur / in the glass storefronts," and as hazy and private as the lines "I hold on to the rail / and he goes down again," which seem to rise out of nowhere and refer to something ineffable.

Shoetown is a book with an overall vision—a kind of macramé in which the individual poems are knotted to each other to form an intricate design. In fact, the vision may exist almost completely in the mind of the reader, so careful is McCarthy *not* to give away his sense of what it adds up to. The memory of war, the return of Vietnam veterans, the lives of factory workers, prisoners, and migrant laborers, the personal life of the poet, the longer life of the natural world—all are held in suspension until, willy-nilly, they collide with each other and set new thoughts in motion.

War, so central to this volume, is treated obliquely. The first reference is in "Rangoon, 1944" when someone (father? uncle?) tells of bailing out and carrying the wounded co-pilot for six days. The child's mind sees through the transformative power of the experience—"As if for those few moments / you were above it all again— / the house on West Main, the factory / downtown. / As if standing there / another life still held." This romanticized version is replaced in "Ghosts" by the specter of the one-legged vet with his poppies on Memorial Day: "I know I'll never really find you, / dark brother from another time."

So it is that "Children of the dust" becomes not so much a poem about a mental institution as one about the horrifying effects of war, the fears that rise up with no referent in the world we know:

And the night, the night
we had names for, its breath
was our breath, the long sweep
of oncoming wave, a sigh
lulling us with promises.

We called it friend, brother,
because sleep tricked us
like a sorrow with one eye.

The veteran come home is invisible. "Here I am," he calls, and no one answers. "Riding Fence" voices the emptiness and the anguish: "Oh anyone, anyone. Silence is the steam / rising, the word half-finished. // This would be the hour of silence, / this unfilmed episode of gray dawn." "The Hooded Legion," finds him standing before The Wall:

There is only the rain
as it streaks the black stone,
these memories of rain
that come back to us—
a hooded legion reflected in a wall.

They are caught riding fence, belonging to neither world.

McCarthy does not overplay the fact that he was in Vietnam. For the most part, the reader is left to do the work and make the connections. The poems hardly mention the fact, and yet it functions in his *need* to reexamine the lives he left and returned to—those of the workers, the uncle who does piecework, the arc welder, the man from the local salt mines, the nameless field hand from "Migrant Labor Camp #6." McCarthy pays homage not only to their work, but to the way that work shapes their days. Not once does he give in to the impulse to close the poem with the self-consciousness of his own insight. He seems to be stating (by not stating) that those lives are intact, that the world goes on, that he cannot shape their vision for them. Often, as in the evocation of the migrant camp, the poems end with an ongoing image, like the "tinny scrape / of the wind / flapping the plastic windowpane."

In the few clearly autobiographical poems, McCarthy allows a more intimate voice to assert itself. But the intimacy is not so much with the subject of the poem as with the reader. For example, "Smoke," a poem addressed to his mother, who died when he was four, seems almost to be directed to a larger audience. There is a fine moment when, as McCarthy speaks to his mother, the reader seems to experience an intensely personal lyric overheard within a more public poem:

> We must have dreamed together
> you and I, I remember
> my fingers touching your dark hair,
> the snow filling up the backyards,
> the first cold flakes on my mouth.
> Oh, I have gone asking for you,
> embracing what I could
> as the first green deepened
> the still fields.

Gerald McCarthy's voice is confident and convincing, unselfconscious yet fully in control of its emotionally rich material. The book's power derives in large measure from a matching of voice, line, and vision. McCarthy's lines seem familiar rather than experimental. They gather into stanzas without strain; there is ordinary syntax and, typically, each line is sustained for only three or four stresses before folding into the next. Yet, despite the sureness of voice here, these poems don't tell us what to think; they simply present occasions for thought. Even with the most openly political poems, the reader must participate in the making of meaning. "Flag Burning (A Prayer)" is one such poem:

> The Sherente of South America
> believe the stars
> are their dead children
> who have climbed into the sky.
> Let each star
> be a hundred children,
> a thousand.
> Let their innocence
> keep rising above us
> so we may remember
> who we are, how we came here.
> Let the clear cold air
> be filled with them,

because the names have fallen
off the old pictures now,
and the newsreels have faded.
As another autumn
turns toward winter,
and we pause to look skyward,
hoping to glimpse Orion's belt
or Cassiopeia,
let us pray to remember
these lies we've lived with
for so long in such earnest.

The reader must return to the title and imagine the action that accompanies this incantation.

"Threnody," the final poem, is a blend of interior and exterior voices, moving between private reflection ("Sudden snow, sudden moment / of grace, / let the wind come on") and public irony ("Oh come on snow, / you can do better than that"). Listening to voice rather than watching for line, the reader is lulled into the final stanza where, in a recapitulation of imagery, the individual life blends with that of the natural world. The poem ends with the speaker's desire to walk through the snow as if it were smoke:

Let me sit beside you
until my breath is yours,
and I am nothing
no one.

Shoetown is short—only thirty-seven full pages of poetry—but it shows how the line can effectively be effaced in service of a vision and, at the same time, become the instrument of that vision. *Shoetown* is a mature—and *moving*—book; the Cloverdale Library should be proud of its choice.

And now, a "short talk" on *Short Talks* by Anne Carson—tiny prose pieces that blur all genre distinctions. These could be called essays (they were classified as such for *Best American Essays 1993*), but in this collection they are presented to us as poems. Never longer than a paragraph, sometimes only one or two sentences, they range from the abstract ("Short Talk On Hedonism") to the concrete ("Short Talk On Orchids") to the unexpected ("Short Talk On The Sensation Of Aeroplane Takeoff," "Short Talk On Walking Backwards"), with talks on Gertrude Stein, Sylvia Plath, van Gogh, and Brigitte Bardot thrown in for good measure.

In her introduction, Carson writes "I will do anything to avoid boredom." If these were meant to fend off boredom, she should ask whose boredom matter's most—hers or the reader's. There is nothing more boring than something too clever, too amusing, too contrived. As is the case for most prose poems, these pieces either fly or fall flat.

One that works well is "Short Talk On The Mona Lisa":

> Every day he poured his question into her, as you pour water from one vessel into another, and it poured back. Don't tell me he was painting his mother, lust, etc. There is a moment when the water is not in one vessel nor in the other—what a thirst it was, and he supposed that when the canvas became completely empty he would stop. But women are strong. She knew vessels, she knew water, she knew mortal thirst.

It succeeds because it sheds new light on an old subject, moves from what we know of the painting to what we know of human nature, extends that to the concept of "mortal thirst." The artist's mortality is instantly set against the longevity of the art. And the piece has managed to establish an intimate speaking voice, one that is not afraid to be didactic. When the pieces work in this way, they disclose a strong sense of play and a lively imagination. They are, quite simply, fun.

When the pieces fail, they do so miserably—and in a variety of ways. Often they lack substance or become too fanciful. Sometimes they simply don't "connect." In other instances, the worldview presented makes a kind of deliberate nonsense. One such piece is "Short Talk On The Youth At Night":

> The youth at night would have himself driven around the scream. It lay in the middle of the city gazing back at him with its heat and rosepools of flesh. Terrific lava shone on his soul. He would ride and stare.

The problem here is that the piece relies too heavily on the *techniques* of poetry without having any of the essence of poetry. It does not temper the strange with the familiar; the surreal scene is given no justification and the similes come from left field. This isn't even fun. It sounds too much like the author's note: "Anne Carson was born in Canada and teaches ancient Greek for a living. She spends most of her time otherwise painting volcanoes."

Occasionally, as in "Short Talk On Sylvia Plath," Carson resorts to the syntactic flexibility of Faulkner or Joyce, running her sentences together until they eventually break down. In "Plath," Carson moves from external observation (a restatement of Plath's mother's perspective) to internal awareness (where she virtually begins to speak for Plath)—all within one unruly, inconsistently punctuated unit. The point seems to be that Carson "gets" what Plath's mother missed about the violence of her daughter's inner life. Such irony is both too easy and too self-congratulatory; it offers neither exploration nor explanation.

Carson's short talks rely wholly on her angle of vision; the line plays no role at all as these pieces unfold. They are organized by the sentence, and any shift in tone or image takes place within that period. Neither the eye nor the ear is invited to take note of or stop at a line end. Most prose is utilitarian in this way; it wants to get its "message" across. Carson's message (though sometimes obscure) is the whole point. She plays with idea, trying on and discarding stance after stance. In the end, she's playing with her audience, too, refusing to engage her sometimes-intriguing attitudes the way a full creative essay might, and pulling back from the glimpses of personal disclosure with which she only teases us—but which a poet, using the full materials of poetry, might develop powerfully. It is an old truth that commitment to the *means* of the art—in poetry, to the full range of craft—allows a writer to go anywhere (to the very imaginative or to the very personal) without losing the reader's interest or confidence.

Ah, here's the rub: when the pieces are considered as "essays," a greater percentage of them are successful than when they are read as "poems." Carson has inadvertently defined the importance of the poetic line—the tangible thing that Wayne Dodd calls a "visual demarcation" of the music. Confronted with its absence, we suddenly realize the myriad ways in which the line is integral to how we read a poem. It is the poet's signature. It displays the energy or the grace of the skater. It leaves its telltale mark long after the lights are out.

The Ladybug and the Universe

On Stanley Kunitz's *Passing Through: The Later Poems, New and Selected*; Donald Justice's *New and Selected Poems*; Gerald Stern's *Odd Mercy*; and Michael S. Harper's *Honorable Amendments*.

EVERY SUNDAY MORNING we watch CBS's *Sunday Morning*. Well, almost every Sunday morning. With *The New York Times* waiting, I wait, somewhat impatiently, for the final minute of the show—that minute where Charles Kuralt used to say, "I leave you now near Omaha, on the banks of the Missouri," and the camera would simply sit there, looking at the long sweep of the river on a clear day in November with the sun lowering itself in the west. Then, a goose or two would come into the range of the lens, followed by more until the screen was filled with geese wheeling and banking, skein upon skein threading themselves through each other, the air filled with yelping as they came in to land. Or else he'd say, "I leave you in the mountains of Vermont," and the camera would start up close, focused on ice melting, so that a drop would slowly form, take on solidity and weight, tug at its own surface tension, elongate, then drop to the stream below—over and over, the accumulated shedding of winter until, finally, the camera would carefully pull back, and we'd see a rushing stream and then, at last, the mountains in the distance.

Those moments mattered. In a busy world—one in which we do all too little sitting in the middle of the forest, or standing at the edges of rivers—they put us in touch with ourselves. With the self who had once been the child on her stomach in the grass watching the precarious progress of a ladybug, or the adolescent suddenly struck by the ever expanding universe as ranges of hills unfolded before her and the wind made the only sound for miles around, lonesome and austere. You only need to have had one of those moments in your life—one clear, fixed point at which you fit yourself into the larger world—for that final minute of CBS *Sunday Morning* to matter. It gave you back to yourself, briefly, even as it took you somewhere new.

Things have changed a bit since Charles Osgood took over. For one thing, he comments more, can't seem to resist using words to tell us that here in the flatlands of Western Washington we are likely to see what the Spokane saw long before the white man, etc. In other words, he directs our thoughts just at the moment when they should be most free to roam. And the camera has changed, too—more radically, and far more destructively. It's a nervous camera now. Instead of letting things come into the range of its lens, it takes on life as an active verb, flitting from branch to branch, flirting with nature. It pounces on its images—one recent Sunday I counted six different animals in less than a minute—then darts away in search of something more interesting. The eye cannot rest, cannot take in, cannot settle and savor. We are no longer participants, but spectators.

Sometimes an individual poem can act as the fixed lens of a static camera. It can put us back in touch with ourselves by inviting a sustained attention, transforming its subject by the quality of the attention being paid. Once we've entered its field of vision, that poem opens to us others by the same writer. A poem we encounter in the initial stages of becoming familiar with a writer's work can have predictive power; it acts as a genetic marker, a key to open the door. We see more *because of* that earlier poem; we are attuned to nuance that *comes from* that earlier poem. We assume a kind of direct lineage, an underlying sensibility that links one with the other.

Reviewers, almost by definition, look at an expanding universe: the world created by the poet as the poems accumulate. When we make a statement about a book, it is necessarily abstracted, defined by what we think the individual poems add up to. So we tend to forget that the way they add up is poem by poem, drop by drop, and that how we read the individual poem is the way we once looked so hard at the ladybug—with intense scrutiny, amazed curiosity, passionate response.

Interestingly, it seems to be possible to agree on the cumulative effect of a poet's work without agreeing on the particulars. Joseph Brodsky's essay "On Grief and Reason" (1994) takes a long, hard look at two poems by Robert Frost. Brodsky finds a dark vision in Frost that leads, in the end, to the isolation of the poet as maker: "he stands outside, denied re-entry, perhaps not coveting it at all. . . . And this particular posture, this utter autonomy, strikes me as utterly American." But on the way to a conclusion with which I concur, Brodsky fails to read the tone of "Come In" to such an extent that he gives the poem a particularly Catholic reading. I would venture to say that "repent" (which Brodsky would substitute for "lament") was not much in Frost's vocabulary. Yankee Protestantism would dictate an even darker reading of the poem—one where a recognition of nature's indifference eclipses any religious yearnings. And when Brodsky reads the "darkened parlor" in "Home Burial" as a metaphor for the grave instead of what it clearly is—a darkened parlor—he also takes himself (as reader) outside the timeframe of the poem. The child's body is still in the parlor; the husband is outside digging the grave with an abandon that offends the wife; the reader of the poem is expected to understand the simultaneity of the events in order to preclude any tendency to "take sides." Frost stands *with* the reader; to make a metaphor would be to violate his impartiality, to force meaning. The greatness of "Home Burial" has always depended on its maker knowing "not to sing."

Both the mystery and the individuality of reviewing, it seems to me, lie in how the leap is made from the particular to the abstract. For each book, there must be several discrete moments of recognition: moments in which the poem itself acts as objective correlative, as an entry to the way the poet's world comes to meaning. You look through the viewfinder, adjust the focus, and click: the lens flies open to take in the world of someone else.

This is especially true when you are reading poets with an established body of work, poets whose work you have followed over the years. How easily your voice slides into theirs. Maybe you've heard them read in person, made some adjustments in how you hear. Maybe you've simply grown used to the cadence, the rhythm of their thoughts. But there was a time when the work was new, when you walked into a strange landscape and didn't know which way to turn. And what you did was what nearly all readers do: you let one poem speak to you so deeply that it speaks still, and goes on speaking.

"As one who was not predestined, either by nature or by art, to become a prolific poet, I must admit it pleases me that, thanks to longevity, the body of my work is beginning to acquire a bit of heft." This sentence, from the author's note to *The Poems of Stanley Kunitz, 1928-1978*, was written almost twenty years ago. Now his longevity is celebrated once again in *Passing Through*, marking the occasion of Kunitz's ninetieth birthday. This book collects the poems from three books (including a Selected) written after 1958. It also contains the long major poem "The Wellfleet Whale," which appeared as a separate chapbook, as well as nine new poems. "Three Floors," first published in *The Testing Tree* in 1971, is one of those poems that serves as a lens; it speaks to—and through—the later poems.

Three Floors

Mother was a crack of light
and a gray eye peeping;
I made believe by breathing hard
that I was sleeping.

Sister's doughboy on last leave
had robbed me of her hand;
downstairs at intervals she played
Warum on the baby grand.

Under the roof a wardrobe trunk
whose lock a boy could pick
contained a red Masonic hat
and a walking stick.

Bolt upright in my bed that night
I saw my father flying;
the wind was walking on my neck,
the windowpanes were crying.

Over the solid warp of the poem—a strict stanzaic and rhythmical structure placed there to support the sweep of memory and imagination—the poem is a sea of shifting images and associations. In sixteen lines, Kunitz has peopled the house with ghosts. The small boy is literally caught in the middle between the past (the loss of his father) and future (his sister's marriage, his own manhood). The poet re-creates the various claims on his affections as he presents the immediate moment of the poem—the darkness and the visionary sight of his father flying. The reader is drawn into the poem's emotional complex in such a way that childhood itself, with all its confusions, is awakened in memory.

"Three Floors" is a study in variation. Alternating between four- and three-stress lines (with slight differences in syllabic count), each stanza is at once familiar and surprising. There is a contrast between the strong masculine end rhymes of "hand/grand" and "pick/stick" and the haunting feminine rhymes of "peeping/sleeping" and "flying/crying." "Whose lock a boy would pick" is iambic trimeter, but the strong beat is muted so that each word must be read in a slower, more measured cadence. The child picks at the metaphorical lock of the family, hoping to discover his own identity.

The final couplet creates a sense of closure by returning to the strict meter of the poem and, at the same time, by moving into the realm of fantasy. In this way, the make-believe sleep of the first stanza is contrasted with, and equated to, the wide-awake vision of the last. The poem thus feels complete in its metrical package even as it opens up a strange emotional world where nothing is quite what it seems. "Three Floors" itself has become a vehicle for the imagination, creating a father for the son. But even as the father apprehended, he seems to be leaving. In a frenzy, the child perceives an elemental loss where the external world reflects his own amorphous grief. And behind loss is a question: *Warum*—why? The father's death, the mother's anger, the child's internalized conflict—nothing makes sense. Without an answer, the child is fated to ask this question throughout his life. The imaginative act, then, is seen as a way of discovering meaning, of making a divided house, however briefly, whole.

Twenty-five years ago, "Three Floors" harked back to a still earlier poem, "Father and Son" (1944), in which the poet searched for the lost father who had committed suicide before the son's birth—and found, at the bottom of a pond, "the white ignorant hollows of his face." But it also pointed to a companion piece in *The Testing Tree*, "The Portrait," in which the mother jealously, even angrily, denies the child any access to his dead father. But now, in 1996, "Three Floors" seems to prefigure the new and important final poem of *Passing Through*:

Touch Me

Summer is late, my heart.
Words plucked out of the air
some forty years ago
when I was wild with love
and torn almost in two
scatter like leaves this night
of whistling wind and rain.
It is my heart that's late,
it is my song that's flown.
Outdoors all afternoon
under a gunmetal sky
staking my garden down,
I kneeled to the crickets trilling
underfoot as if about
to burst from their crusty shells;
and like a child again
marveled to hear so clear
and brave a music pour

from such a small machine.
What makes the engine go?
Desire, desire, desire.
The longing for the dance
stirs in the buried life.
One season only,
                    and it's done.
So let the battered old willow
thrash against the windowpanes
and the house timbers creak.
Darling, do you remember
the man you married? Touch me,
remind me who I am.

"Touch Me" connects directly to its antecedent, but it is a connection made as much by contrast as by similarity. What makes these two poems coalesce, for me, is sensibility—and the poet's desire to fix the moment in memory. Once again he is lying in bed, haunted by wind and rain, by the branches thrashing against the windowpanes. And once again he sees *through* to the heart of things. This time, however, the present is meditative as opposed to visionary. He reactivates the child whose questions haunted the earlier poem by recovering the child who paid attention to the crickets. Both poems contain the large underlying questions of identity, but the later poem poses, first, the simple question of being.

Opening with a reference to a much earlier poem ("As Flowers Are"), "Touch Me" is a bit less formal than "Three Floors"; the structure is more subtle, its music even more varied, and its methods more sure. There are the same intricate rhymes—more a crochet than a weaving—slant rhymes that make a pattern like the fluid course of a soccer ball as the players work it down the field: "rain/flown/afternoon/down" and later "again/machine/done," or the initial "air" echoed in "clear/pour/desire, desire, desire" and then, as in a reprise, caught up again in "remember"—the operative word of the poem. But the ending is not elevated as in "Three Floors," where the poet tries to make language fill the void. In "Touch Me" he falters at the edge of the visionary, falters where the song has "flown," pulling back from the urge to fabricate in favor of the urge to resuscitate. At the exact moment when the earlier poem would have made the transformative leap, this one settles back. The poet foregoes rhyme and rhythm in favor of statement, a deflated kind of poetry that makes the end both terrible and moving: "Darling, do you remember / the man you married?"

The line break is crucial. Because if she remembers, then he has identity; if she remembers, she connects with the person who was "wild with love"; if she remembers, she is the link between the old man, his younger self, the child, the cricket, the very earth in which he has been gardening all afternoon. She connects him to his life through touch—the very thing that was withheld in "Three Floors." Even as he interrogates, he answers his own question: "remind," not "show."

The act (if it comes) will remind him of what has already been fulfilled. The gesture of *poetry* is superseded. "Touch Me" is a poem of completion and incompletion: poetry can only do so much, makes the link for the poet but it isn't sufficient. With great honesty and great vulnerability he admits to a need for another to restore him fully to a sense of himself, but it is a self rooted firmly in the present tense: "who I am." Such a simple poem (a study in monosyllables almost comparable to Frost's) for such a complex thought.

Speaking of poetry as a form of blessing, Kunitz tells us (in an introduction to *Passing Through*, which he calls "Instead of a Foreword") that "it would be healthier if we could locate ourselves in the thick of life, at every intersection where values and meanings cross, caught in the dangerous traffic between self and universe." Time and again, as this volume shows, Kunitz locates himself at that intersection, still asking why and still discovering that, although it has "one season only," life is worth the living.

Donald Justice's *New and Selected Poems* also collects work from a relatively small number of books—six, including a previous Selected. As for Kunitz, book publication has been infrequent and each volume has made an impact. Justice has earned his reputation as a master of the art through careful attention to the craft. Over fifteen years ago, when I first heard his "Absences" (in *Departures*, 1973), I could not believe that so much could be said—and not said—in only twelve (or thirteen) lines. It seemed to me then, and still seems now, a study in how what is absent from a poem can fill it with its presence.

Absences

It's snowing this afternoon and there are no flowers.
There is only this sound of falling, quiet and remote,
Like the memory of scales descending the white keys
Of a childhood piano—outside the window, palms!
And the heavy head of the cereus, inclining,
Soon to let down its white or yellow-white.

Now, only these poor snow-flowers in a heap,
Like the memory of a white dress cast down . . .
So much has fallen.
                                And I, who have listened for a step
All afternoon, hear it now, but already falling away,
Already in memory. And the terrible scales descending
On the silent piano; the snow; and the absent flowers abounding.

The first thing I notice is the plural of the title, the sense that more has been lost than can ever be retrieved through the act of memory—and that memory itself is elegiac. As the snow falls in the present (*this* sound of falling), the flowers of the past both bloom and wither; the visual image of the snow outside calls up the sight of a dress—the active memory of the poem; the room fills with music held in memory so powerfully that it obscures whatever step the poem has been listening for. The speaker's own absence meant that he was present in another time, another place. Thus the past is more active than the present. In fact, the absences are so realized that the reader feels as though the speaker is courting loss, counting on loss to fill him. The present tense of the poem—"hear it now"—is caught between the immediate past (the afternoon), the distant past (the piano, the palms, the memory) and the future in which this loss too will bloom with the others, will be relived in the active voice of memory.

So the presences of the poem reside in innuendo, in image and imagination. They are conjured through sound, as though the vowels of the language could refashion the past and make it palpable. The long *i* of "quiet" intrudes on the musical *o*'s of the first two lines. It is picked up again in "white" and from then on the two play tag, circling each other, circling the long *e* of "heap" which contains the potent image of the poem. The middle two lines shorten to pentameter in order to hold their images—white petals, white skirts—in opposition. Then, the *e* shortens to that of "memory" and "step" and "terrible." Everything ends in ellipsis. The broken line emphasizes that the "I" also has fallen. Sound, too, seems to fall away, only to be revived in the last line with its opposite—"silent"—and then the echo of *o*'s again, a reminder of what is present—the snow, the absent flowers abounding.

With so much music, such a poem seems to savor its subject. Loss is a muse. The voice dances around it, making of nothing something so all-encompassing you feel you could turn and touch it.

Sense (or meaning) would send me from this particular poem to "Invitation to a Ghost" in Justice's *New and Selected*. Written in memory of Henri Coulette, it begins, "I ask you to come back now as you were in youth." This poem, of all the new ones, names the active desire to remember, to be alive in a past almost more vivid than the present. But I'm not following sense in Justice: I'm letting sound send me in other directions.

The Artist Orpheus

It was a tropical landscape, much like Florida's, which he knew.
(Childhood came blazing back at him.) They glided across a black
And apathetic river which reflected nothing back
Except his own face sinking gradually from view
As in a fading photograph.
                                        Not that he meant to stay,
But, yes, he *would* play something for them, played Ravel;
And sang; and for the first time there were tears in hell.
(Sunset continued. Years passed, or a day.)
And the shades relented finally and seemed sorry.
He might have sworn that he did not look back,
That there was no one following on his track,
Only the thing was that it made a better story
To say that he had heard a sigh perhaps
And once or twice the sound a twig makes when it snaps.

Here is a perfect example of how one poem informs another. By moving the myth into the landscape of his childhood, the speaker of the earlier poem now equates himself with the figure of the artist. The impersonal poem is made personal. And once again the vowels call the tune. The long and short *a*'s flicker through the lines like darting fish. Taking their cue from the word "landscape," almost every line contains a combination of long and short sounds, a syncopation of vowels as in "came blazing back" and "fading photograph . . . stay." Over this pattern of sound, Justice has imposed the structure of a sonnet with its expected rhyme scheme. The rhythm varies, but there are three pentameter lines (two strictly iambic) to suggest a scaffold through which the rhythms wind their skein of sound.

The epigraph for the entire collection refers to the traditional myth of the poet:

Orpheus, nothing to look forward to, looked back.
They say he sang then, but the song is lost.
At least he had seen once more the beloved back.

In "The Artist Orpheus," however, this is subverted. Whereas the traditional story shows the consequences of looking back, here the variations on and repetitions of rhyme ("back" with "black", "back" with "track") imply not only the direction of the gaze, but also its circularity. The near rhymes alert the reader to what might have been, but isn't. "Might," "perhaps": the poet poses an alternative myth, one that is more in line with his own sense of loss. With a kind of gentle wit, he suggests Eurydice may never have been following at all. Story is more powerful than the real physical loss that generates it. Version becomes reality: loss, not Eurydice, is the muse. This, it would seem, is the necessary condition of art.

With this in mind, the reader can approach such new poems as "The Miami of Other Days" or "Pantoum of the Great Depression" as further manifestations of absence. And "Sadness," which begins "Dear ghosts, dear presences . . ." reminds us yet again that the lost world has its own imaginative power, doubled somehow, like lanterns in the river—the shimmering reflection that is the poem—until presence equals absence squared. *New and Selected Poems* reminds us that Donald Justice is still an important presence in American Poetry.

The title of Gerald Stern's most recent book, *Odd Mercy*, is a variation on a theme—or, more accurately, a concept—that has threaded its way through his work ever since "The Dancing" first appeared in *The Paradise Poems* a dozen years ago. In a long sustained sentence, that poem sweeps from junk shop to holocaust in the space of nineteen lines (and from fart to God in eight). Full of exuberance, the poem virtually rollicks on its way to its surprising ending, its sudden and sobering empathy.

The Dancing

In all these rotten shops, in all this broken furniture
and wrinkled ties and baseball trophies and coffee pots
I have never seen a post-war Philco
with an automatic eye
nor heard Ravel's "Bolero" the way I did
in 1945 in that tiny living room
on Beechwood Boulevard, nor danced as I did
then, my knives all flashing, my hair all streaming,
my mother red with laughter, my father cupping
his left hand under his armpit, doing the dance
of old Ukraine, the sound of his skin half drum,

half fart, the world at last a meadow,
the three of us whirling and singing, the three of us
screaming and falling, as if we were dying,
as if we could never stop—in 1945—
in Pittsburgh, beautiful filthy Pittsburgh, home
of the evil Mellons, 5,000 miles away
from the other dancing—in Poland and Germany—
Oh God of mercy, oh wild God.

"The Dancing" unfolds through accumulation, and as in any good junk shop, anything goes. In a freefall down the page, held together through the illusion of the spoken voice, the lines follow a process of association from object (coffee pot) to remembered object (Philco) to music to remembered dance to a conjunction of specific time and place that sends the speaker reeling outward in his imagination. The poem is Jewish to its core—especially in its enigmatic closure, which is worthy of whole pages of the Talmud. Instead of hoarding experience, the poem is expansive. It opens ever outward, moving from the "I" in the junkshop to the shared experience of millions and finally to the unknown (and unknowable) mind of God.

"The Dancing" is more a middle than an early poem; in fact, it occupies the exact center of Stern's selected volume *Leaving Another Kingdom* (1990). When I first read it in 1984, it was reminiscent of the wholehearted embrace of experience in "Lucky Life" as well as the self-conscious celebration of "Behaving Like a Jew," two even earlier poems with which I was deeply familiar. But its ending was new precisely because it was equivocal. What were Stern's definitions of "mercy," of "wildness," and of "God" himself? Until then, God had been as likely to appear in lower case, a "god of rain," a "god of tears." Until then, Stern's Jewishness was a condition—something he shared, celebrated, examined—that linked him with a longer history. Suddenly, in "The Dancing," he was speaking not *about* it but *through* it—speaking out its painful wrestling with the nature of a god who can spare or condemn as part of the same dance. Although I can find no earlier mention of mercy, there's no question that, from this poem on, the enigmatic concept of mercy has become one of the underlying—and driving—questions behind Stern's poetry.

To some extent, this query was ever present but muted. The vibrant voice of *Bread Without Sugar* (1992) seems, in retrospect, to be shouting down some nagging doubts. Now, in *Odd Mercy*, the question surfaces over and over like a whale rising for air. The opening poem of the collection states that a craving for light is "the first mercy," raising the issue of what is the second? the third? The title poem quickly follows, taking a sidestep into an oblique angle of vision by looking at the *quality* of the mercy—its oddness—not at its ranking in some ordination of mercies. The poem is too long (seventy-nine lines) to quote in full, but its opening lines move immediately inside the speaker's ruminative range.

> I kick a piece of leather; except for the claw
> it's mostly sky. Let the silkweed bury it.
> and let the silkweed bury the silkweed. There isn't
> a particle of life there, that's if leather
> can have a life. Silkweed sends its seed
> to cover the body—there is grease; there are
> feathers on the claw. Juice, I think,
> juice of the cat, juice of the silkweed. The pods
> are empty, there is no cream, only a little
> white left over, dry and fluffy. Let the
> nail bury the nail, let the helmet
> of someone named Knute bury the helmet of someone
> named Si or Cyrus. Inside the bliss is gone,
> the mind is empty; it has moved from one form
> of grasping to another. I lift it up,
> it is a kind of football, something between
> a dry tongue and a ball. I execute
> a perfect dropkick, claw after claw—there still
> are dropkicks in Pennsylvania. It could be
> the self growing more aloof that gives me the courage,
> something I can hide behind.

This is quintessential Stern, raucous and daring. He's kicking dead cats and singing about it! He's going into one of his deep underwater dives and who knows where—or when—he'll come up? He's playing with Ecclesiastes, playing with nature, playing with death itself. And he knows it. He makes claims for a "self growing more aloof," but I'd argue that he finds a self growing less and less aloof. As in "The Dancing," connections are being made; the poem is spiraling inward to where self and history are intimates. "Odd Mercy" also uses Stern's typical associative method of progression, but by now he so trusts his ability to be far-ranging that what is association for him might be disjunction for anyone else. The poem explores the relationships between self and cat, self and the past, son and father ("he will spend his lifetime / waiting"), moving from literal to figurative with lightning speed: seed of the present, seed of the past, seed of the seed, seed of the self, self suddenly facing the self as it kicks a dead cat like a football . . . no, like a suitcase. In a moment of fusion, the suitcase filled with books and underwear is also packed with the images of the poem and these, in its final lines, open not so much to hindsight as to retrospective insight:

. . . the cat
is in a rage, there is silkweed, it drifts
like insulation over the brushes, it falls
like snow in the farthest pockets, there is toothpaste
and Neutrogena and Solex; there is a clock
I bought in Sienna, it is a German clock
a *Peter*, with three stars and a kind of forties'
face; it ticks like an ancient bomb, the size
is perfect, the paint is a little chipped, it is
a second heart for the cat and after a day
of odd mercy another one for me.

Memory, and the consolation of memory. Stern has returned to the junkshop of the past only to come face to face again with the inexplicable: he has packed his imaginary suitcase with an object that harks back to the forties—and the clock's ticking sets in motion an "odd" mercy, as enigmatic as the wild god who conceived it.

The world contains all things: the cat that killed the bird, the boy who waited for his father, the clock that ticks away the time, the lives we lead, the lives we might have lived, the man who waits, now, for answers he knows he will never have. To love that world is to forgive it. And Gerald Stern loves with all the passion of someone who refuses to drown. It's interesting to note that both this poem and the earlier one culminate in a single defining moment around 1945, one which stops the imagination cold. For Stern, I think, this moment is one he must live—and love—his life against.

The concept of mercy is the linkage between the poems, an idea that plagues rather than consoles the poet. Notice that it's always qualified (*first*, *odd*) as though he has no strict definition; however, it's a quality that must exist if Stern's universe, with all its pain and irrationality, is to have room for the joyous, the redemptive. Perhaps the poet dispenses the mercy after all, and that's what he finds odd about it.

Odd Mercy marks a change in tone. It has all the wit and vitality of Stern's other work, but it's a quieter book, more contemplative. And Stern is harder on himself, over and over pointing an honest finger at his own direction, worrying away at the edges of a contemporary culture that lets the dead bury the dead as it turns its back on its homeless, its disadvantaged. "Hot Dog," the long last poem that takes up half the book, threatens to get out of hand as it flits from point of view to point of view, from Augustine to Whitman, from oppressor to oppressed, with a kind of deflated mania. Near its conclusion, the speaker repeats "Never again" and the reader suspects he's heading for deeper water. It will be interesting to see where Stern's voice—which over the years he has come to trust so completely—will lead him next.

Black man:
I'm a black man;
I'm black; I am—
A black man; black—
I'm a black man;
I'm a black man;
I'm a man; black—
I am—

This is the opening stanza of "Brother John," the first poem in Michael Harper's first book, *Dear John, Dear Coltrane*, published in 1970. A first poem necessarily informs all others, but Harper has actually used fragments from this poem that act as a refrain in subsequent books. So the poet himself has highlighted this lyric, expecting the reader to know how—and why—it reverberates. Beginning with a blatant statement of condition, the stanza then pulls the statement apart, emphasizing and deemphasizing in turn "black," "man," and the combination of the two, ending on an assertion of identity—the affirmative iamb of "I am." From there, the poem continues to celebrate both jazz and the jazzman in a series of riffs on Charlie Parker, Miles Davis, and John Coltrane, each time reiterating part of the first stanza as a refrain. Then comes a harmonic progression to Brother John, who is simultaneously universal—"he's a black man; black"—before the variation on the opening that ends the poem:

I'm a black man; I am;
black; I am: I'm a black
man; I am; I am;
I'm a black man;
I'm a black man;
I am; I'm a black man;
I am:

Each punctuation mark dictates a timed pause, creates a rhythm that approximates jazz, allows Harper to create a syncopation of his own—a celebration of being that includes blackness as part of its meaning. Whereas Stern seems to *discover* a defining moment, Harper's, in a way, was from his birth. But as a poet he has undertaken the task of looking beyond—or beneath—historical condition to discover the existential.

From "Brother John" forward, Harper has explored what it is to be black in our society and, in so doing, has opened up to all readers the wealth of black contributions to our history and our art. His work has never flinched as it faces the hard questions of racism and race relations. In a dense, staccato style, Harper has taken another look at American history, collapsing time and condensing fact so that the juxtapositions often startle us. At he same time, he has offered up personal experience in conjunction with national events. In making us more aware of our differences, he has made us more aware of similarity. "Tranetime" is for anyone who can listen and respond.

Honorable Amendments is Harper's first book in ten years, and its appearance makes us suddenly aware of the too-long absence of this strong, energetic teller of truth. Harper's style has been one of syntactical compression, of declarative statement, of fact superimposed on fact building layers of ambiguity until they make demands on the reader just at or beyond the breaking point. The effect is discomfiture. We do not know what we need to know to read these poems, and somehow our not knowing is a part of the way they open up the world. First, we are asked to realize how little we know of what has shaped this country; second, we are treated to what we *do* know from another perspective; third, we are asked—no, required—to alter our own perceptions to encompass those of the poems.

In *Honorable Amendments*, the range of epigraphs, historical notes, and dedications covers Ralph Waldo Emerson to Ralph Waldo Ellison, Eugene McCarthy to Martin Luther King Jr., the dictionary to traditional oral formulations. Harper's subject matter is eclectic, moving from Grant's autobiography to Lincoln's second inaugural address to the poet's own trip to South Africa to the plight of the Cherokee to the art of Romare Bearden to Langston Hughes's boyhood to Frederick Douglass to Coleman "Hawk" Hawkins (for whites) and Coleman "Bean" Hawkins (for blacks), and right down to Jackie O—which is to say that the book is about (if books can be said to be *about*) a refiguration of American history in order to expand, adjust, redress, inspire. Amendment is necessary if we are to understand each other, and this book presents some alternative aesthetics through which we may also *make* amends.

So how are we to read the provocative ending of the long last poem, "Prologue of an Arkansas Traveler"? After a litany of historical events, the poem concludes:

District of Arkansas
set up as partial payment for Louisiana Purchase; Quapaw Treaty
and ceding of lands between rivers, Arkansas and Red; Cherokee
agree to leave Arkansas; Sam Houston's revolution plan; Federal troops
burn Napoleon (look that up!); Poll tax; Convict Leasing Law;
Elaine race riot; state-owned bridges made toll free: quilt that!

One believes that Harper has looked it up—has looked up everything—and found it wanting. One also believes that he is offering up his version, his unique slant on American literature. The challenging "quilt that!" takes on more of the tone of the imperative: turn this, too, into art.

The years since 1970 have been stormy, and they've seen myriad changes. But "I'm a black man" still haunts me, forces its rhythms on me, its insistence and its assertion, its triumphant otherness. So I turn, now, to "Laureate Notes" from *Honorable Amendments* to see what, if anything, has changed. Written to the Providence *Journal*, it raises all the old questions.

Four papers a day, *Globe*, *Times*,
Monitor are not enough,
this is a personal editorial,
this is demise. Update your photo
gallery; all the black people do not
appear in the negative, and in broad
daylight, let's say, on Broad Street,
a rainbow a cliché, but a full range
of coloration.
Which is your slant
on dry and wet news, please, give
us the facts; save the attitudes
for the collection plate,
which in the old days,
was a hammer, a trestle,
and a boy in the dark
unable to make change
because he was folding the news,
in the hot, in the cold.

Your police news lacks how you treat
the rich, how you make fun of
immigrants, who count out their
change in the women's room,
which is often out of paper:
this is the paper of the numbers,
this is the paper of the rich.

I will not comment on the police:
they are brown, sometimes on horses,
and often patrol: my boy watched you chase
a 15-year-old up Chestnut Street
in a heisted car, and, when he lost
control, watched him beaten into
submission, and because he was upstairs,
and not at ground level,
with a perfect view for justice,
and my answers, which came quickly,
because he stutters, looks Cape Verdean,
has been hassled by men in brown
for their amusement.

I realize these men have their own children;
I realize they are not in love with mine;
when it comes to protection, editors,
one must get one's blows in early,
If you want to make sense
to a kid about justice,
about the law.

This is one or two incidents,
it must stand for the whole;
it is all he knows about order,
it is all he speaks of the law.

Tomorrow: car theft; tomorrow: trash
collection; tomorrow: judges and juries;
tomorrow, the IRS, BVA, MLA, PAL, CVS, NBC, BRU
tomorrow: happened today.

Possibly the most accessible poem in the collection, "Laureate Notes" could be said to "stand for the whole" as it makes its simple claim on our humanity. The police (their brown uniforms have connotations of fascism) stand for the whole of society. Twenty-five years later, "Laureate Notes" does not end with the strong identity of "I am" but with a series of impersonal acronyms and the scary prediction of what "will be." Yet here "will be" equals "is": Harper lets us know that time has run out. "Justice will take us millions of intricate moves," said William Stafford; in this poem, the perfect angle to view justice is from above—and it's clear that most of those intricate moves have yet to be taken.

"Laureate Notes" is another assertion of identity: a personal editorial made public, a pronouncement. And it predicts future assertions. Fact: there is more than one "slant." Fact: the newspaper was built on the backs of the boys in the dark "folding the news, / in the hot, in the cold." Fact: the police can be seen to use excessive force. Fact: a boy has been hassled. Fact: from now on, it will be difficult to talk to him about justice, about law. Fact: the rhythms make a jazz of the experience, the music of a future that, if we don't heed its warnings, will spell more misunderstanding. As time present is torn between time past and time future, so the language is torn, charged with pun and double meanings (e.g., newspaper / toilet paper; film negative / negative stereotype), like the double vision of history/today Harper makes us see.

If "Brother John" was celebratory, in some ways "Laureate Notes" is one of Harper's most pessimistic poems, its ending definitive. The poems of *Honorable Amendments* are difficult to read—even in "Laureate Notes," the third stanza fuses pronouns to the point of confusion. The poems can be daunting, at times condensed to inaccessibility, yet the book does not exclude me from its experience. It invites me to learn more, to learn the limits of my knowledge. And this is probably because I sense that Michael Harper stands with Ralph Waldo Ellison in refusing to play what has come to be called the "race card": "and who knows but that on the lower frequencies, I speak for you."

Harper's voice—honest, penetrating, combative, censorious, exultant—is to be welcomed back. His is a voice of reason, I think, but impassioned reason. The ending of "Late September Refrain," yet another praise for Coltrane, could almost be called the poet's self-portrait:

> A mouthpiece is different from a reed,
> which flanges into the spaces of the mouth
> where even spit evaporates to the song.

The mouthpiece is the tunnel,
viaduct, headband of the sun;
it is the fields, and the call of the fields.
It is the shining in your example:
I say your name; John William Coltrane.
I say the refrain: *a love supreme!*

Michael Harper just might be the mouthpiece through which American history and American literature can find a way to reconciliation.

So an earlier poem may be reflected, enlarged, in a later one; it may, even by contrast, illuminate the shape of a poet's vision. When we look long enough, the two become reciprocal. Which is the ladybug, which is the universe? We do not always read chronologically. It occurs to me that the reverse could also be true: upon discovering a significant later poem, the reader might, with hindsight, be able to discern its roots.

I pick up a recent issue of *The Georgia Review*: first, I turn to Fred Chappell's review (what books did he look at, which did he like?), then the essays, then some of the poems—and I encounter, mid-magazine, a poem by Philip Booth that is so chillingly beautiful I'm suddenly afraid for us all.

Views

Walking, you thumb the remote
to scan news,
watch the weather girl
dance both hands, pivot,
smile, and point to
the other coast.
So what does morning look like?
What does the world.
From this motel:
an anywhere town, across the bay, shining.
Elsewhere mountains.
Miles beyond hills,
the capital cities, their walls behind walls.
Monuments to our lies,
to our self-blinded lives.
Above us now, two fish hawks, cheeping musical shrieks,
the risen sun easing their wingbeats.

Over us all,
daylight's invisible satellites, shamelessly
bouncing back from space the emptiness we feed them.

It must be Sunday morning, I think, a Sunday in transit, waking in a motel room in a strange town. Time to let the world in—a world available by remote control. The weather girl is speaking about another city, other conditions, and with the sound on mute she becomes a dancer—the most poetic act of the poem. But she's as impermanent as the weather, a part of the larger system: TV, motel, satellite. If the speaker looks out, he can see what's across the way. That world—the one he might call the world of reality—is framed by window, framed by unfamiliarity.

The title implies more than one: views within views. The gap between what is on the screen and what is outside the window widens. The poet becomes aware of the fish hawks above him and, above them, "over us all," the unseen presence of the satellites that bring yet another reality—information about what he cannot see. In a transient world, the capital cities—centers of power that encircle us like an environment—take on permanence. Yet they are walled, inaccessible. We've constructed our own vast impersonal lie and now it holds us in its cage.

In the end, "Views" is a poem of limitation. The poet's act of seeing the grace at hand is not the act of seeing the whole world. The tone of the poem, both ironic and elegiac, is a little sad, a little angry—but not with an anger that could transform anything. Yet "Views" also opens wider and wider vistas with an intimation of the universe. Now that I've read this poem (written after the publication of Booth's eighth book, late in a career that spans over forty years), I'm going back to the early books to look for the ladybug—for the early poems that, through this Sunday morning insight, might now shine with new significance.

What Persists

On Charles Wright's *Chickamauga*; Robert Hass's *Sun Under Wood*; Maxine Kumin's *Connecting the Dots*; Paul Zimmer's *Crossing to Sunlight: Selected Poems*; Lisel Mueller's *Alive Together: New and Selected Poems*; and Leslie Norris' *Collected Poems*.

> The most obvious and salient fact about the natural separation of poetry from criticism is that in the greatest ages of poetry there has been little or no criticism. Criticism comes, if at all, after the art.
>
> Karl Shapiro

THINGS HAVE CHANGED since Karl Shapiro's time—and this *is* Karl Shapiro's time. But during his long career of writing both poetry and criticism, the gap between the two has simultaneously widened and narrowed. Theorists have discovered what writers always knew ("The meaning of poetry, as far as language is concerned, is the meaning of *hey-nonny-nonny*. To the poet, *hey-nonny-nonny* means what the other words in the poem failed to say."—Karl Shapiro, *In Defense of Ignorance*, 1960), but they've added a complex new vocabulary to the old insights. In fact, sometimes "old" vocabulary isn't what it seemed. A previously unpublished essay by Randall Jarrell (which appeared in the Winter 1996 issue of *The Georgia Review*) reveals that prominent "modernist" critic to have had quite a few insights we have always termed "postmodernist." The point is that critical ideas, including a poet's ideas about his own work, evolve across time with overlapping strands rather than clear or sudden breaks.

We think of theory as not being the same as criticism. But for the poet, especially today, theory, criticism, and practice are often one. Poets who last have inevitably evolved not only their own aesthetic principles, but an ongoing critique of these principles. In effect, their work is a kind of "practical theory" (in place of I. A. Richards' "practical criticism"). Some poets elaborate on their conceptual underpinnings within their poems; some have a kind of invisible structure that governs their choices. In either case, the reader is often made conscious of the *process of writing* as much as of the *subject matter*. Together, these add up to what we might, for want of a better term, call *content*.

I am convinced one of the things that makes a poet have "sticking power" is the sense the reader has that the poet knows what he or she is about. The poems themselves may be full of questions, but the poet is sure of what to ask. (This is different from the "sticking power" of an individual poem, which may or may not be written by a poet who persists.)

And how do we assess persistence in an age when publishing houses are "downsizing" their poetry lists in favor of blockbuster political or TV personalities and the latest legal wrangle? Excellent poets often have a hard time finding a publisher for second, third, even fourth books. Others have found a publisher with loyalty but often also with an insistence that they produce more to keep them in the spotlight. And meanwhile, it takes a spot on NPR or an invitation by Bill Moyers to pull a book of poetry out of the ho-hum category of negligible sales.

The bottom line is a bitter lesson. The place of poetry in our society has been debated for decades with no apparent answers and no lessening of the urgency of the question. But it's useful to remind ourselves that the question remains urgent to all too few of us. And what about the Internet, with its allure? Will young readers want—and need—the physical presence of the poem on the page? Will they see enough by any one writer to understand the poetry as well as the poem? Or will all our thoughts be scattershot, forays into the unknown?

A writer's poetry is always more than the sum of his or her poems. One can talk about this only when there is a large enough body of work to reveal an ongoing aesthetic. In a poet who persists, a critical overview simultaneously arises from the poems and governs their inceptions. It links those that will be written to those that have been, however different these may sometimes appear. In this essay, I will look at six poets whose work has persisted over time. A key part of their persistence has been their work's ability to judge and, if necessary, correct itself. In other words, this is writing that teaches us how it is to be read.

Three years ago, in the afternoons,
                    I used to sit back here and try
To answer the simple arithmetic of my life,
But never could figure it—
This object and that object

Never contained the landscape
                                        nor all of its implications,
This tree and that shrub
Never completely satisfied the sum or quotient
I took from or carried to,
                                    nor do they so now,
Though I'm back here again, looking to calculate
Look to see what adds up.

I'm instantly in the presence of, inside the voice of, Charles Wright. How do I know this? Even without the black-and-white cover of *Chickamauga*, even without the potent associations of the title, I know this is a "Southern" voice, a voice that will take the time it needs to think the things it wants to think. Speculative, contemplative, the poems of Charles Wright move across the page with the unhurried pace of a porch swing.

Wright is a poet for whom subject matter is subsumed by process. He can, it appears, begin anywhere, with anything, and a poem will emerge if he gives himself enough time and space to ponder the imponderables and to follow his own train of thought through its curious patterns, trusting it to find its way. At the same time, the poems probe and posit and penetrate even as they seem willing to follow a course of natural logic. (I can't help but think of "Snow," one of my early favorites, which begins with the structure of logic—"If we, as we are, are dust, as it will, rises"—and moves through the "then" clause with a sweep of religious and scientific history to end, six lines later, on a surprising note: "white ants, white ants, and the little ribs.") Logic, in a poem, is not always synonymous with "rational." Wright takes us on associative journeys which open the rational world to new and different interpretations.

Chickamauga was awarded the 1996 Lenore Marshall Poetry Prize, only the latest of Wright's many recognitions. Divided into six unequal sections, each of which embodies the fluidity of time, the book is a kind of stock-taking, a middle-aged reflection. The first section, "Aftermath," is a series of responses to the ideas of other writers—T. S. Eliot, Lao Tzu, Celan, Li Po (and even Yeats, if a poem called "Easter, 1989" could be said to be referential). Yet each response is filtered through the here and now of landscape, a view through orchard to the Blue Ridge mountains beyond, which colors the response by narrowing it to the specifics of season and circumstance. The second section is a deliberate foray into the "known land" of memory, the exactitude of 1959 and then 1963 in Italy, and the inexactitude of a number of fleeting memories finding a place together in my favorite of the poems, "Sprung Narratives." Memory—including the impossibility of "fixing" memory, of finding its proper place in the order of things—becomes a motif. But it is the concept that engages the mind, not the event. And memory is not the moment held, but a movement of its own:

> This text is a shadow text.
> Under its images, under its darkened prerogatives,
> Lie the lines of youth,
>   golden, and lipped in a white light.
> They sleep as their shadows move
>
> As though in a dream,
>   disconnected, unwished-upon.
> And slightly distorted. And slightly out of control.

The other four sections twist these strands to form a thread comprised of memory, response, careful observation, and surprising images—until, in a religious sense, it connects "everything with everything else" and, in a more literary vein, "constructs us and deconstructs us."

"An Ordinary Afternoon in Charlottesville" is exemplary. The somewhat generic title, paying homage to Wallace Stevens, could serve for many of the poems in the book. The ordinary, the title implies, is sufficient; everything is important. The scene is a close-up of an orchard, with birds "combustible / In the thin leaves incendiary—," and the tone is meditative, a bit melancholy:

> Or so they say. We like to think so
> Ourselves, feeling the cold
>   glacier into the blood stream
> A bit more each year,
> Tasting the iron disk on our tongues,
> Watching the birds oblivious,
>   hearing their wise chant, *hold still, hold still* . . .

The poet mediates between the "now and not-now" of the earlier poems; the afternoon is tinged with the familiarity of Dante's *Purgatorio* and the premonition of a final holding still. Meanwhile, the afternoon "fidgets about its business" as the sunlit feathers of the birds flare in the branches, everything a part of everything else, reminiscent of the Eastern poets Wright has been reading throughout the book.

If Wright's concerns are religious and philosophical—and they are—they are also painterly. He suggests that his poems, like Elizabeth Bishop's, are "descriptive." Light is doubly important, serving as insight, intelligence, intuition, and also as illumination. In "Still Life with Stick and Word," the poet examines a broken stick along with whatever word is the word of the moment:

> Inside now. The word is *white*.
> It covers my tongue like paint—
>   I say it and light forms,
> Bottles arise, emptiness opens its corridors
> Into the entrances and endless things that form bears.
> *White*, great eviscerator.

These lines are characteristic. The reader is invited to participate, to say the word and to watch the thought unfold. To see what form can, and will, bear.

In Wright's case, form allows a freedom of thought. His distinctive lines help him to move from the particular to the abstract—and back again. Even as they break, they continue. Sometimes thoughts falter, then resume; more often they veer away from themselves, catching up the lint of other thoughts, moving outward in associative circles until they embrace idea. Wright's abstraction is built on so many specificities that the reader settles comfortably into its center. But Wright is never satisfied: by noting the repetition of the seasons from the fixed centers of his successive backyards, he can take his own measure from a number of perspectives. (Titles like "Looking West from Laguna Beach at Night" and "Looking Across Laguna Canyon at Dusk, West-by-Northwest" show his obsession with getting it right, even in memory.) His answers are answers only for the temporal duration of the poem. What pertains today may not pertain tomorrow. What Wright sees on a winter afternoon may be contradicted by a summer morning's song. "Structures are wrong," he declares emphatically on page 6; relenting, he admits on page 63, "Everything flows toward structure, / last ache in the ache for God." The poems may say one thing at any given time, but the *poetry* is all about not-knowing, about impermanence and flux.

This brings us to "theory" as Wright practices it. His method becomes his message. He does not show us *how to* (if we were to do it, it would not be like this) but *that it can be done*. Wright's images, like Sylvia Plath's, are arresting in their uncanny accuracy; the reader discovers a way of experiencing the world that, even in its strangeness, seems incongruously *right*. Afterwards, we see things differently. While Plath's images are intense, even desperate, each linked to an emotion, Wright's are intent on an internal perception and restrained passion: "The sea with its one eye stared."

Since Wright's poems are about movement, they let the reader in on the movement even as they self-consciously annotate their own progress, even subvert it to see if the opposite will reveal yet another possibility. Wright's images occupy a juncture; they are the vehicle, moving thought from concrete to abstract and back again. Accompanied by patterns of sound, these images feel as fluid as music, as in "Cicada":

> Noon in the early September rain.
> A cicada whines,
> his voice
> Starting to drown through the rainy world,
> No ripple of wind,
> no sound but his song of black wings,
> No song but the song of his black wings.
>
> Such emptiness at the heart,
> such emptiness at the heart of being,
> Fills us in ways we can't lay claim to,
> Ways immense and without names,
> husk burning like amber
> On tree bark, cicada wind-bodied,
> Leaves beginning to rustle now
> in the dark tree of self.

The whole point of all this thinking seems to be to "answer to / my life." Not to answer, or to find an answer for, but to speak to its conditions, both physical and spiritual. The poems approach the age-old question of the nature of the universe and the place of the individual life within it, each time opening wide vistas, and often coming back to the inevitable: "There's only this single body, this tiny garment / Gathering the past against itself, / making it otherwise" and, in another poem, "One life is all we're entitled to, but it's enough," and in yet another, "When we die, we die. The wind blows away our footprints."

Like Wright's ten other books of poetry, *Chickamauga* is not so much a collection of discrete poems as a long meditation. And Charles Wright's body of work really could more accurately be termed a body of thought. From poem to poem, book to book, his work has taken on the thickness of thought. That is, the poems accrete; they weave in and out of one another. Wright effaces himself before the immensity of his questions, his mind asserting its presence through the clarity of his images. The result is not a "shape," nor is it formless—it's an approximation of human consciousness. Wright teaches us how to listen to him: attentively, with an inward ear and eye. I cherish this work as a whole more than for its specific poems. I count on its being there.

Another poet with whom the term "meditative" is associated is Robert Hass, who has just completed his tenure as poet laureate of the United States. His well-known "Meditation at Lagunitas" was one of the first poems to acknowledge contemporary theory and, at the same time, to rail against it. Its final three words—"*blackberry, blackberry, blackberry*"—not only demonstrate the gap between the thing and the word for the thing, but almost defiantly—and joyfully—partially bridge that gap by inducing memory through invocation.

Sun Under Wood, Hass's fourth collection of poems (he has also distinguished himself as the writer of essays and as a translator of Czeław Miłosz and others) takes its title from the "sonne under wode" of an anonymous twelfth-century lyric—a stark mixture of religious feeling with the natural occurrence of the setting sun. Hass blends intense feeling with a precise knowledge of the natural world as though the two were mutually dependent on each other—and in Hass's case, they are. These poems might best be described in his own phrase, "navigable sorrow." But if it's a sorrow, it is mitigated by the impulse to sing, the felt necessity for poetry in spite of its inability to change anything. Private pain (from which the book does not shrink) gives way to a generalized knowledge: "I had the idea that the world's so full of pain / it must sometimes make a kind of singing."

Sun Under Wood begins with a poem called "Happiness," so the pain is given a context: it is retrospective, reflected upon, realized not in its intensity but in comparative tranquility—something to be examined with the same curiosity with which the poet looks at dragonflies mating or the same precision with which he names the mariposa lilies. From within the happiness of a new marriage, Hass uncovers the sorrow at the heart of his first marriage, but not without first revealing the sorrow *of* the heart streaming from his mother's alcoholism.

It's interesting to note the progression of this personal narrative within the collection. In "Dragonflies Mating" a memory surfaces concerning his mother's coming into his school gym and his humiliation over her "bright, confident eyes" and slurred words. Then the poem pulls back from memory, tries to "fix" not the moment but the stance:

> When we say "mother" in poems,
> we usually mean some woman in her late twenties
> or early thirties trying to raise a child.
>
> We use this particular noun
> to secure pathos of the child's point of view
> and to hold her responsible.

Who is this "we"? How many people write poems? How many people reduce a word with such powerful associations to a "noun"? Here Hass displays the self-conscious attitude of the writer, always aware of the activity even as he engages the emotional source. In his case, he has built that self-awareness into the poems, breaking into them with an editorial eye ("It is summer as I write" or "This morning I am pretending . . . ")

So it's an easy step in the following poem, "My Mother's Nipples," to begin with improvisation. The provocative title is undermined immediately with a precise description of bulldozers in "the upper meadow at Squaw Valley," which leads to farmers and roofers and the eventual green sign reading "Squaw Valley Meadows." Only in the second segment (an enigmatic couplet in quotes which seems to come out of nowhere) does Hass intrude on his own reverie:

> "He wanted to get out of his head," she said,
> "so I told him to write about his mother's nipples."

From there, it's another easy step to a playful riff on how various poets might write about *their* mothers' nipples—the cosmopolitan's song, the romantic's, the utopian's, the philosopher's, the misanthrope's, the saint's, and so on—and then to the distanced study of a photograph before he finally faces his curiosity about and aversion to his own mother. At this point, the poem breaks into (blossoms into?) prose, a mix of past- and present-tense memories of his mother in an institution and, in another section, her oddly solipsistic response to her husband's (the poet's father's) death.

But the poem continues to undercut itself—and it knows this. No sooner has Hass found a lyric moment in which he can come, quite naturally, to the conclusion (spoken in direct address, to himself), "I said: you are her singing," than he begins the final segment of the poem, "You are not her singing, though she is what's / broken in a song. / She is its silences." Then, after a stanza break, the qualification: "She may be its silences." Words, lo and behold, do not suffice; they always need to be shaded to nuance, and then the nuance itself needs further shading.

At some point, Hass's acute sense of the impossibility of his task becomes a part of the way his poems are fashioned. They intrude on themselves, reminding the reader that these are, after all, only poems. They examine the power of poetry, and find it wanting. At first, this is somewhat disconcerting because the interruptions are just that—they disrupt what is otherwise a more traditionally coherent lyric. But Hass is teaching us, through interruption, to expect his "other" voice, the one that questions, dismantles, pricks its own bubbles. This happens early in the book when he writes not only the poem ("Layover" and

"Iowa City: Early April") but the alternative poem ("Notes on 'Layover'" and "A Note on 'Iowa City: Early April'"), giving us yet another view of the same place, person, event. "Layover" may be just a bit too politically correct in California terms for me (I remain unconvinced that the native Alaskans think of their snowmobiles, CBs, and prefab sheds as being imposed by a "colonizer"), but "Notes on 'Layover,'" with its sequences of *I could have saids* and *And thats*, is stimulating in the way it fills in the spaces, poses alternatives, moves through a series of associations in the manner of all minds in all airports, then catches itself short with its final insight that the speaker doesn't even recognize his own life, with its unfamiliar vases full of mauve hydrangeas.

This technique has hardened into pattern by the last half of the book, so the reader is prepared for two of the most significant poems, "English: An Ode" and "Interrupted Meditation." The former is imaginative and far-reaching. It begins in Spanish and moves through a number of English words with their derivations, connotations, and unnatural origins to end with an English translation of its opening. Along the way, we learn what Hardy meant by a *madding crowd*, the reason we say we are *at loggerheads*, how Hodgkin's lymphoma got its name, and even that the suffix *-math* (as in *aftermath*) comes from the Anglo-Saxon word for mowing. And all this is buried in an imaginative "story" generated by finding a secondhand book with two names (one English, on Spanish) written on the flyleaf. If this poem is also a bit politically correct, it points the finger at my resistance:

> There are those who think it's in fairly bad taste
> to make habitual reference to social and political problems
> in poems. To these people it seems a form of melodrama
> or self-aggrandizement, which it no doubt partly is.

But I remain steadfastly guiltless since it is never politics per se I object to, but any specific agenda that assumes universal agreement with "accepted" stances.

Luckily, Hass is willing to undercut himself as well as his poems. The final work in *Sun Under Wood* is titled "Interrupted Meditation," and it is here that Hass's method finds a true home. The poem begins with short interruptions:

> Little green involute fronds of fern at creekside.
> And the sinewy clear water rushing over creekstone
> of the palest amber, veined with a darker gold,
> thinnest lines of gold rivering through the amber
> like—ah, now we come to it. *We were not put on earth*,
> the old man said, he was hacking into the crust

of a sourdough half loaf in his vehement, impatient way
with an old horn-handled knife, *to express ourselves.*

In one fell swoop the old man has put us all in our places. The poem goes on to reveal a narrative in which the old man and his friends, in wartime Poland, had left scraps of bread where they thought a family of Jews might be hiding. *Thought. Might be.* The young friends didn't raise their voices, didn't know if people or dogs took the food, whispered about "art" and "truth" even though each meant its own kind of death. The remembered conversation is juxtaposed with the poet's observation of the mountainside until soon the "dialogue" is dense, intense with the necessities of the man's acquired knowledge: "*To Czeslaw I say this: silence precedes us. We are catching up.*" Hass goes on to let the man critique his (Hass's) poetry:

. . . *you can express what you like,*
enumerate the vegetation. And you! you have to, I'm afraid,
since you don't excel at metaphor. A shrewd, quick glance
to see how I have taken this thrust. *You write well, clearly.*
You are an intelligent man. But—finger in the air—
silence is waiting. Milosz believes there is a Word
at the end that explains. There is silence at the end,
and it doesn't explain, it doesn't even ask.

The poem might end there, but doesn't. Hass goers on to recollect the failure of his marriage and to think of how we "live our half lives / in fantasy, and words." So why not resort to words? The speaker says, "I am a little ashamed that I want to end this poem / singing, but I want to end this poem singing . . . "

Still, this is *talk* about singing. Hass's real "singing" is a singing of the mind aware of itself and a singing of the natural world, which he describes with affection and accuracy and, often, a kind of remorse. Hass's nature isn't just nature observed, nor is it nature idealized. It's another act of the mind where we learn as much about ourselves as we do about the nonhuman. What persists in Hass is his awareness of the obstacles to song and his desire to sing. "The Woods in New Jersey" is a song in every sense of the word—musical, personal, and shaped, but more. Addressed to Supreme Court Justice William J. Brennan Jr., the poem defines the law as something so ephemeral, so intricately ordered, that it mirrors the natural order of the forest. But there's something else as well—the life that makes any order, including a poem, matter. Here, for once, Hass has mastered metaphor:

And what of those deer threading through the woods
In a late snowfall and silent as the snow?

Look: they move among the winter trees, so much
the color of the trees, they hardly seem to move.

Sun Under Wood was awarded the National Book Critics Circle Award for 1996 and, as poet laureate, Robert Hass worked tirelessly for poetry and for the cause of literacy in this country. Because of the honesty and seriousness of his own work, the standards he expects of poetry, and his dedication to the work of others, Hass's legacy is—to date—a generous enhancement of the life of literature in America.

Maxine Kumin was awarded the Pulitzer Prize for poetry in 1973. She served as poetry consultant to the Library of Congress in 1981, and in 1995 she became a chancellor of the Academy of American Poets. *Connecting the Dots* is her eleventh collection of poetry. The book's dust jacket suggests that she "expands on themes that have engaged her most strongly," but I would suggest that, though this is certainly true, there's more than expansion going on. There's a kind of rejuvenation. These poems have the energy and urgency of youth; they are active more than reflective, leaving the reflection to take place after the fact, in the mind of the reader. Even memory seems to reside very close to the surface in this new collection.

Kumin's poems have always been toughly clear-sighted; nature, for her, is wonderfully complicated and complicating, never romanticized. And humanity is seen as part of nature. *Connecting the Dots* opens with a crown of sonnets called "Letters," placing the emphasis on the human. The letters are, if anything, silent missives written to a deceased mother who might or might not have understood them, a recitation of the poet's thorny, shifting relationship with her mother until they eventually "pulled even," and a retrospective appreciation that leads, full circle, to the final line where the mother sends a brief message to the daughter. Because of the circular motion of the repeated lines in a sonnet cycle, the first and last lines combine to acknowledge—at last—a reciprocated love. From this perspective, the speaker launches a series of poems in which she links her life not only to her parents but to her children and grandchildren, then enlarges the circle by finding connections with other poets, friends, neighbors, historical figures, animals—in short, everyone and everything. A good example of this panoramic view comes at the end of "Rehearsing for the Final Reckoning in Boston," where the Berlioz *Requiem* is filling the Symphony Hall:

Like a Janus head looking backward and forward,
pockmarked by doubt I slip between cymbals
to the other side of the century where our children's
children's children ride out on ranting brasses.

Kumin's poems assume continuity. That is the backdrop against which she can voice her religious doubts and her principled beliefs.

"After the Cleansing of Bosnia" sees those beliefs mirrored, even magnified, in her daughter's chosen mission with the UN in war-torn countries (this time Bosnia), but the poem moves ever outward to its enigmatic ending in the dream of an owl with a mouse in its talons:

We saw there was no obstacle
he-who-looks-behind-without-looking,
he-who-looks-ahead-without-blinking
could not thread through, backward or forward,
and we were falsely comforted.

In some ways Kumin also appears to have set herself the task of unblinkingly looking both backward and forward in order to assess and repossess the world. In the book's last section (but at the emotional center), two poems about her friendship with Anne Sexton are seminal, possibly even the source of Kumin's newfound energy. The first, "New Year's Eve 1959," recalls Sexton dancing with Jack Geiger, the "Physician / for Social Responsibility." Anne kicks off her shoes, and the dance ("setting all eight gores of her skirt / and twirling") begins. But the scene is replayed in memory, and the poet gives the evening a context it didn't have when the notes of "Chattanooga Choo-Choo" filled the room. "This was after Seoul and before Saigon," she says, placing the moment in the flow of human history, placing herself in the role of observer and, even, in the role of survivor:

madcap Anne
long dead now and Jack snowily
balding who led the drive to halt the bomb
and I alone am saved to tell you
how they could jive.

"October, Yellowstone Park" follows directly—elegantly formal in its rhymed and slant-rhymed (*abba*) quatrains—as an elegy to Sexton on the seventeenth anniversary of her death, but also as an affirmation: "Of sane mind / and body aged but whole I stand by the sign / that says we are halfway between the equator

// and the North Pole." At the halfway point of the poem, in full sun, on the 45th parallel, Kumin (as woman, as friend, as poet—but not as "speaker," which would distance her from her own lived life) declares:

> Fair warning, Anne, there will be no more
> elegies, no more direct-address songs
> conferring the tang of loss, its bitter flavor
> as palpable as alum on the tongue.

Despite her assertion, she lapses almost instantly into direct address:

> I've come
> this whole hard way alone to an upthrust slate
> above a brace of eagles launched in flight
> only to teeter, my equilibrium
>
> undone by memory. I want to fling
> your cigarette- and whiskey-hoarse chuckle
> that hangs on inside me down the back wall
> over Biscuit Basin. I want the painting
>
> below to take me in. My world that threatened
> to stop the day you stopped, faltered
> and then resumed, unutterably altered.
> Where wildfires crisped its hide and blackened
>
> whole vistas, new life inched in. My map
> blooms with low growth, sturdier than before.
> Thus I abstain, I will not sing, except
> of the elk and his harem who lie down in grandeur . . .

Even the rhyme scheme is altered; it shifts dizzily through a series of permutations, then resumes for the final stanza. Kumin moves from the tang of personal loss toward incantation. Her declaration of independence ends with a vision of Sexton hammered into memory. But the residual—and enduring—image is the sweep of Yellowstone and its resolute regeneration.

The present-tense immediacy of the poem brings it close to the reader, even as the formal aspects allow the writer a certain distance from the material. The result is a tension that energizes the work. It is experiential, not referential. The book's two sestinas—one early on, one after the poems about Sexton—also benefit from the constraints of form. "In Praise of the New Transfer Station" may be the only poem to celebrate a dump since Wallace Stevens did it—and what a dump this is! Kumin remembers the "pre-ecological days" when it was actually called a dump, but now recycling makes for a social occasion. This poem is pure fun—and its repetitions are so subtle that at least this reader was brought up short at the final three lines, suddenly (and only then) made aware of the form.

"The Riddle of Noah" is more noticeably a sestina from the beginning, so Kumin feels free to take liberties with the words, substituting rhymes, antonyms, and combinations to form an intricate network of sound and association which can sustain the content without trivializing it. Spoken directly to her grandson ("You want to change your name"), the poem moves from the child's wish for another name to a memory of the poet's brother (who did actually change his name) and then on to its central memory:

> The names that we go by are nothing
> compared to the names we are called. *Christ killer*! they mocked
> and stoned me with quinces in my bland-looking
> suburb. Why didn't I tattle, resist? I guessed
> I was guilty, the only kid on my manicured block
>
> who didn't know how to genuflect as we lock-
> stepped to chapel at noontime.

Again, the present-tense framework of the poem, combined with past-tense recollection, revives memory. Present and past exist simultaneously. The logic of association governs the poem and allows for its surprising turns, as it moves well beyond personal memory into a shared history that implicates not only the present but the future:

> Spared being burned at the stake, being starved or gassed,
> like Xuan Loc, Noah is fated to make his mark,
> suffer for grace through good works, aspire to something.
> Half-Jewish, half-Christian, he will own his name, will unlock
> the riddle of who he is: only child, in equal
> measure blessed and damned to be inward-looking,
>
> always slightly aslant the mark, like Xuan Loc.
> Always playing for keeps, for all or nothing
> in quest of his rightful self while the world looks on.

And so *Connecting the Dots* concludes by filling in the picture. From Kumin's vantage, looking at the progress of time, the world requires balance. On the day Sarajevo falls, she appreciates the music of a student orchestra. There's continuity in the changing seasons, the sense of the seed's tenacity even as she tucks the garden in for the winter. And always there's the word: reading Hopkins, she finds the "priest's sprung metronome" keeping descriptive time with the emerging landscape; poised on horseback, she sees a fox with its brood, wishing she possessed the word the vixen uses to call her young out of the den:

> Its sound o-shaped and unencumbered,
> the see-through color of river,
> airy as the topmost evergreen fingers
> and soft as pine duff underfoot
> where the doe lies down out of sight;
> take me in, tell me the word.

Kumin's own words feel unencumbered—lithe, shaped, charged with purpose.

Maxine Kumin has achieved by now a kind of wisdom based in honesty and grounded in her love of nature—her appreciation of its fruitfulness, its unruliness, its almost willed persistence. Her poems ask us to assess them in a complex manner, employing our intellect, our sense of form, even the biographical knowledge she has shared with us in other books over the years. For those interested in Kumin's overall accomplishment, *Selected Poems 1960-1990* (covering work from her first nine books) has just been published by W. W. Norton, and a collection of critical essays, *Telling the Barn Swallow: Poets on the Poetry of Maxine Kumin*, edited by Emily Grosholz, was recently issued by University Press of New England. But there's nothing retrospective about *Connecting the Dots*; it has the feel of the transitional, building on and extending the themes of earlier work even as it seems to be embarking on a new venture characterized by an active voice and a genuine curiosity about the future. Kumin teaches us, by example, to survive.

When the poet's "practical theory" has been flexible enough to allow for change and yet consistent enough to provide a framework, the resulting "selected" volume may achieve a unity that has been undetected (or only fleetingly glimpsed) in the separate volumes. The poet has had an opportunity to assess earlier work, make choices, put the poems together where they can—and most often do—speak to each other. The very act of giving the poems new life may, in fact, give them a different life. This is certainly true of Paul Zimmer's *Crossing to Sunlight: Selected Poems*, in which he provides even a third life for some of the poems that had appeared in his first selected, *Family Reunion* (1983).

Over the years Zimmer has given us a number of memorable personae, including the delightful "Zimmer," in whom we instantly recognize ourselves.

In Zimmer's second collection, *The Republic of Many Voices* (1969), "Zimmer" emerges as one of the "many voices," plagued to some extent by his own *inner* voices: guilt, fear, regret. But the persona is somewhat enigmatic; it figures in the titles, then recedes in favor of the first-person singular of the poems. "Zimmer's Head Thudding Against the Blackboard" begins "At the blackboard I had missed / Five number problems in a row." "Zimmer" and "I" are clearly equated, yet somehow removed from each other. When the exasperated nun throws him back into his seat, the speaker of the poem discovers the source of power: ". . . I hid my head and swore / That very day I'd be a poet, / And curse her yellow teeth with this." Moving from the past tense of the recollection to the present tense of "this," the poem realizes its own secret ability to create a new reality, to give the nun those yellow teeth for all eternity. The speaker of the poem is not quite the Zimmer of the title, who functions to place the self in memory and who allows the poet to take a slightly distanced stance on his own life.

This technique is perfected in the third volume, *The Zimmer Poems*, where the persona dominates almost all the titles. We see Zimmer not only in the ongoing narrative of his life (who he was/is) but also inside his dreams (who he would be). It's an age-old story: the awkward child in an insensitive world, the bullied boy dreaming of revenge and, always, the fearful sinner under the domination of the Church. "The Day Zimmer Lost Religion" begins with the small sin of missing Mass on purpose, waiting for Christ to "climb down / like a playground bully" to beat him senseless. The ending, though, shows the subtle shift in perspective, indicating that the speaker knows more than Zimmer does:

> But of course He never came, knowing that
> I was grown up and ready for Him now.

At the same time that Zimmer (the poet) creates Zimmer (the persona), he sets him against a long tradition of poetry. Sometimes playful, punning on the name itself ("Zimmer Is Icumen In"), sometimes with ribald seriousness ("Leaves of Zimmer"), Zimmer takes his own measure as well as that of "The Tradition." That "Zimmer" has entered this tradition is evident in recent poems like John Engels' "With Zimmer at the Zoo," where Engels counts on our knowing the original in order to play off our expectations.

Someone picking up a single Zimmer volume would probably take pleasure in it—it would be hard not to—without gaining much sense of the ongoing project. It may be that Zimmer himself didn't know where this playfulness would lead. But he persisted. Over the years, the distinctive world of Zimmer has evolved as a means of expressing and framing very human desires and ambitions, the kinds of things that many might consider too mundane (or profane) for poetic treatment. In that middle ground between first and third person, the Zimmer persona makes the unimportant significant precisely because it does not demand attention to the self. The titles deflect any implicit solipsism. We can watch the performances, each of which gives us a glimpse of a never-completed figure, almost antimythology: The Myth of Zimmer.

In subsequent volumes, Zimmer expands his repertoire. His "Wanda" poems explore sexual desire and fantasy with unashamed self-knowledge. After these, there is a gradual shift to the third person. Reversing the earlier method, now the title sets the scene (as in "The Duke Ellington Dream") and Zimmer appears as a central "character":

> Of course Zimmer was late for the gig.
> Duke was pissed and growling at the piano,
> But Jeep, Brute, Rex, Cat, and Cootie
> All moved down on the chairs
> As Zimmer walked in with his tenor.
> Everyone knew that the boss had arrived.

The introduction of this third-person Zimmer has the effect of establishing yet more distance—this time allowing for a stance on the subject matter as well as the self. There is also room for compassion. But even this enlarged Zimmer can sometimes be constraining. Certain circumstances do not lend themselves to parody or irony, and distance would trivialize their importance. So the deaths of the poet's parents are treated with the first-person immediacy and the honest respect they deserve.

From this point on, Paul Zimmer is able to step out of his created persona and write a fully personal poem. That's not to say he doesn't resort to "Zimmer" again, but he has gone unmasked and discovered the freedom of wearing his own face. "But Bird," another of the many tributes to jazz and blues, is an example of what happens when he leaves the persona behind. In the autumn of 1954, Zimmer heard Charlie Parker play and found something he could believe in. Five months later, the poet was stationed in Nevada where he witnessed tests of the atomic bomb:

> The bones in our fingers were
> Suddenly x-rayed by the flash.
> We moaned together in light
> That entered everything.
> Tried to become the earth itself
> As the shock rolled toward us.

The red-cheeked boy who heard that tenor had lost his innocence. Five months later, Bird was dead: "But Bird. Remember Bird." If the poem were written in the Zimmer persona, it would lose the mythic power found in the juxtaposition of the two overwhelming realities.

Unlike many volumes of selected poems, *Crossing to Sunlight* does not begin with new work. Paul Zimmer has sensed that the new poems belong at the end of the book where they can make their own profound statement. By then "Zimmer" is gone, replaced by a "he," a "you," and an individualized "I" to look the world squarely in its eye. Nevertheless, the persona haunts these poems, makes them more poignant, possibly more heartfelt. Now the third-person hero of "Entrance to the Sky" contains the vestiges of an earlier self who might have used a less resigned tone. This character, too, occupies the middle ground between "he" and "I"—but the effect is not so much a distancing as it is a blending of perspectives:

> He has faith in whatever the sky brings—
> rain, heat, snow, ice, dark.
> He believes in morning, noon, and night,
> in sunrise, sunset, and midnight.
> Even these small, unnerving lights
> might bring down to his life
> some sudden, lustrous conclusion.

Faith, rejected in the earlier poems (at least in the form the priest presented), now seems possible.

The speaker of these new poems admits he has had a cancer scare, a detached retina, and asthma, that he is overweight and wears hearing aids. In short, he admits to aging. And the poems vacillate between acceptance of and resistance to death. In "The End before the End," he contemplates "the vast, chilled foothills of age." In "And Then I Drove On," the title itself tells the aftermath, while the poem details the near-accident that "makes my chest echo when I think of it." A new awareness of mortality makes for renewed observation, and for Paul Zimmer the observation is heightened by his years of seeing life through a double lens of Zimmer & Co. All those years of practice have made way for a poem that is intensely personal yet not confessional, a poem that, even with a detached retina, retains its peripheral vision. Zimmer has emerged from "Zimmer." (But wait: in a recent long sequence called "Poems from the Old Republic," published in the autumn 1996 *Gettysburg Review*, the old gang is reconvened in death. The sequence ends with a "paunchy guy / slowly dragging off in the dust / a tremendous letter Z . . ." So we might expect to see him again.) *Crossing into Sunlight* assures us that Paul Zimmer, like the Orpheus of his opening poem, can cross the infinite boundaries between selves, between darkness and light.

Lisel Mueller's *Alive Together: New and Selected Poems* was awarded the Pulitzer Prize for poetry in April 1997. The book opens with the new material, almost as though Mueller's own sense of her career is a bit like peeling an onion, working down to the core. But it's an onion that has grown over thirty-five years and six previous collections—each new volume adding density and weight to the previous ones, enlarging her themes and accumulating detail as though memory itself were taking on importance in inverse proportion to the distance between the event and the memory of the event. While the earlier books explored the power of "story," the later books have become more and more aware that the poet's own story is symbolic of its time.

If it's true that all happy families are alike, then Mueller's family shouldn't be called happy. But it was—and happiness takes its own convoluted turns. "Ordinary life: the plenty and thick of it"—over many volumes the story unfolds: a gentle, happy family living in prewar Germany; their flight to America, leaving the grandparents behind; the immersion in a new language; grief at a mother's death; marriage; motherhood; the loneliness and pain of the father, his impending death. As if aware that the reader of Mueller's earlier poems is familiar with the details of her life, "Curriculum Vitae" opens the selected poems with a reiteration—twenty numbered one- or two-sentence statements that summarize the "story." These are nearly all in the first person. Only the thirteenth (the unlucky one) slips into third person, the pain still necessitating distance: "the death of the mother hurt the daughter into poetry." Echoing Auden's poem in memory of Yeats ("Mad Ireland hurt you into poetry"), Mueller's third-person story simultaneously removes her from the event and reveals it as the source for everything that is to follow.

The "new poems" portion of *Alive Together* is no longer than in most selecteds; it acts almost like a "book," with three distinct sections: the first with its focus on place and time (memory), the second with its emphasis on things, and the third a long sequence about the plight of Patty Hearst. So memory persists, bringing with it quiet reflection on the *meaning* of memory. In "Place and Time," Mueller begins with the moment when she hears a man on the radio telling that the business district of his hometown had been plowed under, then moves to the thought of what can—and cannot—be eradicated:

My mother is dead, and the piano
she could not take with her into exile
burned with our city in World War II.
That is the half-truth. The other half
is that it's still her black Bechstein
each concert pianist plays for me
and that her self-taught fingers
are behind each virtuoso performance
on the stereo, giving me back
my prewar childhood city
intact and real.

If the man on the radio has his own version of "some music that brings back" his town, he can recall with equanimity what is now gone. "Pillar of Salt" expands this theme as the poet compares herself to Lot's wife, looking back at destruction. She brings back her family in "brilliant moments" of memory—a show set up for herself "so I can change the ending, / stop it short of hell, / give them bearable old age, / a decent death." But the ruse doesn't work—history is unalterable:

Memory is the only
afterlife I can understand,
and when it's gone, they're gone.
Soon I will betray them.
Think of it as the solid pillar
dissolving, all that salt
seeping back into the sea.

Along with (and probably related to) the poems of memory are poems about failing eyesight—cast in first person. This theme has been implicit in earlier volumes (perhaps best known is "Monet Refuses the Operation") but now it is made explicit. As the poet's world goes dark, her ears compensate, opening *new* worlds: "Tonight the crickets spread static / across the air, a continuous rope / of sound extended to me, / the perfect listener." Not only the perfect listener, but the perfect describer of auditory experience. The poems are filled with alert attentiveness to sound: soft-spoken daughters, a far cry, querulous murmurs, laughter of women, wind howling, clocks striking, and always the radio with its music. The sounds here are almost tactile.

So it is with empathy that Mueller begins "Captivity," her poem about Patty

Hearst, imagining the darkness ("Eight weeks in that closet: / a child's worst nightmare, / being locked up in the dark") and the intrusion on the darkness ("the radio always on / blaring just out of reach / of her useless hands"). And it is with empathy that Mueller imagines Hearst learning another language—the language of fear and dependency: "*Green*, she said to herself, / a beautiful word in another language, / devoid of meaning." But there's more going on here: Hearst's story presents a contemporary version of the fairy tale—the maiden in distress, translated into modern terms. However, Patty Hearst has foiled our expectations because her story was more complicated, more human, than our sense of myth could bear: "We wanted kitsch, / the easy split into black and white, / a story in which the heroine, / bruised but pure, throws off / the Tania skin . . ." Mueller examines the subsequent lack of empathy on the part of the public—"She turned into Tania and we turned against her"—including herself in the all-encompassing "we":

> We could not cope with the huge
> complexities of the heart,
> that melting pot of selves.

More than most people, Lisel Mueller is aware of the selves that make up an individual. Her own entry into a new language has been a source for her understanding that everything is a kind of translation, and her method has often been what I would call "indirect metaphor"—an implied metaphor that works subtly through the choice of vocabulary. The Patty Hearst poem is about Hearst, not about fairy tales, but the frame of reference is such that the reader realizes something about the way anecdotal material, through human necessity, becomes myth. The new poems in this book serve to reinforce Mueller's ongoing concerns and to provide an umbrella under which *all* her poems can be seen to be "alive together." (It's interesting to note that the title poem for this particular gathering is taken from her second book—sure testament to the fact that the various poems stem from the same source and build toward a cohesive statement of being.)

Finally, each volume represented here reveals a steady and steadfast love for her husband which takes the form of delicate love poems that honor both the difficulties and the sustenance found in an enduring relationship. "Together we make the equinox," she says of her husband's optimism coupled with her caution. "Midwinter Notes" quietly—and beautifully—extends love for someone else into love for the world: "As the world grows darker / before my eyes, the sun / sends me sharper, harder / glances off glass, off ice- . . ." Set against her failing eyesight, the poem offers something that will not fail:

Another chance to wake up together,
accepting the invitation
of one more morning.

And the world itself, as if by association with this fidelity, reveals yet more of its secrets:

At twilight, water in roadside ditches
pulls down the last light
to be transformed from lead
into softly gleaming silver.
It has taken me years to discover
this slant conjunction of sky and water
late in the day, when the dead
are allowed their brief shining.

In Lisel Mueller's case, what has persisted is her life, but her life is recreated in poems that couple present and past in a continuing commemoration of what could have been viewed as historically broken. Because of her biographical circumstances, she has "translated" herself from one language and one culture to another, but her sensibility provides continuity. Over the years, she has held herself to a standard of clarity and truthfulness in language as well as in emotion. Her appreciation of the persistence of her life takes the form of celebratory lyrics—love poems to the world. And she couples the lyric with the concept of story, bringing old tales into the present and making them new. It is especially gratifying to see the Pulitzer committee recognize this achievement and give one of our highest honors to this poet whose experience is quintessentially American.

The Welsh poet and short-story writer Leslie Norris, born in the industrial and mining town of Merthyr Tydfil, has taught for many years in the United States, most recently at Brigham Young University. He, too, has undergone a kind of "self-translation"—this time not so much in language as in landscape. Norris' early poems contain not only the pit ponies and slag heaps but also the fields and moors, the curlews and cattle, the bracken and barnyards of his native landscape. And these poems reflect, in their formal construction and lush sounds, the influences of early Welsh poets as well as both Dylan Thomas and Edward Thomas. *Collected Poems* incorporates seven previous volumes along with new work, moving from the "secure horizon" of his childhood to the great expanses of the American West, and from the security of a mastered form ("I believe that craft is more than anything, almost," he said in a recent interview) to the challenges of a more Americanized "freed" verse.

Norris' work is not as well known in this country as it should be. In 1994, Camden House (Columbia, SC) issued a critical assessment of his work, edited by Eugene England and Peter Makuck. That collection, *An Open World: Essays on Leslie Norris,* with contributions by Glyn Jones, William Matthews, Sue Ellen Thompson, Brendan Galvin, Richard Simpson, Fred Chappell, and Christopher Merrill among others, places Norris firmly in both landscapes and celebrates the range of his vision. Maybe *Collected Poems* will now introduce him to a wider audience.

"Autumn Elegy" (from *The Loud Winter, 1967*) demonstrates Norris' early ease with form and rhythm. Looking at the September hillsides, the poet turns elegiac:

> Young men of my own time died
> In the Spring of their living and could not turn
> To this. They died in their flames, hard
> War destroyed them. Now as the trees burn
>
> In the beginning glory of Autumn
> I sing for all green deaths as I remember
> In their broken Mays, and turn
> The years back for them, every red September.

Such passages show Norris' skill with enjambment, his subtle ear for rhyme, his sure ear for meter. They also sound rather old-fashioned. Another characteristic of his early work is that the poems tend to sum up their own contents, ending on a definitive note as though the speaker had, in the process of working through the poem, found an answer to whatever question spawned it.

Elegy is one of Norris' repeated themes—not only for his dead companions, but for other Welsh poets (Dafydd ap Gwylim, Dylan Thomas) and for the land itself:

> Whenever I think of Wales, I hear the voices
> Of children calling and the world shrinks to the span
> Of a dozen hills.

Then, six stanzas later:

> Whenever I think of Wales,
> I think of my leaving, the farewell valleys letting go . . .
> ("Postcards from Wales")

Reading Leslie Norris, for most of us, means entering an unfamiliar landscape but familiar territory. He is decidedly the poet of childhood (boyhood, to be more exact), almost as though it were yet another landscape. Maybe it is—a landscape of the mind, of a certain kind of freedom. The sweep of these poems is extensive, but they return, almost always, to the particularity of boyhood—one not frozen in amber, but fluid and lively in the imagination. So when, in "Dead Boys," he imagines his friend returned to the town of their youth, he talks as if they were all singular ("he" / "the boy"), and the reader is made doubly aware that the poet's own childhood is represented as being universal:

> Days are long to a boy;
> Nights buried his foundered sadness in their tides
> Till the black hulks slept in softness, as he slept.
> Once he was thoughtless to an easy friend. The roads
> Of summer led them away and they broke in a rough moment,
> Never to meet again. It was here that he said goodbye
>
> To his angular childhood . . .

By the time Norris published the work that appeared in America in *Sequences* (Gibbs Smith, 1988), he had been living in Utah for quite some time. The initial sequence is "The Hawk's Eye," eight poems in which the land is seen from above, almost mapped in flight. The landscape is explored from a position of self-imposed exile. If writer and raptor are not fully equated, the hawk's viewpoint is at least equivalent to the perspective of the poet, allowing Norris to collapse the distance between childhood and the present, between somber Welsh mountains and the high Sierras. "I could use that harsh gaze / above the crested summit . . ." says the speaker, and "I could see the men / I might have become. . . ." In "Hawk Music," he obliterates all boundaries. From above, the land appears flattened, untouched by political demarcations, and the isolate eye of the soaring hawk "is concerned with what's visible":

> Its happiness is to watch
> the intricate valleys weathering
> and the wearing down
>
> of upturned faces of rock.
> Let me lean into this wind,
> so rare that its demands
>
> are those of music. I would
> give it a note on the thinnest
> string of air, a sound

so high the ear cannot
support it. But I
will hope to hear it.

With these poems, Norris seems to have found not only a new vista but a new kind of music—freed from the demands of form and, at the same time, firmly tethered to meter and sound. As they shed some of their didacticism, the poems gain authority; the final section of the book, "New Poems, 1996," touches on earlier themes but with new, more subtle dimensions. "Bringing in the Selves" looks hard *at* the eight-year-old self (seen in third person—"He has in his mind / the names of waterbirds / mallard, swan, moorhen: / he discovers and murmurs / their incantatory syllables") and, at the same time, looks *with* the eyes of the child ("Mild rain polishes / the skins of new leaves"). The final couplet adds an overlay of adult sensibility, completing the self: "Come in, child, come in. / The circle is made." And for those of us who love soccer, "The Night Before the Game" captures the magic and anticipation found in practice—whether it be sport or poetry:

So he runs around
in the ring of light, a small thin boy,
until his running is automatic and the ball's
response is to something other than his feet,
something different, a sudden unity,
a harmony, like happiness.

On the brink of sleep, he imagines the next day's game when the "moving thread of playing" will link him to everyone (even "Arthur Ferguson, / who's gone to Australia") in a web of intricate connection.

The new work contains a major poem, "Borders," written in memory of the poet's friend John Ormond. It begins with the "bridge between the town and Breconshire" where the boy "lived a moment in adventurous limbo" and about which the man asks,

Did I stand on air then, invisibly
taken to some unknown world, some nowhere?
Where was I then? I was whole
but felt an unseen line
divide me, send my strong half forward,
keep my other timidly at home.

Then this memory is emotionally fused with other times, other places. Driving in America, Norris once stopped to buy a Navajo belt buckle and found himself at the meeting of four states, placing "a foot in Utah, / a foot in Arizona, my palms flat / in the dust of Colorado and New Mexico." Having thus experienced the insubstantiality of border, the poet feels free to let the poem flow, like "the river's neutral water." He recalls his friend—"When he left, / it was to see his place from a distance / and peacefully go home"—and the way Ormond saw his mother through to her death. In a final breathtaking shift, the poem sheds narrative in favor of narrated meditation, reminding the reader of the poem's source:

Border, boundary, threshold, door—
Orpheus moved either way, the living and the dead
were parted by a thin reflection
he simply walked through. But who can follow?

For all the boundaries I have crossed, flown over,
knowingly, unknowingly, I have no answers;
but sit in the afternoon sun, under mountains
where stale snow clings in shadowy patches,
remember my friend, how he had sung,
hope he is still singing.

So it is that last poem, "His Father, Singing," is all the more poignant as it catches up multiple associations. The title—ritualistic, almost archetypal—creates an interval to be bridged. The first lines tighten the focus by claiming a more personal connection: "My father sang for himself, / out of sadness and poverty . . ." The single instance of his singing—"He sang for us once only"—stands out in memory: a moment when the poet saw his father holding his younger brother, and "what he sang / above his baby's sleep / was never meant / for any infant's comfort." As the poet's song merges with that of his father, the younger man accepts what he cannot understand; his father's life remains a mystery and the poem resigns itself to the unanswerable:

For the first time raised
his voice, in pain and anger

sang. I did not know his song
nor why he sang it. But stood
in fright, knowing it important,
and someone should be listening.

The memory is so precise that it creates a landscape of its own—one which not only recovers but illuminates the lost.

Content—so important in Norris' poems—is nonetheless secondary to form, which orders memory so that it's not just an accumulation of detail but an aesthetic experience: the poems perform on the page. Yet over the years of sustained discipline, Norris' form has somehow softened; he has moved from the constrictions of end rhyme into the subtler patterns of internal rhyme and a "sprung" meter, with the accompanying freedom of insight that comes when a poem's form does not demand an expected epiphany. By refining his craft, by staying true to his true material—more, by redeeming the past—Leslie Norris has demonstrated why he continues (and will continue) to persist.

. . . *after the art*

19 April 1912
Dear Madam
I am only one, only one, only one. Only one being, one at the same time. Not two, not three, only one. Only one life to live, only sixty minutes in one hour. Only one pair of eyes. Only one brain. Only one being. Being only one, having only one pair of eyes, having only one time, having only one life, I cannot read your MS three or four times. Not even one time. Only one look, only one look is enough. Hardly one copy would sell here. Hardly one. Hardly one.

Many thanks. I am returning the MS by registered post. Only one MS by one post.

Sincerely yours
A. C. Fifield

We do not know of or remember A. C. Fifield. But we know exactly to whom he was sending his rejection letter. There's something in her style (and something in his imitation) that endures. Something in her style, some thing, not any one thing, but some thing that makes for something. Well, you get the idea. I am only one. One reader. Reading one by one. Only time will tell.

Against

On Mary Karr's *Viper Rum*; Billy Collins' *Picnic, Lightning*; Thylias Moss's *Last Chance for the Tarzan Holler*; and Ted Hughes's *Birthday Letters.*

FOR THE PAST WEEK, I've seemed—even to myself—to be against everything. Well, not quite everything, but a lot more than usual. I've been against little things: the way you can never—ever—get a real human on the phone when a company has voice mail; the people who don't like the color of the new lampposts where I work; the way the bank can't give me an answer because the computer is down; a student who told me to please print my comments on his papers because he can't read cursive. I've been against bigger things: the other side of the "argument" I've had with a university press about "gender neutral" language; the fact that not one of my students has read, or will be asked to read, *Moby-Dick*; the rudeness that has crept into ordinary conversations. And I've been against really important things: lying under oath; our country's failure to act when innocent people are being massacred in Kosovo. It's not that I'm going through a cantankerous period; I've been a bit cantankerous all of my life. But the accumulated effrontery of contemporary life seems to have caught up with me.

In all of this, I have realized something about the nature of being *against.* In most instances, it implies something *else* I am *for.* I have a position—one I've come to through thought and contemplation—so that I cannot remain neutral (though if I didn't really quite like those bright red lampposts, I might be neutral in that small battle). The quality of opposition presupposes an alternative—except concerning things so awful you have no idea what to do, and even then you have an option of speaking out. "Against" is not always contrary. Sometimes it's truly resistant, sometimes only pointing up a contrast, sometimes, even, *in anticipation of*. . . and it's occurred to me that all this is not unrelated to art, including poetry. Being "against" is, after all, one mindset out of which art gets made. And I don't just mean subversive, political art, but the kind of art that defines itself as necessary precisely because it views itself as an antidote to the tired, the outmoded, the superficial, the false. The kind of art—and the kind of criticism—that is, in its own right, an alternative.

Mary Karr offers both art and criticism. At the end of *Viper Rum*, her third collection of poetry, is a twenty-three-page critical essay on the aesthetics of contemporary poetry. Entitled "Against Decoration," this courageous and provocative essay first appeared in *Parnassus*. That such an essay could be termed "courageous" says something of the state of the art of criticism. By all rights, "Against Decoration" should be part of an ongoing dialogue, one more challenging voice in a vigorous larger discussion. Instead, it proffers a somewhat lonely sanity, asking the hard questions that others have seemed content to leave unasked.

Anyone who has read Karr's memoir, *The Liars' Club*, knows that she does not pull her punches. In "Against Decoration," she dismantles some of the poems of the "new formalists," risks criticism by taking on such people as Helen Vendler, Anthony Hecht, and others. Karr pointedly critiques some of the poetic practices (and their practitioners) in the contemporary canon, talking of "the highbrow doily-making that passes for art today." Referring to Amy Clampitt's "purple vocabulary" and to the "glib meaninglessness" of John Ashbery and the language poets, Karr examines ornamentation and formalism "as an aesthetic value in and of itself"—and finds it wanting. In addition, she questions Vendler's enthusiasm for poetry as a kind of academic "game," a puzzle to be solved. Karr calls for clarity rather than obscurity, depth rather than surface. She wants a poem that does not shy away from its emotions, is not afraid to be memorable, acts as though its content matters.

Indicting much of what she finds to be excessive, even evasive, Karr does not blame individual critics, but rather laments the state of criticism—or the lack thereof. She raises the age-old question of why poets write, and for whom. If too much power has devolved into the hands of too few reviewers, we need to think about venue and about audience. Who reads reviews? If they are only for poets, then why do we not have the lively interchange of ideas that characterized the not-too-distant past? If they are for readers of poetry, why do we hear no murmurs of concurrence, no growls of dissent?

"Against Decoration" is important not only for its message, but for its informed and astute logic. Karr examines the work of the "new formalists" not in the light of free verse, but *against* other formal poems such as Yeats's "Easter 1916" or Seamus Heaney's third sonnet sequence, "Clearances" (*The Haw Lantern*). In doing so, she exposes the soft belly of large parts of the movement.

(At one point, she even pits James Merrill against himself.) And by refusing to equate form per se with a political stance, she interrogates not only the formalists, but Ira Sadoff's leftist outrage at form itself as well as whole schools of critical theory. No poet writing today should proceed without at least noting Karr's legitimate misgivings and taking them into account.

Karr's list of what she is against (obscurity of character, foggy physical world, overuse of meaningless references, metaphors that obscure rather than illuminate, and linguistic excess for no good reason) can be translated into a positive list of what she is for: clarity of character, a strong sense of the physical world, clear references, metaphors that illuminate rather than obscure—and linguistic moves that enhance a poem's meanings. Referring to what sounds suspiciously like good old-fashioned "authorial intention," she invites us to explore the *reasons* for a poet's choices.

We cannot help reading one book against another, one poem against another, one idea against another. It's how we make distinctions. So, in exposing others, Mary Karr naturally exposes herself. To include such a challenging "manifesto" at the end of a book of poems is to invite its application to the work at hand. The poems of *Viper Rum* stand up well under her self-imposed critical scrutiny. Using Karr's standards of evaluation, it would be safe to say there is very little linguistic excess here. These poems intend to be hard-hitting, toughly iconoclastic, blunt, and unflinching almost to the point of repulsion. If they are excessive at all, they are excessively blunt. They look hard at the effects of alcohol, a failed marriage, an impulse toward suicide and self-destruction. The speaker of the title poem toys with temptation and turns aside. "The Last of the Brooding Miserables" calls up a litany of other deaths:

> Lord, you maybe know me best
> by my odd laments: My friend
> drew the garage door tight,
> lay flat on the cold cement
> then sucked off the family muffler
> to stop the voices in his head.
> And Logan stabbed in a fight, and Coleman shot,
> and the bright girl who pulled a blade
> the width of her own soft throat,
> and Tom from the virus and Dad
> from drink—Lord, these many-headed
> hurts I mind.

Unrelenting, the list unreels a not-so-pretty picture, ending close to home. The intimate voice says "Dad," refusing to let the reader hide behind the formalities of "my father." Karr does not recoil from the truth. She goes on to give her reason for compiling the list: "I study each death / hard that death not catch me / unprepared." Taking its cue from its invocation, the poem ends speaking directly and intimately: "Let me rise // to your unfamiliar light, / love, without which the dying / wouldn't bother me one whit." The tone is both prayerful and belligerent until, in a final gesture, the speaker bows her head.

In *Viper Rum*, Karr returns to the themes that haunted *The Liars' Club*—her parents' drinking and dependence, her sister's forced and cheerful practicality, her own troubled loving. In her urgent need to claim the life she's led in its own stark terms, Karr not only faces it head-on, she almost rubs her own face in it. Calling funeral homes "for the best cremation deal" from her father's hospital room, noting her son in his Dracula cape as her friend phones with news of a cancer diagnosis, remembering the "dead space" only alcohol could fill, recounting the night fears that call up fields of skulls (she knows they're there—think of "Adolf and Uncle Joe") that envy the very flesh covering her head, Karr almost hurls these moments at her readers, daring us to avert our gaze. Daring us to ask for decoration, something to redeem the moment, clean it up for public consumption. But Karr refuses. In doing so, she runs the risk of elevating her bluntness to the alternative status of high impoverishment—a dark negative space that forms its own misshapen doily. This rarely happens. Karr's intelligent—and *reasoned*—portrayal of life as she knows it shapes the collection.

The poems of *Viper Rum* may be blunt for bluntness' sake, but they are not exploitative. Karr stares hard in the face of hard fact. There must be a place in poetry for the honesty that knows what it's after, and what it's after here is the tough, gritty, physical world in all its inarticulate confusion. These poems make something of what we've been handed, not something of whole cloth. They rip up the Hallmark card and replace it with the difficult, demanding claims of love in an imperfect world. Her ear is part of this. The staccato, onomatopoeic music in the middle of "The Pallbearer," for example, accentuates, rather than masks, the stark realities of a burial:

> The cherrywood cover got pittered with rain,
> glossy with swirls in the grain
>
> as with great red rivers risen to flood.
> I too was flooded. My eyes brimmed
> the green world blurry, though my face stayed flat.

The rhythm of walking took all my thought.
Later the shovels of dirt fell splat
on the cover, and they left a nice mound

like the start of a rose garden.

A hard-won religious impulse runs throughout the collection; any sense of redemption comes after Karr has refused all easy answers. In "The Wife of Jesus Speaks," an unnamed woman faces Christ's denial and her own eventual suicide. From hell, she announces herself:

In these rosy caverns, you worship
what you want. I have chosen that time

in time's initial measure, history's
virgin parchment, when with his hard
stalk of flesh rocking inside me, I was unwrit.

"Christ's Passion" opens with a cocky, almost-strident voice ("Sure we're trained to his suffering, sure / the nine-inch nails, and so forth") before it gives imaginative space to the nature of the suffering, the taking-on of everyone's fears and sorrows, the burden of human doubt. And "The Grand Miracle" continues in this vein ("Jesus wound up with his body nailed to a tree— / a torment he practically begged for, / or at least did nothing to stop"), calling his resurrection one of a long line of hoaxes, and then ending with the gospel of the "prospect of love"—a shared space where humans learn to trust in faith and in each other.

For 2000-near years
my tribe has lined up at various altars,
so dumbly I open this mouth for bread and song.

Dumbly. At the heart of the book is the speechless awe at a world that must be taken on faith, the wordless acceptance of someone who has contemplated its opposite—the noisy clamor of death—and come back to make the best of those moments of grace (basketballs swishing through the air at a family picnic, bumper cars at the county fair, a chorus of voices rising in unison) that only this world can give to us.

Writing against decoration, Karr has made her case for the emotive voice, for a poetry of feeling. She has not shunned form; many of her poems find stanzaic structures that enhance their meaning, call subtle attention to slant rhymes and the cadence of spoken voice. Karr has found a form in which she can explore the qualities of language—its sounds and its metaphors—that will lead toward clarity. Her final message—and there is one—is so simple that only simplicity could convey it. "Chosen Blindness" depicts a time when she noticed nothing, not even fields of dandelions gone to seed. She herself had gone to seed, paralyzed by drink, sucking smoke into her lungs, waiting for death to catch her unprepared. That was the past, the chosen blindness. The second section shifts to the present: "Now I go to church. Who'd think it?" The third section ends with mother and son holding a hymnal, matching their voices. Written for her son, the poem attests to her willed survival and the strengths of those people we know to be America's promise:

My forebears
forbore this way, in company. Bread fed them,
and they had to practice hope to keep

plowing up the Dust Bowl's
starved earth in rows, year
after fruitless year, till the cotton came back.

To say something this true and this moving in anything but the plainest of language would be to do it—and them—a disservice.

The work of Billy Collins opposes the abstract and the pretentious. His poems, which seem casual compared to Karr's intense ones, balance humor and emotion; they are lucid, easy to read, amusing and amused. Their complexities lie in their ability to surprise: one thought flows easily into another with humorous good nature until, suddenly, the poem takes an unexpected turn. *Picnic, Lightning* takes its title from *Lolita*, in which the young nymphet gives a two-word parenthetical explanation for her mother's death. Its telescopic combination is both ominous and somehow humorous—one can almost hear her offhand tone—and Collins uses that to establish his own tone in the title poem:

It is possible to be struck by a meteor
or a single-engine plane
while reading in a chair at home.
Safes drop from rooftops
and flatten the odd pedestrian
mostly within the panels of the comics,
but still, we know it is possible . . .

As he shovels compost into a wheelbarrow, he thinks of the ways the body can betray itself so that the "instant hand of Death" becomes the reason for detailed marveling at the soil: "bits of leaf like flakes off a fresco." Because the combination of picnic and lightning is inherent in everything we do, the thought of death heightens the speaker's awareness of the things at hand: "Then the wheelbarrow is a wilder blue, / the clouds a brighter white." He can hear plants singing, and the "click / of the sundial / as one hour sweeps into the next."

The click of the sundial is characteristic of Collins' poetry—the impossible made possible through an imagination that never veers far from reality, but simply reinforces the wonder of the actual. The result is not decoration, but a shaped necessity. The opening poem of *Picnic, Lightning*, "Fishing on the Susquehanna in July," with its satisfying rhythms, sets the stage for such incursions into the imagination.

> I have never been fishing on the Susquehanna
> or on any river for that matter
> to be perfectly honest.
>
> Not in July or any month
> have I had the pleasure—if it is a pleasure—
> of fishing on the Susquehanna.

The nearest he's come to fishing on the Susquehanna is in a museum in Philadelphia when he contemplated a painting of just such a scene, thinking that was something he was never likely to do. Then he moved on, to other American scenes, to "one of a brown hare / who seemed so wired with alertness / I imagined him springing right out of the frame." In just this way, the speaker has, in fact, been fishing on the Susquehanna, in July, the blue sky filled with clouds and the trees dense along the banks. And yet Collins has not appropriated the experience; he has remained true to his honest admission of what he did—and did not—do. The poem is not about fishing; it's about what it is to imagine oneself fishing, about the power of art to transform.

For all his easygoing informality, Collins is not afraid to be moving. He admits to emotion and to the validity of emotion and, beyond that, to the validity of imagined emotion. "I Chop Some Parsley While Listening to Art Blakey's Version of 'Three Blind Mice'" completes its thought in the first line—"And I start wondering how they came to be blind." From there, Collins is off on a riff—wondering at the circumstances that caused them to be blind, wondering how they found each other, wondering about the farmer's wife, wondering his way right through to dicing an onion which might, just possibly, account for the "wet stinging" in his own eyes although the "mournful trumpet" of Freddie Hubbard isn't helping. By now, with the help of the music, he's overcome the cynic in himself and feels real empathy for the sightless creatures "without tails to trail through the moist grass."

Jazz blows its own ubiquitous trumpet throughout this collection. "Jazz and Nature" manages to fuse the internal and external worlds in one of those exceptional moments when, with Art Pepper's "speedy, mellow alto / pouring out of two big maples" and a bee driving the speaker indoors, he moves from memory into his own present tense. In a few swift stanzas, the poet progresses from biography to autobiography, from listening to jazz to listening to his inner voice, from a consideration of nature to a contemplation of his small family tree:

> the work whose pages are turned
> every day like a wheel that is turned by water,
> the thing I can never stop writing,
> the only book I can never put down.

Jazz also informs poems that are ostensibly about something else, as in "Snow," where a slow Monk solo becomes the falling snow: "the notes and the spaces accompany / its easy falling / on the geometry of the ground." The poem turns playful as the poet imagines the composer imagining a winter scene while he sits at the piano, or, in turn, imagines that the music could also go with rain and falling leaves, or, conversely, that the snow could go with "an adagio for strings," a swirl of thoughts to mirror the fusion of music and weather. In a characteristic gesture, the poem turns serious when you least expect it, so that there is delight in the seriousness and delight that it could come so quickly to alter the mood. Thus the ending of "Snow" is all the more moving for the playfulness that preceded it:

> It falls so indifferently
> into the spacious white parlor of the world,
> if I were sitting here reading
> in silence
>
> reading the morning paper
> or reading *Being and Nothingness*,
> not even letting the spoon
> touch the inside of the cup,
> I have a feeling
> the snow would even go perfectly with that.

The snow shapes itself to mood, to music, to the perfect title of the book to read in such a snow, to the internal stirrings of the spoon that rests nowhere as the poet's imagination discovers it ready and waiting, an image that links the parlor of the world with the interior self.

Collins can make you almost laugh out loud while feeling pain, as in his brilliant rewriting of Auden, "Musée des Beaux Arts Revisited." From real Irish cows in a field to reincarnated peacocks, he gives us the benefit of a whimsical mind working over the mundane. But it's more than that. It's the precision of language used to surprise with its rightness, enlighten us with its insight. At his best, Collins is *seriously* funny. For example, "Lines Lost Among Trees" invokes lines that came to him when he couldn't write them down and which he can't recall: "They are gone forever, / a handful of coins / dropped through the grate of memory, / along with the ingenious mnemonic // I devised to hold them in place—." Has ever the limitation of "ingenious" been more clear or more familiar? So Collins in his distinctive voice gives us an elegy for the lost lines:

> those six or eight exhalations,
> the braided rope of the syntax,
> the jazz of the timing,
>
> and the little insight at the end
> wagging like the short tail
> of a perfectly obedient spaniel . . .

Collins plays against the artificial, usually predictable, self-importance of contemporary poetry. His self-consciousness seems unselfconscious. He handles image with the deftness of a juggler tossing in another ball, catching it effortlessly, integrating it seamlessly into the act. His inventive metaphors illuminate as though the world had been glimpsed in a flash of lightning.

Humor is tricky, especially in poems, and some of these work better than others—though I suspect the list would differ from reader to reader. I'm not as entranced with "Victoria's Secret" as I am with the wet dogs that will repel people in the future as much as they do in the present ("To a Stranger Born in Some Distant Country Hundreds of Years from Now"), and I'm not as entertained by undressing Emily ("Taking Off Emily Dickinson's Clothes") as by the oddball facts the poet has found in reading a one-volume encyclopedia from *Flannagan* to *flatheaded* to *Flavian* ("What I Learned Today").

My personal favorites illuminate not only the world but also a sense of the temporal within it. There is a doubling of time in "I Go Back to the House for a Book." The speaker returns for something to read in the doctor's office and, while he's inside choosing the book, another self goes on without him, always, now, three minutes ahead of any experience the speaker might be about to have: just ahead of him, the perfect double, although less schooled in "the love poems of Ovid." This playful conceit becomes something profound—that sense of possibility we all know, not presented here as earthshaking, but rather as the quiet choices continually made that in retrospect become the life we have led.

"Lines Composed Over Three Thousand Miles from Tintern Abbey" are also lines composed many years after first reading Wordsworth's poem. "It was better the first time"—when it was fresh, when the image hadn't diminished through familiarity, when the body was full of energy, so that now, when "we" (he's included us all by now) put down the book and sleep, when we wake "a little before dinner," something will be missing. We will wake older, no longer virgin, noting the slightly acrid aftertaste of relived experience: "Nothing will be as it was / a few hours ago, back in the glorious past / before our naps, back in that Golden Age / that drew to a close sometime shortly after lunch."

Unfolding like a black-and-white newsreel, "The Death of the Hat" follows the long and distinguished history of hats: "The day war was declared / everyone in the street was wearing a hat." The poem pivots—"But today we go bareheaded / into the winter streets"—and suddenly the memory of the poet's father wearing his hat to work every day is coupled with the image of spruce trees wearing "cold white hats of snow" until the poem resolves itself in heartfelt elegy:

> And now my father, after a life of work,
> wears a hat of earth,
> and on top of that,
> a lighter one of cloud and sky—a hat of wind.

In unforgettable moments like these, *Picnic, Lightning* proves again that poetry can be accessible *and* significant, that perhaps one depends upon the other.

Thylias Moss is, ironically, writing against the written word. Anyone who has heard her read her work is struck by the significant difference between the words as they appear on the page and the words as she performs them. This is the case for most poets, of course, but not to this extent. What usually happens is that the spoken voice of the poet quietly informs our subsequent readings of his or her work; the reader remembers cadence and tone and inflection, and makes subtle adjustments. With Moss, the spoken voice comes alive in Southern Baptist glory—rising at times to chant, to song, to exhortation, falling at others, to whisper, to love-babble, to inarticulate moan.

The question for such a poet, playing simultaneously with the written and the oral tradition, is how to mediate between the two, how to capitalize on the strength of one without overshadowing the other. Through the years, Moss has experimented with a number of ways to indicate her interest in the oral even to the silent reader who has never heard her voice. One has been a kind of syncopated spacing, phrases set off from other phrases, sentences broken open to force the reader to add rhythm, to punctuate with silence or added emphasis. Another has been the long flowing line, a groundswell of sound and cadence to carry the reader along on its current. Still another is the use of repetition, a single phrase repeated (as in a sermon) until it reaches the pitch of urgency. Along with these, Moss has often dealt with biblical subjects so that the very vocabulary and concentrated concern has been that of the church—and, by extension, the pulpit. Her poems are meant to convince, in the way that the oral is meant to convey conviction.

Last Chance for the Tarzan Holler uses all of these techniques—and something more. The poems of this volume do not experiment so much as demonstrate: they announce themselves as full-blown examples of something new. At the same time, they are more than ever written *for* the page: dense with reference to biblical and classical themes, the colloquial superimposed on the formal, these are poems that must be *seen* to be heard. On the cover jacket, Harold Bloom calls the book "profound and disturbing"—which it is— and says "its difficulties are necessary and rewarding." He does not define the difficulties, but I will say they are the difficulties of tackling hard philosophical and ethical choices, not the difficulties of deliberate obfuscation. So if there are places where the sense seems to break down—and there are—then it breaks down into the nonsense of human dilemma.

The title poem is a good example. Moving from fairy tale (Hansel and Gretel) to the contemporary drama of Susan Smith's decision to send her two young sons strapped in their car seats to the bottom of a lake, it wrestles with such ideas as assisted suicide, infanticide, abortion, and sexual abuse, as well as the more positive concepts of bone marrow transplants and the urgent will to live. Just before death, when the body is most alive, it can give the "Tarzan holler," that long, wild, nearly human sound that issues from the lungs at birth, at death, at a few untrammeled moments in between. Moss finds a way to delve into the understory:

> Susan, I don't mean to be cruel
> but   as you know   it is inevitable. She
>
> once took the boys on a picnic near water
> cool and effervescing with motherhood
> that blew bubbles that emerged

from Michael's right ear when she whispered
in his left, a rummage

of secret disappointments in school, so much
to remember, fix; life imprisoned in ego. Susan
likes Mr Quixotic, *psst, pass it on—does not—does too*
and wants the time of day from shrugging shoulders,
silhouette

like iron monument in the park.

The ordinariness is betrayed by knowledge. That Smith was a real person, her life, too, filled with *pssts*, complicates the picture and adds yet another moral dimension. Add to that the fact that to execute her might be to rob a relative of the marrow she needs for survival, and you have a modern-day tragedy. But Moss is not milking the dramatic; she's exploring it, turning up the stones so that we see what lives underneath, refusing to let us reduce a complex human situation to something as easy as "right" or "wrong." The narrative moves from direct address to past-tense narration to present tense (albeit locked in the past), and then the syntax, instead of reinforcing idea, begins to work against it. And the oddly reductive lines are so compressed that they will not fully yield up meaning or make an exact equation:

Humperdinck's
Rubylips, witch, bitch ≈ Gretel, baker, widow-maker

At the heart of *Last Chance for the Tarzan Holler* is the human body, with its own urgencies. Lactation, defecation, copulation—you name it and Moss has explored its function, its counterpart in nature, its place in our mythologies. She does this with precision, as "Ant Farm" demonstrates: " . . . such a narrow world it was, pressed between / sheets of Plexiglas no bigger than standard issue composition paper on which / I took notes on their progress that in my notebook never was, for I kept looking / at them from my perspective had I been as restricted; they could not open the world, reach / for stars though their tunnels longed to be telescopes." But she also explores with imagination—the poem goes on to talk about a number of the 5,000 species of ants, forcing us to see ourselves as she has seen them.

Postmodern in the best sense of the word, engaging the slipperiness of language rather than exploiting it, Moss's poems move quickly from reference to reference, always circling back to the individual experience, the body as home. The residue is bone, and "Those Who Love Bones" looks at bone as history:

Even after long silences they may be exhumed
and even if the surviving fragment is just a piece of skullcap
no bigger than a nicotine patch, William Maples
still can tell how alligators gnawed it at the bottom
of a river two years after the hatchet man put it there; there's
a bible of bones in a barn in the former Yugoslavia

5.
and thick as grief around Pol Pot's feet.

The section numbers interrupt the train of thought, announce that one bone just leads to another, leads to "*Hey, Hambone; Hey, Daddy*," leads to how we are all alike under the cover of the skin:

Somewhere out there also: catacombs, decay, decay, half-
lives, promises, a finger on a string to help a more perfect knot
come into being on Wilma's wedding day, marriage to bone,
faithful, uncompromising truthful bone
—the mind cheats, soft
and dreaming, inventing words bone can't say, not even a simple
forensics-defying word: *race*.

This collection takes on too many topics for one review to cover them adequately, and Moss's informed, curious mind encompasses too much to be roped into any one category or pronouncement. In fact, she suggests that for every idea there will be a counter idea, for every belief a skepticism. So, the religion she presents here is many-faceted. Rooted in the dark angers and the deliberate injustices of the Old Testament where the stories take on the power of myth, it can be traced into the present where "Glory" praises flame, asks God to "burn himself again for the sake of light," and the poem is charged with instances of fire, given up to the "glory raging":

I don't mean to say embrace it, but if it looks when it detonates
like glory, then take no chances, fellowship
with what little colored boys know
lashed and gasolined on the branches, imperfect crosses
with all the limbs intact, the wood undisciplined, the boys
a wild offering and given to God who could use them
since he's not the God he was in the past when he rejected certain
burnt offerings, clad his favorites in asbestos, outfitted the others

in salt; now he takes whatever he's given, revision into neuter
in the Oxford *inclusive language* new testament
without old biases, without tradition, and without passion.

The New Testament may lack passion, but its God has softened somewhat. "A Man" calls to its congregation through its refrain—"he was a man"—until you can almost hear the church resound with Christ's humanizing presence, until God himself is "more like / what God needs to become, so moves also, / so God moves also // because a man moves."

"Advice" rejects a former professor's admonition: "Do not write about the Holocaust / young sable lady: some subjects must be earned / not dreamed." And "stay out of that region of abjection; / you have misery a-plenty in your zone . . ."

Professor, this poem is not revenge;
it is forgiveness

The poet asserts her right to enter the world of experience *and* imagination, to add to her "echoes of lamentation" all she knows of man's inhumanity to man. Thylias Moss may not yet have found the perfect balance between the oral and the written, possibly because her language tries to have it both ways; what comes to life on the tongue can seem at times imprecise on the page. Portions of these poems may remain obscure to any reader. Moss often elides traditional syntax, and sometimes sense, but her objective is evident and, I think, important. She is a poet of many gifts and she produces a poetry that takes risks. *Last Chance for the Tarzan Holler* is strikingly expansive, especially when read against some of the narrow, self-obsessed or ideologically rigid poetry that is all too prevalent, and the ending of "Advice" indicates that Moss is still evolving:

. . . I will not abandon this poem
that attempts to touch much of what keeps touching me
shaping me into a woman who hopes to finish knowing herself
in time to begin to know something else.

You are ten years dead. It is only a story.
Your story. My story.

Now it has been thirty-five years since Sylvia Plath's death. In *Birthday Letters*, Ted Hughes is writing against his own silence. He is also, inevitably, writing against the myth that has grown up surrounding their marriage—a myth fueled by his silence and by those who have appropriated her life to their own causes more than they have honored her poetry.* The first half of the book recapitulates the story of their meeting, their marriage, their first few years of partnership. And the last half explores the hardships and psychological disintegration. By breaking his silence, Hughes invites our natural curiosity—even prurience—and the book will be read as much for its attitudes as for its poetic quality. That is probably appropriate since Hughes clearly is making an effort to tell his side of the story, to give balance where, before, there were only the fires of speculation.

In these eighty-eight poems, Hughes addresses Plath—the "you" that (even when it hovers in the background) is central to each. Her presence is palpable and Hughes speaks directly to her, eradicating the grave even as he often invokes it. The poems are filled with a tragic sense of loss, with anger, with passionate memory, with regret. In other words, they convey the tumult of the marriage and its aftermath—a haunting sense of something uncompleted which these poems, as they rework the events, attempt to piece together. What was incomplete was Hughes's understanding of the emotional events that were unfurling around him and, by extension, of his part in them.

Birthday Letters is bound to be controversial. It is impossible to read it in any way except against Plath's *Complete Poems*. Ten of the poems share a whole or partial title with hers, many refer to places or events that are familiar from her poetry, several use her own lines or phrases (as in "Night-Ride on Ariel," where bolts of moonlight are "Crackling and dragging their blacks / Over your failing flight"). This technique is not (as some might say) derivative, nor is it thievery. Rather, it creates a sense of dialogue. There are two sides to every story, it says, and these poems, like hers before them, are subjective versions, rife with the metaphor and image of shared existence. Hughes carefully introduces fragments of Plath's poetry in order to *claim* that life as much as to establish his own version of it. Plath is everywhere in these new poems—muse, partner, patient. The complex relationship of two great artists is laid bare.

In "The Rabbit Catcher," clearly the counterpart of Plath's poem of the same title, he talks of a time when she tore up a snare, clearly an act with which he has no sympathy. Yet the poem asserts both points of view:

* *Editor's Note: Along with much of the world's literary community, we regret the recent death of the poet Ted Hughes. This review had been written and was in production at the time of his death; Judith Kitchen has subsequently added a final paragraph, "Coda," (page 142) to put* Birthday Letters *into a larger perspective.*

. . . I saw
The sanctity of a trapline desecrated.
You saw blunt fingers, blood in the cuticles,
Clamped round a blue mug. I saw
Country poverty raising a penny,
Filling a Sunday stewpot. You saw baby-eyed
Strangled innocents, I saw sacred
Ancient custom. You saw snare after snare
And went ahead, riving them from their roots
And flinging them down the wood. I saw you
Ripping up precarious, precious saplings
of my heritage, hard-won concessions
From the hangings and the transportations
To live off the land. You cried: "Murderers!"

There is no way to close the gap. The poem ends with her ability to catch the poem, while he stands outside her imaginative space.

So how do these poems work? It's impossible to strip them of Plath and substitute another more generic "you" in order to analyze their effectiveness. They rely on specificity of time and place and event. This is important in a dramatic and almost an evidentiary way, for the book's reason for being is the accumulated weight of memory and insight. *Birthday Letters* is the product of memory revisited so that each remembered scene is now colored by subsequent knowledge—the face of her suicide:

Till your real target
Hid behind me. Your Daddy,
The god with the smoking gun. For a long time
Vague as mist. I did not even know
I had been hit,
Or that you had gone clean through me—
To bury yourself at last in the heart of the god.
"The Shot"

Hughes's analysis—if that's what it is—will probably be called a rationalization. Many of the poems convey a sense that there was nothing he could do, that he was a player in someone else's drama. In this version, Plath had so completely identified him with the father who died when she was eight that Hughes was destined to fail to meet her needs. In effect, he re-creates "Daddy"—her daring, and deliberate, fusing of the two men. Hughes pounces on this psychology to explain what went wrong: in reviving her father through her poems, she was transferring her anger onto her husband. This may very well be true, and certainly the picture Hughes paints is one her poems could also lead us to suspect: an erratic, vulnerable, brilliant, volatile woman, trapped in a body wracked by hormonal swings—blood driven, moon driven, ecstatic one minute, despairing the next. I wish, though, that Hughes had explored a bit more his own role in the scenario, understanding through hindsight what it must have been to be so bright, so energetic, so creative, so ambitious, and with so unformed a self that the responsibilities of family and finances became unbearable. He lets himself off the hook a little too easily—and lets her off, too, opting for chance over choice:

> Sometimes I think
> Finally you yourself were two gloves
> Worn by those two hands.
> Sometimes I even think that I too
> Was picked up, a numbness of gloves
> Worn by those same hands,
> Doing what they needed done, because
> The fingerprints inside what I did
> And inside your poems and your letters
> And inside what you did
> Are the same.
>
> "The Hands"

And Plath remains both the woman he first met (lively, engaging, reenergized in memory) and the woman she became in their marriage (uncertain, furious, plagued by memory)—in each case more objectified and observed than internalized and understood. Throughout these poems, Hughes makes some simplified pronouncements that have more the ring of the expected than the surprise of true perception: "We thought they were a windfall. / Never guessed they were a last blessing" ("Daffodils").

That said, it should be possible to look at *Birthday Letters* without forgetting to whom the letters are addressed and still assess the project—and the poetry—as art. These are powerful poems, as much for the force of their own vision as for our interest in their subject matter. But there are too many of them and some are better than others. By all rights, these poems should have appeared singly or in small groups over the years, as a record of his sensibility and a chronicle of his grief (though possibly the pressure of silence is the rootstock of this collection).

Birthday Letters gains power at its midpoint, as though Hughes needed to write his alternative "version" before he could begin to write from within his own experience. Every so often, there is a poem with Hughes's distinctive voice, his raw, animal vision. And every so often he gives himself over to his unique way of seeing the world with his own intuitive imagery. In the end of "Daffodils," the description of the flowers is wholly his: "Propped their raw butts in bucket water, / Their oval, meaty butts, / And sold them, sevenpence a bunch— // Wind-wounds, spasms from the dark earth. / With their odourless metals, / A flamy purification of the deep grave's stony cold / As if ice had a breath—." When this happens, the poems truly do what some of the more deliberate ones do not—they find a deep, communal nerve. However, an earlier version of "Daffodils" (published in *Flowers and Insects*, 1986) presents the same material, and many of the same lines, in the first-person singular—a fluff of a poem which he may later have plundered in order to wrestle it into his agenda, which hardly makes it the poem his publicists claim was written and tucked away as part of an ongoing grief. This raises crucial questions about the sincerity of the emotions, the art, or both.

As the book gains momentum, Hughes emerges as a character in his own right. I find it interesting to experience Hughes's America, to see with fresh eyes what are, for most of us, the commonplace images of the country—the Grand Canyon, Yellowstone, the vast and terrifying landscapes of the West. And he finds in the sea off Nauset the clean and cleansing fragments of Plath's past. But I find it even more interesting to watch Hughes watch her as she experiences his England. All his lonely Yorkshire landscapes thrown into question—the rabbit snares, the remains of Elmet, the drab oceanside—everything he loved fodder for her scathing eye, her glittering intelligence. It's only when his own intelligence matches hers that *Birthday Letters* comes alive not as psychology but as *poetry*. Then we taste the Hughes of *Crow*, the mystical acceptance of a dark Fate that colors the language and the landscape of the heart.

"Epiphany" is the most problematic of such poems. A form of self-interrogation, the poem poses its questions in uncompromising terms. As Hughes tells it, walking over Chalk Farm Bridge on the way to the tube station, he met a man with a fox cub who told him he would sell it for a pound. The poet's temptation is unmistakable as he describes "eyes reaching out / Trying to catch my eyes." Retrospectively, the "you" intervenes (at least in his thoughts): "What I was thinking / Was—what would you think? How would we fit it / Into our crate of space?" and thus Hughes reaches a decision: "Then I walked on / As if out of my own life." The poem could end here, but it doesn't. Its larger implications are disturbing, possibly because the poem contains a vision of marriage that, in most instances, would doom it to failure:

If I had paid,
If I had paid that pound and turned back
To you, with that armful of fox—

If I had grasped that whatever comes with a fox
Is what tests a marriage and proves it a marriage—
I would not have failed the test. Would you have failed it?
But I failed. Our marriage had failed.

Here domesticity and family are set against the feral sense of the self. By turning his back on his own nature, the poet asserts his own needs even as he pronounces judgment on them both. (It's instructive to remember that "The Thought-Fox," the opening poem in Hughes's first collection, *The Hawk in the Rain*, equates poetry with a lone fox in the wood: "Brilliantly, concentratedly, / Coming about its own business // Till, with a sudden sharp hot stink of fox, / It enters the dark hole of the head.") As a present-tense retrospection, the "epiphany" rings false. As a fierce statement of individuality, it is powerful and true. A split urge—a wish to be exonerated and a strain of defiance—runs throughout the book. I prefer the defiant.

Perhaps my favorite poem in this collection is "Error." It blends impulse for a retrospective understanding with insistent, almost archetypal description. Its sounds are packed like a snowball: hard consonants, tongue-twisting alliterations, and off-rhymes mirror the language of the "bundled women" who "Jabbered hedge-bank judgements, a dark-age dialect." Calling the move to Devon a "wrong fork," it ends by watching the two of them there, locked in the bubble of the past: "Gazing out of the transparency / At a desolation." But the penultimate stanza reveals Hughes's own deep, resurrected love of the land:

The world
Came to an end at bullocks
Huddled behind gates, knee-deep in quag,
Under the huddled, rainy hills. A bellow
Shaking the soaked oak-woods tested the limits.
And, beside the boots, the throbbing gutter—
A thin squandering of blood-water—
Searched for the river and the sea.

Birthday Letters cannot be assessed as poetry only. It is a document at once personal and public. Many people have already made up their minds, and this book won't change them. But these poems, written against a tide of public opinion, do try to be balanced and fair. They present Hughes himself as young, insecure, and often ineffective. If, when they met, Plath thought of him as a masculine god, he thought of her as from another world, bred to a sophistication and class which he lacked. The result of their union is a legacy of poems whose pain is amplified when they are read together. Poems are richer than biographical fact, and these spring from the inner landscape of a mature poet as well as from this painful part of his life. *Birthday Letters* adds an elegiac and necessary voice to our understanding.

CODA: Time has a way of melding stories into one: the individual experiences of Romeo and of Juliet emerge as the singular tragedy we know as *Romeo and Juliet*. In retrospect, and with our knowledge that Hughes knew the nature of his final illness and impeding death, the questions surrounding his decision to publish *Birthday Letters* are answered. Breaking a long and dignified silence, this book speaks not only to the critics who accused him but to all of us who consider our "story" *the* story. In the face of death, the particulars are everything—and nothing. *Birthday Letters* is only one part of a legacy of poetry larger than any single book. As we read it now, we must also consider *The Hawk in the Rain*, with its elemental authority, and the dozens of subsequent books that forged Hughes's reputation. In "Fox Hunt," published in 1970, Hughes envisioned the field ahead in which, like the fox, his talent would roam free: "As I write this down / He runs still fresh, with all his chances before him." But all foxes are transitory. Perhaps Hughes wrote his own fate in these lines from "The Morning Before Christmas" (1983):

> A flood pond, inch-iced, held the moment of a fox
> In touch-melted and refrozen dot-prints.

J.K.

Tensions

On George Szirtes' *Portrait of My Father in an English Landscape*; Paul Muldoon's *Hay*; Albert Goldbarth's *Beyond*; Suzanne Paola's *Bardo*; and Naomi Shihab Nye's *Fuel*.

It's early morning. I'm sitting in a corner window on the thirty-fifth floor of a hotel in San Francisco. Outside, nothing but fog, saving me from my own strong fear of heights. Where yesterday I could look out on city streets, moving lights, water in the distance, today there is nothing. No little cat feet, but a dense gray wall of impenetrability. Though if I should go down in the elevator and walk out the door, I could move through it easily enough.

Suddenly, a whir in front of me, and a wire mesh cage holding two men appears from above. They move past and disappear; I only know they are there because the ropes outside my window sway back and forth, revealing the tension of the cage in its circumscribed movement below me, thirtysome floors above street level. Looking through the window on my right, I see two more men in a similar cage, though theirs is narrower, surrounded by what looks all too much like flimsy green canvas. They wear hard hats—one yellow, one white—and are tethered to their narrow walkway by yellow fabric straps. For fifteen minutes, with black tape and a razor, they work on one section of a ledge. Holding the building together with black duct tape, or so it appears, though now they are rubbing and rubbing. Out of the fog, the sudden appearance of the technicians who hold the structure together.

When I look out again, one of the men is gone, the one with the white hat. Where did he go? and how? He's thirty-three stories up, and the windows don't open, do they?

Sometimes the world hands you metaphor. For the past hour, I've felt a bit unsettled, the way I feel when reading Robert Hayden's "Those Winter

Sundays"—the mystery that still resides in the phrase "fearing the chronic angers of that house." I've also felt astonished, the kind of astonishment that quickens every time I hear "In the room the women come and go / Talking of Michelangelo" and think, Where did that come from? And I've been unexpectedly delighted, as in "Time held me green and dying / Though I sang in my chains like the sea." At my window I have, I now realize, experienced the underlying tensions of a poem.

What has happened to tension? That tug of war between the line and what the line can contain? The standoff between form and content? The tectonic slippage between what is stated and what is implied?

Tension is not simply a matter of craft, but of something internal—the poet's willingness to launch him- or herself into unknown territory. All too often, I open a book to find what I have come to call the "standard poem of self-expression"—slack lines of reportorial poetry in which the poet recounts circumstances with the assumption that, because he or she is thinking "correctly," the reader will, by definition, agree with what is being said. And I may. But I do not read only for confirmation of my own ideas. So the sameness—if not of content, then of technique and, worse, stance—worries me. What is the future of an art whose practitioners won't take genuine risks, including the risks of self-discovery, and who congratulate themselves for speaking what amount to no more than preconceived or prepackaged "truths"?

Randall Jarrell worried about something similar—but he was concerned about the critics: "May one of them say to the others, soon: 'Brothers, do we want to sound like the Publications of the Modern Language Association, only worse? If we don't set things straight for ourselves, others will set them straight for us—or worse still, others won't, and things will go on as they are going on until one day even you and I won't be able to read each other, for sheer boredom.'" Now poets seem to have left themselves vulnerable to the same charges. Sometimes I suspect my own abilities to keep an open mind, but mostly I've come to realize that my boredom *is* at stake—and that contemporary poetic practices have done little to alleviate it. In a profound way, boredom is the ultimate test in art: if the work stops being genuinely interesting, it doesn't *matter*. Art that disturbs us is always more interesting than art that proclaims, or just solicits approval. I like the risk-takers. The poems that hold my interest are the ones that exhibit some form of tension.

The one remaining man (the one with the yellow hat) pushes a button and one side of his walkway drops a few inches. He's standing on a sloping board! I'm terrified by the very thought of it. And then a hand—only a hand, seemingly dis-

embodied—appears through the railing above him, handing him something—more tape? some putty?—but whose hand is it, and how did it get there?

When Robert Frost wrote in his Notebook "for my pleasure I had as soon write free verse as play tennis with the net down," it was necessary to think about what he conceived of as his "net." Surely it was not merely the empty husk of traditional forms—the sonnet without substance—but a second net of his own devising. Jeffrey Meyers, a recent Frost biographer, has stated that "he maintained that his verse sprang from the strain or tension that evolves when a strong rhythmic pattern, based upon strict or loose iambic meter, is played against the irregular variations of common speech." So Frost built his own net, a warp of form through which to weave the weft of colloquial speech, the "sentence sound" that gave his poems their particular flavor. Note the surprising force in the ten one-syllable words that open the blank verse of "Directive": "Back out of all this now too much for us."

The concept of warp and weft is a useful one—although it's often impossible to tell one from the other in the finished fabric. Still, we do know that the warp provides a structure across which the weft has been woven. Form, of course, supplies one external frame, but often the warp is internal. The poet may choose any of a number of aspects of craft—patterns of speech, patterns of sound, an appeal to the visual, extended metaphor, image, tone, narrative, lyric intensity—and then put them together in any of a number of combinations. That is, one poet may seem to work sound against a structure of "given" metaphor while another may do the opposite, working metaphor against a pattern of sound. The problem is to tell warp from weft, and possibly it can't be done in any ultimate sense. Yet it's an interesting way to think about poems, and it may be that readers intuitively understand when a poet is working in more than one direction. The result—the individual poet's unique blend—can be seen as one source of tension in a poem.

In the 1960s, when both Robert Lowell and Sylvia Plath shifted from formal structures toward free verse, the result was an emphasis on content. But it was content enhanced by the way their lines became more compressed, their imagery more raw and urgent. Interestingly, their poems remain compelling when so many modern-day "reruns" do not, so it cannot be merely the confessional mode (now all too familiar) nor the content itself (the ante of victimization has been raised in several successive rounds) that makes their poems survive the test of time. I suspect that, for both Lowell and Plath, the poem was a quest, a necessity, rather than a statement.

Personal experience makes a natural warp, but over the years I've realized that, without some other element of craft, content is what is ultimately boring. Content-driven poems are good for the first reading, but they often have little to fall back on—and any retold story usually does begin to fray. The poems that remain as surprising the twentieth time as the first (and perhaps more surprising for some newly perceived nuance) have elements that hold our interest over and above content, and in the face of shifting attitudes. Pablo Neruda infuses his work with the magic of metaphor, welding the abstract to the concrete. William Carlos Williams and Marianne Moore intrigue the eye, while Wallace Stevens and Theodore Roethke pique the ear. In this way, they create intricate spaces for new and ever more intricate readings.

And now the hand is hitching a strap to the railing and the second man (the white hat) is climbing back over it into the cage. The scene looks exactly as it did before. If I'd looked away, I might never have known what had gone on, how they went about their business in and out of the cage. And in front of me, still the fog, still the ropes that sway with the weight of what they are holding, out of sight below me. And beyond them, the city I cannot see, but know is there.

Portrait of My Father in an English Landscape by George Szirtes is one of the most elegantly formal books I've read in recent years. Szirtes is a master of iambic pentameter, of the sonnet in particular, and seems to have found ways to make English rhymes sound new. One way he does this is through innovative use of enjambment; the stanzas unfold seamlessly while the intricacy of the pattern establishes itself, as in the second section of "Busby Berkeley in the Soviet Union":

This music is in your blood, slithering through your arteries.
It's no longer 1934
but whatever you want. Call it today if
it pleases you. You're watching TV, some series
about hospitals or cops, an investigator
on the scent or a plaintiff

in a court case of a documentary about fish,
it doesn't matter what kind of tripe
you fancy, you get it all, good quality.
So you think you are safe, but under the rubbish
it raises its head. Sweet music. Suddenly you wipe
your face. Electricity

courses through you, or is it nostalgia?

The rhymes here, almost invisible (though not inaudible), constitute the poet's "net" or aesthetic game. But it is the wedding of form and content that gives the book its characteristic tensions.

The title of the collection sets up the classic opposition of father/son, homeland/exile. At the heart of this book is the family's flight to England during the Hungarian revolution in 1956 when the poet was six, and his growing realization that his parents speak not only a different language but a different experience. Here, on exhibit, is the son's mastery of the father's second tongue. Doubled by the barriers of language and politics, the gap between what Szirtes can know and what he can never know of his father is what this work *can't* master. So, for all their linguistic shimmering, for all the clever puns or references to art and literature, the poems crackle with the tension of the inaccessible.

The sonnet is Szirtes' natural form, and this book culminates in three separate Hungarian sonnet sequences—each sequence a series of fifteen sonnets, every sonnet beginning with the last line of the previous one, and the final one incorporating all the repeated lines in order. That Szirtes can do this once is impressive enough; that he created three such sequences is staggering. But here again the question of tension raises its head. By increasing the aesthetic stakes, Szirtes almost forces us to examine these three long sequences not for their similarities but for their differences. "The Looking-Glass Dictionary" is a postmodern look at language itself, opening with the obvious: "Words withheld. Words loosed in angry swarms. / An otherness. The whole universe was / other, a sum of indeterminate forms / in motion. . . ." These flat statements *about* language do not have the force of the lived experience *in* language, and the poem suffers from this, though it seems to know what is at stake. In the ninth sonnet, Szirtes stares into the mirror of words and then movingly describes his father with the simplicity of pure sight:

> The language outside meets the ur-language within
> with the consistency of dream
> which sits like a faint moisture on the skin.
> My father's voice. A gentle coaxing lost
> in the depths of his chest. His musculature
> is iron swelling in his arms. Thin frost
> covers him in a Russian forest. Pure
> narrative lines run through him. He stands
> in the street with the city in his hands.

But in this sonnet sequence overall, the content pales before the perfection of the form, and the form feels somewhat empty when its content is language—

and writing—itself. In the final and title sequence, "Portrait of My Father in an English Landscape," content and form blend in such a way that the tensions are perfectly balanced. The variations in the repeated lines and the repetition of images in different patterns add to the formal pressure, giving form an equivalency with the biographical material of his father's exile. The poem tugs equally in each direction (though sometimes loses sight of itself in such lapses as "Language slips, words slide / and take pratfalls"—a carry-over from the former sequence). In a series of fragmentary snapshots, Szirtes creates the collage that must stand in for the portrait—the incomplete picture of a man seen in the context of European politics, experienced and partially understood.

Form, however, allows for another kind of understanding. Szirtes gives us not only the historical perspective but also the wonders of our own language. The final sonnet (the one that seamlessly weds all the first lines of the other fourteen) reveals the power of this particular form. It's the old chicken and the egg—which came first, the conclusion or the individual lines? How and when did the poet construct the rhymes so that they would play themselves out in the final sonnet? The reader is asked to peel away the layers of abstraction by remembering each line in its earlier incarnation while seeing it fresh in a new one. This must be the hardest of poetic tasks, and Szirtes is one of the few poets writing in English capable of such a synthesis.

> The classic shot of my father is one
> easy to destroy. Historical whim
> preserves a secret well worth sitting on,
> though even on clear nights its stars are dim
> particularities of luck and guilt.
> He is a light that must be interpreted
> through chains of command, cracked bones and blood spilt,
> through women crippled, and often left for dead.
> A presence, like the ghost in a photograph,
> a surfeit, a core that can't be truly known.
> The wolf is in his lair. The children laugh
> in the high street at the old loner with his bone
> and bandana, his edges neither straight nor true.
> Their father waits for them and calls them You.

And now the fog is lifting a little, and two more men in shirtsleeves are standing by the railing, kibitzing, and everything looks ordinary, almost commonplace. They're even drinking coffee.

Paul Muldoon is America's master of form. (That's right, he has become a citizen, though Ireland may not gladly give him up.) He is so adept, has so much dexterity, that in fact form doesn't serve as much of a "net"—he seems to need to generate increasingly elaborate superstructures (forms within forms), almost as though in building them up he can create the effect of tearing them down. For Muldoon, it's *ideas* that matter. He is so referentially brilliant that idea and form together can strike spectacular sparks—but only sparks. Muldoon needs to engage emotional as well as intellectual material in order to create the great poems of which he is capable. In his previous book, *The Annals of Chile* (1994), he gave us one of the most important poems of the last half of this century in "Incantata" and a significant long poem in "Yarrow." I find it hard not to read his new book, *Hay*, in the afterglow of this accomplishment.

But what is a poet to do after he or she has written something of genuine importance? Wait years for the next great poem? Or follow William Stafford's advice to "lower your standards and go on"? Muldoon seems to have opted for keeping his engines idling, demonstrating once again his ready wit and facility with words as he explores just about every aspect of living. "Sleeve Notes" is a commentary on twenty-one pop musicians or groups from Jimi Hendrix to Dire Straits; a sequence of one hundred haiku chronicles the changing seasons in New Jersey. Some of the latter work beautifully in the traditional sense:

> Beyond the corn stooks
> the maples' firewood detail.
> Their little red books.

Others have the feel of mere reportage:

> I've upset the pail
> in which my daughter had kept
> her five—"No, *six*"—snails.

Rhymed haiku, perfect syllable counts, but to what end? The enterprise does not quite live up to its promise, reveals nothing new about the old form, marks time but does not remake it.

In *Hay*, Muldoon reveals his linguistic agility, his erudition, his knowledge of pop culture, his cunning wit, his playful perceptions, and his ability to toss them all into one grab bag and pull them back out in innovative poetic exercises. What this collection hints at, gives us glimpses of but does not truly provide, is *poetry*—the kind that takes off the top of your head. The poems of *Hay* are mental puzzle-making, material looking for significance, causing me to suspect that this book was published too soon after the last one, that his publishers have done him no favor exhibiting his facility without demanding more depth. Even poems with the immediacy of personal content, like "Longbones," end up feeling a bit contrived, orchestrated to fit their rhymes rather than allowing form to reveal inner urgencies. The long finale, "The Bangle (Slight Return)" is so playful—it takes its cue from Oscar Wilde, adds Australian geography and slang, incorporates an earlier play on "errata" to undercut its own vocabulary—that, while it is decidedly a tour de force, one wonders what force it is touring.

Oddly, the book's two concrete poems are among its most moving. "The Plot" simply spells out "alfalfa" over and over until the empty space in the middle of the poem asserts its "alpha" between two "alfas," and something begins to sprout. "A Half Door Near Cluny" takes "stable" and makes the reader see *stables, table, tables, able, lest, stab, blest,* until the brain cannot but add *blessèd, establish*—house and stable meshed with what the door reveals, conceals. With stark simplicity, Muldoon has shown us how a word can contain multitudes.

Three poems in *Hay* demonstrate the tensile strength of Muldoon's best work, easily walking the tightrope of craft while below him content swirls and boils. "Wire," a sestina in which the repeated words become increasingly ominous, superimposes memories of war-torn Ireland on an innocent walk in the Connecticut countryside until the speaker imaginatively enters the territory of the terrorist, all innocence transformed by the distorting lens of suspicion: "the endless rerun / of Smithfield, La Mon, Enniskillen, of bodies cut // to ribbons as I heard the truck engine cut / and, you might have read as much between the lines, / ducked down here myself behind the hide. As if I myself were on the run."

"Third Epistle to Timothy" also contains an imaginative entry into the life of another, as Muldoon reconstructs his father's days as an eleven-year-old servant to the Hardys of Carnteel. The boy is subjected to hard physical labor and the fire and brimstone of his boss's religious fervor, coupled with the fervent history of the Irish cause. The tenth and final section fuses that experience with those of literature, ending with as dark a vision of the future as of the past:

> That next haycock already summoning itself from windrow after
> wind-weary windrow
> while yet another brings itself to mind in the acrid stink
> of turpentine. There the image of Lizzie,
> Hardy's last servant girl, reaches out from her dais
> of salt hay, stretches out an unsunburned arm
> half in bestowal, half beseechingly, then turns away to appeal

to all that spirit troop
of hay treaders as far as the eye can see, the coil on coil
of hay from which, in the taper's mild uproar,
they float out across the dark face of the earth, an earth without
form, and void.

In a substantive and quite astonishing feat, "They That Wash on Thursday" rhymes each of its fifty lines on the word "hand"—fifty lines in which Muldoon moves from the initial gamelike quality of his rhyming to a hard look at the hard life of the speaker's mother and the hands of the women he has loved, from wry self-mockery toward a serious conclusion where Ireland and America coexist in his daughter's freehand drawing of "a green field on a white hand."

I believe that Paul Muldoon will be seen as one of America's finest poets (as he is already considered one of Ireland's); added to his previous accomplishments, the range and substance of these three poems confirms this prediction. For Muldoon, content *is* the tension because he always plays his tennis with more than one net.

And now there is a third figure—a dark-haired young man without a hat, wearing blue straps—in the cage. The two others are lowering the cage and he is leaning out, examining the corner of the building, testing the windows for tightness. The two stand by with their razors and tape. Now the one without a hat is talking on a telephone. He cups his hand around his ear, as though to hold some sound at bay. I, of course, can hear nothing.

If Paul Muldoon has a counterpart it is, oddly (or perhaps not so oddly), Albert Goldbarth. Each is an aficionado of pop culture, each has a supremely quirky mind, each plays with ideas to create a style that is absolutely unique. While Muldoon has form and meter, Goldbarth has a natural rhythm—one both physical and mental. His natural rhythm might be called "fairly iambic not-quite pentameter"—but really it's the rhythm of thought, of the way one thought leads to the next so that reading him is like watching a three-ring circus. It's not that his verse is freed, but that poetry itself is freed. Freed of preconception or expectation, freed to become whatever this most free of minds might discover it to be. In *Beyond*, Goldbarth articulates his responsibility for rescuing singular events from the fate of "data chaos," which

leaves me wildly trying to think of pockets adequate
to *everything*: The ashtree staff of the hermit
on his mountaintop for seventeen years. The latest Nintendo

epic, *Callow Drooling Wombat Warriors*. The doctors
cracking open Nicky's sternum like a matzoh—he was five.
The perfect wedge of brie John found one day on his car hood.
Gunshots. Twill weft. Owl-hoo. Storm, and calm.
The poem as fit receptacle. Sure. Right.
I'll know what to do with them.

A Goldbarth poem *is* a common denominator, *does* become, in his own words, a "megamatrix substrate (God, / or atoms, or Imagination)" holding the "infinite unalike dots"—or their equivalents—in the whirring mixer of his mind. So his tensions are those of one idea in relation to another, concept as it clashes with belief, notion wriggling out from under judgment, science as it faces the unanswerable. *Beyond* is no exception to this rule, and in some ways there is little new to say about this book because it's been said about the previous books. Goldbarth has not embarked on some new project, nor has he deviated from his regulation beyond-the-norm fare—but just that he can maintain his wonder at the multiple facets of this world (and the worlds beyond our comprehension) is, in fact, *our* wonder. He opens to us the cosmos with all its mysteries; as old mysteries are explained, new ones unfold, and Goldbarth is there to see even mystery in a new light. "The Red Shift" finds an equivalence to the universe in motion in a man standing in the heartland thinking he still smells of the fish in his hometown, what he was born "away from." "Even; Equal" moves from the real world to the netherworld, as the speaker watches snow bridge the gap of class until he imagines his deceased father playing poker with the tailored oil barons on the other side of the cemetery: "Death—the way snow makes the ditch / and the window sill even; equal."

Those "other" worlds—where things remain unknown, possibly even unknowable—intrigue Goldbarth and become a part of his ongoing cosmology. He likes to look at what cannot be easily explained, to contemplate the profound along with the mundane. His lightning-quick shifts between one realm and another are part of his poetic bag of tricks; the resulting implosion in the reader's mind make reading this poet a joy, but an arduous joy. Perhaps this is why he hasn't received still more attention, which this work deserves. I only know that I can't describe the pleasure one feels in reading a poem like "Believing a Resonant Chord Exists Between His Work and the World, Pieter Bruegel Attempts to Help Banish the Tarantella." Goldbarth brings to bear everything he (and we) know of Bruegel's work, as well as new "factoids" such as how the Dutch once tried banning the color red and pointed shoes to stop an epidemic of dancing. In the first section Bruegel banishes red from his paintings, in the process altering the world. The middle section questions cause and effect as the poet imagines a contemporary woman who dances in a nude bar, a woman with a six-year-old daughter to feed, a woman who's been banished from the world of PTA and parish bazaars even though, as the poem points out, over $42 million a week are spent in nude bars—on cover charges alone:

> Because someone is marrying, someone
> in another painting is walking on stumps. Because somebody
> is an entomologist tweezing a living dot into the light,
> somebody else is resolving the orbits of planets. Because
> this happens, that doesn't. Listen. . . . Quiet. . . . You can hear
> the Possible issue its tiny cries at the edge
> of our actual world. Because somebody's dancing,
> somebody isn't: somebody's *painting* dancing, in a room,
> in a mood, in a head-encircling cloud of linseed and solitude.

The final section strips the paintings down to black and white, to the ghostly shadows of black and white, a "silence as stark as this duochrome world" where life suddenly intrudes with its sounds ("pain, perhaps, or sexual fervor") and Bruegel paints in the dancers, in red, for "who is he to stop them?" And the reader ends up pondering the purpose of art, the very act of imagination (with a capital *I*).

In *Beyond*, Goldbarth seems to want to test the powers of poetry: "When / Ginsberg writes 'I declare the war in Vietnam over!' // —*is* it over? in the 'real world'? or in the poet's own / apocalyptic and love-marbled heart? I don't know." The underlying tension in Goldbarth's work may be that he knows poetry resolves nothing. Answers nothing. For all his bravado, for all his Imagination, the poem does not redeem the past, does not give life any ultimate meaning, does not bring his father back. Loss is at the heart of every poem, adding its pungency to the mix of ideas, its flavor to what it is to be alive.

Beyond ends with a long sequence in many voices called "The Two Domains." It won a science fiction award, and it's Goldbarth's version of *Ghostbusters*. The narrative is simple: an agnostic woman hires an "exorcist" to rid her hotel/warehouse of the ghosts of two young lovers who were killed there a century earlier before they could consummate their marriage. You guessed it—the prim and proper warehouse owner is seduced by "otherness," and the resulting lovemaking somehow assuages the itchy ghosts. The idea is fun, the poems are fun, the voices are fun, the idea is fun all over again—but for me this sequence lacks the atomic explosion of real, and surprising, insight. I'll vote high honors to the first half of the book and give honorable mention to the inventiveness of the rest. Meanwhile, cause and effect: because Goldbarth is, somebody isn't. Albert Goldbarth has the all-encompassing vision of Whitman or Ginsberg, the precision of Bishop, the knife-edged refinement of Stevens or Plath. This is a recipe for originality, and Goldbarth just may be the American poet of his generation for the ages. He's out there now, without his hat, winging it over the city.

And now all three men are gone, dropping somewhere below my sight level—and with them half my morning. What of the window in front of me, those first ropes that appeared from nowhere and sway, now, as mere evidence of another drama somewhere below? Sometimes they whip back and forth, or jerk crazily, and I imagine the wire mesh cutting through fog, making a pattern, a filigree of fog moving in to fill the incision.

Suzanne Paola's *Bardo*, winner of the Brittingham Prize from the University of Wisconsin Press, looks to the Tibetan bardo journey (where the soul wanders through various realms trying to avoid rebirth) as its central metaphor. Paola effectively fuses this with classical Western tradition, and her explanatory notes in the introduction give just enough information to enhance the reading of the poems. Unfortunately, the biographical material supplied in the same introduction diminishes the element of surprise necessary to some of the poems. Discovery—or revelation—is undercut by prior knowledge.

The bardo journey, especially the various colored lights associated with different "heavens," serves Paola well as the warp on which she weaves her story—itself relatively simple: youthful indiscretions, drug usage, a depressing death of the spirit followed by renewal and education, an emerging self eager to enter womanhood, desire for children and despair at the body's inability to bear them. But Paola has managed to make a poetry of innuendo and implication so that the story unfolds in fragmentary sketches, filtered through the associative vagaries of the mind, as much a poetry of what is unsaid as of what is stated. Consider the fifth (and last) section of the opening poem, "In the Realm of Neither Notions nor Not-Notions":

> Pale, painted, body
> geographic with bone: this girl who lived
> as myself—
>   She's become
> a thing I carry: unsure, watching her sleep
> from Coeur d'Alene to Seattle to Bellingham. Hip-
> bone, ribcage, imperishable breath.

We looked too hard then: we boarded the wrong ships.
In the one drive
for a stillness so tangible even the shadow stops.

All things, as the Buddha said, of one pure Suchness
free of arbitrary conceptions derived from sense

& inconceivable, as a river of rock, as a mountain opening its
drecked passage,
the small shadow frantic there, & our car's shadow
crossing, seemingly at will, the stygian black.

Paola carries that self with her through the rest of her journey; oneness of spirit will contain her former self as well as who she has become. She never quite frees herself from the arbitrariness of sense, however, finding herself in a sensual world composed of the odor of "singed onion," the "soft flesh" of poppies, the sound of rain drumming its "bored fingers" on the roof. Again and again, the poems draw us into that tactile world even as they resist it in their search for the spiritual.

If anything mars these poems, it is the writer's self-conscious awareness of their extended metaphor, spawning such lines as "I've interrupted with my mind / the elegant flow of one thing to the next" or "I failed in what I tried to do: / I looked for something that is less than God." I suspect that what looks like (but does not function as) an intuitive leap is not so much a part of the associative process as a concerted attempt to *make* one thing flow into the next, less a reflection of the spiritual world than a willed representation of it. I prefer Paola's more spontaneous moments—for example, the celebratory sound and the quick wit of observation found in "Fall Landscape, with Empty Places & Sound":

Gulls yawp, strung
like worn teeth on the power lines.
Crows *awk*, & the porch swing
rasps a vowel in the wind.

And I cherish the all-too-true description in "Seeing It All as the Bardo":

Sometimes there's a stammer in my ear
an *I,I,I,I* bird of self chirping through the lips.
The soft red light of the jealous gods. The ones
who are always softly bickering. A realm

where envy pulls. But I didn't realize
how much and how truly I enter it—

A university. I work here.
My words, the bird says. My
articles. I, I.
High-pitched song
but my own.

Suzanne Paola achieves her tensions through indirection and a seemingly natural ability to leave things out. The poems float on nuance—and thus I reiterate the point that her introduction detracts from the power of the poems to *imply* narrative. "Columbines," perhaps my favorite, is a simple lyric which demonstrates the elasticity of metaphor:

I promised myself I wouldn't love you
anymore, being beyond you: little
spoonfuls of impermanence.
The flowers I could never stop looking at—
tiny flutes honeycombed
with tinier pleating, five
nectar-swollen spurs, five petals
unfolding like a cartoon cry around your mouth.

Such a terrifying articulation of a small idea—

I would never have done
what I've done, if I'd heard you—understood
you, then—what it takes
to make one small, barely visible, quickdying thing.

With no overt reference to infertility, the poem gathers up its grief in imagery and in the accumulated long *i*'s that culminate in the quick "dying." The longer poems in *Bardo* contain shorter sections that function much as this poem does, and it is in these moments that Paola successfully bridges the tensions between lyric and narrative. Of far more interest than the subject matter of these poems, this balancing act catches the attention as Paola struggles to say, without saying, what needs to be said. The tapestry of *Bardo* is a wall-hanging in which there are gaps; the warp is revealed through the absence of weft. There's a kind of disjunction—details omitted, narrative leaps beyond the ordinary. The result risks obscurity, but rewards us with a vision that reveals the holes to be part of the whole.

And now they are back, risen again to my sight, three men pointing to windows, gesturing with their hands, a high-rise mime show with an audience of (as far as I can tell) one. It's clear they don't quite see eye-to-eye. The yellow hat looks down toward the street, the one without a hat makes an adamant gesture, the white hat opens his hands in conciliation. Something is at stake—but what? Oh my god, the one without a hat is suddenly standing on the ledge, outside the railing, turning around to say something to the others, standing there (okay, so what if he has a short strap holding him to the rail) having the last of his conversation thirty-three floors up on a ledge no wider than the length of his (what look to me to be) fine Italian shoes.

Sometimes there is a spontaneous response to being alive that manifests itself in the natural use of language, the world seen anew in simile or adjective, deliciously varied, offering up its mysteries through the tilt of the head and the slightly altered angle of vision. Neruda's "perpetual cup of water" or his "elusive butterfly of time," his "red noise of bones" or the "day withdrawing to its own local cemetery" are examples of such a response. In contemporary America, the poems of Naomi Shihab Nye have this special kind of spontaneity. They leap from the pages with their exuberance and their genuine delight in looking hard at anything and anyone that comes into view. In fact, a quick glance at some of the titles in her latest book, *Fuel*, would suggest Neruda's *Odas Elementales*—"Morning Glory," "Luggage," "Feather," "Butter Box," "Bill's Beans," "Alphabet," "String." And a sampling of phrases underscores this affinity: "From this distance every storm / looks like a simple stripe"; "We're fat with binders and forgetting"; "the high bouillon surge of joy"; "& only birds with their sharp morning notes / had the sense for any new day"; "Daily the long wind brushes YES / through the trees."

Nye's particular challenge is to shape the material so that it speaks for itself. The risk here is the risk of the ordinary. As her previous book *Red Suitcase* suggests, Nye is a traveler and her poems record her encounters with other people, other places. *Fuel* continues in this vein, feeding on her experience of the actual world. There's universe enough right here on earth, she seems to say in "Luggage," surveying the basket of apricots, the smiles of strangers, "thinking / how this world has everything and offers it / how it is good we only have two hands."

There's courage in writing of the human, of the everyday: your young son's first ride on a bicycle, or attending an estate sale, or the pancake breakfast with Santa, or no. 2 pencils. There's either courage or confidence that, whatever the topic, something interesting will happen. And something always does happen in the hands of this poet who trusts her instincts, trusts her observations to lead her into new territory, another place to "visit." Nye finds the complex in the simple, as the small vases from Hebron which "tip their mouths open to the sky" become vessels for the history of the Palestinian struggle. Conversely, she finds the simple in the complex, moving from the complicated human emotions of "Snow" (a poem about sledding with her younger brother in order to avoid family tensions) to the realization that "there can be a place / so cold any movement saves you." From there, it's simple to break the frosty barriers between people, to unravel the complex maze of disaffection in the name of love.

The poems of *Fuel* are refreshingly easy to read and understand, yet they continue to haunt you, insisting themselves long after you've finished reading. They force you into unexpected corners and hand your own ordinary world back to you tied in a shiny ribbon, curled with the scissors of Nye's acute eye, held in place with her perfect adjectives. This is a collection of disparate poems; there is no continuous narrative here other than the story of active receptivity. The lesson seems so simple—live fully, contemplate what others say, let that lead you into your own interior spaces—but few of us remember it so wholeheartedly. Here's what happens when you do:

The Rider

A boy told me
if he roller-skated fast enough
his loneliness couldn't catch up to him,

the best reason I ever heard
for trying to be a champion.

What I wonder tonight
pedaling hard down King William Street
is if it translates to bicycles.

A victory! To leave your loneliness
panting behind you on some street corner
while you float free in a cloud of sudden azaleas,
pink petals that have never felt loneliness,
no matter how slowly they fell.

How skillfully Nye identifies herself as the rider, acknowledges her own experience of loneliness, pays homage to that of others, and, in the final gesture, moves from inside to the exterior world with its tiny messages of hope.

These inviting poems are optimistic, but Nye is not Pollyanna. She does not shrink from the realities of the Middle East, from the pain of memory or empathy with the grief of others. She enters the human drama knowing that, as in "Wedding Cake" when she is asked to hold a stranger's baby on an airplane, she will be left with a crumpled skirt and an aching lap. But she's had the pleasure of an hour with a baby in a frilly dress and observed with wonder that "already she knew the small finger / was funnier than the whole arm."

Fuel leaves the reader with a new appreciation for the ordinary made extraordinary, a feeling that the lives we live do matter, a sense that poetry is in the beholding rather than in what is beheld. They leave us with our own version of an aching lap. We want it back—that way of connecting—knowing that falling pears make a "round, / full sound in the grass," or that painted signs dry more quickly in English than Arabic (the thick swoops and curls stay moist), or that her uncle, in his adopted coffee shop, is still shaking his head "back and forth / from one country to the other." We want the simple pleasure of "Eye Test" where the letters, "tired of meaning nothing," long to become words. And we want the complex pleasure of the long elliptical lines of "String," wound into their own ball of perception:

> though so many days have driven in between us and original hopes
> as a boy stands back from his earlier self mocking it
> and the light of fireflies blinking against an old fence has become
> as sad as it is lovely because so many hands are gone by now
> it is not that we wanted the light to be caught   but reached for
> *that was it*
>
> Tonight it is possible to pull the long string and feel someone moving
>   far away
> to touch the fingers of one hand to the fingers of the other hand
> to tug the bride and widow by the same thread . . .

The poem ends with a delicate fusion of lives in the first-person plural, including the reader in its realized spaces, tugging us, through language, into the world at large:

> Just then a light clicked on inside tall windows   draped tablecloth
> pitcher of flowers   lace of evening spinning its intricate spell
> inside our blood and what we smelled was earth and rain sunken into it
> run-on sentence of the pavement   punctuation of night and day
> giving us something to go by   a knot in the thread
> although we did not live in that house

Sensuous, imaginative, and surprisingly surprising, Nye is a poet who spans cultures. What scholars call "otherness" dissolves in her embrace. *Fuel* begins with "Muchas Gracias por Todo," giving thanks for everything. And at the book's conclusion we must give thanks to Naomi Shihab Nye for reminding us that our everyday lives can be the source of infinite wonder, that the simple juxtaposition of noun and adjective puts the lie to pretension, that in thinking about our own lives we would be wise to echo her last line: "I would not trade."

Now the dark-haired man is back on his side of the rail, and the other two are in their cage, and all's right with the world. White hat and yellow hat are working away, rubbing and wiping and, yes, lifting off the tape and throwing it into their trash can (the cage has a beige plastic container for just such a purpose) and suddenly there is an array of familiar-looking tools—screwdrivers and sandpaper and measuring tape—to reassure me. There are patches of sky. A gull traces the canyon of the street. The city is emerging from fog, spreading itself out block by block under the absent noontime sun. And I go back to my book.

In Pursuit of Elegance

On Les Murray's *Selected Poems*; Yehuda Amichai's *Open Closed Open*; Derek Walcott's *Tiepolo's Hound*; Jane Cooper's *The Flashboat: Poems Collected and Reclaimed*; Robert Wrigley's *Reign of Snakes*; James Richardson's *How Things Are*; Gregory Djanikian's *Years Later*; and Stephen Dunn's *Different Hours.*

> Bertolucci called me when I was about to start shooting, and he said, "Have you learned that everything is form and form is emptiness?" No, I'm always the last to know.
>
> Martin Scorsese

I'VE ALWAYS SUSPECTED THERE was an affinity between soccer, mathematics, and poetry. For twenty-five years, I've watched soccer whenever I could. I've lost two whole summers to the World Cup. I was once a hopeless fan for the hapless Lancers (who were in the same league as the moneyed Cosmos) and now I'm a raging fan of their successors, the Rochester Raging Rhinos (who won the 1999 U.S. Open Cup). In the old days, as we sat on the bleachers, we could hear at least five different languages spoken by our neighbors. Italian, Spanish, Russian, I could recognize. The others were what? Greek, Serbo-Croatian, Ukrainian? Who knows. The Lancers' game was not beautiful to watch; they were not good enough for that. But sometimes an individual play would stand out: the ball placed perfectly, the players imagining the ball—no, becoming the ball—in order to let it find its way into the net. The crowd would rise of one accord. That's how I knew. When the crowd rose to its feet, its many languages were one. What we had simultaneously witnessed could only be called elegance.

I can't think of anyone who uses the term "elegant" as matter-of-factly as a mathematician. "That's an elegant proof"—and other mathematicians know exactly what is meant. Mathematical elegance takes many forms. Sometimes the proof is short, moving straight to the point with surprising ease and clarity. Sometimes it meanders, picking up nuance along the way, until the result is a proof that expands and enlarges the original premise. Sometimes it is surprising, coming from an angle so different from what is expected that it demonstrates the versatility—and variety—of logic. Sometimes it is referential, building on the accumulated knowledge of the field. Often it contains a metaphorical aspect, bringing together in a symmetric way ideas that do not appear to be directly connected.

My mathematician friend tells me that elegance is overused as a term, that perhaps it is better to think of proofs as "satisfying." That word, he contends, allows for a messy or unwieldy proof that has genuine importance, for the hundreds of pages of the proof of Fermat's last theorem (possibly the *Ulysses* of mathematics) that demand further scholarly analysis and exegesis. There is even room, he says, for the "outrageous" proof, the one that goes against all intuition.

What might be the definition of elegance in poetry? It's not merely fastidious adherence to form or high-toned rhetoric or elevated diction or lofty subject matter that makes for elegance. That would be a sociological definition, perhaps. Poems build their own aesthetics, and the standard of elegance varies to fit each one. Like mathematical proofs, poems sometimes move without an extraneous gesture; sometimes they eddy and circle in spirals of sound and accumulated nuance. They can surprise with metaphor that opens up the world. Even with the rise of public readings, there is usually no crowd to rise to the occasion. There is only the lonely reader, caught in his or her own sense of what has happened. So how do we know what we've experienced? And yet we know. We know we know. And we know we have no words to describe that deep sense of satisfaction. Others have tried—Dickinson's taking off the top of your head, Frost's ice riding on its own melting—but those senses are theirs, and ours resist formulation, though still we strain for it. In the end, we hope to find someone—anyone—to whom we can say "let me read you something," and then we hope that whatever magic struck us will strike again.

Searching for the nature of elegance in poetry, I turned first to recent works by established masters who have long mattered to me. I quickly realized that *Learning Human: Selected Poems* by Les Murray would not meet my needs—or certainly not in book form. In collecting "the poems he considers his best," Murray (a poet I adore) has not included some of what *I* think are his best, proving again that maybe poets do not know what their best work really is. Yes, this new book contains such memorable poems as "Midsummer Ice," with its poignant memory ("'Poor Leslie,' you would say, / 'your hands are cold as charity—'"), and "Dog Fox Field" with its chilling reminder ("Our sentries, whose holocaust does not end, / they show us when we cross into Dog Fox Field"). But without "Walking to the Cattle Place" or "Aspects of Language and War on the Gloucester Road" ("I am driving *waga*, up and west. / Parting cattle, I climb over the crest / out of Bunyah, and skirt Bucca Wauka, / A Man Sitting Up With Knees Against His Chest: / *baga waga*, knees up, the burial shape of a warrior"), the book fails to encompass the full innovative range of the Australian experience. And without "Ill Music" it loses one of the most technically perfect and heartbreaking poems I know.

Learning Human is too broad a title for this reduced selection. This book cannot be considered definitive. It is a pale, Yankeefied version, fit for the formal confines of its publisher, but without Murray's customary "quality of sprawl." Still, a reader new to Murray's work will find here "The Buladelah-Taree Holiday Song Cycle" with its expansive, free-ranging lines, the pure sound-play of poems like "Shoal," and at least six poems from "The Idyll Wheel," including the taut metrics that demonstrate Murray's mastery:

> Grief is nothing you can do, but do,
> worst work for least reward,
> pulling your heart out through your eyes
> with tugs of the misery cord.
>
> ("The Misery Cord")

Likewise, Yehuda Amichai's *Open Closed Open*, translated by Chana Bloch and Chana Kronfeld, does not reveal what I consider his essential strengths: wit, linguistic surprise, and an unnaturally natural metaphorical way of thinking. In what is hailed on the jacket cover to be his "magnum opus," Amichai gives us an Israel filled with the glory of living detail, but stripped of what I have always described as awe—that is, his surprise at his own condition. Just when I glimpse one of his characteristic internal landscapes ("Oh, the small interrogatives of my life, / hopping, chirping, flitting about, / eluding me since my childhood"), it is clouded by a more didactic external analysis ("The gap between the names / of streets and the people who live on them is growing / and hope gets more distant from those who are hoping"). Maybe Amichai has become older and somewhat repetitive, but inventive lines like "Sometimes Jerusalem is a city of knives" or "I want my son to be a soldier in the Italian Army" make me suspect that the problem lies somewhere else. Part of it may be that this book takes as its base familiar Jewish verse, but part, I suspect, is due to these particular translations, which lack, in English anyway, Amichai's usual energy and verve. They have the feel of possibly too much precision, a literalism which fails to liberate in the second language the power of human emotion his poems have always before conveyed.

Author's note: Since this review was written, Yehuda Amichai has died. My quibble with his most recent book should thus be put in a larger perspective. The world has lost one of its greatest poets—a man of peace, a man of supreme imagination. Amichai raised his glorious, secular voice, filled with religious reference and metaphor, to call on all of us to love one another. We should be grateful to the late Ted Hughes for calling our attention to this unique voice and helping to make it available in translation. Leafing through the pages of *Open Closed Open* or *Love Poems*, I sense that almost any poem could serve as elegy. Every line shimmers with meaning. "There are candles that remember," Amichai says as he recounts his relationship with Israel, the country he loved that was younger than he was. "Late in my life I had a daughter that will be twenty-two / in the year 2000. Her name / is Emanuella, which means 'May God be with us!'" From *The Selected Poetry of Yehuda Amichai*, translated by Chana Block and Stephen Mitchell, I light these candles to pay homage:

> My soul is experienced and built like mountain terraces
> against erosion. I'm a holdfast,
> a go-between, a buckle-man.
> ("There Are Candles That Remember")

> He will die as figs die in autumn,
> shriveled and full of himself and sweet,
> the leaves growing dry on the ground,
> the bare branches already pointing to the place
> where there's time for everything.
> ("A Man Doesn't Have Time")

> Look, we too are going
> in the reverse-flower-way:
> to begin with a calyx exulting toward the light,
> to descend with the stem growing more and more solemn,
> to arrive at the closed earth and to wait there for a while,
> and to end as a root, in the darkness, in the deep womb.
> ("Look: Thoughts and Dreams")

Derek Walcott's *Tiepolo's Hound* is a more interesting and complicated disappointment. Beautifully produced, with twenty-six full color reproductions of Walcott's paintings to accompany its one long poem (164 pages of couplets), the book lays claim to elegance from the outset. In what Walcott continually admits is a "fiction," he chronicles the life of the artist Camille Pissarro, a Sephardic Jew born in St. Thomas who left the island to become a painter in Paris. Self-conscious in the extreme, the poet, as narrator, intrudes on his tale with the consciousness of postcolonial theory. The word *colonised* proliferates, suggesting that Pissarro betrayed his native land in favor of more "artistic" landscapes.

But what is native to one who is already outside, or transplanted? So Walcott, both under the cover of his subject and in the guise of narrator, confronts the issues of Art and origin. He describes the techniques of the various impressionists in such a way as to give a brief art history lesson, invoking Cézanne, van Gogh, Courbet, and Corot, among others, to say nothing of the now-problematic Gauguin. Yet somehow the paintings—and the painters—rarely come alive in the telling: "There is something uxorious in Pissarro's landscapes, / as if his brush had made a decorous marriage // with earth's fecundity; her seasons and gates, / the snow-streaked mud of fabrics whose soft cage // held Vuillard and Bonnard in the speckled interiors / of the bourgeois sublime, wine, linen, bread, and flowers . . ." They serve as *idea*, as painter in the abstract, just as Pissarro serves as *concept* of exile, as emblematic outsider.

What *would* have been Pissarro's fate had he stayed? Would he have become an obscure painter of the Carribbean? His position is not lost on Walcott. Referring over and over to his couplets (which rhyme not in the traditional closed fashion, but *ab//ab//cd//cd*, etc., employing a dominant iambic beat and enough pentameters to establish a pattern from which to depart), Walcott alerts the reader to his knowledge that as he "mounts the stairs of the couplets" he is using borrowed Western forms with which to examine his nameless origins. Wresting conclusions from the reader, Walcott recounts his struggle to create an art that is not derivative, that is true to his "roots." But all art is derivative. Nothing comes untainted by the imposed name: not the breadfruit or the frangipani or the poplars shivering in the fields of France. At some time, someone stamped each thing with the thumbprint of its signifier; at some time, someone gave up the essence of simply being to the process we call Time. (Sometime someone invaded France . . .) And Time, as Walcott admits in this poem, "is not narrative"; it "continues its process even for the masters . . ."

The disappointment I feel here is that instead of taking off the top of my head, the poem calls forth my love of argument. It says, in verse, what Walcott has said better in critical prose, in a review of a new anthology of Caribbean writing in *The New York Review of Books* (15 June 2000): "That was the afflicting torment of successful colonials, that the deeper our education, the more it moved us away from the people. As it divided, though, so it enriched." I recognize in *Tiepolo's Hound* a slick academic version of what I have formerly loved in Walcott. Where is the painterly quality of "Midsummer, Tobago" with its pure imagery that evokes both place and feeling? I find echoes in phrases ("Heat. Scorched boulders.") that instantly expand into intellectualized description, not evocation ("Dust in the rutted roads, / stumbling to the crunch of gravel, clay shards, and shale, // mica or quartz in the sun, dry, papery reeds / of leaves whose hues vie with autumn's. I swore: I shall // get their true tints someday. Time, in its teaching, / will provide the bliss of precision . . ."). And where is the energy of the patois that brought to life the island life? Gone, into the realm of analytic statements on the nature of loss. Where is the driven energy of "The Train" or the sustained drama of *Omeros*? And where is there room for the reader's participatory insight?

Walcott's presiding assumption is that there is an equivalency between the blank page and the gessoed canvas. But if a picture says more than a thousand words, then Walcott's paintings have the last say. They punctuate the difference in the two modes, showing us the color and shape of island life. For all its elegant presentation, *Tiepolo's Hound* breaks no new ground—and every soccer player knows that the goal comes from a surprising variation on a set play.

Elegance may not be a property attributable to an entire book of poems—or, if it is, it may occur so rarely that we can think of the consummate examples. Wallace Stevens' *Harmonium* for one. But no individual volume by Robert Frost, who included too many stock poems alongside his masterpieces. Galway Kinnell's *The Book of Nightmares*, but none of his other volumes, which do not have the benefit of such thematic continuity. Sylvia Plath's *Ariel*, Robert Lowell's *Life Studies*—in short, the groundbreaking books that changed our way of reading. Or, conversely, the quiet culminations of a lifetime as in Thomas Hardy's late poems, Elizabeth Bishop's collected. So maybe I am looking for something I cannot expect to find with any regularity. Maybe I need to search elsewhere.

An elegant proof is sometimes just one of many perfectly serviceable proofs a mathematician has produced, sometimes the singular inspired product of a lifetime's cumulative work. Or, as in Fermat, the theorem itself may be evidence of genius. And a goal is hardly the only example of elegance in a soccer game. Good defense has its own aesthetics. A near goal is sometimes far more satisfactory to the aficionado than a mess of bodies in front of the net resulting in an accidental score. Maybe the individual poem is where the quality of elegance will reveal itself.

Jane Cooper's *The Flashboat* offers up a rich variety within which to begin my search; its subtitle is "Poems Collected and Reclaimed," suggesting that the author has had time to rethink earlier choices, to see her work in a larger perspective. The early poems are strangely formal, intricately and delicately complex. They make it easy for Carolyn Heilbrun to call her "an astute, elegant poet" on the jacket cover. "You thought yourself alone," Cooper says in "For Thomas Hardy," joining him in the risky venture as she enters the tradition.

Yet the poems here are emphasized by several sections of prose—some in the form of prose poems and autobiographical anecdotes, some by more conventional essays on origin or intent. As the poems change in character, experiment with new and different modes of expression, these prose sections serve as lines of demarcation. Thus Cooper is able to orchestrate her move from formal to free verse, along with a growing social awareness shown in her studies of Willa Cather, Georgia O'Keeffe, and Rosa Luxemburg. Some of the later sections (and even individual pieces) combine poetry and prose, as though to chronicle the struggle for articulation. What interests me here, however, is the poet's understanding and acceptance of her single life—not isolated, but nevertheless single. Poetry is seen as a way of being in the world, a sufficiency. "Each word, each solitude, cracks open."

So I'm drawn to a specific poem—one from the middle of Cooper's career, neither as formal as her early work nor as experimental as her later—which shows the quality of attention it is possible to pay:

The River in All Lights, from an Upstairs Window

The river in all lights, from an upstairs window:
The river sometimes like a ribbon of blood.
The river with water hyacinths, blood-brown stems
and lilac heads, iron rusting to blue.
The river blue on blue under the sun.
The river nicked with white as the wind rises.
The river darkened to steel, with copper glints,
or elephant-blue under a thunderous sky.
Now the horizon is lost, the opposite shore
lost as the river roils and mirrors itself.
Now there is only a ribbon of glistening mist
we call the river. Now there is only sky.

I am tempted to talk about alliteration and assonance, about the repetitive accumulation of sound as well as of recognizable "rivers," but those aspects of the craft are secondary, it seems to me, to the way this poem presents the condition of isolation. The seclusion here is not necessarily reserved for women, though in the book as a whole Cooper certainly gives a balanced and intelligent account of a female response to living alone. Here, though, the upstairs window serves not so much to imprison but as a vantage from which to observe the changing river, the effects of wind and weather.

The river is known yet mysterious, a storm about to boil, a disappearance. As it moves from red to blue to dark to nothingness, it also moves from the life of blood and flowers to the inert elements of rust and steel and copper. Yet the poem, initially devoid of verbs, suddenly glints and roils even as the river loses the colors of life. The "now" of the poem takes over, subsuming all those other remembered "lights" in the moment of erasure. The center of the poem is the absence of the river. Effacement is manifested, here, as a powerful presence. In what this poem says without saying, in what it knows of the world and the human condition, its elegant bursts of color and movement merge into something refined—a perception which itself becomes a structure. Of course the patterns of sound are part of this, but I especially like the way the poem posits one thing and becomes another.

One poem does not make an elegant book, but this poem is representative of the qualities to be found in *The Flashboat*. Neither strident nor driven by ideology, the book moves from a passionate desire for connection through a personal grief and into a mature acceptance of how the individual life has been lived. It does a genuine service to women as it meticulously examines both the public and the private, the ways in which the ineffable can and cannot be celebrated.

Odd how elegance seems to change its stripes depending on its context. Maybe it's linked to the contrarian in the reader. In a book of short, simple poems, a sudden expansiveness strikes an appreciative chord; in a book filled with openness, we begin to value restraint. But surely it's more than obvious contrast that distinguishes one poem from another.

Robert Wrigley's *Reign of Snakes* is rhetorically charged, especially so in the five longer poems that are italicized, as though they were giving voice to an inner sensibility expressing itself in its love of language and vocabulary. The opening lines are a good example: "*Spring, and the first full crop of dandelions gone / to smoke, the lawn lumpish with goldfinches, / hunched in their fluffs, fattened by seed, / alight in the wind-bared peduncular forest.*" And that is just revving up for lines like "*Plum and umber, dumb phlox spilling*" to show Wrigley's love of vowels and consonants. Such lines strive for something opulent, but they also run the risk of sounding too lush for their own good. So Wrigley has made of contrast a virtue, tempering these inner voices with a more sinewy narrative line in the body of the book. "This wedge of county land shows up / every year on the tax bill"—and we sink back, relieved of the pressure to maintain the intensity.

So I select a poem that seems to hover halfway between the two modes, one foot firmly planted in detail and the other in sound as it winks on and off through the lines. The first half of the poem accumulates specifics: of weather, of nature, of intent and attitude, culminating in the repetition of "snow" to remind us of how it heaps up on itself. Wrigley gives us the visual accumulation of the flakes even as he is talking about their pervasive smell—their overriding, isolating, anticipatory odor.

Prayer for the Winter

I place two pennies, one on either rail:
warm from my pocket they melt the frost there
then harden into place against the coming tremors.

The ties too are tufted white, and fibrous mounds
of coyote scat, and the next occasional spike
worked loose, which I fling like the others in the river.

A crooked volunteer tree offers up its last
or its only apple, hard and thick-skinned,
bitter still but sweetened a bit by the cold.

Along this mile-long arc of track, four springs
and four steep chutes choked with blackberries,
and four cold pools crowded with cress.

It's a black fly wind, all ice and bite,
and the usual fishermen have all gone home.
Trainmen hate those pennies. I'll hide

until the engine's past, hide again
for the obsolete caboose this short-line throwback
still uses. They hate the clunk and jump,

the eighty-ton shudder pummeling their bones.
But I want something to show for this day
other than a mile of awkward walking,

a wind so fierce and relentless the chimney smokes
lie out in rigid lines and vanish and the only smell
is snow, snow, snow, like a fat and generous relative

coming all day but still too far off to see.
And when it arrives, the lead cloud billowy and black,
the first icy spits will sting like little fires.

A succession of sounds catches us almost unawares. The coyote scat and the spike worked loose go almost unnoticed—just more detail in a litany of details—but for the hard *k* sound that won't let go. The ear is energized. And so the succession—*crooked, thick-skinned, arc, track, choked, blackberries*, even *cress*—make their own clack of wheel on rail. But sound alone is not enough. I like the speaker's intimate knowledge of this mile-long arc of track, his knowledge that the trainmen hate those pennies, and the knowledge (both his and ours) that he has placed them there against this knowledge. This is not a poem about remembered childhood, but about adult persistence. And we know all this (if we're old enough) because of that wonderful "obsolete" caboose. We see it there—like a good period at the end of a sentence—because we've *seen* it there.

So far the sounds have been in service of sense, in service of an almost literal evocation. But they have attuned the ear and now they can lend their power to something larger.

Already the downstream train plows from under it
and rounds the corner flocked, a thunderous cake,
a mile of steel, a birth-water umbilicus

harkening storm, and I, who must ply
the deadman roads and walk the skin-tingling
right-of-way corridor, I don't ever want it to stop.

Not the train, not the snow, not the winterkill wind
that blows and blows. No, let it snow,
let the earth go blind and the highway unlined.

Let it come down like sleep, let the deep drifts
extend their leeward fingers and the springs spill
into long random sculptures of ice.

Wouldn't it be nice, marooned in a frozen world
for a night one long winter long, home
where the fire burns the years and wind

sings its one note wavery aria over and over,
and we are alive, alive, in a place
where nothing matters but that we are warm

where the children toss their gossamer
untenderable coins against the weather,
and never lose, and never, never lose.

The vocabulary becomes elevated—*umbilicus*, *harkening*, *winterkill*, *leeward*, *aria*, *gossamer*—as though to remind us not of the winter of the title, but of the prayer. This is the interior space of the mind, the place where meaning is made from all those details. The echo of sound builds its own pattern, emerging as an intricate series of internal rhymes that work equally effectively within the line, within the stanza, or spilling over from one stanza to the next (plows/rounds; I/ply; snow/blows/blows/no/snow/go; blind/unlined; sleep/deep; finger/springs; ice/nice) until the poem is a loose weave of sound. "Over, over, alive, alive, never, never"—the *v*'s hover over the poem like an incantation, transporting it from the specific time and place into the realm of supplication. Wouldn't it be nice? To dream the long winter long, to never lose. The poem not only creates its own world, it plays against of what it knows of the world.

If *Reign of Snakes* is striving for this particular balance between the inner and outer worlds—and I think it is—then Wrigley has found his form in "Prayer for the Winter." Too much of the overtly lyrical or the assiduously narrative pales in contrast. Elegance, here, is the right mix of impulses, the tipping over and the pulling back.

So now I feel as though I'm on the track of elegance, but its footprints are surprisingly unlike what I had expected to find. I might have *said* that form had little to do with it, but still, I guess I had half expected to find it in form. Or a variation on form. But Bertolucci was right: form *is* emptiness—shaped emptiness, waiting for eloquence to fill it, waiting for the moment to rise to its occasion.

So now I'm trailing something else—the shape of thought—and I find it in James Richardson's *How Things Are*. I would assert that Richardson is one of the most exciting poets writing today. Still, it's a quiet excitement, an acquired taste. His poems are intellectual in the best sense of the word: philosophical, contemplative, rational. But their rationality is modestly undercut by a thinking-man's acceptance of his own irrationalities. In other words, Richardson works out his thinking before us, and we usually concur—understanding, as we do, that some percentage of thought resides in emotion.

So the long title poem in twenty-six sections that Richardson calls "How Things Are: A Suite for Lucretians" takes into account both science and sentiment. In something that mirrors scientific syntax, this poem follows the discourses of logic: *because, therefore, thus, similarly, for example, but then, whereas, as if, if then, if, if, if.* Syntax is the key to reading Richardson. He surprises you with variations: "I have every disease. / I have heart shutting down. / . . . I have the undone. / I have August, terminally. / I have sleeping on an open magazine. / I have white, chronic dawns." And more than that—he creates what I can only call syntactical inflection. The periodicity of his sentences, the pacing, the qualifiers, the sudden shifts of attention—all conspire to emphasize his quiet wit, to force the voice to register the weight of a particular word, to give it shape and significance. And so I choose a poem that demonstrates the mind in progress.

A Disquisition upon the Soul

It doesn't register the kid on rollerblades,
or two on the bench that wind sends lightly together,
or the *Times* they leave, or who sleeps under it.
No, those are the heart's. The soul is an old, slow camera
that shows which way the waveless ocean was,
and the day, and darkness, and again the day;
but all things moved or moving, us or ours,
it sees through. Therefore it does not see them.
Is it the restlessness, then, that in the thick of our lives
sends us to windows, wishing for the end
of all that has made us happy? That, sadly,
is also the heart. The soul would not know
which dying friend you thought you could leave for dead,
what shattering love you could leave your daughter for,
or that you stayed, since no one stays long enough,
and, being immortal, hardly knows it was alive
when it is back where it came from after all our years,
as faintly blued as snow is from the height of our skies
and heavier only by the sound of waters.

From its inception, the poem announces its intellectual query, its entry into the realm of thought. But here thought is carefully orchestrated, or else documented (it's hard to say which), so that the poem proceeds in fits and starts, primed by the commas of *old, slow,* and *and the day, and darkness, and again the day* to sense the timeless infinities of the soul. The short, quick sentences belong to the heart.

They occur in real time. They know what life is all about. The short *e*'s of *restlessness* and *then* and *sends* and *end* are mere diversions, an interval that echoes the soul, but knows nothing of its patience. Life, to the soul, is the blink of an eye, a timelessness where everything is put in perspective, except that the perspective does not take into account mortality. The driving force. The heart. The human heart that leaves, or stays. The heart that is ruled by the period, not the comma. The heart that can stop at any minute. So the poem upends itself, relegates the soul to where it belongs, which is somewhere outside the temporalities of "us or ours." The soul is useless. Thus (and how can we avoid such constructions in the middle of this book?) Richardson mirrors Frost's "Earth's the right place for love," and this disquisition upon the heart stays long enough to register in human time what it is to be alive.

So what do I mean by syntactical inflection? Take one line: "when it is back where it came from after all our years." The emphasis (very slight) on the present tense of *is* and (somewhat more) on *our*, is determined by the past tense of the preceding line, by the earlier emphasis on the first person plural pronoun, but even more by the falling cadences of *being immortal* and the stress on *hardly*. Like T. S. Eliot, Richardson teaches us how to read the poems so that they are easily read out loud, keenly orchestrated by an ear so fine-tuned to the *thinking* cadence that it produces thought.

And Richardson knows he does this—or voices the hope that he does. In the ending of one of my favorites in the book, "For the Birds" (a long poem, in seventeen fragmented parts, built around the songs of various birds), Richardson illustrates the parenthetical nature of our interior asides, the human tendency to hear speech in the sounds that birds make, the ability of language to capture pure inflection, the way meaning will impose itself on sound:

> (As for the secret English on my English:
> inaudible, I've learned, to anyone else:
> let it go? What no one else can tell me
> how can I stop whispering to myself?)
>
> *
>
> somewhere in the tuliptree
> *has been*   *will be*   *has been*   *will be*
>
> *
>
> *Is this the end*   *the end*
> one says
>   one says
> *No this is*   *this is*

There's wit and insight and sheer love of language (to say nothing of love of punctuation marks) in *How Things Are*—and best of all there is audible English on his English. But Richardson puts a spin on the human condition as well, and the resulting balance of conjecture and emotion is a true definition of mind and heart in concert.

It's easy to think about the emptiness of form, harder to think about how everything *is* form. That would force us to find the underlying form for everything we read and to expand our definitions. Gregory Djanikian's *Years Later* acts a bit like a movie, giving us the wider sweep, the multifaceted characters we find in film. The book is not so much governed by a presiding sensibility as by a central notion—that of "two neighboring solitudes" suggested by its epigraph from Rilke. The poems begin in circumstance and move to insight. Djanikian looks at the undersides of unrequited love, the boredom that is in marriage, the unexpressed desires of neighbor, stranger, and self, as well as the odd, crazy, joyous coincidental moments of our lives.

The book's title implies the long view, and many of its individual titles have the ring of distance: "Good Neighbors," "Court Scene," "Tourists of Dolor," "The Man Who Was Always Sad," "Histories." One could think of *Years Later* as a series of persona poems, but the project is far more subtle than that. The imagination here serves as a kind of postulation. Djanikian's "camera" pans the crowd, employing every possible pronoun in order to try out various angles of vision. His pronouns do not act as a stand-in or mask for the writer as they do in so many contemporary poems; rather, they attempt genuine exploration of otherness. Although Djanikian may begin with a "character" or a situation, however he frames the scene there is always some part of him inside it. These poems enter not only the lives of others, but the possible lives of the self. If there is a further lesson to be learned, it's in how completely the persona (whether the generic *you*, the third-person *he* or *she*, the editorial *we*, or the more conventional *I*) becomes a part of the *reader's* psyche.

Break Up

It's I AM at the Golden Grill
and he's looking down at his bourbon
as though he might stick his nose in it,
what the hell, before he gets to the bottom.

From the dark booth in the corner
someone's yelling, "Where have I put my love?"

and that sounds right to him, this sense
of having misplaced, having lost
the location of: if only he could think back,
gesture by gesture, word by word.

Lorrine and the True Sensations
are about to sing "Barrelin' Down to Your Heart"
and he's grateful for something loud and raucous
to keep him together, push
against him on all sides: along the bar,
everyone turning around, giving
his loneliness to Lorrine, all he's got.

If his wife walked in just now
from wherever she was—Idaho, Wyoming?—
he'd do something extravagant, take
half his clothes off, sing *Sweet Wilderness of You*
and dedicate it to the one he loves.

He's been quiet and still so long
he wants to cause a riot, something physical,
maybe meanness sitting on his stool for a change
and having a drink with everybody.

It could go on all night, this feeling
that he's missed something along the way,
something now the couple getting up to dance
might have, all hands with each other,
all thigh-muscle and crotch, tight with the music.

And when he walks out of anyplace now,
he'll know if it's for the last time:
he's seen that walk,
and the door it passes through.

Love turning away, love running out:
he'll be here till morning thinking about it.

Rhythm makes this poem easy to read; the muted iambics carry the narrative thread, culminating in their emphatic "he's seen that walk" (which veers toward spondee)—and you can bet he has. But by then you are already inside his head, inside his "what the hell." And you're simultaneously outside, just another customer at the bar, watching him, noting that his loneliness is "all he's got." The neighboring solitudes coincide. So the meanness he dredges up reflects both what we know from observation and what we recognize from somewhere deep within.

The dualities are highlighted by the progression from concrete to abstract—Golden Grill to anyplace, someone in the dark booth to everybody—and back again to the reality of "here" where he'll sit all night thinking. They range from the solid certainty of his glass of bourbon to the imagined riot, from the specificity of what he'd do if his wife walked in to the vagueness about where she even is. We are given some of the "facts" and even more of the "figments," and this is all we really know of most people—what they choose to show us mixed with what we know of ourselves. This double "take" on life is punctuated by the colon, that visual equal sign that fuses two thoughts around its fragile hinge. The mark is introduced early to show external evidence of interior thoughts, then reappears at the end where it connects the objectified man to the subjective knowledge of the reader.

Years Later is a study in irony—things are never quite what they appear to be. However, the irony is, for want of a term, light-handed. It's not the objective, but the result. It's what rises up to greet us at the end. This collection reveals the supreme irony: because it is so clearly about everyone else (including the author), we find ourselves facing the neighboring solitude of the mirror. With its gentle handling of psychology and its playful speculations, *Years Later* is even more a study in tone. Tone dictates what attitude the reader will take toward content, and Djanikian masterfully modulates tone, playing something in each key in order to give us the full range of experience.

The difference between the elegant and the satisfying may be relevant to poetry. If a mathematical proof can be recognized for *what* it accomplishes, then some poems might be termed satisfying for their significance, their orchestration of meaning.

In Stephen Dunn's latest book, several poems fit that description. That is, they manage to become more of an already good thing. *Different Hours* has a lot of what we've come to expect from Dunn: wit and wisdom in equal measure, playful banter between epigraph and poem, serious dialogue between epigraph and poem, serious encounter with idea and concept, love of life. But there's a newfound sense of mortality that governs its message. On the back cover, Dunn states, "I am interested in exploring the 'different' hours, not only of one's life, but also of the larger historical and philosophical life beyond the personal."

Yet Dunn has made his trademark the idiosyncrasies of the personal. A few years ago, in a review of one of his books (see *The Georgia Review*, Winter 1996),

I said, "My suspicion is that Dunn's inner landscape is even darker and more honest than his guileless speaker is willing to reveal—an idealess, imageless, almost wordless space in which he knows that the fragile body prays to an absent God and goes unheard." As if in answer, *Different Hours* admits some of that terrain—one poem is entitled "The Death of God"—and then explores it.

Dunn's poems never call attention to their craft, but he combines an ease of grace and wit, a simplicity of diction, and a rhythmical flow so that, neither image-ridden nor highly metaphorical, still his poems manage to mean more than they say. They reverberate with a kind of "aftershock," the surprise that keeps surprising. This is true for this collection as well, so the difference here is one of degree: the poems have become a fraction more serious, a smidgen more contemplative, a speck more solemn. And there is a slight shift in emphasis—*Different Hours* is not quite as interested in self, or others, as it is in the realm of ideas. He alerts us to this with certain gestures, as at the end of "Irresistible," where the simple description of the events in a movie gives way to his own interpretation:

> That would have been understandable
>
> and simply moral, and I wouldn't
> have walked out into the welter
> of the night, into the fraught air,
> so happily implicated and encumbered.

Diction dictates stance, and the elevated language alerts the reader to the fact that something is at stake (although how many times can a word like *fraught* appear in one book?). The speaker is encumbered—happily so—by the complex, even perverse, ways of the heart. Never willing to settle for the "simply moral," for what Dunn later calls the "virtue" of the seldom-tempted, he is happy in his implication.

So this time I select a poem that ostensibly conforms to Dunn's own directive. Certainly its title announces something beyond the personal. In fact, its title raises—before the fact—all the red flags: of exploitation, of the possibilities for expected response or false insight, and of the poet's appropriation of the subject matter.

> *Oklahoma City*
>
> The accused chose to plead innocent
> because he was guilty. We allowed such a thing;
> it was one of our greatnesses, nutty, protective.
> On the car radio a survivor's ordeal, her leg
> amputated without anesthesia while trapped

under a steel girder. Simply, no big words—
that's how people tell their horror stories.
I was elsewhere, on my way to a party.
On arrival, everyone was sure to be carrying
a piece of the awful world with him.

Not one of us wouldn't be smiling.
There'd be drinks, irony, hidden animosities.
Something large would be missing.
But most of us would understand
something large always would be missing.

Oklahoma City was America reduced
to McVeigh's half-thought-out thoughts.
Did he know anything about suffering?
It's the naïve among us who are guilty
of wondering if we're moral agents or madmen

or merely, as one scientist said,
a fortuitous collocation of atoms.
Some mysteries can be solved by ampersands.
Ands not *ors*; that was my latest answer.
At the party two women were talking

about how strange it is that they still like men.
They were young and unavailable, and their lovely faces
evoked a world not wholly incongruent
with the world I know. I had no illusions, not even hopes,
that their beauty had anything to do with goodness.

Dunn manages to avoid the pitfalls precisely because this poem *is* personal. The speaker is on his way to a party. Life goes on and, in this case, its banality accentuates the import of the larger issues. So the difference here is in the *way* Dunn is personal. He has always wryly pointed the finger at himself, but now he seems a bit more willing to implicate others as well. The poem circles and circles, moving from the inconceivable event to the all-too-conceivable self and back, as though trying to find the "something large" that it admits outright will always be missing. And still the poem itself probes for an answer.

At work here is what I would call a deliberate deflation. The event in all its horror is undercut by the fact that it is being reported, then re-reported at the party, reduced to small talk even as it occupies the center of attention.

The speaker, rather than imagining the victims, the devastation, the aftermath, simply recounts the words of the one who experienced its reality. "Simply, no big words—" a prescription for poetry, for how to make it real. Poetry, then, might be able to do justice to the rippling implications of Oklahoma City. The echo of Auden in stanza four at least suggests that the masters know more about suffering than does McVeigh; poetry is, after all, thought-out thoughts. But that would be far too obvious for a poem by Stephen Dunn, and so we are forced to turn to the last stanza, to the way "the world I know" occupies the same line as the lack of illusions or hopes. Although the poet describes his own lack of hope, the "I" becomes generic as we face our own dark honesties. Under Dunn's subtle direction, we implicate ourselves.

How has he accomplished this? With orchestral legerdemain, the poem alternates between the world of the party (which ironically contains the world of ideas) and the world of half-thought thoughts (which overlaps with the physical world of pain). We are never in one place for long. Instead, we are forced to see the event in a context—and it happens to be the context in which most of us find ourselves most of the time: we participate peripherally, as observers, and we try to make sense of it. We want to know *why*. Rights and wrongs eddy in these stanzas. They mix with each other until they solidify: an alloy of competing loyalties and conflicting ideas. The hole at the center of rationality is set against the very rationalism of the Constitution. Science, religion, politics—nothing will serve up an answer. Nothing is transformed.

We're happy enough to watch someone implicate himself, but less willing to walk out of a poem fully encumbered. Yet, under the right circumstances, we appreciate the weight of obligation—and that is precisely what gives Dunn's poems their satisfying quality. The significance here is the mesh in which we see our lives and their often-unacted-upon insights so deftly reproduced.

I think I am still holding in my mind some sense of the *form* of elegance. The poetry of poetry. On the radio, the sportscaster calls the plays. In my mind's eye, I see the game unfold. Players I have come to know move on an imaginary plane. The ball laces the field. The team has found its form, the announcer says. For a moment, the game is beautiful.

Interlude

On Madeline DeFrees' *Blue Dusk: New and Selected Poems*; Linda Gregerson's *Waterborne*; Li-Young Lee's *Book of My Nights*; Philip Schultz's *The Holy Worm of Praise*; and Natasha Trethewey's *Bellocq's Ophelia*.

LOOKING AT BENJAMIN was like seeing my own sons all over again. A physical memory swept over me: the long nights, the worry, the overwhelming sense of responsibility. But this was different. I found myself doing what grandparents have done from time immemorial; I reassured, I reminisced, I recalled how quickly things change. Benjamin's parents can't imagine, now, that he will ever sleep through the night. They can't imagine he will drive off in the car—alone. I have a different perspective now, so I don't mind sitting for an hour, holding a sleeping child, listening to the little sounds he makes, noting his tiny fingernails, the way his downy hair stands straight up, feeling him shift into deeper sleep, his mouth twitching with whatever dream newborns have. I remember, though, when I coveted that hour, wanted that hour for myself. My life had been usurped, and I wanted it back.

Why don't I feel that way today? If anything, I am even busier than I was back then. And maybe that's the reason. How could I be too busy to hold Benjamin as he squirms and begins to cry? I can laugh at his howl. It will stop. It's only a matter of months and we will have all forgotten. Interval, hiatus, lacuna—there's something to be said for a distance in time that allows for simultaneous recollection and prophecy. Benjamin's very existence alters my point of view. The world he has so recently come into captures my attention and I see things in a different light.

Interval, hiatus, lacuna. Interval hints at a space of time between events—the thirty-five years (to the day) between his father's birth and Benjamin's. Hiatus suggests a break in continuity, but this baby *is* continuity, the sense that life goes on in some predictable fashion. The hiatus, then, was in me. Lacuna implies a missing part, a gap. Lacuna is recognized after the fact. We didn't know we missed him until he was here.

Many of today's poets, pressured not so much by the urgency of their material as by academic structures or their publishers' bottom-line exigencies, seem to be putting out books at the rate of approximately one every two or three years. They leave themselves little time for genuine assessment of the very project they have set themselves, following instead what often looks like the path of least resistance. So when a poet returns to the publishing scene after quite a few years between books, it's difficult to know which word to select. Was it interval, the natural spacing of books in an on-going—and comprehensive—*oeuvre*? Was it hiatus, a necessary break for the poet to take stock, to assess the direction of the work, to experiment with new directions? Was it lacuna—a crisis of confidence, failure to find a publisher, what is commonly called "writer's block"? There are several possible reasons for such an interlude, so let's just call it *interlude*. Let's look at some poets for whom an interlude occurred—and at what resulted.

Blue Dusk by Madeline DeFrees covers fifty years of poetry, yet the selections have been made so carefully that the book feels freshly minted. As in many "selecteds," the new poems come at the beginning, and this turns out to be fortuitous. The new work reveals a history that informs the whole collection, as in the opening poem, "Going Back to the Convent," which begins: "This time it is no dream. After twenty-three years away / I wake in a Spokane convent in my Black Watch / plaid pajamas. . . ." DeFrees left the convent in 1973 after spending thirty-eight years as a nun. The fifty-year span of the poems ensures that readers will experience both the religious and the secular, as well as the inevitable tensions that accompany the decision to leave. At the onset of this collection, one can see how deeply the past is embedded in the present. The dreams of that life (that habit of living) haunt the poet's sleep, sometimes as inclination, sometimes as guilt, sometimes as resistance.

In these magnificent late poems, appearing ten years after her previous book, DeFrees examines root cause. At their center is memory awakened with such clarity that it bridges the years, casting itself in a living present. At their heart is a lost love, or a lost possibility of love, brought to life in such a way that it asserts itself, this time giving the poet access to earth as opposed to heaven. In "Visiting Sunday: Convent Novitiate," she remembers how her cousin played the piano for her. In "Elegy for Arnold," her cousin is so alive in her mind that she knows "you've come back / to guide me, reading the difficult score, breathing / the rarefied, music-drenched air / of a love come into its own." These poems are reclamation. They recapitulate, and amplify.

One of the advantages of going over old territory with new perspective is that what was earnest can become ironic, what was obvious can become complicated, what was cloudy can become clear. This is the benefit of interlude. One clarifying element is humor. Framed Blue Nun wine labels now hang in the poet's home. She can watch Marilyn Monroe's movies at will, whereas before, "Convent movies had to be clean as / bleach. Even your titles // went wrong: All About Eve, / The Seven Year Itch, The Asphalt Jungle, / Some Like it Hot, How to Marry a Millionaire. / Sex was a bullet I dodged, that shot on the subway / grate!"

Another vehicle for clarity is style. DeFrees manages to create a conversational tone in poems that are, somewhat obliquely, formal. Breaking free from the forms themselves (earlier books are represented by sonnets, a villanelle, couplets, intricate rhyme schemes, versatile enjambment), DeFrees orchestrates these new poems through carefully balanced stanzas, a delicately iambic bass line, and almost-imperceptible internal rhymes. The first stanza of "Still Life" employs these devices in order to create tone:

> After your letter arrived I left the oven on
> all night and never once
> put my head in it. After your letter arrived
> I let one foot follow the other
> through the better part of the day. Your letter
> lay on the kitchen table by the paring
> knife on the stoneware plate with the apple core
> like a Dutch still life restored to
> its muted color.

The heavy iamb of the second line gives way to its echo. The obvious sounds of *letter, never, letter, better, letter* are themselves muted in *paring, stoneware, core, restored, color*. These dominant sounds are interwoven by vowels: the *o* of *oven* and *on* and *once* and *one* and *other*, then the long *a* of *day* and *lay* and *table* and *plate*. Couple those with the many instances of alliteration and you have a recipe for overkill, yet here there is the resounding simplicity of voice, the crispness of detail, one object placed next to another as in a still life, to re-create the bravado that leads, with psychological precision, to the final lines:

> Sang
> wash of sunlight on the sill and apple core,
> sang water glass half full of emptiness. Sang body
> all in shadow that I must bathe and dress.

Madeline DeFrees not only strives for stylistic balance, she explores the very concept of equilibrium. For all the evenness of routine the convent afforded, it represents something out of balance. The opening section of *Blue Dusk* ends with a poem entitled "Vermeer's *A Woman Holding a Balance*"—a kind of still life of a still life. Against a backdrop of critical speculation about the woman's "meaning," the speaker notices, "The woman holding / a balance keeps her silence." Vermeer did not sign this painting, yet his vision hovers in the interstices. "Light loves the woman's face," says the poet, though even through a microscope the viewer cannot tell what is being weighed on the scales: "It echoes with incertitude." The speaker would warn us against drawing too many conclusions, but how tempting it is to see the poet as the woman standing "pensive and alone," to assume that the "impassable gulf that widens as we try to cross it" exists between poet and reader as well. And yet we try to cross it, finding in the poem's final sentence a manifesto: "The painting means: itself."

The new poems act as a kind of retrospective overview; in the light of their honest appraisal, the earlier works, which appear in the order of their publication, chronicle a changing state of mind. The poems set in the convent show a nameless self—or rather, someone who has taken on another name—aware, always, that her questioning personality disrupts the very balance she has sought. Even as a poet, she is the exception: "Nuns are the fictions / by whom we verify the usual contradictions." The introduction of English into the Mass is welcomed, but it foreshadows her own mutability:

> Schooled in an ancient language, I've no word
> to grieve its timely going.
> Voices I had not heard
> through reams of psalms on Sunday
> revive and stir,
> fragile as doves and whiter
> on the morning air.
>
> ("Whitsunday Office")

The ensuing poems explore the desire to regain identity—as a woman, and as an individual. They celebrate a secular world made spiritual through living *in* it, being *of* it. The Blue Nun emerges as a character whose oddball circumstances and offbeat rhymes signal a healthy attitude and a lively imagination: "You may have noticed / how the walls lean toward the river / where a veil of fog hides a sky diver's / pale descent. The parachute / surrounds her like a wimple. / That's what happens when Blue Nuns / bail out. / It's that simple."

Unearthing her own meanings by returning to family stories, by examining in depth what she had once taken on faith, DeFrees demonstrates the truly contemplative life. Often she finds herself wanting, and often she turns to the natural world for solace. Slowly, she builds a set of personal symbols, most notably the color blue (a blue more serene than that of Wallace Stevens, more the blue of infinity) and water in all its various states (a fluid medium in which she can immerse herself, and from which she can emerge with new understandings). What she discovers is somewhat contradictory: "The sea is a source. Consider / the subterfuges of the sea . . ." and "Water followed you inside / your second skin" and "I am my own / barometer, and like the water, always falling" and "water seeks its own level, water / holds its peace." For DeFrees, nature is not quite indifferent—it's something to be contended with, learned from, talked back to. And religion is not so much rejected as incorporated into the lived life:

Bless me, Father,
under heavy sun and hoping
still to make your life my own. I cannot nullify
the work this body's done
nor call each act religion. Wherever one road
joins another, blind, I think of you
and conjure up the loss. When two roads, gaining
speed, speed up to intersect, I cross
myself and lay the body down, arms open for what comes
to pass. Father, I am signing in.

("The Register")

Blue Dusk (the very title reveals a state of mind and being) is a study in self-examination. Madeline DeFrees has taken an unflinching look at what has made her tick. In probing deep, she has opened up wide vistas. The book ends with a poem from her 1991 collection, saying, "I cannot love my yield / the less because of this / late gathering," and we can only love it more for the interlude that allowed for such a generous perspective. Taken together, these poems name the writer. Their aim was not so much song, but singing. They say, "the poetry means: itself."

Linda Gregerson's *Waterborne* is her third book over a twenty-year span. There's something to be said for giving oneself time as a writer—time to ponder, to live, to realize that reconstruction is not the same thing as recording. Reconstruction carries with it a long view. In Gregerson's case, there was a definite hiatus between her first (1982) and second books (1996) that resulted not only in stylistic changes, but a sense that the intervening years had provided her material. *Waterborne* now manages to carve out its own specific territory. By orchestrating her entire book in three-line stanzas, tercets that allow for fluid thought, thrusting the mind forward and backward simultaneously, connecting past and future in their immediate presence, Gregerson makes a stylistic statement that she expects us to treat this book as more than an ordinary collection of recent poems. Style itself urges us toward synthesis. The task of reading *Waterborne* is not so much to discover each poem's significance as to find a context in which all the poems come together.

What Gregerson has achieved is a sentence that is casual without being conversational—a sentence she breaks into at will with parenthetical addenda. Sometimes these take the expected form of qualifications or asides, sometimes of interior thought or unspoken dialogue; sometimes they are framed as direct address, but usually they are contrapuntal—phrases taken from classical texts to add an over- (or under-) melody. These phrases come from such various sources as the Bible, Shakespeare, Thomas Morton (who came to America in 1625), Sappho, and early religious or political documents. Everyday events are not so much elevated as enlivened by the juxtapositions, with history thus providing the backdrop against which experience is tested. In "Maculate," for example, the poet not only quotes the Bible, but distorts it:

> we always had the Red Cross drive in March
> (*consider*
> *the lilies how they grow*). The snowmelt
>
> frozen hard again, and cinders on the shoveled
> walks.
> I was wearing your grandmother's boots.
>
> (*Consider the ravens, they have neither storehouse*
> *nor barn.*)
> The grocer gave a nickel, I can see him yet,

some people had nothing at all.
And I came
to Mrs. Exner's house (*no thief*

approacheth, neither moth).

Gregerson establishes the device early, and the reader begins to look forward to the way the contemporary story will play itself out when it is held up to the light of the past. When Mrs. Exner (who is poor, and stooped, and an object of ridicule) gives three dollars, the speaker is chagrined, but the understanding of what has just occurred comes through biblical associations.

All the poems in *Waterborne* share the same form and, to a large extent, the same technique. Hovering gingerly between the obscure and the obvious, the poems take us into fluid territory where information is not so much withheld as deferred, leaving the reader hungry before the fact, poised at the tip of knowing. This is, I suspect, because the story itself is not what interests the poet. The story alone would not suffice. The mind at work on the story, the past brought to bear on the present—these are Gregerson's objectives. The effect is not pretentious—it is enticing.

The underlying story is the simple duplication of all our lives: the death of a father, family lore, a sister's chronic medical condition, a child determined to ride her bicycle, a growing relationship with one acre of woods and with the river that determines so much of its ecology. Today's waters, at once threatened and threatening, do not offer up the solace of the past, although under certain circumstances (as in the final section of the title poem), it might look as though they could:

Turning of the season, and the counter-
turn
from ever-longer darkness into light,

and look: the river lifts to its lover the sun
in eddying
layers of mist as though

we hadn't irreparably fouled the planet
after all.
My neighbor's favorite spot for bass is just

below the sign that makes his fishing
rod illegal,
you might almost say the sign is half

the point. The vapors draft their languorous
excurses on
a liquid page. Better than the moment is

the one it has in mind.

Speaking directly to her readers, Gregerson closes the distance between her thoughts and ours. At the same time, she opens wide spaces with her unabashedly cerebral approach. She, too, has something "in mind." Precisely *because of* her scholarly bent, the book coheres; it becomes a study in how the body comes to knowledge—and this is knowledge that can only be gained over time. "Eyes Like Leeks," the opening poem, discusses how we come to understand social constructs; it ends watching a play within a play: "Reader, it's / sharp / as the lion's tooth. Who takes // the weeping away now takes a delight as well, / which feels / for all the world like honest // work. They've never worked with mind before, / the rich / man says. But moonlight says, *With flesh*."

My three favorites in this book demonstrate the embodiment of historical fact. "Cord" re-creates a day of stacking firewood while the speaker's father is dying. The poem talks directly to the dying man, speaking to the reader through indirection. "Double Portrait with American Flags" traces family history by penetrating a photograph, infusing it with Norwegian history—and finding there the reason why the father cannot bear to look at his own daughter. "Half Light" obliquely tells the story of George Wishart, a Protestant martyr of the Scottish Reformation. Here the poet states—in a philosophical voice that can only be said to represent herself—the overriding issues of the collection:

Backward

longing not so much for death-by-proxy as
for that
which makes the dying incidental. Hence

our beggarly rapture at stark divides: the cliffs
on one side, North
Sea on the other, and the mutilated

body (there is nothing quite so good at this)
for scale.

Somewhere between her dense and rigorous first book and this new collection, Linda Gregerson found a way to bring a lifetime's accumulation of knowledge and her own study of Renaissance literature to bear on contemporary issues. It is always well worth the wait to see a poet break out in new and original forms. *Waterborne* is a case of practice made perfect. By positioning the past within the present, the body within the mind, Linda Gregerson shows us the power of confluence.

If the ineffable could be put into words, there would be no need for the word *ineffable*. Li-Young Lee has always given us the unsayable through striking juxtapositions of the spiritual and the mundane. With *Book of My Nights*, Lee has broken an eleven-year silence as a poet. During this time he published a memoir about his experiences as a very young child in Indonesia and his coming to America. In this new book he seems to want to eliminate the world and go directly for ideas. Lee's work has always been inclined toward the visionary and, for some, his immersion in what might be called the transcendental may be what is most valuable, but I am troubled by the way these new poems refuse to be pinned down. The move into full abstraction is a new direction for Lee—and what the new direction denies him is the very particularity that often led to unpredictable but inspired connections. Gone are the trout with slivers of almond, the braid of hair that becomes the rain, the butcher's knife that reveals the immigrant's essential schism. Gone are the things of this world that led to thoughts of the next, as in "I no longer hear the apples fall. But how // they go! Incessantly, though / with no noise, no // blunt announcements of their gravity." Instead, *Book of My Nights* contains such phrases as "when clocks frighten me with their long hair" or, more convolutedly, "Your voice, the size of the heart's / first abandonment, / is for naming // the span each falling thing endures. . . ."

Ostensibly, *Book of My Nights* is a chronicle of sleeplessness, and sleeplessness, we know, has an almost surreal quality. In the dead of the night, the poet can look into his own dark thoughts: into memories of destruction, fears of inadequacy, the mysteries of death itself: "And then that question / from which all the other questions begin." Like Linda Gregerson, Lee has carefully orchestrated his collection, filling his insomniac hours with the worries and insecurities that do not quite disappear with sunrise. He calls out to an invisible God, and the darkness at the other side of the pane is his only answer. Occasionally, he stands face to face with his inscrutable God, and the poems act as though the right words might unlock His inscrutability. There is no doubt that mortality is a central issue—and that the quest for completion (the matching of the name with the silence that surrounds it) has a heightened urgency. But this book begs the question. It prettifies the angst.

"Heir to All" is a good example:

What I spill in a dream
runs under my door,
ahead of my arrival
and the year's wide round,

to meet me in the color of hills
at dawn, or else collected
in a flower's name
I trace with my finger
in a book. Proving

only this: Listening is the ground
below my sleep,
where decision is born, and

whoever's heard the title
autumn knows him by
is heir to all those
unfurnished rooms inside the roses.

The urgency takes precedence over the *source* of urgency. And the answer cannot be found in the deep image, no matter what depths it seems to have come from.

Individual poems here often snatch at meaning in ways that delight. And yet, within the book's conceptual integrity, they have a kind of sameness. How many roses, how many wings, how many silences can one read before they lose their power? I suspect that such images are diminished because they connect the abstract with the abstract. The world recedes, taking second place to mysticism.

There are emotionally engaging poems here—mostly in the final third of the book—though they have a tendency to become lost in the welter of easy assertions that surround them. The middle of "Echo and Shadow," for example, echoes the strengths of Lee's previous books in its transition from the sight of a woman standing in a doorway to the larger questions of purified desire:

A world and a world.

Dying and not dying.
And between them
the curtains blowing
and the shadows they make on her body,

a shadow of birds, a single flock,
a myriad body of wings and cries
turning and diving in complex unison.
Shadow of bells,

or the shadow of the sound
they make in the air, mornings, evenings,
everywhere I wait for her . . .

The beginning of "Praise Them" weds John Berryman with Mark Strand in a way that could almost make a convert:

The birds don't alter space.
They reveal it. The sky
never fills with any
leftover flying. They leave
nothing to trace. It is our own
astonishment collects
in chill air. Be glad.
They equal their due
moment never begging,
and enter ours
without parting day. See
how three birds in a winter tree
make the tree barer.
Two fly away, and new rooms
open in December.

The ending of the poem suggests that humans should aspire to the birds' "untroubled and untroubling gaze." Surely, though, the "troubled" human condition occasions the entire book.

Years ago I went on record in these pages (with words now on the back cover of *Book of My Nights*) as feeling that Li-Young Lee is one of our finest younger poets. Perhaps Lee received too much attention too early in his career. Perhaps this occasioned some loss of direction. At any rate, I sense the intervening years as "troubled"—a lacuna that marks a wavering or change of vision. At stake may be what will happen to the power shown in his earlier work. Poets must write without taking the critics into account, and critics must remember that such changes often prefigure further development. *Book of My Nights* may have been published too soon, without enough editorial intervention. If it reflects—as I hope it does—a poet in transition, let's hope the next book will bear the fruits of what seems to have been a fallow period.

After a hiatus of fifteen years, Philip Schultz has published his third book, *The Holy Worm of Praise*. What's changed, for Schultz, is not the expansive, breakneck, gloriously rhythmic sentences that characterize his style, but his fundamental stance toward his material. Gone is the amusingly boisterous doom and gloom that occasioned the need for the invention of Guardian Angel Stein. This new collection begins with praise, giving thanks for a long list of experiences and influences. The list tumbles down the page in first person plural, a litany of communal circumstances, given voice in Schultz's inimitable fashion. Just a few examples from the title poem demonstrate the cadence that provides his distinctive momentum:

> our Nijinsky leaping off the tongue's springboard
> our Talmudic rapture and musical pajamas
> our brass candlesticks gleaming like Statues of Liberty
> our circular journey to singular moments
> the organ crescendoes of our lies and promises
> our crawling dubitably along godless lifelines
> our daily umbrage and masticating jaws and death row memoirs
> our Euclidean fornication and obsessive sucking
> our forgiving no one anything

By the end of the poem, though, the "us" is acknowledged as being "one among many," and it is in this spirit that *The Holy Worm of Praise* continues its expedition.

Schultz admits that "I lived in a monologue a long time," that "it remembered every insult," and that "the past was its domain." The fifteen-year interval, then, marks a division. The slightly bitter undercurrent is gone. This book has the future as its domain. Schultz takes us through this process of transformation to the moment when "something is different, / refined like an eyebrow dormer, enhanced / like a slap on the back at the right moment, / a smile thirty years late and therefore all the sweeter. . . ." That "something" is later given a name—Monica—with a marriage and children (and a future) to celebrate. The speaker can, by the end of the book, say goodbye to Stein, consigning him to another less fortunate soul.

There's more to this shift than just outlook. There's an essential optimism that alters the terms of the poems: the similes move toward light rather than darkness; the ampersands have become *ands*; the poems have given up their bravado in favor of bravery. This does not mean, however, that Schultz no longer tackles the difficult material of his past. It just means that, even when the poems return to familiar territory (Grandma, the old neighborhood, the ill-fated inventions of the speaker's father, his mother's loneliness and, later, her Alzheimer's disease), the past is at last forgiven.

I find it hard to say "speaker" when discussing poems set in the Rochester, New York, of Schultz's childhood. Let's say "poet" here, allowing him the real and vivid aural memories in "Stories": the water jumping in the bathtub (*raau-uummppphh*) and his mother's singing (*lala aaa uuiieeoo laaa*) as she tickles him into his pajamas and tells the old stories that are, in the end, her legacy. The resurrected past is freed from blame. Even the faces in the photos of children in "The Children's Memorial at Yad Vashem," stoic in their resignation, may, in some way, forgive the God who wrote them "in one of his glistening books":

> Philosophy cannot help us,
> nor wisdom, or time.
> Or memory.
>
> We look at their faces and their faces look at us.
> They know we are pious.
> They know we grieve.
> But they also know we will soon leave.
> We are not their mothers and fathers,
> who also could not save them.

The final section contains one twenty-five-page poem entitled "Souls Over Harlem." Its epigraph is from Wallace Stevens, but it owes everything to William Carlos Williams' "Paterson." It's not as long or as full or as quirky, but it accomplishes something equivalent to that masterpiece. It's a complex poem, not so much in structure as in the layering of experience, weaving the life of the speaker—personal memories, anecdotes, letters, a news bulletin on the car radio, the suicide of an old friend twenty-seven years ago, the history of resistance to the Vietnam War, the difficult history of racism, the hard history of immigration—with the story of an actual crime. "Souls Over Harlem" is an important poem; at its center is an instance of mass murder and arson to which the poem repeatedly returns, elaborating not only the causes and consequences of this event, but also the imagined stories of the participants—their backgrounds, their daily lives, their dreams. In a poem both brutal and compassionate, elements combine and recombine to gather many disparate threads into one shared history:

Tonight,
in bed, Monica remembers
her mother's argument
with memory (whether
her mother's cattle car had a stove,
she recalls something burning)—
I say, of course the mind
demands a stove, only so
much reality can be sustained
before the mind disappears
inside its dreams. I think,
of course Abubunde Mulocko
owned an argument, a stove
he couldn't forgive.

. . . .

My father's
immigrant eyes
flashed in the slats
of shivering rain
as he torched
a clothing warehouse
for insurance

. . . .

Napoleon
the doorman
is interviewed on TV
on his way home from work,
stands on 125th Street
in front of a black hole
in the ground, shakes
his head, "Will this community
survive? Man, you
gotta be kidding."
Behind him, screams
(I imagine) ricochet
and tinsel angels
float
in a whoosh of red air.

This surprising new volume deepens Philip Schultz's vision and registers a shift in attitude as, after an admittedly self-imposed silence, he enters the realm of dialogue. Simultaneously sobering and ebullient, *The Holy Worm of Praise* is proof that patience has its own rewards.

Natasha Trethewey's second book, *Bellocq's Ophelia*, demonstrates another kind of lacuna—one between kinds of texts as well as the historical periods in which they were created. Here the author bridges a century-wide gap, taking as her subject E. J. Bellocq's photographs of prostitutes in New Orleans in the early 1900s, collected in a book called *Storyville Portraits*. *Bellocq's Ophelia* raises issues of narration and invention. Trethewey has provided the imagined life of one of these young women, Violet to the men who frequented the brothel, but Ophelia to herself. Ophelia is the daughter of a black woman and a white man, has endured a childhood of hard work and poverty, has managed to acquire some education, and has fled to New Orleans to find employment. Starving, she is selected by Countess P—, and her new, interior life begins.

There are many ways to tell a story, and Trethewey has chosen to give us Ophelia from several angles, almost as though the poet, too, were posing her. The opening poem is an account of the origin of the project. One photograph reminds the poet of Millais' painting of Shakespeare's Ophelia and, in this leap from one art to another, she names the unknown subject whose life gives voice to this book. The poem exposes the imagination of the writer as she creates not so much a persona as a character: "Her body limp as dead Ophelia's, / her lips poised to open, to speak." The next voice we hear is Ophelia's, writing home about her difficulties in finding work. And after that, "Countess P—'s Advice for New Girls":

> See yourself through his eyes—
>
> your neck stretched long and slender, your back
> arched—the awkward poses he might capture
> in stone. Let his gaze animate you, then move
>
> as it flatters you most. Wait to be
> asked to speak. Think of yourself as molten glass—
> expand and quiver beneath the weight of his breath.
>
> Don't pretend you don't know what I mean.
> Become what you must. Let him see whatever
> he needs. Train yourself not to look back.

The obvious application to photography is not lost.

Two series of poems dominate the collection, "Letters from Storyville" and "Storyville Diary." In this way, Trethewey is able to make subtle distinctions between what one tells (and the voice one uses) to another, and what is kept for the self. Ophelia remains essentially the same in each—refined, somewhat proper, articulate, attuned to nuance. The letters, written by Ophelia to her former teacher, allude to the other women, memories of the farm, even her "work" and how she is able to remove herself into the realm of fantasy. In her precise, ladylike language, Ophelia even confesses, "It troubles me to think that I am suited / for this work—spectacle and fetish—a pale odalisque." The prostitutes—featured for clients as "octoroons"—are seen as exotic, and in these letters the presence of Bellocq is first mentioned. The section ends with a distanced description of one of his photographs, all carefully told in a narrative third person until the voice of the writer intrudes, just slightly, in the last three lines:

> It's easy to see this is all about desire,
>
> how it recurs—each time you look, it's the same moment,
> the hands of the clock still locked at high noon.

The diary entries are private, self-absorbed, meditative. Each is given a title as well as a date, indicating its particular focus. All fourteen lines long, these "sonnets" reveal the internal thoughts that were not stated in the letters. Here we see Ophelia's state of mind, the way each white man calls up her memories of her father until

> I search now for his face among the men
> I pass in the streets, fear the day a man
> enters my room both customer and father.

In these entries, we learn how Ophelia responds to being photographed, how she learns to be still, to "wear skin like a garment, seamless." She realizes that she is as much the creator of the photograph as he is. Gradually, Ophelia begins to see with a photographer's eyes, and the world opens up to her in darks and lights, sunlight and shadow. She thinks in terms of how to stop time, how to capture the moment as she has been captured on film:

> No sun, and the city's a dull palette
> of gray—weathered ships docked at the quay, rats
> dozing in the hull, drizzle slicking dark stones
> of the streets.
>
> ("Spectrum")

The final poem, "Vignette," imagines Bellocq and Ophelia preparing for what became the cover photograph. Throughout the book, a scattering of poems written in third person act as a kind of frame, as if representing an objective eye. The third-person narration here, however, differs from the declarative mode of its earlier appearances. The voice is clearly speculative, proceeding from "perhaps" to "maybe" to "suppose" to "imagine." In this way, the poet again asserts her presence:

> Bellocq takes her, her brow furrowed
> as she looks out to the left, past all of them.
> Imagine her a moment later—after
> the flash, blinded—stepping out
> of the frame, wide-eyed, into her life.

The implication is that there was a real woman, a real life. Ophelia, briefly made real through the imagination, is again relegated to the realm of the photograph—at once factual and unknowable. She looks past all of us, with her secret, forgotten name intact.

That the author understands her own subtle interaction with Bellocq's photographs is undeniable. Clearly she feels responsible both for her own creation and for what we know of historical truth. She does not offer up this work in the cavalier spirit of postmodern play, but with what could almost be called a reverence for the irreducible individuality of the unknown, unnamed woman whose being she has taken as her subject. The few poems told in what approximates Natasha Trethewey's own voice bring a twenty-first-century perspective on a time fraught with significant history—that of the immediate past (abolitionism, Civil War) and that of the immediate future (desegregation, civil rights). Trying on various points of view, Trethewey positions her subject, much as a photographer would, caught in the crux of change. *Bellocq's Ophelia* is orchestrated so precisely in order to pay homage to interiority. And it does so in measured, musical poems of unusual complexity. If Trethewey takes sufficient developmental time between books—the creative interlude—she may well find other subjects and structures worthy of her considerable talent.

The Fact of the Room

On Albert Goldbarth's *Budget Travel through Space and Time*; Quan Barry's *controvertibles*; Joseph Stroud's *Country of Light*; Ann Townsend's *The Coronary Garden*; Kevin Prufer's *Fallen from a Chariot*; and Linda Bierds's *First Hand*.

RECENTLY, ON THE RADIO, I heard about an experiment. Several people were told they would be participating in a study and would need to be interviewed. They were each, in turn, brought into a waiting room where they sat for a few minutes before being called into the interview room. The interview, however, consisted of asking them to describe the waiting room. That was the experiment.

There were interesting differences in the descriptions—and they broke down, to a large degree, along gender lines. The men were usually quite vague. It was just a room, after all, and they were only waiting for the interview to begin. Pressed, they might guess at the colors of the walls. There were a couple of chairs, they thought. A desk. A window to the left. Yeah, looked out over the parking lot. Asked about the size of the room, they were more specific. Fourteen-by-sixteen, they guessed. Maybe sixteen-by-eighteen.

The women, on the other hand, had no idea about the size of the room. Medium-sized, for a waiting room. Reminiscent of the old breadbox routine, it was bigger than the dentist's, but smaller than a classroom. Medium. The walls, oh, they could argue about the tint, but they knew the color—mauve—or a variation of mauve, with white trim, and they remembered the curtains as having a kind of mauve and gray pattern. And Venetian blinds. On the desk there were three books, maybe four, placed near the outside corner, some paper stacked neatly, a phone. Some pencils, in a holder. It was an orderly desk. Pressed, they might be able to tell you the color of the book jackets. A couple had even peeked at the titles. They went on—the colors of the chairs, the design, where they were placed. The pictures on the walls.

Without getting into whether these differences are brain- or culture-induced (though the recent mapping of the X chromosome suggests greater differences than previously thought), it is clear that, for the few minutes that the room became a part of their ongoing stories, different people noted its details in varying degrees of specificity, and they noted different details depending on their own interests and inclinations. Thus the men's ability to gauge dimensions, the women's sense of the décor. And they had varying degrees of curiosity, or decorum, that led them to snoop (or not) at the contents of the desk.

If it had been my experiment, I'd have asked for more than detail. I'd have wanted to know what they had been thinking about while they sat in the room. Why did they notice certain objects? Had they speculated about the interview? The interviewer? What kind of person did they think worked at such a desk?

We all pour the facts of the world through the sieve of our interests and inclinations. Now that I have young grandsons, I notice other people's babies and toddlers. A few years from now, I'll notice kindergartners at play. Now that I live in the Northwest, I remark on how small the trees seem when I drive through New England. My world has expanded to include orcas and the warning signs that tell you to go to high ground during a tsunami. On the other hand, the facts of mid-April snowstorms and white-tailed deer have been tucked into something we'd call "memory," but which is really facts-in-absentia—something to be called up when needed, though no longer part of daily living.

By the same token, we've come to expect that our poets will give us a special filter through which to experience the things of the world, one that employs the lens of insight, or the shaping frame of metaphor. We believe that they will hand us back the room—the fact of the room—somehow transformed. We will see it with fresh eyes, will note its details and make meaning of them. We will imagine who is beyond the door and what other worlds will open when we open it. I'd like to look at the "things on the desk" of six very different kinds of poets: at how, and why, they handle facts—and how, and why, they hand them back to us.

In Albert Goldbarth's case, the desk is more than cluttered; it has shoes and ships and sealing wax—a jampacked ecstasy of found objects spilling over its edges, stuffed into the drawers, piled knee-deep on the floor. Comic books, nudie magazines, 116 postcards of the Eiffel Tower (one for each year of its existence), a windup sushi.

The cover art for his latest book, *Budget Travel through Space and Time*, is a 1727 print called "A Voyage to Cacklogallinia," used with permission of the Ordway Collection at the U.S. Space & Rocket Center in Huntsville, Alabama. I've been to the center, and it's full of fascinating detail of man's probe into space—but I never saw the likes of this eighteenth-century imagination that pictures a palm-covered shoreline, galleons in the bay, and above, looking a bit like migrating geese, a flock of chickens bearing a canopied litter with one (he must be) scientist off into the cloud-filled sky. It's the perfect cover for what happens on the pages in between.

At first glance, it might seem that Albert Goldbarth seeks out the oddball tidbit, the strangest of the strange—the clothes Martin Van Buren wore to campaign in 1828, the nation of Tuvalu sinking into the Pacific, the (by now) myriad test tubes growing HeLa cells named for Henrietta Lacks, whose tumor furnished them—in order to take us on a kaleidoscopic romp through the outlandish. True, but only partly true—because Goldbarth feeds on fact. In fact (ha!), a direct IV line of fact flows constantly into his imagination, creating something new, something of Goldbarthian proportions, which is to say something both wonderfully fanciful and devastatingly true. And we are the lucky recipients, transported into realms we hadn't thought to think of. Budget travel, yes, when for a mere fourteen dollars you can go out so far and in so deep.

Goldbarth goes to fact for some of the same reasons he went, in "Scale-Model Sketch," to a Mexican village:

> And why
> I was there?—the skin I'd been born into
> wasn't enough, I guess; its far-outfurling mesh
> of connections wasn't enough. I wanted more
> inside me, more digestion stones, the way the owl has,
> and more for them to go to pulverizing
> work on.

Why do I act so confidently as though the "I" of the poem—the one who saw the moon reflected in a jar of water on his backstairs in a village "unmasked of anything urban"—is as close to being Goldbarth himself as it's possible to be on the page? Because *Budget Travel* makes of this "I" not so much a narrative persona as a prober and prodder and synthesizing sensibility, in short, a roving imagination in the process of putting things together. It enters the poems at will and it speaks directly to the reader, both in offhand comments ("Was she a clock? Well, yeah: *of course* / a body's a clock) and direct address ("Now this is the part where you / enter the poem. You heard me: // you"). And this "I," in turn, becomes the object of its own inquisition: "God, / Did *I* write that? Did I *write* that?" Like the cells in the body that keep changing, this self is protean, constantly revised and renewed and reconsidered.

Albert Goldbarth may be interested in facts, but *Budget Travel through Space and Time* is far more concerned with what can never be known, the spaces where edges blur—as in all the lost histories in the old people's home, as in the moment when twilight banks toward night, as in the inaudible inspirations between life and death, as in fog (the operative image in the book), as in the air through which the present self reaches back to the adolescent he was (now "only a hole in the air"), as in "the moth / invisible against a ground of jungle moss and guano," as in all things (Goldbarthianly graphically) indistinguishable, "*like spit on cum*." All the facts crowd around, putting pressure on meaning. But nothing means more than the invisible arc between the facts, the energy generated simply by touching one wire to the other, and the belief—yes, belief, as in the moment when you *know* (there's no other word for it) that the derivative exists, that you've crossed the indefinable territory between Δ and *d*—that something new has come into the world. Not just the poem, but new *meaning*.

Budget Travel shifts its emphasis from the micro and macro of Goldbarth's earlier books ("the far perimeters—the bugs; the stars—inside of which our little, loopy / human selves get lived") to the selves themselves. Using his own "self" as a ground, the poet names himself, his friends, his family, his haunts, his various activities (topless bar, library, late-night conversation), or calls up historical figures or events, in order to establish the substantial through which the insubstantiality can be measured. He is unadulteratedly the writer of the pieces, often reminding the reader that he's mentioned something before, remarking on the typo in the epigraph he's used as a point of departure, inserting the notes he's written for himself, footnoting the poems, even forcing the reader to look back ("But it wasn't a deer / I was talking about in section 3"), or into ("But aren't *all* prayers aerosol?"). He even takes on a reviewer—enough to make you worry about what you say—and he does all this to establish the umbilical link between writer and reader. These poems *demand* not only our attention, but our participation. For Albert Goldbarth, the facts he unearths are merely a vehicle for the journey they will launch—budget travel inside the brain. He gives us the facts as he encounters them, and thus we take part, traveling along the dendrites to unknown worlds. The ubiquitous question mark that reveals his thinking process also asks that we follow its logic; we write ourselves into its foggy ambiguities and emerge still questioning.

Part of our willing participation comes from the enticing informality of the voice, its conversational style, and part comes from the way Goldbarth continually startles us with his coined combinations. Nothing is more fun than when he goes through a list of antiquated words, imagining a future when "clit ring" has gone the way of "pinafore." There's a balance even in the universe of language; we can't gain "wonky" without the loss of "sillibub." And nothing is more moving than when Goldbarth touches some part of our shared humanity, as in the ending of "Scenes from the Next Life" when he speaks for the boy whose mummified body was found with the wing of an ibis attached to its shoulder:

> To be half a bird is to be
> completely a monster. Even so, I love to feel this delicate
> comb of bone—that I've been given instead of an arm—
> accept the rush of evening air; and if I lift it then,
> I can be played on like a harp. If I don't know
> the euphoria of flight itself, at least
> I know the quieter joy of its blueprint.

Paying homage to both space and time, Graywolf Press has found the perfect format for these poems. The oversized pages do justice to the lines and allow the poems to remain visually intact. *Budget Travel* is a long book (162 pages), but its nine sections seem to float on air—like skipping stones hovering over water, marking time in quicker and quicker intervals. And Goldbarth pays homage to the past (about a quarter of the poems are written in segments comprising "a sonnety fourteen lines") even as other poems leap into a future of omitted letters, long prose sections, embedded research, and the implied questions to which imagined answers abound.

To demonstrate the spandex elasticity of these poems, one would, well, need to print an example in full. But Goldbarth's poems are long, complex, unwieldy beasts, averaging around four pages. Thus the reviewer is reduced to some approximation of an approximation.

The back jacket of *Budget Travel* claims that Goldbarth is now "creating at the height of his powers." If this is so, what can Goldbarth do next? Offer up more of the same (which he more deftly phrases "enough the same / to be the same") until it ceases to amaze us? Luckily for us, it will cease to amaze Goldbarth first, so we can predict that he'll find something new to do. Meanwhile, he gives us a book that shimmers with love and sex and friendship and aging and death and a zillion other things in equal measure. Hovering over this particular collection, the BIG QUESTION accumulates its own power. "Some Ways" puts it this way:

It happens as many ways as there's us.
The image I prefer is simply the end
of an ordinary day, when the colors are deep,
and we stand outside, and silently, as one,
the shadows are called back into our bodies.

As if to confirm the singular experience of death, Goldbarth provides a matching definition of life: "For this we fight, to be a single cohesive perimetered thing. And if not?—'senescence,' we call it. 'Transcendence,' if it's desirable." *Budget Travel through Space and Time* encompasses the very recent technologies that can take us to the first instants of time and space, and also to the mysteries that remain mysterious, as in the individuality we bring with us on our journey through the fallopian tube. The book's aim is wonder—a wonder that, in an age of "überglobal, multizillion-dollar, telecyberfiber transport system(s)," taxes the imagination at ever-increasing speeds. And its aim is unadulterated joy—at the whole shebang, the gist and jism of the universe.

Quan Barry's desk is divided into two distinct areas: on the left, one pile of objects—a velvet-lined box, carved ivory, a blue and white porcelain vase, but also a neon-yellow highlighter and a pocket radio; on the right, another pile of objects, slightly less defined but including driftwood, a marble with a green hue, cotton batting. In between, the slippery space in which the mind flits, making connections between the two piles.

Each of the forty-nine poems in Barry's second collection, *controvertibles*, juxtaposes disparate things/events/concepts, viewing one in terms of another. Each title (e.g., "the seahorse as transubstantiation," "the Great Molasses Flood of 1919 as allegory," "Vietnamese Dictionary Definition as Self-Portrait," etc.) provides the framework for a kind of large-scale *logopoeia*. The word *controvertible* (Barry has borrowed the noun Dickinson made of an adjective, and even the adjective is somewhat elusively defined in my dictionaries) seems to claim some element of the debatable—the competing emotions/responses that swirl up when two images/ideas collide. The rhetorical construction is not quite a conceit, but a vehicle by which each side of the "equation" informs the other, somehow in the mix defining a new, and hybrid, space. Even before entering the poem, the mind rushes quickly to bridge the gap.

And here lies the rub. The "facts" are given primarily in the titles. For the most part, we can follow the generated sparks that arc between the two poles of the poem's inception, and can feel the combustion, if you will. But some of these poems work better than others simply because they *depend* on the reader's knowledge or sophistication. Suppose one reads "snow angels as Michael Furey" having made angels in the snow (thus responding to the question "What makes the short-lived / beautiful?") but without having read Joyce? Or maybe having read "The Dead," but having forgotten the name of the man in the distant graveyard over which the snow is falling? What would you then make of these lines: "Why does everyone need to believe that someone / would die for them?" The generated space of the poem rapidly loses intensity when the concepts or images through which things are transformed are rarefied. This happens most often when the second half of the "equation" is abstract or theoretical (as in "metempsychosis," "psychostasia," "resipiscence," "semiotics," or "jeremiad"). Yet this cannot be the only indicator, because two of the most powerful poems in the collection are "purdah as polemic" and "ultrasound as palinode." In the latter, Barry names her own nemesis:

> Or the dilemma of having a critical language before the poem physically exists—
> i.e., theory superseding the line.
>
> Yes, there is a beauty in transparency, in explanation,
> in rendering.
>
> But I want the difficulty, the *first there was nothing*
> & the *then there was light.*
>
> In my hands the image of her body like the prow of something
> wriggling into being.
>
> Because poetry should inform theory & not the other way around.
>
> *Sophie.*

The naming of this "small moon" supersedes any theory the poet has previously called upon. And Barry positions the poem near the end of the book, as a kind of overarching commentary on her own methods.

The facts in *controvertibles* are often high-toned (paintings, theater, music), sometimes making the poems feel a bit too clever or esoteric. A few are culled from more recent history or pop culture (Richard Nixon's 1972 Christmas bombing campaign, Doug Flutie's 1984 Orange Bowl Hail Mary pass), thus making of the poem an intermediary between the public event and something intensely personal. The reader is transported into an arena where, as in "the seahorse as transubstantiation," private associations are given context:

I imagine it was a creature like this at the annunciation, something mysterious & derivative & spiked w/grace. Something extracted from the sea five thousand by five thousand times. Something medicinal & tidal. A conveyance.

Who doesn't want to be altered?

When I take you into me, I become you, we are thirded & furious. The night spreads like oil. When we rise salt-skinned from the water, everything is demonstrative.

Interestingly, the most private (even obscure) poems benefit most from Barry's rhetorical device. By filtering experience through an intervening image, the "I" seems, somehow, more available. Vietnam ("that some of us were foundlings / & that some of us were given up freely") becomes a window to perspective ("Who made this shard-filled thing winged like a butterfly? // All week I expected to see that light, to put my foot down on the earth / & come away changed w/what only the body knows: // emanation. The fallacy of closure"). Or the poem can reveal the undersides of what inspired it, as in "domestic violence as Noh play," where brutality is all the more shocking presented in this formal guise:

Don't let the stylization confuse you—the *koken* cloaked in black, how each stagehand
materializes in the scene, deals the protagonist his weapon,
& vanishes.

That night the only music was the phone's ringing.

Afterward I remember looking at her face—the carved wood's deepening azure—
& the moonlight slashing through the window
like a sword.

The poems of *controvertibles* are best read two—or three—times so that the carved space they generate becomes a solid sculpture of its own. These poems are smart and savvy—perhaps, as the saying goes, too clever by half. They smack of the academy (no blurb should use the word *contextualizing*), so they may deter as many readers as they entice. And they suffer slightly from their formulaic conception. But to turn away too quickly from the intellectual challenge they present—or to miss the lyric impulse that fuels them—would be to overlook Quan Barry's genuine achievement: the recombinant DNA of metaphor that hands back fact, transformed.

Joseph Stroud's desk is orderly, even ascetic. Three white sheets of paper. A black pen. On one corner, near the back, there's a globe. And the room—its white walls, its simple rug, the hand-hewn rafters. Stroud's fourth book, *Country of Light*, is a study in various simplicities. He uses facts not as a springboard for imagination but to ground us in the slow, steady reality of daily living. They are as cleanly, and as honestly, given to us as the potato handed to the poet by a peasant on his way to Machu Picchu. They serve to remind us that things are sometimes simply what they appear to be, surfacing in his poems the way the turtle surfaces in "At the Well of Heavenly Clarity": "It turned its head a moment, looking around at the world, then sank back into the well." For Stroud, the naming is sometimes enough. The holding to the light.

The informing spirits of *Country of Light* are Li Po and Neruda, and Stroud moves easily from the concise to the voluptuous, from "I have much to learn of patience" to "Like a hand / from the dark house / arose the intense / perfume / of firewood. / A visible scent / as if the tree / were alive." He also moves easily between the lyric and the narrative, the compression and brevity of his series of six-line observations and the expansive informality of the prose poem—one whole section consisting of prose poems in the voice of Giotto. Stroud's poems roam the world—Latin America, Spain, thirteenth-century Italy, a cabin in the high Sierras, Vietnam. Along the way, they explore a range of emotions, embracing the capricious humor of "The Old Poets Home"—

> What do you do if you're a poet and you come to that place where there are no more poems, when the words are all used up for you, when the muse won't give you the time of day, or night, what do you do, do you go to the Old Poets Home, sit around with Orpheus and Homer and all the other silverbacks, Sappho in a bouffant blue-gray wig sipping sherry, Eliot with his mouth like a prune, and what do they do there, trade images, recall great lines, complain all day how all the new poems seem so slick, so enameled, so gussied up, so much *froufrou* and decoration, such silliness strutting around acting important . . .

—along with the contemplative reflection of "Reading Wallace Stevens" (printed here in full)—

> I close the book and look out the window
> up the hillside from the cabin where a stag
> and two does pass through the sunlight
> and through shadows between the pines,
> disappearing among the colors they are,
> appearing among the colors they are not.

—as well as, in "Stitching the Woe Shirt," the stark *factual* facing of grief:

Inconsolable

*

As if a word could name it

*

As if sorrow were an ax

*

As if a prophet opening the body could read the future

*

As if a god reached in and scattered her across time

*

Inconsolable

*

As if *grief* and *anguish* and *desolation* were threads

*

As if this poem were a needle

If these poems are about learning how to live in the world, part of the learning process is reading other poets. Stroud almost literally communes with earlier writers, bringing them to life by fitting his moods to theirs. "Reading Joyce in Winter" brings snow to Shay Creek ("the silence so huge / I can hear snow falling over the Spur") until it falls also on the Shannon waves, ending with the final words of "The Dead." "Late Night, Year's End, Doing the Books with Tu Fu" rather raucously takes the Chinese poet into his balance sheet: "Instead of numbers, let me enter words / into the ledger, this account of our friendship, this little poem from me to you." And "Dancing with Machado" moves through personal grief to celebration:

Machado danced
the color of light on the mountains—
I danced the silver of leaves—together
we danced the sun on the river—
just the two of us, two men
dancing alone in the shimmering
fields of Baeza.

However, in "The Death of Lorca" imagination is usurped by fact, and the poem ends with this account: "An hour after the executions, the gravedigger arrived. He recognized the two bullfighters, observed that the third man had a wooden leg, and the fourth wore a loose tie—*you know, the sort that artists wear*. He buried the bodies in a trench, one on top of another, in no particular order." Stroud finds fascination—and horror—in what the world has to offer up; he seems more intent on the experience itself than on making something of it.

In Stroud's hands, the poem itself becomes a fact, with the weight and solidity of a made object. Within that object, however, there is a fluidity, a sense of its coming into being, something like watching as the potter spins his wheel and the bowl is pulled up out of the clay. "Wintering" is a good example. Time ebbs and flows. The poem slowly unfolds, beginning in the recent past—"Woke this morning"—and touching lightly on details: woodstove, coffee, silence. Looking ahead, the speaker makes plans for the day, then steps back into a memory of the day before—stacking firewood, the clouds, the impending storm—only to arrive at the present moment again ("now this morning the first snow"). Dipping into a more distant past, he recalls a line from an ancient poem, then pictures the future—"I think of the winter to come." Again detail, but this time it's anticipatory: light, canyon, woodstove, logs, silence, where he can envision himself "honing my spirit / in the country of light."

The book's fourth section, "Passing Through," ends with a sequence of six poems set in contemporary Vietnam, a combination of travelogue, conversation, dictionary, history, and hallucination. Whether through the violent imagery of the war and its lingering effects, or the six tones of *ma* that differentiate *ghost* from *mother* from *which* from *rice seedling* from *tomb* from *horse*, the reader steps into the poet's shoes. We travel together, moving from AK-47s, bomb craters filled with water, and white silk *ao dais* up through the jungle, the mist, and the mountains, until, in "Country of Clouds," we hear an echo of "Wintering": "so we climb higher / until at last we come out // into a country of light." Although the poem goes on and we descend, Shay Creek and Vietnam are linked linguistically—as if, in Joseph Stroud's perception, all poems are one poem, and we can watch it crystallize around the stark, salient fact of his being in, and of, this world.

Ann Townsend's desk—rich rosewood with a teak inlay, a deep blue old-fashioned blotter, a photo in a silver frame—fits neatly under a window looking out at a garden basking in the stilled, late-afternoon light. Three leather-bound volumes, open, with bookmarks at specific pages. A yellow pitcher, filled with bright red tulips. The tulips have been gathered from Townsend's second book, *The Coronary Garden*, which takes its title from an unfinished chapter in a seventeenth-century botanical treatise with a focus on flowers that can be fashioned into garlands or crowns. And the poems, likewise, have the formal elegance of an English garden.

The cover jacket praises this book for its love poems, and it's true that love is their subject. The speaker pays attention to its every detail (her lover's short-cropped bristling hair, his muscles as he mows, the missed heartbeat of the first kiss), and she perfectly captures the giddy charge of physical attraction in "Mindful of You," where the odd setting only fuels the speaker's awareness of the other: "It was a funeral / but I felt happy shame pressing / against my eyelids." Yet love threatens privacy and complicates the emotions, so these poems are really best characterized by one of the titles, "Love Poem, Unwritten." "Something keeps me / from saying the words," the speaker says, then she says them instead in image, in her rapt attention to the sound of the neighbor's earthmover whose stutter calls up memory, becoming the "stammering letter to you / that I fail and fail to send." Often, as in the final lines of "Your Body's Weight upon Me," the idea inherent in the image remains deliberately mysterious, unable, quite, to bridge the gulf between fact and implication:

> Exactly how you claimed me
> is best left to the ellipses, the silent margins—
> better to say
> that in the market place
> the vendor wraps his flowers in butcher paper
> and twine, and ties the knot twice:
> when you buy it you take it out into the cold.

The operative image of flowers often serves Townsend as an objective correlative: "They Call You Moody" looks into a "proneness to sadness," and suddenly everything—the jack-pine, the crows, the whole turbulent sky—seems to mirror the mood while "the crocuses snap open on their crazy / hinges." Or, in "Geraniums," the flowers "fail to thrive," reminiscent of what a doctor said when speaking about a baby. By the end of the summer the geraniums have withered, and the speaker, haunted by the terminology, says, "I watched the boy die, leaf by leaf." The world is too much with us in these poems: it presses against the eyelids with its colors and sounds; it hurts us with its knives. No wonder that, in "St. Veronica's Trials" and "Just Toast, Thank You," Townsend explores the ascetic impulse to renounce such a world. Love is continually undercut by its own fragility. It is fraught with death, with the unbearable beauty of a transitory garden.

This is never more true than in the title poem, on which the book opens. The speaker is addressing someone who has attempted suicide, someone whose bandaged wrists are seen as tulips. It's a poem of helplessness, handled with reticent dignity. The speaker moves in and out of time, fascinated by the properties of blood, fascinated by the botanical descriptions of the various flowers, alternately courting and fending off the poem's understated anguish: "and if

I loved you better // would this mortal scene stay unwritten?" But love is not sufficient:

> Despair needles you with its whisper,
> it is agnostic, it believes in irony,
> like a fly's buzz it is perception, a busy
>
> blood clot that stays alive, alive.

The speaker remains mindful of the separation: "I'm not the stopped motion, the straight line out." To love is to be vulnerable, and throughout the collection the narrating sensibility explores that vulnerability, never quite learning to live with the questions it raises.

The "things" of this book are not so much facts as they are the markers of everyday living: food (there's a deliciously acerbic poem about cooking for a guest), garden (which extends to field and the nameless horse who owns it with such presence), immediate family, friends. The "facts" here are emotional truths, and Townsend feels her way delicately through them. She distinguishes her poems from more traditional pastoral poetry by complicating the emotions, embracing human complexities, and introducing an inquisitorial narrator, as well as by liberating the line so that everything—detail, description, and doubt—floats free and unfettered. The poems link interior to exterior in the hesitant spaces surrounding the lines. For example, in "Mouse's Nest" the cumulative facts, as such, are subsumed in the larger movement of the poem, so that its ending, in which the speaker tosses the baby mice outdoors, juxtaposes a dozen solid images in such a way that the result delineates the ephemeral:

> so with a shudder
> my hand apprehends
>
> the scoop
> and spoons them furiously out
> the open door,
> into snow melt,
>
> first light, grains scattering
> with the bodies,
> grain wriggling with the life
> that feeds on it.
>
> My breath's a scattershot,
> an arrow, her answer.
> Now, breeze:
> silence wisping in the barn.

For all its emphasis on frailty, this collection is unflinchingly tough, and the candor here is layered with a subtle musical intelligence. Like the two arteries of the aorta, Ann Townsend's poems supply blood directly to the heart; the dichotomous threads of *The Coronary Garden*—passion and its terrifying counterpart—force us to face the thorny nature of our lives, and loves.

Latin texts are strewn all over the sleek modern surface of Kevin Prufer's desk. Stack upon stack, interspersed with yellowing newspaper clippings, back issues of *National Geographic*, and a worn copy of *The Rise and Fall of the Roman Empire*, so that to find something you might need to dig down through the ages, so to speak. A bullet casing. A box of matches. A glass of red wine.

Prufer's third book, *Fallen from a Chariot*, seems to pick up where his previous one, *The Finger Bone*, left off. It is filled with images of violence, not least of which is the cover photo "Corona del Mar," which shows a mangled car that has clearly careened over an embankment and crashed into a telephone pole. Its engine and hood are crumpled into the shattered windshield, and the viewer cannot help but imagine the rest. The title poem opens the book with a scene that seems—except for the snow—to emanate from the photo, as though memory itself has been stirred:

> There is, first of all, her body,
>   and the snow around it
> so, at a glance, it is the glittering body of a god who fell
> too far
>   and can no longer rise, cannot transform—
> a bird, a deer—away.

Throughout the first section of the book this body and this snow and then the ensuing ambulance take on transformative lives, moving through the subsequent poems, shape-shifting, seen first from one angle, then another. Sometimes Prufer speaks in the voice of the dead, sometimes from a narrating persona who recalls scenes from his childhood and his mother's own death, sometimes in the vast impersonal third person ("To the body, the snow is neither cold nor gentle. To the body, there's / a zero where the field should be"). The "I" of these poems is always "the speaker" because Prufer positions himself outside the poem as a presiding sensibility. Thus, as the snow becomes a fallen angel and the angel becomes a doomed airplane and the plane becomes a bird, open for dissection, the roving "I" slips from observer to the one to whom it is happening, the one who can buy a drink as the plane goes down, musing to himself: "that America loves a doomed and falling / populace as much as it loves anything."

So it is that the second section takes the rise and fall of Rome as a presiding metaphor. The lives (and first-person voices) of the emperors play themselves out against a contemporary backdrop. Caesar, Augustus, Nero, and Caligula hover over the conversations of Gracie, Paula, and Wilson, along with the ubiquitous "I" (who sometimes appears in self-referential third-person, as in "He looked up from his book"). Thus the reader comes to understand that the child's history book informs the man's sense of a nation in trouble, probably doomed. These devices are exciting, but the poems must be even more intensely felt by someone who knows the specifics of Roman history. Almost as if to make this point, images from the first section begin to inform the second so that, when we see a horse that has fallen in the streets of ancient Rome and "did not rise when it blew snow against its back / and buried it," we cannot help but associate the horse with the mangled car.

"Facts" abound here, but they are provided from outside instead of originating in lived experience, thus acting more as symbol. Rather than weight the poems with their solidity, the facts seem to liberate them from specific contexts. Prufer's method is collage—a kind of REM amalgamation that is almost, but not quite, surreal. Sentences begin, but do not always end. The poems proceed through association, mixing history with contemporary images of bombs and falling buildings, Nero's fires with modern conflagration, until they act as warning: "The watch ticked on its chain, / but who could read it? Not the Romans, who loved the lukewarm air / of the trepidarium, / who sank, one by one, into the elegant baths." As in "Caligula, Clairvoyant," it's impossible not to conflate our time and theirs, not to read prediction in Prufer's images of the destroyed city:

> And under the park bench, the shadow of the man
> looked toward the ruins of the square, where the cafés had closed,
> the umbrellas folded away—
>   It was a lovely city,
> in its gold coins and arches, splendid where the fires
> spread up the walls like vines.
>   Triple exposure, rot
> where the dulled brain died. And distance
>   made a drama of it.

Distance allows Prufer to dramatize his warnings. The third section posits the endgame. Death comes calling, trailing all the old images

> Snow will continue   to sift into my eyes   fill my eyes
> or rain like hot glass   or wind

and introducing a new one: death by drowning. The speaker stands on the shore, singing like Nero, as the dead have their say.

The fourth section, not surprisingly, reassembles the imagery to build further pictures of destruction. In one poem, the empire is a hidden bomb, ready to split the airplane "like a milkweed pod"; in another the empire is already falling, along with the businessmen, "their red ties streaming behind their necks"; in another it has fallen and, when it fell, "the internet closed / like a refrigerator door." The "chord of bombers" has left smoldering cities, the gladiator's blood has "feathered" on the pavement, in contrast to the active first image in the book, the cars in "Apocalyptic Prayer" are now

> dead on their empty tires,
> their needles on zero and still. The bridge folded
> and the grass grown wild—

The facts of this particular closed world have been made public—and their symbolic implications are unmistakable. Personal nightmare has been transformed into a societal vision.

As *Fallen from a Chariot* catches up the confusion and insistent energy of a mind trying to make sense of the inconceivable, it has the feel of Apollinaire's "Zone" (certainly lines like "The airplane lands at last without folding its wings" or "You have had enough of life in this Greek and Roman antiquity" would fit perfectly into the book's method). "Lemure," spoken in a voice from the tomb, concludes: "The plow goes overhead like an excellent idea, fading when it reaches the corners of the field, then rumbling back." So, too, the excellent ideas of these poems resound. But Prufer's achievement—the beauty he carves out of horror, and the brooding distance through which he compels us to confront our times—could also pose a problem. Precisely because they share a deliberately common imagery, the poems begin to blur into one poem, giving the book the cumulative feel of a project more than discovered insight. And precisely because they stem from a preconceived political position, they seem to want to prove a point. The apocalyptic note may, in the end, prove visionary, or it may date this collection. What will unquestionably not be dated is Kevin Prufer's invigorating talent—the energetic force of his lines as they sing their way across the page.

Linda Bierds's writing table is one clean sweep of mahogany—computer, printer, keyboard, strong black tea on a lacquer tray. Books in floor-to-ceiling cases, perfectly alphabetized. You have to walk into the study, inspect it closely, to see the ancient telescope folded neatly in the corner by the window, to notice the dog's bed covered with a Jacquard quilt, slightly worse for wear.

Outside, the sound of the sea, or less than a sea, but still a muttering of water. It swirls up to fill the cover of her seventh book, *First Hand*, with its watery hues of blues and black.

Bierds opens the book with an author's note that recounts her peering into the microscope in the biochemistry lab at the University of Washington. Recalling her first flawed microscope, Bierds finds in her own experience a version of the scientific strides that have opened our understanding of who and what we are. *First Hand* contemplates a variety of historical figures who have opened scientific doors, beginning in "Prologue" with the child Galileo, who slices through a hailstone with his father's violin string in order to see into the mystery that made him think *horses*, hearing them on the cobbled street. Yet the layers of ice blur even as they are revealed, and the child wishes for better instruments, more perfect conditions, something "without a hint of song." But song accompanies science in this breathtaking book, becomes its companion as Bierds's own meticulous rhythms extend the mysteries of art.

The operative device is repetition: phrases recur in carefully worked patterns, but they mutate, rotating on their stems until, like a helix of DNA, the words themselves recombine to produce new meanings. And certain images reappear in different guises, connecting scientists across the centuries. What is the source of insight? Does art mirror, or predict, the science it so closely resembles? Using a scientific method of her own devising, Linda Bierds tackles the large questions, moving continuously between insight and its inception, trying to bridge the gap between conjecture and proof, the leap of faith that precedes confirmation, that space between teakettle and condensation that is, in fact, the steam. Invisible reality, and the knowing that makes it visible in the mind's eye, unfolding in "Elegance" as definition:

> Elegant, that formula, that sudden click of harmony
> when facts aligned, and matter, from the bee or from
> the bath, lost not itself but simply its perimeter.
> Elegant, that sudden shift beyond the eye, that soundless
> click: clear stone across some greater clarity.

Greater clarity is what *First Hand* is all about. Bierds looks to those moments at the brink of the discoveries that form the foundation for contemporary exploration: Archimedes, Newton, Mendel, Curie, and Watson, along with a number of more obscure scientists. She adds to these the voices of artists and inventors—those whose explorations also realigned our sights, from electricity to moving pictures, from the chiseled stone of Bernini to the chiseled words of Keats. And she looks beyond, through all the "if onlys" that lead to new technology, to the ever-increasing rate of change as the cloned lamb (now old hat) leads us back down into the dark world of doubt. Taking as its representative figure that of the monk Gregor Mendel, whose experimentation with pea plants led to an understanding of genetic heredity, *First Hand* delves into the twin impulses of science and religion. From matins to vespers, Mendel prays to a God he takes on faith; from morning to evening, he thwarts the natural propagation of the peas (some called it heresy) in order to see behind their mysteries. Bierds captures his voice and his meditative mind so that he emerges wholly human in his complex needs. Nothing—not the abbot tending his sheep, not the cat with its sleep-filled eyes, not the patternless petals spilling on the floor—escapes his notice. One good example is "Spillikins: Gregor Mendel at the Table." Note the way the poem—in its mapping of the elaborate spill of the pick-up sticks, in its hesitant, hovering dashes—hints at the helical structure intimated by Mendel's rudimentary experiments:

> On the table, a nest of fretted sticks:
> trefoil, knife blade, horse head, bell,
> snake on a staff, bird on a branch,
> miter, bucket-yoke, fork.
> And at my elbow, black tea,
> the mahogany sheen of contentment.
>
> All afternoon, to train the hand,
> I lifted the snake from the branch,
> the yoke from the horse,
> the bird from the yoke,
> each carved bone such weighted weightlessness.
> And then, through the window, it came—
>
> for a moment, through the window—
> that silence so still it is holy. That stillness
> when the world's swirl suddenly stops
> and everything—wind and whinny and cough—
> is gripped by respite's harmony.
> Then the grip loosened
>
> and all down the hillsides the church bells spilled.
> And under the bells, the birds,
> and under the birds, the metallic chitter
> of knife blades, forks,
> and I rose
> for the body's sustenance.

World and representation shimmer in the hologram, each signifier caught on its way toward the stillness of sign until, with a flick of the wrist, the world emerges in the vibrant energy of sounds repeated (still/stillness, gripped/grip, hillsides/bells/spilled/bells) and sound itself is sustenance.

The inquisitive voices chime across the centuries, their individual, lonely pursuits now fitting neatly together, tongue in groove. How one thing—or fact—informs another over time and space becomes a focus for Bierds's attention. In "The Monarchs," the "shifting, clicking tines" of the multifaceted chandelier heard by Bishop Berkeley become the frozen butterflies falling to the forest floor in modern Mexico. In "Ecstasy," the eerie fact that the actress Hedy Lamarr invented a magnetic code for torpedo guidance systems is played against her filmy magnetism on the screen:

> Look, she whispered,
> there is nothing between us—until nothing
> stopped her airy touch, and nothing
> stirred, and nothing cast its rhythmic clicks
> high in the darkness above them.

From 1942 to the current microchip is hardly a blip on mutation's radar screen. "Sunderance" links the rotor blades Russian fishermen use to cut through ice with the helicopters that saved them from the floes (those "motes // afloat in God's compound eye") in a moment when "all that was mercy could be forged firsthand." "Firsthand" becomes first hand—the originating force we swim our way back to. Science and religion seem inseparable. The dilemma is actually framed in "The Trinity Years":

> How, in light of Creation's complexity, could devotion
> stand free from inquiry, vast love from articulation?

The answer, it seems, lies in the potent imaginative space Bierds carves around her own inquiry. The various personae speak as though the poet had managed to find, in the articulated facts of their lives, the roots of their curiosity. "In how many ways might shape take shape?" is answered by the range of her subjects, the diverse ways she manages to push the poem to the brink of the ineffable, and then beyond. Not until page 54 (of a 71-page book) does Bierds enter these poems as a speaking persona in her own right. Contemplating the physicist Charles Vernon Boys, who in 1879 "touched to a spider's quiet web a silver tuning fork" and watched the spider's response, she becomes an additional respondent. Standing before a painting of a saint, she introduces an "I" who hears her own long A ("although the note I hear / is organ-cast, cathedral-bound") and comments on herself as "Godless in this god-filled room," attuned to the way "like instruments vibrate sympathetically."

Bierds displays the like instrument of her own mind in the measured cadences of the penultimate poem, "Sonnet Crown for Two Voices." These are not Albert Goldbarth's "sonnety fourteen lines," but a tightly sung descant between herself and Mendel, her century and his, as she comes full circle to the moment in the biochemistry lab where a "gloved guide" reveals to her the microscopic world. Speaking first for the self (as the first eight lines resound in their almost iambic beat, "The glow, how can I express it? My god, / it lifts from protein flecks, up and across / this crafted lens"), and then for Mendel (in the more closely iambic sestet), each sonnet balances the scales of what is known—the cyclone of 1870, the cyclone-spun chromatin of 2004—against an unknown future. Just as the cyclone gave Mendel a glimpse of symmetries yet to be discovered, Bierds looks deep into the nucleus and senses the ultimate mystery. As she gives Mendel's enduring faith the final word, even the fact of death takes on a kind of incandescence:

> Silence, then through the frost of shattered glass
> an afterglow arose—or pressed—fully formed
> but borderless. As I will be, the swirling world
> subtracted from the I of me: wind, chalice,
> heartbeat, hand . . . Weightless, measureless, but beautiful
> the glow. How can I express it, my God?

The book, however, has a final word of its own. In its poetic "epilogue," a collage of detail links Ortelius' early maps of South America with Bruegel's landscape of games, the first tulips brought from Constantinople to Antwerp with the rising tide of invaders, until its final image—the Nuremberg Peace Fair of 1650 where fifteen hundred boys on wooden horses rocked in the square, filling it with color "like tulips, some said. Like soldiers, said others"—reveals the subtle moiré patterns of history. As though everything were part of a conscious blueprint, the world reveals "the whole of itself." Like Bernini's marble bees, the poems of *First Hand* fly in the face of gravity. With an austere elegance worthy of a mathematician, Linda Bierds communicates her wonder at the natural design, repeatedly achieving "that sudden click of harmony" where the intellect and the lived fact find congruence.

And my very real desk, cleared now of these six books? The usual mess of paperclips, pens, and index cards, coffee mug and calendar. Nothing remarkable. So I look up. On the windowsill, a glass paperweight: a swirl of pink blossom in a deep blue helix, sun caught on its dome until the rays splay their iridescence over my computer screen. Outside, apple blossoms in the early morning light, white against white. Later, the sky will turn blue over snowcapped mountains—and on the walls, the family photographs, gene pool expanding until I recede, a child in patent leather pumps on the day of my Aunt Margaret's wedding. My mother smiles down enigmatically. My three grandsons watch from behind their mysteries. She would have loved them, my boys' boys. I state it as fact—the fact of this room—and it is.

Raindrops on Roses . . . *

On Albert Goldbarth's *The Kitchen Sink: New and Selected Poems, 1972–2007*; Carl Phillips' *Quiver of Arrows: Selected Poems, 1986–2006*; Robert Wrigley's *Earthly Meditations: New and Selected Poems*; Rebecca McClanahan's *Deep Light: New and Selected Poems, 1987–2007*; Bruce Beasley's *The Corpse Flower: New and Selected Poems*; Paul Zimmer's *Crossing to Sunlight Revisited: New and Selected Poems*; and John Engels' *Recounting the Seasons: Poems, 1958–2005*.

. . . and whiskers on kittens . . . doorbells and sleighbells . . . girls in white dresses . . . silver-white winters that melt . . . —you really can't stand that tune, and it's probably because the tune carries the words, and the words just drive you crazy, going over and over in your mind like that. Not that you don't like raindrops on roses, but once those raindrops have been paired with those kittens they become so . . . well, the only word you can find for it is *twee*, and that's a word that defines itself by resisting definition—because your twee is someone else's bright copper kettle, and vice versa. Anyway, the tune drives

* With apologies to W. B. Yeats, Marianne Moore, Emily Dickinson, Robert Frost, Jean Cocteau, Samuel Johnson, and Archibald MacLeish, for what I've done with their definitions of poetry.

you crazy carrying on all day in the back of the brain, and pretty soon, as a kind of antidote, you begin to think of your own favorite things, but then they, too, instantly fall prey to the all-too-familiar: your grandson's bright hair in the sunlight, the nutmeggy smell of pumpkin pie baking, a blue glass goblet on your windowsill, one of the three tenors, your twenty-nine-cent Elvis Presley stamp, your ten-cent Robert Frost stamp, and, right now, the amazing snowdrift of cherry blossoms right at eye level across the street from where you sit wishing you could forget that song.

What's not to like about wild geese that fly with the moon on their wings? Nothing. Nothing at all. In fact, the line's rather gorgeous; rhythmically, it rivals Hopkins' "Long live the weeds and the wilderness yet." Well, maybe not when you couple the latter with "This darksome burn, horseback brown" and Hopkins' ability to "spring" his rhythms into something that transcends mere song. Those geese, combined with a bevy of simpering girls in blue-satin sashes, lose their gravity and take on an aura of sentimentality.

So now you start a list of what you don't like, over and above not liking that tune, persistent now, whirling noisily in your head. The problem with "favorite" is that it doesn't really have an antonym—and if it did, maybe its opposite would not be quite what you need. After all, pure loathing is not what you're after, but things that—simply because you don't really like them all that much—help to define your character or sensibility just as much as the things you want to savor. Even your negatives make a list that sounds all too much like a song: gum on the sidewalk and Muzak with dinner, letters that say that you aren't quite the winner, long-distance walks from the car to the mall, these are the things that you don't like at all.

All this riffing, just so I can ponder the process of selecting poems for a Selected. By the time poets are contemplating a Selected, they know you probably either like their work or don't. So, do they merely hand us a list of their favorite things, or do they consider more than their versions of schnitzel with noodles, sifting past work for evidence of a poetic trajectory or life span, so to speak? Maybe they want to chronicle the evolution of their craft, or highlight the consistency of their themes, or call attention to a dramatic shift in outlook. Even though the tasks they've set themselves might look similar—define your poetic self by selecting a compact, comprehensive look at the whole from among the poems of your first five, six, or seven books, your last twenty or twenty-five-plus years—it's interesting to note how differently diverse poets go about tying the strings of their particular brown paper packages.

When the lid clicks,
When the toad's real,
When the top of the head is gone,
I just remember that certain poems will
Remind me I'm not alone.

Albert Goldbarth lets us in on the process, telling us what rules he set for himself, how he went about sorting through thirty-five years of work in twenty-three books and twelve chapbooks (23 + 12 = 35, I note). He's also written five (5) collections of essays and one (1) novel. (I insert the arabic numerals here just to watch the numbers buzz around my head like flies.) So . . . *The Kitchen Sink* is quite possibly the best—the only—title for this pulling-together-of-disparate-everythings. Goldbarth takes a couple of pages to tell us what he's left out—the longer poems (not surprisingly, since he allowed himself no excerpts) and a fair percentage of his earlier poems—and what he's included—more of the later poems, more of the shorter poems, more of the later "self" and less of that "Albert Goldbarth" who is recalled fondly as an "out-of-the-loop, completely unnetworked, wide-eyed, trusting licker-of-stamps-beyond-counting and habitué-of-mailboxes-at-midnight." In other words, Goldbarth invites us to imagine him with a wild head of hair, a poet about to become The-Poet-Who-Can-Write-Everything-But . . . and now he includes the *But.*

That said, in *The Kitchen Sink* Goldbarth has a bit of fun mixing everything up, stirring the pot of the accumulated poems the way the large index finger on the book's cover stirs the swirling clouds above a spinning earth. The book is divided into four sections. The first, "Love and Cosmology (1983–2005)," is organized roughly by theme—or, in what is a more Goldbarthian approach, by varied like-mindedness—with eight subsections to further emphasize that he has often revisited certain concerns over the more than two decades represented. The second section ("The Rising Place for the Dough") simply contains forty-eight one-page poems from those same years. The third section ("The Fossil of an Omelet") steps back in time and, in Goldbarth's word, "excavates" thirteen poems written between 1972 and 1983, approximately one poem for each of those early years of production. The last eighty pages are new poems (a new book!), thus flummoxing the reviewer who would like to comment on the overall achievement and, at the same time, note new directions. So I simply note that the recombinant DNA of this collection flies in the face of whatever tradition there is in putting together a Selected. And why not? Who could select from among so much without making some statement about what had been selected? Or omitted? In resisting the norms, Goldbarth establishes his norm—everything *including* the kitchen sink.

There's no way to talk about 350 pages in an omnibus review, and I am already on record as thinking that Albert Goldbarth is producing some of the most innovative, entertaining, and devastatingly moving poems from both the end of the old century and the beginning of the new. Yes, the early poems do reveal a less confident writer: the lines break more conventionally ("Faucets / hover over the sink / like the short sleeves / of an amputee / remembering what it was / to wash up"); the sentences are more serviceable ("Sometimes, summer rain makes sky a closing / iron maiden"); the humor is a little strained; the experimentation is more tentative; and (this really interests me) the music is far less sure, so that idea presides over rather than resides within the poem. The ending of "Animal Functionsong" is a good example:

> But if I pray too huge this morning
> *buffalo, mountain gorilla, white rhino*
> Asking one gift too outré
> *tusk, milk, civet-musk, panther-silk, ambergris*
> Thieve me a least sweep scrap of fatback
> *packrat, jackdaw, jay*

This is a far cry from the sure swagger of Goldbarth's now-inimitable music, the cadences of a mind indulging its subtlest nuances with the rhythmical, parenthetical, emphatical, comma-riddled, dash-filled daring of the later poems.

Beyond a mounting confidence, a willingness to let out the stops come what may, a readiness (maybe a wish?) to risk all, Goldbarth's poems do not "grow" into themselves, but quickly evolve as though their author had discovered a secret: the poem *is* the self. By 1983 (where this collection begins), we see him at full strength, rolling the sounds of the words over his tongue, climbing the rolling hills of his thoughts as they undulate across the landscape of the line. We hear the voice in the head as it insists itself on the page, sometimes WRIT LARGE, sometimes caught in the slipstream of emotion, a ghost rhythm that chants an old Hebrew prayer behind the smokescreen of contemporaneity.

In becoming the sum of all his parts, Goldbarth unleashed a brand new voice on American letters—a voice that seemed to be practicing for what would come, a voice with the capacity for pity and rage, a voice to encompass more than any single life can bring. The next-to-last subsection of part one is entitled "July 23, 1995," and its three longish poems deal (in part) with the death of Goldbarth's mother. (We're glad to hear her speak of his "poetry-hokeypokey," saying he'll even put her IV hookup in a poem.) Here, we see all that practice brought to fruition:

> The following day my sister holds her hand
> for hours, while whatever "self" is left of herself, inside of herself,
> flutters like a moth in search of an exit,
> wearily beats at the cancerous lumpgrown underside of the skin.
> There is no magic elixir for this, no out-of-the-empyrean
> deific intervention—no, there's only the pissy arguing now
> with a clod of a doctor over what he airily calls "pain management"
> (too little too slow), and the true heart-sundering moments
> when her eyes clear and that twenty-three-year-old life-fixated woman
> on the lion statue stares at me from out of this sunken-in form.
> That's it. That's everything. That's the whole world today.

The rhythms here are a great, heaving keening, an open-armed embrace that speaks volumes and is orchestrated so the simple "that's it" will contain her present and her past and fuse them forever in a son's whole world. That world, in turn, can encompass comic strips, Egyptian death rites, science, sex, and the buttons his mother saved when the shirt wore out—in short, "that's everything."

The one-page poems of section two are a delight as well, serving up familiar Goldbarth in bite-sized chunks. Sometimes overshadowed in their original contexts, these shorter, sonnet-sized poems have been given new room to breathe. But the new poems ("Human Beauty") draw me to them like a moth to the flame, hungry to know where this mind has recently been going, just how it *keeps on* going. There are no real surprises here—though, by definition, everything Goldbarthian is a surprise and more of the same is not synonymous with old hat. No, these poems wear the new(ish) hat of registered mortality. They are deeper, more penetrating, and, if anything, more life-affirming as they tackle the various versions of dying that the human body can think up. "Assisted living," "mini-strokes," "colonoscopy," "bone-marrow"—the language of individual heartbreak peppers this section, and a culminating disquisition on the anachronistic properties of DNA in "Grahamesque" leads toward metaphor:

> And I know
> if we could see the foot that Martha Graham sees
> as a matter of faith—if it were glass, or even only as translucent
> as a molded shape of aspic, with its contents on display—
> we'd see it isn't an anthropometrical matter of how many more,
> but how best used: a filigree
> of focused expertise.

The Kitchen Sink is focused expertise. Best used, it does not give us the broad overview of a "career" that many Selecteds convey; rather, it reminds us that writing poetry is anything but a career—it is a calling. The new poems speak with new authority, as though they have abandoned a raucous overvoice in favor of an equally gutteral undervoice that rises to the surface of this new work as an honesty and an intimacy that no longer feel the need to surround themselves with bodyguards. You read these poems for the same reasons you read the earlier ones, but emerge from the experience both elated and chastened. You confront yourself in the mirror, every nagging doubt and snide aside and lusty laugh of you, and you celebrate. There's no other response to imagine, any more than Goldbarth can ultimately imagine anything but these three lines:

> Why do I write? It's what I do
> with the portion of carbon I am, before it returns to the universe
> of carbon that the trees created even before there were people.

When the lid clicks,
When the toad's real,
When there's a lump in the throat,
I just remember that certain poems will
Untie their Gordian knots.

At the other end of poetry's spectrum, we find the chaste austerity of Carl Phillips' lyric quest. *Quiver of Arrows* contains no new poems, but simply compresses the work of eight books into one, handing up Phillips' version of a mythic journey. Each previous book is represented by a mere eight to fifteen poems, a distillation so subtle and sure that it seems as though Phillips, if he could have known what was coming, might have written only these eighty-four to announce his presence on the poetic stage.

Perhaps because I came to Phillips' work at his third or fourth book, perhaps because his early work was not instantly available to me, I have always been playing catch-up with his "career." So here a Selected does the service it sets out to do: it provides an "overview" of the work in its entirety, while at the same time inviting me to note recurring images, to find the common threads that lead from book to book, to "read" the ongoing saga of one poet's struggle to find and make meaning in his world. Two hundred pages is just about right for such a project—comprehensive enough that I don't wonder what I'm missing, compressed enough that I trust it to be the poet's best *statement*. I take this book at face value; it exists so that I can honor one man's twenty-year process, one writer's maturing voice—his tussle with craft to find a way to say what would otherwise be forever silent.

Reading the early poems fascinates me, partly because it becomes clear that even by his second book Phillips had found distinctive elliptical methods for unlocking his poetic material. The first book is a bit more direct, but even there the poet's discretion creates the sense that one is being invited into private spaces, private thoughts and feelings and associations. "X" opens *Quiver of Arrows* with a cascade of associative half-hints of erotic moments, anonymous and fleeting: "X is all I keep / / meaning to cross out." Although the poet alludes to racial and cultural issues in "Passing," the speaker resists group appropriation: "I want to tell the poet that the blues / is *not* my name, that Alabama / is something I cannot use / in my business." His business, the subsequent poems imply, is myth. It's also orchestration. The poems begin to open out, spreading their lines over—and down—the page, a bit like the feathers on the book's cover, drifting in air.

Phillips' sentences hover, pick up speed, spiral to digression, circle back, and finally land. The function of the line, often, is to give visual expression to that orchestration, to emphasize the music of thought, to dissect the intricacies of emotion, to see the sentence through to its potential. Quoting excerpts from any poem becomes difficult because each poem is arranged in such a way that its sentences accrue meaning—and complexity—as they twist down the page. Phillips builds a system of images, then approaches them from every angle, each stone turned and turned again, held to the light, and then the light itself broken, refracted, until the language we use to speak of it is itself broken apart, broken nearly free—held only by the (almost) invisible tether of syntax.

The best way to read Phillips is to quicken the pace of your voice even as your eye is arrested, so that instead of slowly savoring each seemingly unfettered line, you reconstruct the sentence he has so carefully decelerated in order to explore its components. That way, you restore a speaking sense to what is otherwise fractured, as in this section of "The Truth":

> Because
> it still matters, to say something. Like:
> the heart isn't
>
> really breakable,
> not in the way you mean, any more
> than a life shatters,
>
> —which is what
> dropped shells can do, or a bond sworn to,
> remember, once

couldn't, a wooden boat between
unmanageable wave and rock or,
as hard, the shore.

In the early books, Phillips echoes Greek myth, at times using a chorus like a kind of conscience to question motive, including the role of art. But he quickly integrates that conscience in his method so that interrogation is the driving force. To be, or not to be, if this, if that, then . . . a poem by Phillips tips on the knife edge always, always hovers on the brink of its own implications. Using white space to sustain uncertainty, "To a Legend" speaks beyond its own dimensions:

And briefly defines: now you're

the horse, now the snow that veils it,
now the wild signature that the horse
keeps making, startled, inside the snow;

and now its rider—untrained, uncertain,
both.

Quiver of Arrows is thick with desire—and its companion, loss. Phillips picks apart the elements of desire, pares them down to essentials, then finds multiple ways of asking "because how can we not want?" And wanting, in his hands, takes on all the commas and qualifiers of a convoluted sentence, finding in its multiple dimensions a sheer physicality of need. If Phillips sings the body electric, then the descant is sung by the mind:

thinking it, wrongly,

a thing attainable, any real end
to wanting, and that it is close, and that
it is likely, how will you not

this time catch hold of it: flashing,
flesh at once

lit and lightless, a way
out, the one dappled way, back—

The dash breaks off thought, and yet, suspended like this, the mind worries at experience even as experience refuses to yield up its full, embodied meanings.

This book does not have the feeling of pastiche, of cobbling together, that many Selecteds have; instead, it builds its own trajectory—one that covers youthful intensities, powerful loss, mature affection, betrayal, restoration. The author seems to have looked down on his poems and seen them much in the way he describes a field:

> Something at once
> still and rampant, as across the field
> of a coat-of-arms that any field, seen
>
> from above, makes sometimes.

The arrow, the feather, the field: each image takes on significance. Where there is an arrow, there is also the taut bow, the wounded stag. Where there is a feather, the possibility of flight. Where there is a wound, the desire to wound. Nothing escapes this roving mind; nuance is, in many ways, its nemesis. Each poem an arrow, the book itself the quiver, this collection holds—quivering—twenty years of wrestling with the body's demands. It asks, quite possibly, more of love than love is ever able to give, and isn't this the stuff of myth, writ large?

The presiding metaphor is that of the tether, a bond of trust that is tested again and again, held up to the light of parable and legend, or of clear and present danger. The mind and body spar until each traps the other in alien question marks. And what *do* we do with a love that far outlives the body that held/is held by it? The final poems in this collection are fraught with anxiety, with imagined betrayal that, once imagined, threatens to become real. The book ends with "Riding Westward"—evoking the familiar image of the lone rider heading into an unknown future. But if the ending strikes a cultural resonance, it does not quite complete the book's arc; one senses that Carl Phillips has much more to say so that, at the end, the reader feels acutely poised on the edge of new exploration.

When the lid clicks,
When the toad's real,
When the quarrel is with the self,
I just remember that certain poems will
Make of themselves a salve.

Robert Wrigley has elected to orchestrate *Earthly Meditations* in what we have come to think of as the traditional form for a Selected: new poems first, then an abrupt shift to poems from the earliest book and a slowly building momentum toward the present. So I begin by assuming that he does not have so much a larger statement to make as an impulse to highlight his best work over twenty-five years. Wrong. It's not long before I find myself noting that some—several—of my favorites are not included. Why would anyone leave out poems as fine as "Prayer for the Winter" or "Breaking Trail"? Taste, you might argue, but that explanation is not enough to suit me, so I hunt for clues. The first stares back from the book's cover: the two words of the title must in many ways have informed Wrigley's choices as he searched for some way to make one book out of many. And many of the poems he selected do seem meditative, and earthly, and, well, earthy. Even the "other" world of the dead buck in the final poem turns out to be this world—here, and here, and here. Throughout, there's a kind of consistency in subject matter—the rough outdoors, the lives of animals, our animal selves, family dynamics, lust and love—that holds these poems in a loose web of focused attention.

Only after writing those words do I note—really note—the cover illustration: a single barb of a barbed-wire fence (also known as "the devil's rope"), delicately enmeshed in a spider's web, spangled (that's the only word for it) with dew. The ugly and the beautiful, inextricably intertwined. The hard and the soft. The long-lasting and the transient. The inflexible and the elastic. The sharp and the subtle. The anomalous. The opposites revolve until they merge, and Wrigley does not seem so set on contrast as on balance—their equally tensile strengths. The ending of the opening poem, "Slow Dreams," sets the tone:

> And as always I sigh, and dredge it forth,
> some paltry, not even anecdotal sliver:
> the way paper waves gusher off west and east
> from the archetypal mouth of a scissors;
> the tome of unclench, the very continental drift
> of a single kiss beginning to end;
> my own utterly familiar hands approaching me,
> coming straight at my face and filled
> with water that no matter how long held
> never completely spills. My thirst.

Wrigley's thirst is for balance; he holds the cupped water so that it makes a kind of sense, or, as in "The River Itself," he follows it to its source: that "man-sized final slab of melting ice" from which meaning can be chiseled. And in order to find balance, Wrigley must fashion it. The poems are crafted like a cat's cradle, each line pulling intricately at the next as they move through their permutations—the poem itself held in suspension, waiting for each element to settle into the whole. And the elements are themselves the very raucous stuff of life, its splendidly seamy undersides, its awkward elegance.

One consistent element in this collection is humor. Wrigley is able to turn an amused eye on almost anything: the fact that the man who steam-cleaned the carpet must have handled his wife's black bra, the bicyclist he inadvertently came upon while she was peeing, the poets he would not want introduced to his daughter. But there's always a twist, and instead of broad humor there's an inward turn, a wry self-awareness that drifts beneath the surface, then suddenly deepens the poem. There's also attitude: these poems come face-to-face with realities; they acknowledge the indifferences and the anomalies of nature; they refuse to pray. If these are earthly meditations, there's a kind of stoic hardheadedness at their center, an insistence that the poems stay rooted in the earth, find what it has to offer. The title poem moves from its opening filigrees of sound—"Spring, and the first full crop of dandelions gone / to smoke, the lawn lumpish with goldfinches, / hunched in their fluffs, fattened by seed, / alight in the wind-bared peduncular forest"—through a meditation on a series of dead (killed) animals (frogs, and beaver, and fish) and the speaker's admiration for the blue heron's stilled presence. Wrigley ends with a meshing of imagery, having perceived something about the human:

> Slow as an hour hand the heron's leg
> rises, the sun leans into its notch in the west.
> My son calls from the cliff
> across the river. From the drawn distended petals
> of his mother's body, he burst
> into the world and began to mourn.
> The spirit took root in his cry.

The human is, almost always, juxtaposed with the animal so that one informs the other. "Ravens at Deer Creek," for example, slows as the speaker pauses to watch the "caws and cartwheels" of birds that circle something dead in the stand of fir one ridge over. The speaker and the birds exist in proximity, each in a separate sphere that would, should he fall, interlock. The meaning is emphasized by an intricate use of slant rhymes, rhymes so subtle that at first they are hardly noticed until the ear realizes it's been mesmerized. Here's a short passage to demonstrate how subtly Wrigley plies his craft:

> It is a long snowy mile I've come
> to see this, thanks to dumb luck or grace.
> I meant only a hard ski through powder,
> my pulse in my ears, and sweat, the pace

like a mainspring, my breath louder and louder
until I stopped, body an engine
ticking to be cool. And now the birds.
I watch them and think, maybe I have seen
these very ones, speaking without words,
clear-eyed and clerical, ironic, peering in at me
from the berm of snow outside my window
where I sprinkled a few crumbs of bread. We
are neighbors in the neighborhood of silence.
They've accepted my crumbs, and when the fire was hot
and smokeless huddled in ranks against
the cold at the top of the chimney. And they're not
without gratitude.

Neighbors in a neighborhood of sound, the rhymes make their point—and it's no coincidence that the middle line of the entire poem ("from the berm of snow outside my window") is the one without an end rhyme, as though to show the slight disconnect where the two worlds meet. Yet that line contains an internal rhyme that unites man and nature, inside and out.

In the end, craft becomes my focus as I read *Earthly Meditations*. Although the later poems may have managed to sustain their suspensions a little longer, or weave their webs a bit more densely, it's clear that even the early poems were striving for the kind of perfection Robert Wrigley has achieved in his later books. In some ways, it's not clear what a Selected does for Wrigley at this point—except maybe to make that very point, and to announce that he's at that "stage" in the evolution of a poet. I'd have happily waited for the completion of his next book to see what the fullness of another free-standing collection would do to round out the little testings of politics and religion that are hinted at in the "New Poems" section, where "Some days / all I want is no news, none of the time." Meanwhile, I meditate on the meditations, their full-throated joy at being on, and of, this earth.

When the lid clicks,
When the toad's real,
When the dancer becomes the dance,
I just remember that certain poems will
Follow their sounds to sense.

Rebecca McClanahan mixes the old and the new in each of the five sections of *Deep Light*, deliberately eliminating any indication as to the date or the collection in which a poem originally appeared. Thus each poem is "new"—or seen in new light—and the Selected becomes a whole new book in and of itself. (An index at the end gives a list of the new poems and indicates the books from which the others were "selected.") So it is that "First Husband," a poem whose time frame predates many of the other poems and that was originally published in her third book, is found in the last section here. Chronology is not what this collection is about, though it invites the reader to piece together the puzzle of the lived life through careful use of repeated imagery or anecdote, subtle shadings that reveal certain moments from different perspectives.

By electing this method of organization, McClanahan illustrates a point: for thirty years she has been working with a consistent voice, worrying at the edges of human relationships, so that in many ways her poems have been talking to each other for decades. For a while I tried guessing which poems were new, which were old, which voice was young, which was "mature," but in the end I was wrong more than I was right, and that in itself makes an interesting point: McClanahan's evolution has not been one of craft or outlook so much as an ever-widening range of subject matter, accompanied by the emotional maturity to address it in interesting ways. So I find it extremely refreshing to enter *Deep Light* to rediscover certain poems in a new context, and to encounter new ones that add to, deepen, and extend McClanahan's poetic reach.

As in all her previous books, family is central to her Selected. One watches McClanahan's "speaker" as granddaughter, daughter, sister, wife; she marries, divorces, remarries, thinks about her childlessness, attends the deliveries (and the graduations) of her nieces and nephews, ponders the tenuous threads that hold people together: "Without the law, there is no brother, / and no ceremony to mark the breaking," she says in the opening of "Ex-Brother-in-Law," then goes on to imagine his future, and to recount three days in his past as he built a cabinet, perfecting the finishing he could not accomplish in his relationships. Friendship, too, figures prominently in these poems—her friends are often named, included as part of the larger family. But increasingly the poems reach beyond expected ties and take in the lives of others. This may be, in part, a response to McClanahan's move from the family-centered South to a more anonymous life in New York City. People catch her eye, and the result is a fascination with the otherness of those she briefly glimpses. Hovering in that netherworld she explores the unknown life of one of her students, an elderly gentleman she dubbed "James" because he often drove her to the station. "Not James" contains in its title the mix of intimacy and distance inherent in their relationship:

The week
before he died he sent a list of mysteries
I should read, I who always tangle in details
before the end is solved. The paper reported
he was found sitting in his car, the dog
beside him freshly walked. It mentioned
a fiancée somewhere, of which he had never
spoken. "Gentle reader," he would have called you,
this man who used to drive me to the train.

The poem builds on simple declarative sentences, twisting just enough that certain words arrest the eye while the ear reads past them: "never" ever-so-slightly emphasizes the limits of the speaker's knowledge; "reported" and "mentioned" indicate the secondhand nature of what she knows; "you," however, brings the reader of this poem intimately inside. McClanahan's distinctive trademark might be this ability to incorporate us as readers in the poem so that we see everything from within, even how strange things might appear to her. In her hands, it's a shared experience.

McClanahan takes us deep into marital terrain: its ups and downs, its phases; the pangs of separation and the long, slow work of rebuilding. Young love and "old" love exist side by side in this collection, and each is held to the fire and tested, over and over, as though memory and imagination might "fix" things in both senses of the word. I'm so pleased, when I go to the index, to find that "Fortune" is one of the "new" poems; its final response to the fortune cookie serves both to question and answer:

You will never have to buy
another umbrella. Meaning,

we will never lose, or be lost, again?
Or, the sun will always shine?
Or, the umbrella stashed in the back

of the closet, the one we've stood beneath
at burials, at christenings and weddings
when the weather surprised,

is shelter enough. The plain,
black umbrella with a few broken spokes,
the one we keep forgetting we have.

Interesting, to find myself pleased that a poet who seems, in her poems, to be speaking so directly for herself should have the good fortune to find such acceptance. Such happiness—because this assemblage is filled with great good humor and infectious joy, even as it encompasses death and disappointment. Interesting, because I realize that I read this book like memoir, but memoir held to the candle of insight, shaped to the language of metaphor. Yet *Deep Light* resists the "confessional." It wallows in nothing; it expands to celebrate the very diversity of experience it covers—the men in Central Park and the Down syndrome children in the swimming pool, the nephew learning to type and the sister who died just before the poet was born, a father's memories of the Korean War and a cab driver who speaks naturally in almost-rhyming couplets. "Trying to Escape Autobiography" has as its epigraph a quote from a nine-year-old girl, "The truth is sticky," and Rebecca McClanahan's truth sticks to her—and to us—in the sheer weight of detail. Oddly, the mass of countable things is pondered in a poem called "The Invention of Zero," which takes us into a realm where what she can imagine couples with what we know:

> asking nothing of us   taking nothing from us
> cannot divide us   can only multiply   all our somethings
>
> into nothing   rock us   the last lost child
> of the empty-fisted woman   uncounted   unaccountable
> rock us in armless arms   back to where we came from

Because she takes us precisely to where we have already been, Rebecca McClanahan shows us how to see things differently, and because these poems represent thirty years of lived and linguistic struggle, they aspire to the "deep light" of the sea so that they, too, might be "lit miraculously from within."

When the lid clicks,
When the toad's real,
When it rides on its melting ice,
I just remember that certain poems will
Take us to someplace else.

The poems gathered in Bruce Beasley's *The Corpse Flower* cover fewer than twenty years and only four books, making it seem, to me, slightly premature as a Selected. I would have been happier to wait another year for a full-length collection of new poems and then to see a retrospective look later. One reason for this is that new poems often get swallowed up in a Selected, never seeing the light of a review, and, since Beasley seems to be just now hitting his poetic stride, the new poems are what we come for here.

Luckily, the new work, found at the end of *The Corpse Flower*, takes up sixty pages (roughly one-third of the book), so the early poems serve in many ways to predict what we know to be in store for us. They circle and circle themes of religion and sexuality, myth and physicality, until by definition they establish Beasley's orbit. They reveal his love of science, his love of language, and the strange bedfellows the two make in his hands. In poems that are surprisingly moving and personal, Beasley brings the following to bear: his scientific curiosity that dissects words to reveal their genetic makeup; his strangely obsessive need to break open the religious impulse; his quick wit that penetrates the inconsistencies of myth; his verbal acuity in service to emotional multiplicity. Nuanced, playful, almost brutally frank, the early poems establish Beasley as a poet to be watched, and now the reader watches as they move—surely, inexorably—toward their metamorphosis.

Beasley has deliberately omitted all poems from what must be seen as a transitional book—the dauntingly intellectual and linguistically experimental *Lord Brain*, published in 2005—so the new poems here may come as a bit of a surprise. Playing on the word (and concept) "morphogenesis," they can be found in a section entitled "Mortogeneses." This, he gives us to understand, will be a mortal evolution. With a fusion of imagery and vocabulary, "The Corpse Flower" simultaneously describes the flower—its odor and its odd propensities—and human sexuality. The second of its seven sections is representative:

Thermogenesis: stalk
fever-soused to the touch

oozes hot oils & puffs
their stenches from its spike

& skirt, its uncurled shroud,
tuber surging by six

inches a day. *Amor-
phophallus titanium*:

amorphous, labial-
folded & engorging—

Even "labial" reminds us of its more-than-one meanings, and Beasley's density is derived from both the evolutionary sounds of words and the associative side steps that provide new forays into meaning. His implied equation: linguistics = linkage.

At first glance, many of these new poems—spread across the page with a liberal use of white space, broken into component parts, call and response, his and hers—would announce themselves as LANGUAGE poetry. A quick dip into the content, however, reveals something else: an energy so compressed it is ready to spring forth, transforming itself in the process. Story and song and query and lung breathe at the core of these poems; they are exhaled—physically—as the (nearly) visible product of a mind ceaselessly roaming the corridors of meaning, restlessly pacing the halls of experience, hacking away at convention and correlation, fiercely flying in the face of tradition. And to what end? To make, as he has, an amalgam of flesh and spirit, profanity and profundity, of such equal parts that it is impossible to distinguish the ordinary from the astonishing.

"The Craps Hymnal," for example, seems to pit Hawking against Einstein as it sets out to show that God does, indeed, play dice with the universe. Throwing dice to determine to which page he will open the dictionary (the dice are displayed as visual ornaments before the title of each section), the poet then starts with the word as object. In Beasley's hands, however, it soon has its own morphogenesis, piling on associations of boyhood in Macon, Georgia, his adopted son, Old Testament tales, New Testament Apocrypha, gambling odds, aphasia—you name it—in order to make the link between the random and the ordained.

Impossible. Impossible to demonstrate how this poem accrues its meanings, whirling through definitions and redefinings, tilting at the windmills of faith—fashioning, in its own way, a hymnal to the uncertain, and ending with its own earned "Sanctus."

Don't misunderstand. These poems are smart; their play is all work; they make their meanings meaningful. At their heart is a deep questing, religious fervor embedded in childhood, a religious rage for order and explanation. "Mortogenesis" takes the uncertainty relation ($\Delta E\ \Delta t{\sim}h$) for the spontaneous emergence of an electron, positron, and photon from a vacuum as an answer book to the (non) existence of God. "The Vanishing Point" interrogates the restoration of Leonardo da Vinci's *Last Supper* by setting it against a nephew's critical illness, thus asking the Big Question of an absent answerer:

> Should the Supper
> (sandbagged, or scaffolded, or trapped
> at the glass labyrinth's

core)
be forced to *last*?

Or allowed
its vanishing,
its last-known
location
somewhere among the irradiated

blanks?

Religion is at the center of these poems, but central to Beasley's search is (dis)belief (he might even say dissing belief). My personal favorites gnaw at the crusts of conviction. "And Go Into the Street Which Is Called Straight" begins with Twain's observation that this is the only facetious remark in the Bible and, using the Latin *frangere* (to break), splits apart Keats's epitaph with phrases that sound, themselves, biblical. "Not Light nor Life nor Love nor Nature nor Spirit nor Semblance nor Anything We Can Put into Words (—Meister Eckhart, on God)" proceeds as a series of incompleted analogies ("As the ellipse / of a zero // is to nothing. . . . As cadence, to caesura. / Or insomnia // to obsessive dream. . . . As arthritic / fingers to the etude, as // bone-grind / to arthritis. . . . "), culminating with the one relationship that holds everything together, as though the ineffable nature of the pairings does, indeed, find that wordless place we seem to need a name for: "As breath to pleura. As / as is to *as*, I am to You, as / the clitoral / hood, to the tongue." Once again Beasley has wedded the sexual and the spiritual, and made of his quest a striking statement about the nature of the creative urge.

The most ambitious of this set of (ir)religious poems is "Is," which appeared first in *Southern Review*, was awarded a Pushcart Prize, and then was reprinted again in *The Pushcart Book of Poetry* (2006), a thirty-year retrospective. "Male and female he created them . . . " and the poem naturally falls into columns that compare genitalia, imagine the Eve in the Adam and vice versa, working always with the copula—the word "is"—that "unites together subject and attribute," as in copulation, as in coupling, as in the *Is* of creation. A sampling will give some idea of how it appears on the page, but no idea of how its eight pages add up to dialectic:

When Eve was still   in Adam,
when death had not   "come into being"
breasts and vulva buried there inside his sealed-in rib

—Calling
out of the body of the bread (sopped
crusts, in their trapped-air Mason jars) the invisible
teeming,

and out of the Fungus Book, the language I loved:

rhizopus
nigricans,

mycelia, sporangia, hyphae—

Spora, seed *Sporas*, scattered

These are important, innovative poems, although "Rotbox" reconvinces me that we are still too close to 9/11 for any poem to have a long view on political realities. *The Corpse Flower* has been beautifully produced by the University of Washington Press, but I wish some of the longer poems did not break so early that they appear to be complete before the page is turned. This press is a fitting home for Beasley, who inhabits these "so-called Straits." I've chosen to look primarily at the new poems because they have the "feel" of a new and intriguing direction—one that I predict will make Bruce Beasley's reputation as a groundbreaking poet in the years to come.

When the lid clicks,
When the toad's real,
When pleasure unites with truth,
I just remember that certain poems will
Never require a proof.

Paul Zimmer, the author of twelve books of poems and two collections of prose, takes an innovative approach to his oeuvre. In *Crossing to Sunlight Revisited* he revisits his 1996 Selected, choosing just fifty poems from a lifetime of publications, then adding twenty-three new works to total seventy-three—one for each year of his life. With typical good humor, he describes the process in a one-page preface:

> Now I must admit that I am no longer an aging poet or an older poet. I am an old poet. It is time to begin measuring things up for sure. In recent years, for only a brief while, I considered forming a large, collected volume of my work but eventually lost interest in this prospect. Such ponderous books, with their

inclusive dates, have always seemed a bit like tombstones to me. At least in my own case, it did not seem the best course to follow. Georges Braque once wrote: "Progress in art does not consist in expanding one's limitations but in knowing them better."

Zimmer's poems have long reveled in limitation, turning the awkward boy into the inimitable Zimmer of the "Zimmer" poems, a persona he has relied on over the years to shed a humorous and imaginative light on everything from elephants (Zimmer envies them) to angels (Zimmer is bashful in their presence) to poetry itself (where Zimmer is often a stand-in for poets across the centuries). Although the character of "Zimmer" dominates the earlier poems, he creeps sporadically into the new ones as well, this time living out some alternative lives: playing jazz with the greats and spending some time with Blake, when "perhaps he will just be Zimmer, / sitting quietly with the master all day, / listening to the scrape of / his graver and holy ravings, / losing the contest of words again—."

"What Zimmer Will Do" resurrects yet another image from an earlier poem, "The Great Bird of Love," where children are tucked into bed to the tune: "Sleep tight. / No harm tonight. / In starry skies / The Zimmer flies." Now Zimmer becomes "crazy with spring" as he studies a photograph of two young French women sitting in a garden. The sheer exuberance of the bird, swooping in to disrupt the scene, sets him up for what is to come. The girls dub him "Zimmer, l'oiseau absurde," and suddenly he's come full circle, a grown-up version of the Zimmer who faltered before the nuns in grade school, tongue-tied at precisely the moments he would most want to sing.

But sing here he does—a chorus of Zimmers, one for each year of life. It's a slim volume to call a life's work, but there it is, full of fun and fancy, a testament to loving language enough to trust it. The poems are peopled with others: Wanda and Rollo and Lester & Co. They are peppered with a love of the raucous and the lusty and the absurd. Yet the new poems are also tempered with the wisdom that comes from perspective. If there's a statement here, it's that the world has much to offer up and language will be there to meet it halfway. It's also that life is meant to be lived, and loved—in his words, with a "furious love" and in a "preposterous season."

For all the playful qualities of Zimmer's work, for all its mock heroic inventiveness, there's also a nostalgic note. It's not just the steam locomotive he hankers for, but the time when it dominated the scene. "The Old Trains at Night" calls up my own childhood and the limitless distances a train's whistle could evoke. The way its tiny trail of smoke moved across the landscape. The power of those huge wheels and the great huffing presence at the station. For Zimmer (now the poet who sings the aging body lurching from chair to chair and nodding off in sleep), all its imagery suggests the strength and vitality of a younger man:

> They were finest in winter when
> They showed what they could do,
> Slamming their way through huge drifts,
> Chests heaving and great hearts pounding.
>
> But they ran best on moonlight,
> Heaving out steam to secret wildflowers,
> Sliding through ground fog
> As they hauled themselves
> Panting into our dreams.

Crossing to Sunlight Revisited is a quirky collection, one not so much representative of the whole as a thing unto itself. One suspects Zimmer is not looking to present his "best" so much as to offer up poems he still delights in, is *bemused* by. On careful examination, though, the poems selected here (even the early ones) all do seem to begin to point in the direction of age, and of fitting into a longer tradition. They express the hard-won wisdom that poems force on their writers: live in the moment, love the language, leave the rest to chance.

"The Books" catches up the dual nature of Zimmer's enterprise where writer and reader are inseparably linked, Zimmer the character and Zimmer the writer melding into one.

> You knew the rest of your life
> Would be part of their singular flights,
> Vast flocks, brave migrations.

Like his trains, Zimmer leaves a "long, echoing chain of thunder," not so much because he rushes past as because he allows himself time to take pleasure in his "measuring up," and to make that time-taking the essence of his work. One senses he's content to let these few poems cross to the sunlight where we can see what he's seen all along.

When the lid clicks,
When the toad's real,
When the wisdom begins in delight,
I just remember that certain poems will
Teach us to celebrate.

With great sadness I report the recent death of John Engels, in June 2007, during the time I was working on this review. Engels was a poet of great distinction—and a master of several Selecteds that he compiled over the decades. His *Walking to Cootehill* (1993), for example, was arranged in the manner of McClanahan's *Deep Light*—a marvelous mix of old and new, paired across the decades and striking up new conversation. So it seems fitting that his last project was a comprehensive Collected. There is neither space enough nor time to do justice to the six hundred pages of *Recounting the Seasons: Poems, 1958–2005*. But I do want to remark that this nearly fifty-year retrospective was more than warranted; it was necessary.

For this volume, Engels elected to order the poems just as they were in their original collections, preserving their original contexts. I find it imperative to quote a few poems in full to demonstrate their subtle gradations in sound, their sure use of lineation, and their unflinching look at reality. Here are three, almost at random—one earlier, one middle, and one later; notice how, even though I've selected them arbitrarily, they detail the recurring (recounted) seasons of the book's title:

Hawk

I find a redtail's mummy cruciform
on a wire fence, talons fisted
on a strand, the orbits stuck through
with a whittled twig,

beak agape, a snake's tail
protruding, the rest the bird gorged
stripped in the gullet to a hair
of ribs and convolutions

of vertebrae, hawk and snake
this fierce formality, bone
within dead bone.
I watch, my eyes likewise

transfixed. I stare, not seeing
as my eyes see. I see our names. I see
this bird is dead, that
is the first name.

And blind, that is the next.

Sound weaves its long vowels (*a*, *o*, *u*) through the shifting consonants from *r* to *s* and toward the final *i* of "blind," which echoes that of "eye," "eyes," and "likewise," but whose meaning contrasts starkly with the repeated "see." And what is seen? The doubled ironies of "bone" and "dead"—that fierce formality.

Slovenj Gradec

That close to the mountain
at that time of year
the frost came early.
Any who cared to look

could see how close at hand
it had all along
been gathering. The mountains
rose luminous as clouds

above the gibberish color
of the October woods.
In fact, there were no clouds,
but something intervened

for the light did not
make shadows. The planet
had long been cooling.
Already it was beyond comfort.

Normally, I'd shy away from a poem using "luminous," but coupled with "gibberish" it seems positively right, and since the luminosity is questioned and qualified until its mystery remains a "something," the whole of autumn is pared down to elemental cooling, and comfort is more than anyone can expect in the long view of cosmology. All that in sixteen lines, and time slowing, slowing.

Poem and a Near Dream on My 65th Birthday

The shadow of the big dead elm
shines blue as a peacock's breast
against the snow. It's not enough. I've loved

nothing, nothing, nothing
about the weathers of this place:
the summer stink of mildew

in the basements, thin mosses
and lichens blotching the pickets
of the garden fences. Now,

more than ever, the language
eludes me, my tongue's
gone strange in my mouth. Tonight

for all the birthday food
that glues my guts together, for all
the grammarless dream talk,

at this close edge of sleep, I can't
sleep, out of somewhere
bring to mind white fences, an excitement

of beetles clumsy in the weeds, wing-cases
like oil-sheen on water, clambering
eagerly the seed-heads, disposed to fly

straight into the huge
shining beetle-shape of the sun.

—January 19, 1996

"Now," "Tonight," "for all," "I can't," and the moment in time becomes a moment *of* time, a deep-winter calling forth of summer, a near dream that turns the nothing into something, a near death that turns the something into life that might—just might—be enough.

Engels' view of the world was all-encompassing. As the jacket cover states, he is distinguished by his range—"long, short, easy, difficult, philosophical, casual, despairing, joyful, silly, bawdy, heartbreaking, angry, affectionate, uplifting, abrasive, sexy, chaste, polite, and bad-mannered." But it doesn't mention the understated irony that ends one of my favorite poems, "Night Bird." Deep into the night, an unidentified bird ("a night bird of some kind") began to make itself heard; it "until morning / called two hundred times / and more, though surely // it was nameless to itself." With a similar perception, Engels writes of the death of an infant son: "But on the hill / / the pines had strained to a power of wind. / . . . Meanwhile / he is speechless, dark, of no intent."

The final book covered by this Collected, *House and Garden* (2001), is an imagined entry into the lives of Adam and Eve after they were expelled from Eden. Not surprisingly, Engels portrays them contemplating their earthly garden, complete with deck. In these poems, Engels examines what is most human:

our ability to love in an imperfect world, our impulse to name—which originates in loss—and, especially, our "habitable silences."

In his foreword to *Recounting the Seasons*, David Huddle puts this complete volume in perspective far better than I can, noting Engels' subtle humor (Huddle calls it hilarity) and the breadth of his accomplishment. But more, Huddle suggests the larger reason(s) for reading this significant—no, *essential*—book:

> Imagine that as an adult, you become a fan of classical music. One at a time, you buy the recordings and listen to Beethoven, Bach, Brahms, Chopin, Mozart, Vivaldi, Tchaikovsky, and Dvorak; then you find your way into opera with Puccini, Wagner, Bizet, Verdi, Rossini, and Donizetti. But somehow over the years, you don't listen to Mahler. Maybe your friends recommend him to you, but for some reason you don't give him a try, or you listen casually to Mahler's *Symphony Number 9* and it just doesn't grab you. Or maybe you even listen to a few pieces from *The Song of the Earth* and you think they're okay but nothing to get excited about. Then one day—maybe driving in your car and listening to NPR—you hear the divinely grieving fourth movement of *Symphony Number 2 in C Minor*. Suddenly you understand. In a few minutes of listening, you grasp the utterly basic and gloriously complex nature of Mahler's genius. So now you have all of Mahler out there in your future, ten huge symphonies and the song cycles—months and months worth of listening, an opportunity for pleasure you could hardly have imagined.
>
> In the galaxy of classical music, such a scenario is unlikely, but on the planet of contemporary poetry, it's probable. John Engels is a master you may never have heard of, or you may not have given his work the moments of attention necessary to see what it has to offer you. But at this very moment, reader, . . . you've opened the covers, you've begun. Just keep turning the pages.

We could offer no more appropriate memorial to John Engels than to turn the pages of *Recounting the Seasons* and to encounter the ongoing life within them.

When the lid clicks,
When the toad's real,
When it doesn't mean but be,
I just remember that certain poems will
Hand us eternity.

The Omnivorous Omnibus

On Michael O'Brien's *Sleeping and Waking*; Meghan O'Rourke's *Halflife*; Robert Hass's *Time and Materials: Poems 1997–2005*; Philip Schultz's *Failure*; and Stanley Plumly's *Old Heart*.

I KNOW WHAT IT'S LIKE to be on the "other" side of writing, the one where I can do my smug Rhett Butler imitation and mean it when I say, "Frankly, my dear, I don't give a damn." But that's when I'm writing for myself first and foremost, not when I'm writing a review.

Here's the rub: we reviewers write, always, with an audience in mind, twisting ourselves into knots to make sure a point can be understood, to determine whether a transition is necessary, whether we've included enough of the work to give a fair representation, whether, whether, whether. . . . We conjure you, reader—a horde of you, a solitary omnivore—because if you didn't exist, we would be narcissistically wallowing in an exercise in futility. *We* already know what we think about a book, even if we don't yet have words for it. Why would we go to the excruciating trouble to write a review for ourselves?

Is anyone out there to take us in? To take us on? To argue, accuse, anguish, admonish, affirm, or agree? Once poetry reviews have been printed, they seem to float off into the void, along with the books discussed in them. Our silent dialogue with others remains, for the most part, mute. Much of the time, I simply have to assume you are out there, somewhere, wanting to know what I think—not so much because you'll rush right out to buy the book but because you'll be sharpening your own ideas on the whetstone of my assessment. Because you, too, feel the need for some meaningful dialogue about an art that is otherwise next to invisible—even when April rolls around (If you're reading this, you'll almost certainly know what that means.)

I've been comparatively lucky. Twice a year for eighteen years, I've found myself up to my knees in books of poetry, sorting and sifting, shuffling and shifting, finding a pattern, an order in which I can allow my thoughts to progress. That is, I've really been somewhat desperately trying to fit my thoughts to the preordained template (flexible as it may be) of the omnibus review. Which books lend themselves to a more general discussion? Which books speak to each other in interesting ways? Which poets allow me to reinforce a point, or discover a trend, or develop an idea? In short, which books "work" with this form of review?

There are some distinct advantages to reviewing several books in a long essay. For one thing, there is space enough, and time. For another, once I've discovered (or contrived) my "umbrella," once I've found the thread that will carry me through a discussion of four, or five, or six books, I've also provided myself with a presiding metaphor or an encompassing turn of mind—a touchstone that will help to keep me centered. The reader, in turn, can follow the thrust of my argument, knowing what to chalk up to my opinion or observation, what comes more definitely from the writer in question. This is, perhaps, the major strength of the essay-review: readers have the opportunity to follow a reviewer's mind as it delves into the work of several writers, and thus are given time to react and to respond by bringing their own knowledge to the page. They can assess my assessments, can decide more or less for themselves where their own tastes lie on some poetic continuum, can stake out their own position on that line.

A secondary strength of the omnibus review is the way it almost forces the reviewer to think about larger issues and, coincidentally, to make somewhat risky pronouncements about the art itself. I am forced out onto my shaky individual limb to see just how much lofty weight it will bear.

But the omnibus is also a hungry beast. It can eat away at the reviewer until she doles out opinions merely to serve its cause. The omnibus forces us to limit its fare if we are to keep its appetite in check. We write what the creature can stomach, and this sometimes means we leave out books or particular parts of books that don't fit its needs. We often omit the untidy, the oddball, the unmistakably different—which have to fight so hard for room under the umbrella that we'd rather leave them standing in the rain.

Worse, the omnibus can swallow books of poetry whole. They get lost in its vast intestines. Whatever once was unique or unusual can get smoothed over, tamped down, trampled even, by the forced proximity, by the necessity to address one book's essence in terms more suited to another's.

I was never more aware of that ravenous animal than when I began reading for this review. Several of the books that gave me real pleasure did not have much in the way of connective tissue among them. I found books I liked and ones I actively disliked—by poets with whose work I was familiar and poets whose work I don't remember ever seeing before. Okay: something old, something new, something borrowed . . . you can see where this was leading. Maybe I could manage "borrowed," but what would I do with "blue," short of feeling depressed by the books I found troubling?

I tried again. Girl Scout camp, with our young voices rising around the campfire: "Make new friends / but keep the old. / One is silver, / the other gold." Instantly, the inherent nagging questions arose: Does this imply that gold is better than silver, or more lasting? What if there's been a falling-out, into irreconcilable differences? Well, you can see that this notion was also leading me into a misery of my own making.

I could look for thematic connections. Or similar (or differing) techniques. I could try to worry some theoretical point, argue the postmodernism or romanticism or whatever-ism of the ways the poets fit themselves untidily into the tradition. I could spend all my time trying to feed the beast . . . but maybe I would find it easier, for once, to starve him. Easier to grant myself license and leave the books to their own devices.

At first, I wondered why I had never encountered Michael O'Brien's work before, since the biographical note inside *Sleeping and Waking* shows it to be his thirteenth collection. However, no acknowledgment of magazine publication appears in the book, so I feel less guilty for having let him go unnoticed. At any rate, here he comes—this poet two years my senior—with a beautiful book, its cover evoking a dream state with a cloudlike swirl of muted colors from a painting entitled *Slievemore, Curling Fog*. Couple that with the author's name and you might guess Ireland (and there are some poems about Ireland), but this poet is New York City all the way, even if he was born upstate near the Vermont border. He's clearly grown so used to the city—its sounds and sights—that the rural here takes on a precision achievable only when something is not taken for granted.

Sleeping and Waking opens with a prose poem that obliquely describes the poet's working method. In it, there's

> a man sitting in his room writing everything down that comes into his head. Images and sentences. A kind of parade. That ends at the cemetery. . . . The commands surprising in the spring air, as much a part of the rifles as their bolts. . . . Members of the band leaning on their elbows in the grass, among their instruments. And then changing it. What he's written down. The man in the room. So that what happens is the changes.

The rest of the book is made up of short poems—images and sentences—inspired by and reminiscent of haiku. They create the feel of an artist's notebook: a catchall of observations painted with the quick brush strokes of a Japanese calligrapher. Individual poems build by means of juxtaposed sections, each generating its own fleeting sense. The poems accrue, one brush stroke added to another, until there's a suggestion of a whole. Their compression allows the insight (and therefore the sense of the poem as an entity) to take place quietly within the reader. The book itself accrues in much the same way so that what seems, on the surface, to be a series of quick impressions addresses important questions after all: our relationship to other people, our relationship to the earth, what we make of our individual lives. The sketches may be pastoral, but the sense of isolation (and connection) is the product of an urban landscape where "you stop on the sidewalk and the / river of people divides around you, flows on, and you / move and are one with it."

The city—its characters and its character—informs these poems, bubbles and boils under their surfaces, tossing up its variations at every corner: "radio voices from the apartment below"; "little wake in the elevator"; "*Pshaw*! says the huge truck, braking"; "sudden crazy song & dance of the man on 23rd"; "helpless, half-suppressed / smile of the / girl in the / Bleecker Street subway"; "cellphone's blue TV glare"; "bike messengers / flickering like glowworms." In contrast, the countryside serves as a canvas waiting for O'Brien's eye to activate it, as in "Upstate":

Stirred by the
least wind the
wintry, carrot-
colored willow.

*

A pickup
full of snow,
a crow's rau-
cous laugh, the
rapids comb-
ing its hair.

We see the willow branches quiver, as though to emphasize the stillness. Fluid orange against white, though snow is only implied in the hush of wintry *w*s. In the next section, it's there, filling the pickup the way the crow's call fills the air, drowning out the sound of the rapids until they are not heard, but seen. Each element is given equal weight, words themselves are broken into sound, a tumble of *r*s rippling through the long *o*s, until we are pulled physically into the poem's center, shivering a little and stamping our feet for circulation. O'Brien does not merely pay homage to the Zen poets; by simply observing in order to elucidate, through letting what is *stand* for what is, he calls the physical world to our attention, or our attention to the physical world—it's hard to tell which.

I must admit I've never been a big fan of the poem that simply observes. I like a bit of mind brought to bear on the moment. But there's a kind of wit to what O'Brien sees, or at least to the way he sees it. His quick juxtapositions, as in the "rosary / drone of a rapper," activate the poem so that its "moment" of connection or epiphany is either shared by poet and reader simultaneously, or at times happens only inside the reader. His adjectives are at once corroborative and generative, but the real life resides in the verbs. There are many nuggets of precision—too many to quote—but here's a sample sequence of brief imagistic strokes from the middle of "Another Autumn":

> a day gradually effacing itself, perfecting its absence
>
> larval suns, asleep, the handspan of nothing between ribs
>   & pelvis
>
> flaking newsprint, rust's slow fire, a photo yellowing like
>   seersucker
>
> stipple of rain on pond, talking to itself, the day's vacant places
>
> coins of the leaves spangle the lawn, a jet tears off a piece of
>   the sky

Image and metaphor are not the only weapons in O'Brien's poetic arsenal; he uses sound so deftly that we almost overlook it. In its entirety, "Hush" demonstrates his subtle internal and end rhymes, a complex of silence and sound that adds a subliminal effect to the way the poem works its magic:

> black cat darting
> into roadside grass,
> a passing
> car's shadow
>   *
> tiny spider in the
> teaspoon, no, the
> huge chandelier
> reflected there

The sounds rotate until car darts, cat passes, and the tiny and the huge shapeshift in the spoon. One thing becomes another, and shadow and roadside occupy the same space. The tiny and the huge invert in the shallow silver bowl, much as the final two letters of *spoon* reverse: the tongue stopped briefly between one *n* and the next, then voicing the "no" that suspends the action. The poem holds its breath as the commas orchestrate its hush and change its course, repealing what we've already seen until we see again, more clearly.

Although Michael O'Brien establishes his desire to examine the blurred edges of consciousness—the sleeping and waking of his book's title—to my mind his more deliberately surreal poems are the least interesting. I prefer the startling moments of recognition when he has found just the right word or sound to give my ordinary waking days the exhilaration of acute perception.

Here's a vital new voice on the poetic scene—Meghan O'Rourke. Her voice has been heard in its critical mode in the *New York Times Book Review*, but in *Halflife* she emerges from that chrysalis like the moth of her opening poem, trying to "rise to something quite surprising in the distance." Her surprise is the eye-opening inventiveness of combinatorial ingenuity. At times, O'Rourke's next-to-invisible transitions—acting almost like random sense-generators—infuse the poems with the urgency of lived emotion. At others, urgency is generated by the syntax. "Sleep," for example, portrays the insomniac's frenzied state, culminating in verbal meltdown:

> In the bedroom the moon is a dented spoon,
> cold, getting colder, so hurry sleep,
> come creep into bed, let's get it over with;
> lay me down and close my eyes
> and tell me whip, tell me winnow,
> tell me sweet tell me skittish
> tell me No tell me no such thing
> tell me straw into gold tell me crept into fire
> tell me lost all my money tell me *hoarded, verboten*,
> but promise tomorrow I will be profligate,
> stepping into the sun like a trophy.

What distinguishes this from the current "cutting edge" wordplay is the way it wakes the reader to the poem's underlying exigencies. O'Rourke generates lots of energy in this fashion, and the poems of *Halflife* have the passion I associate with first books, along with the restraint that comes from poetic maturity. Their alacrity seems simultaneously to launch and anchor the poems.

"Half-life" is experienced here in a number of guises: persona poems borrow the identities of others, at times adopting the circumstances and sensibilities of historical figures, at times allowing the poet to imagine herself as she might appear to others. These partial lives, dividing and then dividing again, give off bursts of radioactivity as they disappear into the realms of the imagined. One section even delves into the biological phenomenon of the "vanishing twin syndrome," allowing the living child to speak with the sister reabsorbed in the womb.

Perhaps the most memorable of these half-lives appears in the third section of "Still Life Amongst Partial Outlines," in which the poet, while reading an old newspaper, discovers another Meghan O'Rourke—a twelve-year-old girl who, somewhere in Vermont, was repeatedly raped and tortured: "a story that could not be forgotten or owned, / like looking in a mirror and discovering someone else's face." In the eighth section of this sequence, the poet imagines a similar scene from the boys' perspective as they encounter the girl "on the back path from the fields" along Route 4. At that moment, as the title of the entire sequence reminds us, there is "still life"—until a quick cut to the impersonal voice of the narrator serves as transition:

> One takes out a knife and one takes out a rope.
> It is a tired old truth, that death comes to each
> the same, to each alone—
> a solitary, singular act,
> like laying out a tablecloth to eat in solitude—
>
> and all this a few miles from where we pass

All of a sudden the speaker is again implicated as her own experience overlaps the "story" there "by the culvert / and the river splitting into creeks / like a hand spread over the land."

The eight-part sequence entitled "Two Sisters" alternates the voices of twinned sensibilities intimately conscious of each other, nearly interchangeable, so that each has somehow been born into a state of awareness she longs to share with the other. Who is to say, the poems ask, that there is a distinct border between the living and the dead?

In the collection's title poem, the blue TV light in the window seems destined never to go out even as the bodies in the hospitals wink off, so that light itself becomes the focus—the "sodium streets" and the "trees loaded with radium, / colors like guns, // red pock-pock red and the sea yellow up, / yellow down—/ the blue hour, the waiting." Over and over, O'Rourke conjures light, as though she might refine it, as though the poems have a spectrum of their own and emotion is ascribed by color. "The light of the mind is red," one poem begins, and "all that is green must turn to red," says another.

One of the interesting features of *Halflife* is the recurrence of image or occasion, so that the same scene is experienced in more than one way and under more than one circumstance. The similarities force the reader to recognize the overlap as part of a larger tapestry. A good example is the final, encapsulating "Knives of Light," in which O'Rourke looks out and back to look in:

> I.
> In his studio, on a canvas stretched and primed,
> Bonnard kept bits of silver paper
> to catch light: so he could work
> in the poorest-lit hotel or friend's home.
> *Mes brillants*, he called the bits.
>
> He rose, moved to the window, looked out
> into the yellow crescent of lamplight, surprised
> by what he'd made. Outside, the leaves turned from leaves.
>
> II.
> In the variable light of my room
> I stand and in the wind the curtains stir.
> And in the room I see.
> The mind is a stony landscape, which replaces
> need with rock, fact with fact,
> but does not flourish beyond itself:
> is how it always was, bare, wide, cracked,
> capable of knowing small, neat things.

Halflife may be built on small, neat things, but its overall effect is that of Bonnard's paintings: light shed on those things in order to create a whole new world. This is a stellar first collection—filled with the vim and vigor of an active mind. Meghan O'Rourke's verbs are sometimes a bit hyperactive ("flags breeze over tarmac") and her wordplay can occasionally be overly clever ("the wood beneath the green, embarking skin"), but on the whole, the world she creates crackles with a radioactivity of its own.

I've often liked Robert Hass's work and have reviewed it favorably in the past, but *Time and Materials: Poems 1997–2005*, a National Book Award winner, has the tired feel of something the poet has written just to keep up with himself. The poems seem manufactured, ground out with an attempt to prove that poetry matters, and I find them a bit precious. The life described—the one that takes place on streets in France or Italy, the one where the speaker slices nectarines for Moroccan salad, the one where his parents are judged to be crudely materialistic—somehow leaves me cold.

I feel colder still about any need to "listen" to Hass's politics, as though the world should be waiting with bated breath to hear how he thinks we should handle or should have handled foreign affairs. But shouldn't poets have opinions? Yes, of course. Still, the poets Hass quotes—Whitman and Miłosz—cared so deeply that even their laments held visions for their country. Hass acts as though the criticism itself were the vision. It's not.

The poems in *Time and Materials* rarely enlist my participation, but instead remain solely the property of the writer. In doing so, they preach and posture. For example, "I Am Your Waiter Tonight and My Name Is Dmitri" recounts, via Dostoyevsky and John Ashbery, an immigrant family's long, convoluted history of war, but nowhere does it question its own assumed equivalencies. Short of William Stafford's unadulterated pacifism, all wars are not the same. Hass, via Ashbery, smugly elects to keep his protagonist safely in the poem because "you could get killed out there," and I wonder which real soldier he thinks he's saving as he plays this game of words. And "Bush's War" contains this polemical (and prosy) statement:

> The rest of us have to act like we believe
> The dead women in the rubble of Baghdad
> Who did not cast a vote for their deaths
> Or the raw white of the exposed bones
> In the bodies of their men or their children
> Are being given the gift of freedom
> Which is the virtue of the injured us.

Yet this poem does not mention the bones recently exposed in al Qaeda's mass graves and torture chambers, or—given that its setting is springtime in by now well-postwar Germany—consider that the gift of freedom does sometimes involve the loss of innocent lives. When "'Bush's War'" belongs to someone else (as it or some other war almost certainly will), there will still be complex problems to solve, and we will need thoughtful, informed statesmen—not poets—to solve them.

Nevertheless, there are clearly some interesting poems in *Time and Materials*, including several short lyrics that struggle with "the problem of describing," and several that seem to have solved the problem with their lyrical sheen. In addition, Hass achieves an interesting dynamic when he renders dialogue, often between lovers. For the most part, though, the poems do not so much contain passion as recount it. There's a clinical edge as Hass undresses his subjects, so to speak. They talk—and act—in a kind of world-weary, overly intellectualized fashion, as though by breaking their relationships into component parts they might piece together some meaning in their lives. To give Hass credit, he knows this: he orchestrates his characters' malaise. But somehow he gets caught up in his own inventions so that the speakers most closely resembling the poet himself step over the line and join his jaded chorus. Too many of these poems sermonize with a kind of self-important rumination: "What is to be done with our species? Because / We know we're going to die, to be submitted / To that tingling dance of atoms once again, / It's easy for us to feel that our lives are a dream—" Too many drift into lineated prose while resisting the prose poem they aspire to, as in this stanza from "Consciousness":

> Dean had read a book that said that consciousness was like a
> knock-knock joke, some notion of an answering call having
> brought it into being which was, finally, itself anticipating
> an answer from itself, echo of an echo of an echo.

Many other poems here, including "Breach and Orison," try for a self-conscious playfulness that, at its best, allows the reader to watch connections unfold:

> The answer was
> the sound of water, *what*
>
> *what*, *what*, the sprinkler
> said, the question
>
> of resilvering the mirror
> or smashing it
>
> once and for all the
> tea in China-
>
> town getting out of this film
> noir intact or—damaged
>
> as may be—with tact
> was not self-evident
>
> (they fired the rewrite man).

At its worst, however, Hass's play results in the pointless reiteration of what has already been done, and undone, as in these lines from "Time and Materials":

> The object o   f this poem is to report a theft,
>   In progre   ss of everything that exists

That is not th   ese words
  And their d   isposition on the page.

The object   of   his poe   is t   epro   a theft

Well, you get the idea. It goes on, and we never will know whether, in the last line quoted here, there was or wasn't a typo.

Am I too harsh in focusing on the negative here? I do so because Hass appears to have succumbed to the pressures any former poet laureate must feel to remain . . . well, a functioning, public poet. And this brings me to another question: Is it possible we were better off when our poets consulted rather than "laureated," when they were less black-tie and more blue-collar, so to speak? But that would be the subject of another treatise, so I'll bow out here by saying that Robert Hass, with his confident assertiveness, might do well to drive the two-lane back road between Austin and San Antonio. Route 165 winds through hilly ranch country and, at the bottom of every dip, a white pole at the side of the road, a flood gauge, marks the water level—one, two, three, four, five feet—so that drivers won't head into what looks like merely a shallow puddle.

One needs some courage to call a book *Failure*, but Philip Schultz willingly takes the gamble with his fifth full-length collection, the third in quick succession after a relatively long hiatus. This work examines failure in order to come to terms not only with the past but also with the future. In other words, it puts failure in its place, and that place (situated somewhere between past and future) turns out to be remarkably instructive. The father in these poems—he died penniless, a failure—seems finally to be, if not quite understood, at least appreciated, as in the title poem that recounts his funeral:

One called him a nobody.
No, I said, he was a failure.
You can't remember
a nobody's name, that's why
they're called nobodies.
Failures are unforgettable.

In Schultz's hands, this father is unforgettable in his unrelenting capacity for work, for skepticism, and for, somehow, failing to thrive. The rabbi at the funeral fails to show compassion or to understand "that not / believing in or belonging to / anything demanded a kind / of faith and buoyancy." The man's brother fails to honor his spirit; the son "left town / but failed to get away," and the poems are the result of that further failure. Ardently rebellious, angrily driven, larger than life, the father figure haunts this collection even though many of the poems veer away from Schultz's characteristic autobiographical examination of his past. Failure itself now haunts the poems, as Schultz tries to make sense of a life in present tense—a life that contains wife and sons, dreams and dogs, a future lit with guarded optimism. On the serious side, he probes his wife's younger brother's overdose as, from love's vast distance, he watches the lineaments of her grief. On the lighter side, Isaak Babel appears in a dream, fresh from his failure to escape Stalin. As the author interrogates him, Babel reveals a distinctive, pessimistic Jewish humor—"'In a pogrom everyone's a failure. / Our enemies are where our truth is hidden.'"—and then goes on, pickled in irony, to talk about their "big lopsided family" of "relative clauses / who agree on nothing."

Places and people who have failed to stick around come back to the pages of this book, stepping into the poems at will, making themselves at home again: David Ignatow, Leonard Michaels, Yehuda Amichai, a beloved dog, the San Francisco of the past, the old neighborhood in Greenwich Village, the Schwartz boys of memory—all congregate between these covers, preferring the poet's (and our) company to their own.

The first half of *Failure* is orchestrated with such care that one poem flows seamlessly into the next, deepening and expanding the ideas as they speak directly to each other. The stakes build, from "Dance Performance," with its central knowledge that the poet (as father) must step aside for his (as yet) young sons; to "The Traffic," with its oddly humorous sense that we who make it are expendable in our purposelessness; to "The Truth," with its candid mirror. "The Truth" deserves and demands its own space:

> You can hide it like a signature
> or birthmark but it's always there
> in the greasy light of your dreams,
> the knots your body makes at night,
> the sad innuendos of your eyes,
> whispering insidious asides in every
> room you cannot remain inside. It's
> there in the unquiet ideas that drag and
> plead one lonely argument at a time,
> and those who own a little are contrite
> and fearful of those who own too much,
> but owning none takes up your life.
> It cannot be replaced with a house or car,

a husband or wife, but can be ignored,
denied, and betrayed, until the last day,
when you pass yourself on the street
and recognize the agreeable life you
were afraid to lead, and turn away.

From that point we are taken to "The One Truth," which recapitulates his father's life, and then relentlessly on to "Failure," with its funereal revelations. These steps are logical and devastatingly honest, and the reader senses there is nowhere else to go. The study is complete.

Or is it? The second half of the book is a monumental fifty-five-page poem, in four parts and fifty-eight sections, entitled "The Wandering Wingless." Spoken in the voice of a mildly psychotic dog walker who wanders the streets of New York, the poem reproduces the material of the first half from another perspective. This speaker's life bears some small resemblance to the life recounted in the earlier poems, and the speaker's father bears an even greater resemblance to the father we've come to know, but everything is skewed, taking on an aura of madness. The whole story is backlit by 9/11, the day the speaker was given electroshock treatment at St. Vincent's hospital in the Village, then sent back out on the streets because of the sudden expected need for extra beds. The emergency is citywide; the public psyche, irreparably altered by threat and destruction, fuses with that of the speaker. As he wanders the streets, remembering his first dog, remembering what drove him far from family, recounting the social structure of the dog run where he daily takes his charges, and recalling the one day the city filled with smoke and ash and blighted, wingless souls, he drifts in memory and among the issues of class, race, and faith. Ultimately, he asks: "Was this what failure was—endless fear?"

"The Wandering Wingless" is not quite the major poem its parameters would imply, but that's mostly because the fictive protagonist, while he stands in for us (and we might, any of us, become him), fails somehow to include us. Maybe he's too well wrought, too much himself; maybe he's too much a cipher for the country's ills. Still, the lonely, stripped voice of the second half of *Failure* informs the earlier poems so that one can almost imagine shutting the book and allowing both halves to bleed into each other. The poet's life—his family, his city, his past—could easily have been any of those lost lives, peering out from the cracked mirror of his perceptions. The reader comes to understand that the seemingly straightforward poems of the first half arise from/are part of a shattered vision, and that the great good humor and optimism expressed in the first several pages are hard won—a vision of success that can only be realized through a failure of equal proportion. Philip Schultz has shown us what we have to lose, and he has given us the compassionate language by which to save it.

Old Heart. Old friend, I think, as I slide easily into Stanley Plumly's rhythms, the familiar clothes of his voice—and his stance. The past resurrected. His past. My past. My past reading of his past. How he fuses time, calls up the past-in-the-present at every turn, each bird song simultaneously trilled in a *then* and a *now*, each moment held and weighed while the lens of history illuminates it from within.

Plumly's very method is combinatorial: one event sheds light on another until, finally, they are fused past separation. The parable of the Prodigal Son is read against (and through and within) the story of King Lear. Ted Hughes's accomplishment is weighed (and measured) alongside those of Philip Larkin and Robert Lowell, whose selection of Plumly's first book for the Delmore Schwartz prize seemed (in some uneasy back part of the brain) to consign Plumly himself to a similar early death. That's remembered because a renewed sense of mortality dominates this book, from its title onward. Everything mortal fades to something else, and Plumly's own "silent" heart attack merges with his father's louder one. Poetry itself is read against its long past with a preservative fervor.

The old poets haunt these pages, sometimes quoted, sometimes simply as informing spirits; in "Debt," Pound, Stevens, and Eliot become the "three or four dour men" standing around as a young father struggles to save his farm, his son peering through the window as they circle the land, measuring, measuring; and Keats is there, hovering in the peripheral vision of all the poems, his life held up over and over so that he is the impetus behind what might be the most eloquent piece of literary criticism I've ever read—"Nostalgia." In forty lines (five eight-line stanzas), Plumly moves from identifying a tiger swallowtail circling near a dead wren to Pound's dictum, "The natural object is always the adequate symbol," and then on to contemplate how the "natural object" works within a poem. Along the way, he recounts the criticism of Robert Scholes and recapitulates the dismantling of the New Critics, and then goes on to mention what's "worse"—"post-structural, post- / lyrical, post-Derrida and -Barthes, post-Paul / de Man, the Nazi, post-reading of the text"—in order to remember Cleanth Brooks, half-blind, reading with a magnifying glass. Plumly is sure in his knowledge that Brooks "would certainly / have seen the bird grounded on one wing / before the butterfly; truth, then beauty," and Plumly's musical orchestration of the names that would deconstruct his own poetic world puts them neatly in their place. We may be nostalgic to remember when poetry—the best words in the best order—mattered, but by artful use of hyphen and line break, Plumly makes it matter all over again.

Old Heart pays homage to the old poets in a number of other ways. The book is filled with variations on the sonnet. Almost as a contrast, "Meander" stretches its long lines, turning them like a river, actively demonstrating metaphor as it moves to where poem and body are one: "my heart, my spine, my cloud, the X-rays coldly spiritual, the / invisible made visible." Many of the poems are pastoral, including one called "Pastoral," which goes against the grain of expectation. In order to really see, in order to find the adequate symbol, in order to look at the whole (as one does with a painting by first seeing a detail, as one sights "a bird within its song"), Plumly defines his own poetics:

> sometimes, for kinds of beauty, you forgive
> the beautiful, the photographic fragment,
> the small and separate moment,
> even a summer's sunset in a field,
> your rough hand running the tops of thistle
> and wild wheat, domed clusters,
> and complexities of leaves,
> the umbels, whorls, bracts, and involucres.

There's a physical presence in his knowledge, a rough hand that has, in fact, run over the grasses of his childhood. And "Childhood" is experienced as one of those umbels: as a palpable, physical entity that nothing can stop or keep out. It's as ubiquitous as the snow "drifting from one side of the road to the other," worked by the wind, or passing "like the light over your face" at the window, or filling the white oaks that will, in summer, hold the birds that will eventually disappear. The whole of a lifetime is encapsulated in the child's knowledge of seasons, culminating in a mature man's declaration of being—perhaps the very opposite of an *ars poetica*, more a statement of fact. Or an epitaph.

> The body
> piecemeal wastes away, the something soul
> slips from the mouth, muse and sacred memory
> shuts its eyes. I died, I climbed a tree, I sang.

The seamless flow of focus allows Plumly to slip from one time to another, one realm of consciousness to another. But this alone would not make *Old Heart* stand out as different from his other books, and, indeed, in many ways it is an extension of a lifelong proclamation of what it is to occupy a singular body, to sing an individual praise. But in some ways this volume has a tougher edge. It wants to say as well as evoke, yet it wants that "saying" in the form of poetry, not polemics. "Against Narrative," for example, recounts Alfred Hitchcock's *The 39 Steps* to show us how to read meanings through image, against time, within history, by means of what goes unsaid, undone.

Hitchcockian, then, is Plumly's treatment of 9/11. " 'The Morning America Changed' " recounts the poet's actual experience of the event: the Italian Alps, the lake deep and blue, the white boats shining at midafternoon, a day so perfect that even the voice breaking into it sounds like rain in the distance, and then—in only two lines—"on the tiny screen inside / pillars of fire pouring darkly into clouds." From its title forward, the poem announces the event as belonging to others, seen from a distance, and yet that very distance leads to an understanding about the deep nature of tragedy. Plumly's very exclusion from the event, and his subsequent refusal to appropriate, to let it be anything but the "natural object" itself, is the point—and I find this poem far more moving than any of the myriad others I've read on this subject.

" 'The Morning America Changed' " is followed by my favorite poem in the collection, "Long Companions." Spoken in the first-person plural, it recounts the historical framework of those born in 1939—a litany of wars that has defined their generation. The "we" begins to build a collective experience and sensibility, and yet the plural remains peculiarly private; "our" uncles are the poet's uncles. The communal narrative is personal in such a way that "Love our friends / anew, watch them disappear, one by one" has the feel of specific loss, a mortality brought close to home. Then the poem, even as it opens out companionably to include the general, narrows to the one defining moment before it prophesies an acknowledged future:

> Watch the face of the deep darken
> and roll in. Watch the tallest window
> buildings break and fall. The heart bobs
> and breaks. There is fire in the mirror,
> a ghost peripheral profile at the eye.
> Time passes, light pours, in themselves
> a happiness.

The politics here is set against the backdrop of history, and that history is itself seen as only a fragment of a longer line of cause and effect, effect and cause. Mortality is the common denominator throughout this book, and the very fact of death seems to clarify its subjects: Lyndon Johnson; Kafka; Lear; Jan Palach (who committed suicide by self-immolation in protest of the Communist occupation of Czechoslovakia); the poet's father, whose hard death is enacted again and again; his mother, who wastes down to a whistle of will. "We" are caught in mortality's egalitarian eye, and we see everything through its lens, stepping at will into the past, stepping out into time the way the Prague of "Elevens" easily "transforms backwards" in snow, the way the lake remembers the glacier that formed it, the way the man in London is the child in Ohio, the way the whole life is lit on the screen as the heart beats and beats under medicine's scrutiny and the temple of the body is filled with the remembered response to looking up, in the Duomo, when "the terror of / a bird took all the heart out of the air."

Did I fail to mention the birds? They are everywhere—from the hectoring crow and the quarrelsome jays to the nearly invisible songbirds that perch in the branches throughout these poems. Birds appear as spirits (the tissue-thin poems of a dead friend found between the pages of his books) and as metaphor (the sky a "starved black wing"). They chatter and clamor to be heard, or they are quieted, as in "Audubon Aviary," to "stillborn animation." To see something alive "is to almost miss the moment / and have to bring it back / diminished as a memory." Yet Plumly tries for far more than diminishment as he activates memory—not to reconstruct, but to provide texture and intuition. In saying of Audubon that his "silences, / his dark articulate stillnesses / are what we have against what / we'll remember," Stanley Plumly sets for himself his own poetic aspiration. In the end, *Old Heart* serves as a cardinal point on the compass of my reading; it contains the lifeblood of song as it defends the crucial endeavor to give each (re)collected moment its living, breathing name.

Puzzles

On Tony Hoagland's *Unincorporated Persons in the Late Honda Dynasty*; Terrance Hayes's *Lighthead*; Connie Wanek's *On Speaking Terms*; and Peggy Shumaker's *Gnawed Bones*.

IN 1962—THAT'S RIGHT, nearly a half century ago—I was in London, taking a course in what was then contemporary British literature and art. The course consisted of a long reading list that provided fodder for our daily discussion sessions, plus a series of guest lectures, visits to museums (to see work by Ben Nicholson, Henry Moore, Barbara Hepworth), attendance at concerts (including Benjamin Britten's compositions performed in St. Paul's Cathedral), as well as productions of plays by John Osborne and Harold Pinter. But what has stayed with me most over the years is a talk by the scholar and lexicographer Eric Partridge, of *Usage and Abusage: A Guide to Good English* fame.

Partridge told how one day, while walking in the Yorkshire backcountry, he came across an old-timer working in his small garden. While they were talking, the old man suddenly pointed at a cluster of dandelions and said, "See those golden lads and lasses? We call 'em chimney sweepers when they coom to dust." Thus, with one sentence, the gardener unlocked a conundrum that Partridge had been puzzling over throughout his critical career—the nature of a Shakespearean metaphor that had eluded him.[1] Not that he hadn't sensed the flavor of the lines, but the *source* of the metaphor had, until that moment, seemed irretrievable. In Yorkshire, as in the American South, a vestige of sixteenth-century English had been preserved. The dandelions—with their visible life cycle and distinctive

1. Counter to most misquotings, the passage from Shakespeare's *Cymbeline* actually reads: "Golden lads and girls all must, / As chimney-sweepers, come to dust."

shape—provided the missing link to what had, before, simply been a striking linguistic construction.

There are puzzles, and then there are puzzles. I know this firsthand because recently, trying to stave off the boredom that inevitably comes with the lethargy and lightheadedness of chemotherapy, I have become a master of jigsaws. Or, if not master, then connoisseur. I can tell with a glance at the box cover just how long a certain puzzle is likely to take me—whether it's a quick, one-week in-and-out, or will involve a painful three-week ordeal before it finally "yields" to my watchful eye. (Trust me: fireworks launched from the Eiffel Tower will take more than a month.)

Puzzles are strange. They are, somehow, more than the sum of their parts. In fact, I've learned a lot from them. I've learned that there are subtle distinctions among roses, that Times Square at midnight is a single blaze of dark and light, and that hot air balloons are very often indistinguishable from each other. I've learned that there are infinite variations in marble—even painted marble. I've learned that Jackson Pollock must have been certifiably crazy—and a puzzle of his painting can turn you even crazier. I have at times suspected that there is a gnome at the Ravensburger factory who gleefully lifts just one piece from each puzzle and puts it in a different box, or simply pops it in his mouth. And thanks to some anonymous donors from Portland, Oregon, I've learned that it was probably easier to build the Taj Mahal than to reconstruct it in three dimensions with tiny Styrofoam blocks.

Overall, I've learned enough to develop some "rules":

1) Never begin a 1,000-piece puzzle until you've isolated at least 120 straight pieces.
2) Don't forget that the matte blue on the backs of puzzle pieces is exactly the same shade as the sky.
3) Spaces are always bigger—or smaller—than they appear.
4) To paraphrase my favorite riddle: What is the difference between a piece? Answer: One piece is both the same!
5) Puzzles do have one practical application—after working studiously on jigsaws, you will always be able to pack the trunk of your car efficiently.

Reviewing poetry is a whole lot like putting together a jigsaw puzzle—and some books make it easier than others for us to unlock their secrets. My first reading of a collection is the equivalent of looking at the picture on the box—I get an overview, a sense of the whole. The second reading is to sort out the straight pieces, providing a frame. The third reading is to "sort" the rest of the individual pieces, to see how they might "fit" with each other and within the frame. The fourth reading is to tease out any further connections, and to note—with surprise—how some pieces fit where you least expect. The fifth reading is to watch for resolution as the picture comes together again, spread out before you as something you've finally *seen*, intact. And you realize you've handled every single piece, that you know this puzzle intimately.

Tony Hoagland has a knack for making you feel that you know a poem intimately right from its opening lines. His style is easygoing, colloquial—and his subject matter, as almost all the blurbs on his books attest, is eclectic. "It's hard to imagine any aspect of contemporary American life that couldn't make its way into the writing of Tony Hoagland, or a word in common or formal usage he would shy away from," begins the judges' citation for his 2008 Jackson Poetry Prize, awarded by *Poets & Writers*. *Unincorporated Persons in the Late Honda Dynasty* makes the same point simply by its title, and the first two lines of the initial poem reinforce the claim: "A bird with a cry like a cell phone says something / to a bird which sounds like a manual typewriter." But don't be fooled—this is not the easy puzzle that it might appear to be. Hoagland is always more serious than his individual lines seem to indicate.

Humor is one of Hoagland's trademarks, and this new collection casts an amused eye at just about everything: cement trucks, Britney Spears, divorce, foghorns, summer—and in any instance the poem might be expected to sprout a SWAT team, an AA meeting, a credit card, or a "single yellow daffodil." The juxtapositions are always surprising, pleasurable, entertaining. You never quite know what will come next—and that is possibly the first thing you need to know to unlock what Hoagland is after.

Humor is usually more subtle than it is touted to be, and subtle humor is often hard for the reader to interpret. In Hoagland's work, it sneaks up on you: just when you think you're supposed to laugh, the poem twists away, diving into the serious, and just when a poem seems to want you to "take it personal," it turns flippant and makes you smile. Hoagland has mastered the art of contortion, so you almost certainly will not leave a poem on the same note upon which you entered. This is perhaps never more clear than when a poem begins and ends on the same image, as does "My Father's Vocabulary":

> In the history of American speech
> he was born between "Dirty Commies" and "Nice tits."
>
> He worked for Uncle Sam,
> and married a dizzy gal from Pittsburgh with a mouth on her.

I was conceived in the decade
between "Far Out" and "Whatever";

in the precise moment when "going all the way"
turned into "getting it on."

The reader busily engages the sense of history wrapped up in slang and the speaker's unfolding story, while the poet—outside of the quotation marks—plays his own games with the history of speech. The poem relies on idiom to convey the sense of detachment between father and son, which pertains even during their last visit, "in the twilight zone of a clinic, between 'feeling no pain' and 'catching a buzz.'" With the introduction of a setting, the meanings turn somber: the poem ends where it opened, but with the added realities of how all lives fold back on themselves, and of how we never really see through to the person behind the words because no talk is adequate to the task:

For that occasion I had carefully prepared
a suitcase full of small talk

—But he was already packed and going backwards,
with the nice tits and the dirty commies,

to the small town of his vocabulary,
somewhere outside of Pittsburgh.

Because the range of subject matter is so vast, it's easy to think that Hoagland's "puzzle" is the Jackson Pollock—a little paint thrown in spatters at a vast white canvas. But Hoagland's spatters, like Pollock's, are directed—and accurate. He homes in on certain recognizable aspects of American life—the corporate ethos, cellphones, "CNN atrocities," or foreign policy—then pulls in something so seemingly out of context that it provides a new angle of perspective.

There is a thematic connection in "The Story of the Father," where, after the funeral, a father (generic) burns photographs of his son, who has committed suicide. The disconnection grows as the father breathes in the "chemistry of burning Polaroids" and stares toward the horizon, unaware that he is "hogging all the pain." His surprise at the rest of the family's rage is recounted by a narrator who is trying to reconstruct his own imagination and who intrudes on the story in order to comment. The narrator displays empathy, but more important he extends his musings to the universal. In a recapitulation of human experience, "story" itself is internalized:

It is not the misbegotten logic of the father;
it is not the pity of the snuffed-out youth;

it is the old intelligence of pain
that I admire:

how it moves around inside of him like smoke;

how it knows exactly what to do with human beings
to stay inside of them forever.

The distance this father has put between his grief and that of the rest of the family may isolate him forever. And distance—it seems to me—is one of Hoagland's pervasive themes. The very culture that brings diverse people together also serves to alienate. In imagination, Hoagland slams the plane of America into a mountainside, or ties corporate CEOs to the fate of their temps. But his "rant" is not so much anger or resentment as it is a clear-headed glimpse of society's underbelly. His gentle railing against beauty pageants and mini-malls and self-help books is offset by brief moments of perfection, moments when everything seems to coalesce around a fullness of being. Only by being open to all moments can the poet bridge the gaps to find a sense of what finally matters. Only then can the narrator turn his gaze inward, recognizing even the precision of imperfection: "and even my self-righteousness began to wane and lose its torchlike force."

What begins as wry amusement often shifts to bemused wonder as Hoagland works his way toward meaning. "Muchness" begins with watching, then narrating: a woman steps into a boat, which then pulls away. The watcher is left to contemplate the nature of his own heart, how it silently coils, then shocks. But, since story is what is at stake, the speaker must move on to the mind, reflecting:

It was your vanished boat
that gave the scene a shape,
with its suggestion of journey and destination.

And the narrative then, having done its work,
it vanished too,
leaving just its affectionate cousin description behind.

—Description,
which lingers,
and loves for no reason.

The phrase "no reason" unlocks the full puzzle of Hoagland's poems—things simply *are*, and the ability to make something of them is one of life's greatest joys.

The second key to a full appreciation of this work is cadence. Hoagland reproduces the rollicking rhythms of speech with a meticulous ear. His longish lines, heavily iambic, are peppered with trochee and anapest that keep the tongue twisting. But to my ear, Hoagland's subtle and varied use of alliteration is what holds his lines in a taut suspension that delights: "But I couldn't and I didn't and I don't" or "it was the passionate effort of a certain defective trumpet. . . ." Such lines are why I'm ready when one of his more potent statements—"The artist begins to study the art of subtraction"—catches my attention, and I realize that the reasons for the plethora of detail—the poodles and lymphomas and Dewey Decimal Systems and demolition sites of this late Honda Dynasty—are there for us to remove and examine, one by one. Tony Hoagland tosses his paint at the canvas and our job is to "take it personal," to note the infinite variations, the nuance and detail that lead to self-understanding.

The biggest puzzle of Terrance Hayes's fourth collection, *Lighthead*, may be why Penguin chose such a tiny (and light) typeface. These poems are not meant to be taken lightly, and they deserved better in the design department.

In *Lighthead*, Hayes carries on with some of his trademark jazz rhythms and his off-the-cuff riffs on what it is to be black in America, to be American, and to be male. The title of the collection may seem enigmatic, but the poems are concerned with light of all kinds, from "the daze the day begets" to "moonlight juicing naked branches" to images of burning and conflagration. Perhaps the key to this book is really the second syllable of its title: all the poems spring from the head—clever, illusory, cerebral—as they play with forms and language.

One such form is the Japanese *pecha kucha*, which Hayes has adapted in ways that allow for maximum flights of imagination. In these, he is able to tell an extended story with deft leaps that leave it, always, slightly ethereal, framed by possibility and ambiguity. Perhaps most emblematic of these is "Arbor for Butch," where the poet is able to "construct" a meeting with his father and, in some ways, work through one problematic thread of the collection. The father figure is troublesome throughout, and here the crux of the relationship is stated: "Even if I knew this first meeting was our last, I would / have nothing to offer beyond the life I have made without him." A meditation on blood brings the speaker no closer to a man who is "like the road, skid-marked / and distant." In "Bullethead for Earthell" Hayes goes back to Vietnam, to the moments before his father's father's death. For different reasons, Hayes has shared a fatherless existence with his own father, and this bears scrutiny:

And it must be abstract
as dream, pure theory, the moment of death.
. . . .
and the future
scampers down to cover you. Grandaddy,
when my father, the first time I met him,
tried to recall your face, there was nothing
but smoke coaxing our history from his breath.

However, the collection as a whole is marked by the more solid presence of a step-father—a constancy against which the poet often tests his own concepts of parenthood.

Lighthead is divided into four discrete sections, yet each covers similar territory. All the poems, in one sense or another, delve into questions of identity. Their cultural range is somewhat different from Hoagland's, but equally varied. The back bars and railroad tracks of America offer up a range of subjects—from Malcolm X to Satchmo to black tortillas to banjos to chin wool—all of which serve to "record the rumors and raucous rhythms / of my people, our jangled history, the slander / in our sugar, the ardor in our anger. . . ."

Reading through the collection I found myself interested in the ways that Hayes invents new forms out of old. "Three Measures of Time" rings changes on the villanelle, using repetitive imagery and phraseology to look at one late-night scene from the brother's, the father's, and the mother's perspective. There are other experiments with structure and form. "Hide," spanning facing pages as though it were two poems instead of one, pairs both imagery and words:

The tire was like the wet hide of a seal I was the wet hide too in a seal
dropped from the bridge of shadows on broad river bridge
to waters as black as a seal sleepy as the drowned and black
glistening that way in the wake listening that way to the wakefulness

This kind of inventiveness characterizes Hayes's experimentations. He couples these with several distinctive reversals of phrases (one of these can be seen with Harriet Tubman "pointing a finger black enough to be her pistol barrel / toward the future or pointing a pistol barrel black enough / to be her finger"), and the interchangeability disrupts any sense of full completion. The entire collection is restless, unwilling to settle down. Yet this slipperiness gives the book its charm, allows Hayes to call Wallace Stevens his "foe" while stating, "I have a capacity for love without / forgiveness" as he recognizes that Stevens, "with pipes of winter lining his cognition," learned to bring a sentence to its knees.

The poems of *Lighthead* pay general homage to Poetry (capital P) as they make their various linguistic moves. "The Golden Shovel," after Gwendolyn Brooks's "We Real Cool," demonstrates this at every level. Two versions, spanning ten years, where each line ends with the same words as Brooks's modern classic, attest to the poet's shift in emphasis from personal content (the 1981 version narrates a witnessed violence) to a more philosophical stance (as though, in 1991, the viewer of the first version has become street-smart and a bit cynical). Mirroring—but not mimicking—the original poem, Hayes takes his second version into the abstract, breaking apart the end-words to further complicate the language he inherited from Brooks:

Light can be straight-

ened by its shadow. What we
break is what we hold. A sing-

ular blue note. An outcry singed exiting the throat. We

push until we thin, thin-
king we won't creep back again.

While God licks his kin, we
sing until our blood is jazz,

we swing from June to June.
We sweat to keep from we-

eping. Groomed on a die-
t of hunger, we end too soon.

Forced, in this manner, to consider the central words (how "singular" contains "sing"), their linking sounds (as in "thin" and "think"), and the divisions into rhymed patterns (abcacba, and so on), the reader is included in sixteen end-line repetitions of "we."

Lighthead is often a bravura performance, fast-paced and electric in its innovations. There's fun in "Ghazal-head" as Hayes plays games within the form:

You no-good form sucker, that's what.
You no-good backscratcher, that's what.

A blue thumbnail. An old light fixture. A toylike hammer.
A glass or tumbler. Bend your fingers, that's what.

You're one of those sleepers. Those pod people
Poking their noses, those nose blowers, that's what.

Et cetera. And yet sometimes I worry that Hayes's deft moves, his about-face and quick jab, will not make for poems that stick in memory. Individual lines are haunting, but the cumulative poem—with real gravitas—is fairly rare in this collection. One such, however, is "The Mustache." Hayes plays all the same games here, but the mustache ("shadow carved by what divides / the mind and tongue"), with its hint of Hitler at the margins, gives us pause, and its conspiratorial ending seems somehow significant:

The pavement has no way
Of knowing the future leading

Into the valley. The wood of burning
Barnyards and bones, ash coughed out
And covering, gaunt and haunted,

Quiver of rhetoric. Oh, the weight of it,
Possible as grief and hesitation,
As blindness and the wind-struck structures,

Edged and peripheral mustache,
Part fastened fashion, part flag or shadow
Of the flag on this hysterical country.

Terrance Hayes has made it his calling to explore "this country"—how minorities have fared in its hard-won struggle for justice; how it believes and disbelieves its own adages; how, in the end, it creates the opportunity for a poet to write whatever light comes into his inspired and provocative head.

On Speaking Terms is the perfect title for Minnesotan Connie Wanek's third book. Wanek explores almost as wide a range of subjects as do Hoagland and Hayes, and her poems rather clearly divide into those that act a bit like Neruda's *Odas Elementales*—in Wanek's case giving a personal look at such things as umbrellas, blue ink, honey, pumpkins, Monopoly, Scrabble, musical chairs, and jacks—and some longer, more complex (and more personal) lyrics that typically center on some *occasion* that for her becomes a source of contemplation and eventual insight. In every poem, she is on speaking terms with things, emotions, and especially herself.

Wanek's easygoing, controlled, and conversational style results in a kind of modulated intimacy. One specific form of intimacy appears in her metaphors, which feel almost innate as she extends her comparisons to offer up more of the world. For example, a tennis game in "Popcorn" serves to remind us of sunlight and shadow *before* the natural phenomenon strikes its particularly apt chord:

> My shadow swung its shadow racket,
> striking the shadow ball that flew forth to land
> directly under the genuine ball,
> a conjunction perfectly timed, like an eclipse.

With equal ease, pickles become frogs; a tent is a balloon; a comb has been "untangling the night"; and, in a description of cross-country skiing, "behind us / two blue lines unscrolled / and the punctures of our poles / were evidence of chronic instability." Verbs provide further metaphor, as in "water heals behind the canoe" and "a few ripples on the lake / folding themselves over like anonymous notes."

Wanek makes a virtue of simplicity. But in her hands, what is simple also reveals its complexities. One minute a mother is wrapping Christmas presents for her grown children, the silence "so complete that I heard / my scissors sever the very cells of the paper," and in the next we experience an age-old emotion: "the solitude I once craved" has turned into a moment of staring out the window at a pine "topped with a single preening crow / that shone like a black star." The fusion of religious event with personal story makes the Virgin fully human and universalizes the experience of mothers everywhere giving up their children to the larger world. These are not the easy imaginative transformations of one thing into another, but a hard-won recognition of the world at work—an earned emotional insight that fits, like the last piece of a puzzle, with a satisfactory snap.

The "Neruda" poems alone would give readers a sense of Wanek's adept and playful ways with words and images. But what makes this book extraordinary is a series of complex emotional studies, two of which are perhaps the best poems I've read in a long time.

"The Death of My Father" takes the fact that the speaker's father died when she was not present and worries it from the opening lines:

> He died at different times in different places.
> In Wales he died tomorrow,
> which doesn't mean his death was preventable.
> It had been coming for years,
> crossing the ocean, the desert, pausing often,
> moving like water or wind,
> here turned aside by a stone,
> then hurried where the way was clear.

Mourning her absence at the "exact moment" and circumstance of death, the daughter is left to imagine myriad deaths. No memory is free of them. Without finality, the ending of the poem earns its right to upend a well-known hymn:

> The longing to believe is more enduring
> than any truth—truth is so perishable.
> I once was found, but now I'm lost.
> I could see, but now I'm blind.

"A Random Gust from the North" is a sequence of six titled sections, each recalling an occasion somewhere on Lake Superior. The speaker narrates on behalf of an anonymous "he" who has spent years fishing these waters, so the information about the lake is presented intimately and thoroughly—"He went out against the will of the lake. / The water red as sunrise: / he was crossing the sky." The man is so comfortable in his surroundings, learned from the womb, that it is "impossible to say whether the water / speaks from within or without. / Ashore again, he felt the earth / rock on its fulcrum. . . ."

The final section of "A Random Gust" begins with an impersonal interrogation of the North Star ("Can there be such an absolute arrival?"), then resolves all pronouns into an inclusive "we" that universalizes the experience:

> So much light,
> light to spare, light to spread on the ice like salt.
> The pole afloat: we are neither first
> nor last, though perhaps nearer the last.
> We need no instruments.
> The equatorial vertigo subsides;
> the heat of exertion dissipates.
> We have no fear of falling.
> We can never be lost.

Each poem in *On Speaking Terms* is delicately poised, doing exactly its own work, and no more; each tells no story but that of the somewhat timeless present of its narrator. The poems speak to one another only in the way that poems, as they accrue, attest to a way of seeing the world. Wanek seeks something to enter through imagination, knowing that it can never be known fully but that the process may inspire insight, and the outcome might reveal something original. Her poems are similar to her description of open water—"a window to the bottom."

"A Sighting" speaks perhaps most eloquently for Wanek's familiarity and awe as she follows the halting flight of a gray owl. The final three stanzas illustrate her ability to describe and to enter her subject simultaneously:

He flew as though it gave him no pleasure,
forcing himself from the bough,
falling until his wings caught him:
they had to stroke hard, like heavy oars.

He must have just eaten
something that had, itself, just eaten.
Finally he crossed the swamp and vanished
as into a new day, hours before us,

and we stood near the chest-high reeds,
our feet sinking, and felt
we'd been dropped suddenly from midair
back into our lives.

Connie Wanek has such a natural way with the natural world that her metaphors provide more than insight; they take us beyond the ordinary into a realm where we, too, are on speaking terms with objects and where almost anything can happen. Then they drop us back into our lives, enriched and enlivened.

Peggy Shumaker's sixth full-length collection, *Gnawed Bones*, is perhaps her finest. Shumaker, too, covers a wide range—but she casts a far more personal eye than the other poets considered here as she worries at the puzzle of human relationships as well as human connection to the land itself. The first section of the book has poems set in Alaska, Hawaii, western Washington, the Sonoran desert, somewhere in the Middle East, and, yes, the imagination. The last three sections cover, in poetic form, some of the material explored in *Just Breathe Normally* (2007), a memoir in short lyrical prose sections set against the poet's life-threatening accident. In each, setting is important because it becomes an integral part of how the subject matter is presented through image. The second section of *Gnawed Bones*, centered on Shumaker's father's death, is geographically varied; the third, focused on her mother, digs deep into the Arizona desert; and the fourth, chronicling her own slow recovery, stays closer to home in Alaska.

Shumaker's style is far more spare than that of any of the other poets examined here. Her line is typically short and image-laden, so that the "message," as such, is carried (or discovered) pictorially. "The Aroma of Rain in the Desert" is an especially good example because it takes on the difficult task of conveying smell:

Rain so brief
dust puffs up,
each drop
a small hollow
moist as a secret
held under the tongue.

Black and yellow
buzzing sexual,
wide open
false eyes
mariposa wings
not quite dry.

Each drop bursts—bright orange
poppies erupt, flow
molten down the flanks
of Picacho, hot
ocean of small hands
waving from under earth.

Whether simply smelling rain evokes the visual, or whether the visual somehow contains the aroma, the title weds sight to smell. The ear is piqued, too; the slant rhymes of "up/drop" and "hollow/yellow," coupled with the consonance of "mariposa/poppies," the assonance of "flow/molten/ocean," and the resultant blooming contained in "bursts/earth," combine to activate the auditory experience. Throughout the pervasive near-hum of the underlying *u*, Shumaker has sprinkled a repeated plosive *p*, thus making us hear the rain as well. Building such bridges seems to be one motivation for this particular book as it chronicles the struggle—in several areas—to make things whole.

"My Father Never" is the title of one poem, and it seems he never did much to act like a father. But Shumaker is not bitter; she has worked through childhood resentments, has found an adult center. Thus there is something for us to learn from her six-line poem, "Beyond Words, This Language":

The morning I was born
                    you held my hand.

The morning you died
                    I held your hand.

What's left
                    to forgive?

Between the large forces of life and death, the human drama resides. There's still ambivalence in those final lines, indicated by the break. Just how *do* the pieces fall into place? And yet, either way the question is interpreted, forgiveness is the final answer; it may be only a word, but it is something to hope for, something human, something to convey in the language of touch.

The "mother" poems in *Gnawed Bones* are more complex, more haunted. "Go to the Broom Closet and Pick Out a Stick" is the title of one, and those exact words appear later in "Asthma." "Asthma was the reason she couldn't swim, couldn't / push us on swings" and, then, "The reason she didn't want to / be here. The reason she left." "Sky of Souls" pushes the issue: "A holy man / once told me // a child can atone / for her mother's death / wish." Again, the line breaks open the poem to double meanings. If the child cannot atone for the death, maybe for the wish? Shumaker follows this in "You Should Know Better" with the knowledge that she herself will bear no children:

> And the bonus tumor
> growing on a stalk,
>
> odd yellow,
> yolk of all my eggs,
> never ripened into children,
> renegade ovary,
> releasing all through me
> fugitive colors.

These unborn children are nurtured throughout the poems, which themselves become her progeny.

The fourth section is "about" language as much as it is about the frightening accident that left the poet fighting for life. Sight, sound, thought, even touch have been compromised. Deprived for some time of her ability to speak, and longer deprived by her injured brain of the full use of the tool of language, Shumaker makes us aware of what a vital tool that is. "Bubble or clot, hard block / stopping blood to the brain, / blanks out territories / that won't be heard from / again, blanks out / the middle of a sentence, / the whole family / of words. . . ." Again and again the speaker asks what happened. Again and again, patiently, she is told. Finally, words find their objects: "Penny. Paperclip." And with the return of language comes the ability to assess what her life has meant: "*Have I nourished / more roots than I undercut?*" The poems attest to the affirmative, for this reader at least. "For Joe" is the book's dedication, and his presence is evoked at every phase of this difficult last section.

The final poem, "Long Before We Got Here, Long After We're Gone," takes an extended view, finding resolution within multiple images of light; the first-person plural turns this into a love poem as "we" are out on the trail once more. The book ends where it began, circling back to the natural world, filled with gratitude to be able to experience it with full sensory perception:

> In the season blue-white sun
> barely lifts above the ridge,
> limps along the horizon
> then dives out of sight,
> we're changed each day by light.
>
> Someone who's gone before
> broke trail, set tracks.
> With the right kick wax,
> we make our way among birch
> breathing hard rare frosted light.
>
> We make of light arpeggio crystals,
> caribou dance fans, shush
> of bristles. One moment made
> alive, human, unafraid.
> All that's lost not gone.

Perhaps the biggest puzzle of all is how, in an age of "professionalized" poetry, each poet has managed to put a unique spin on the use of image, language, metaphor. It would be impossible to confuse these four poets—and more, I think it is even a sure bet that, given just a single passage, a perceptive reader could quickly and easily identify the person behind the poem. Distinctive poets come relatively early to their "voiceprint," which seems to be the product of cadence coupled with angle of vision. One never confuses Auden with Eliot, Dickinson with Bishop. Exactly how our most accomplished poets forge their voices remains a mystery, but I am convinced the four I've discussed here rise toward the top because of the very quirks that differentiate them. They ask of the world very different questions, adding their puzzling to the long list of puzzlings through the ages. And the world, as always, answers with a question of its own.

Walking the Line

On James Richardson's *By the Numbers*; Robert Wrigley's *Beautiful Country*; Elizabeth Bradfield's *Approaching Ice*; and Robert Cording's *Walking with Ruskin.*

I break lines for no apparent reason
David Grove, suggestion for a bumper sticker on jjgallaher.blogspot.com

I HAVE AN OLD FRIEND who posts bits of poetry on Facebook every day. For the most part, I love this—love the pieces he selects. He reminds me (and all his other friends) that Tennyson, Hopkins, Yeats, Frost, Levertov—and many others in between, and beyond—have a place in our lives. But even as my heart sometimes swells to see something familiar, or to encounter something new, it also falls when something just doesn't "work" in this format, the few lines going flat, refusing to take me into them. I find it's easier to see "flaws" when you only have five or six lines, and these snippets either quickly fire me up or just as quickly dampen any flame.

From this, I make some generalizations. Poets writing in earlier times knew how to engage the ear right from the start. They actually led with the ear, not the eye, but contemporary poets very often engage the eye at the expense of the ear. This may be all well and good when we have the complete poem before us, but when there are only disembodied lines we may find it hard to get a "sense" of the poem. Here's what I sometimes see in current collections: lines that do absolutely nothing to advance the cause. That is, lines that carry very little weight, maybe offering only a noun or two, possibly an adjective. I see lines that are flaccid, devoid of the energy of cadence or chime. I see lines that, quite frankly, are not lines at all—just words strung out or dropped away from, configured for no apparent reason.

I have no firm theories about the line. I have read—and enjoyed—various symposia on the line, the kind that appeared in *Field* maybe twenty years ago, the kind I see cropping up in journals again these days. I am fascinated by what practicing poets feel the line can do for them. But, to be honest, sometimes I do not "feel" their lines, do not fall in love with a poem for what its lines might say.

For example, one of my friend's recent postings contained what clearly could be described as "chopped-up prose":

> Walking through the field with my little brother Seth
> I pointed to a place where kids had made angels in the snow.
> For some reason I told him that a troop of angels
> had been shot and dissolved when they hit the ground.

It may not be fair to judge only four lines of a poem—but that was all I had, and I did not find myself wanting to search out the rest. This excerpt suffers, I think, from what Marvin Bell, in his essay "On the Practice of Free Verse," would call a lack of interesting "syntax":

> Talk about "the line" by itself is never sufficient because lines hold hands with syntax. . . . Syntax provides the occasions for enjambments and end-stops, as well as for caesuras within lines. Syntax distributes the syllables and, in English, the stresses. Thus, the key to free verse may be the sentence.[1]

In recent years, Bell has conducted his own complex experimentation with syntax, and his now-several volumes of "Dead Man" poems dispense with the line almost entirely, using the sentence as their basic unit. Still, I contend that the line can give some indication of how a poem should be read. For instance, in a symposium in *Center: A Journal for the Literary Arts* (vol. 7, 2008), Marianne Boruch muses on the "interiority" that the line reveals:

> That interiority works directly against the bright light, rational feel of the sentence—the very *public* sentence threaded down the page to make those lines. . . . Because the line against the larger wealth of the sentence is a rebel thing which undercuts order. With it comes all that can't be fully controlled: the irrational, the near-deranged, the deeply personal and individual utterance.

That is one of the line's dimensions—it can act as an agent of freedom. Simultaneously, however, it can be a form of restraint. Bell's piece enumerates various ways to take its measure: "A line might be a unit of rhythm, syntax, or breath

1. From Jon Silkin, *The Life of Metrical and Free Verse in Twentieth-Century Poetry*, New York: Palgrave Macmillan, 1997.

(Allen Ginsberg claimed to have written 'Howl' one breath to a line), or it might be a unit of thought, or time, or even a visual unit. One could assume only that, whatever else, a line was always a unit of attention."

So now, as I worry my way around the edges of lineation, I'd like to pay attention to the ways a line can be a "unit of attention" and what happens when we pay meticulous attention to it. Possibly the best way to begin such a project is to think about what an opening line can do to establish expectations, to create what I'll call the poem's "ambience."

Take the first line of William Stafford's "Ask Me"—"Some time when the river is ice ask me"—whose last two words open up the poem, hovering on the brink of a question that has yet to be voiced. We wonder what the question will be and why it is to be asked only when the river is ice. Even before we know what it is, the question is fraught with questions. The ten-syllable line is not iambic, yet its "duration" is familiar, as though the human ear now has a built-in timer for pentameter that recognizes it even in disguise. These rhythmic expectations keep the reader alert to the way Stafford employs subtle (and deliberately unsettling) variations, and his last line—"What the river says, that is what I say"—remains stubbornly enigmatic. Those final ten syllables continue to fend off the iambic as they emphasize the muted spondee at their center, bringing a sense of completion in the sound patterns as well as the sense of the poem. The first and last lines complement each other in tone and weight. Somehow I do not believe that Stafford could have reached his conclusion (in rhythm and in content) if he had not established a unit of thought, with its truncated expectancy, in his opening line.

In a different vein, the opening of Les Murray's "Ill Music"—"My cousin loved the violin"—is so solidly iambic tetrameter that it can't help but establish a meter around and through and against which the rest of the lines must play. No one reading that first line, informal as it is, would fail to note the way it quickens the ear, as though to prefigure the poem's subject. The poem's last line, which repeats an earlier one, is "But these are words." The finality with which the two iambs sum up the poignant inability of the poet to reproduce the physical effects of his cousin's seizures is an aural echo of the opening line; its four syllables take on the same duration as the opening eight, thus giving each of the last words added import. But these are words—and the poem ends knowing what it cannot communicate.

Consider the beginning of Sylvia Plath's "Berck-Plage"—"This is the sea, then, this great abeyance." Ten syllables again, but how differently they sound with the shift, dead center, that leads from the concrete to the abstract. This will be a poem of ideas, the line announces, as it moves from the physical world into the poet's head, into her way of seeing. Plath's ending, 125 lines and seven sections later, does not seem to derive from its opening: "There is no hope, it is given up" can only make sense in the context of the poem as it culminates with the speaker standing at a funeral scene. And yet, there is a continuity in tone from opening line to ending as the speaker allows herself to give her friend's physical body over to that "great abeyance" found in nature. And on a rhythmical level, the pause after the comma seems almost to add a tenth syllable as the line is orchestrated like a bar of music, incorporating its "rest" to put her friend to rest.

In a very recent book by Kelli Russell Agodon (*Letters from the Emily Dickinson Room*, White Pine Press, 2010), first lines reveal some of the reason Carl Dennis selected this work. "Believing Anagrams" opens with "There's *real fun* in *funeral*," and such a line immediately announces that we will be watching the poet at play, that the italicized words are there to help us see not only the anagram but her turn of mind as well. The poem's magic works all the way through to its ending:

> because I want the world
> to *pray for poets* as we are only a *story of paper.*

The anagram is clearly more complicated here, as though the poem has taught the reader how to play the game. Although the anagrams are fun, the penultimate line is what intrigues me—the way it functions alone so differently from the way it moves into the last line. Who doesn't want the world, I think—and, briefly, the poem has opened other, larger doors. Suddenly poets are more than "only" a story of paper.

Some poets experiment with lines throughout their careers, while others establish a kind of "signature" line by which we come to know them. If you are a reader of contemporary poetry, you can't hear the name C. K. Williams without instantly conjuring that long line ambling toward the right margin on the page, or read the name Robert Creeley without almost hearing the staccato near-jazz he could make of his short lines. For formalists the line is determined, in large part, metrically, but I would need more than a short review space to discover all the ways that lines do—and do not—serve the poet who writes in free verse. My intention here is to consider the line as one key element in understanding the work from a few recent collections. I'll look first at two poets with whose work I am quite familiar in order to further understand why I am attracted to it, then branch out to examine two others I've read less often, hoping that I will be able to open and comprehend their work through this (albeit narrow) device.

James Richardson's latest book, *By the Numbers*, announces itself at the bottom of its cover as "Poems and Aphorisms." Whether comprising a single sentence or a whole paragraph, the aphorisms and ten-second essays for which Richardson is becoming increasingly well known speak for themselves; their unit is the sentence, and their method is the pithy observation that serves as adage or axiom. Aphorisms are often characterized by wit or wisdom—or both. For years, I've quoted something I know was coined in the early 1960s—"Wool grows just as fast on a lazy sheep"—and Richardson is fast rivaling that favorite with such one-liners as these:

> The reader lives faster than life, the writer lives slower.
>
> Sophistication is upscale conformity.
>
> You have the right to lie when they have no right to ask.
>
> Nothing dirtier than old soap.
>
> Snakes cannot back up.
>
> When it gets ahead of itself, the wave breaks.

And—my favorite—

> Faith is broad. It's Doubt that's deep.

Until recently, James Richardson may have been poetry's best-kept secret; his work deserves to be much better known, and I was heartened to see *By the Numbers* become a finalist for the 2010 National Book Award. The range of poems in this collection is impressive, extending from retold myths to contemporary ones, but I'd like to examine a single long poem to notice how the sensibility that creates the aphorisms is manifested in Richardson's more extended work as well.

Placed at the center of the book, "Are We Alone? or Physics You Can Do at Home" addresses some popular science speculations in the field of physics. It begins with two substantial epigraphs—one about a prediction that each of us has a "twin" in a distant galaxy, the other noting a growing worry of many scientists that, despite monumental efforts, no radio signals from other worlds have yet been heard. The poem's opening line is "The momentary tightening of your voice," and the first thing I notice is that charged word *your* forcing the question as to whether the poem is addressed to an "other" or is simply referring to the speaker in the second person. The next line, "over your cheerfully expiring cup of steam, maybe it's nothing—," does little to clarify the situation. So this reader lights on *momentary*, which indicates so fleeting a sound (a sigh? a word?) that really only the change in tone can be noted as the voice tightens. Only later does one realize that the first line is also the poem's shortest. From this point forward, the lines grow ever longer, loping across the page in forty-two three-line stanzas, building momentum as the sentences they contain get longer and longer, until we're pretty sure the speaker is desperately trying to reach his impossible probable twin before the latter disappears, hurrying before the sound is lost in that wider universe of sound from which there hasn't been, as yet, any communication. Probability says the galaxy containing the twin will be 10 to the 10^{28} meters away: so little chance to meet the one who knows you better than you know yourself—no, who understands you better than you understand yourself; so little time in this intergalactic (now inter-universal) speculative world. As the speaker reels out the endless distances, he brings the point home in images or ideas (or humanly recognizable moments of incomprehension) that we can absorb:

> Yes, since 1998 it has been known that gravity is failing us
> and the expansion of the universe, governed by a principle of distraction
> called Dark Energy,
> which constitutes 72% of everything, though like Dark Matter it is so far
> undetected,
>
> is accelerating, proving . . . what escapes me . . . and this sense of things
> going downhill
> faster than expected is the cause for what we previously thought was our
> baseless worry
> and the true answer to the formerly soothing question *What's the worst*
> *that could happen?*

The poem itself is going downhill, its wild unwieldy lines held captive to the established stanzaic structure. The basic "unit of attention" is a technically complicated partial sentence, holding just about as much information as any mind can handle without pause. As the speaker, thinking about other life forms, moves into ever more relativistic realms, he translates the technical into the simple realization that "if we find them they'll be gone, and when they find us we'll be gone." Returning to the moment of the first line—a time when the speaker is sitting watching the snow and thinking of that other "you"—he says:

> and yes, at the moment, the world in which I began this sentence
> is impossibly distant, and the world in which I have finished
> and am condemned to what I have said, which is why it is called a sentence,
>
> is impossibly distant but approaching, if that is not a metaphor, faster than
> light,
> and here it is right now.

Even as the poem's improbabilities build, the act of writing becomes a kind of subatomic enactment of its subject. The pen marks its cursive "you," and the poem speaks across time and space. The universe begins to contract; redshift turns to blue. The long lines begin to slow, partially because the poet is no longer using multisyllabic technical words and is, instead, winding down in order to "begin again." After seven pages the poem seems about to return to its opening line, asking the most normal of questions, as though the speaker and his twin are at long last one: "Well, is that coffee you've got there, steaming, or the hell of fusion / in the star-tight grip, in the tokamak of your cupped hands?" Finding the perfect technical word for the natural shape of the hands around the cup, Richardson has returned to the "momentary," demonstrating not only the physics but also the intensity of the human desire for connection.

"Are We Alone . . ." is itself a dizzy whirl of speculation, and the long lines allow for variation in pace as well as complicated syntax. The reader is forced, in part through timing, to discern the poem's sometimes-teasing tone—assisted by Richardson's note at the back of the book in which he claims to have a valid "poetic license from the New Jersey State Council on the Arts." This same lighthearted spirit can be found in the collection's two other long poems, "The Stars in Order Of" and "Songs for Senility." Their shorter (two-word and three-word) lines create opportunities for the visual puns, suspended jokes, and surprise connections that make for almost-aphorism, so the reader can delight in the quick pace—the enjambment of ideas, if you will. And the occasional stanza, as in this one from "Songs for Senility," reiterates the wish to recover the self who *recognizes* the self—the fragile human wish to be wholly aware *and* aware of oneself as whole:

> But that's the trick.
> There was a universe
> where my shoulder brushed the jamb
> of a small child's room
> but I can't get back.

Just as one line does not a poem make, one or two poems do not a book describe. But, buried in James Richardson's riffs on mythology and history, and in his plentiful succinct one-stanza poems, there are many other thematic links to the longer, central poem. In the end, *By the Numbers* wants to play its way into the more serious thoughts of serious readers. Even as the speaker in "Postmortem Georgic" ponders the various possible times of year in which to die, he lists the innumerable (and absolutely identifiable) unfinished chores someone will have to complete in each scenario. Just as death divides spouse from spouse, it also divides the conscious self from the body that contains it, and the poem's final lines—somehow stately in their drawn-out single syllables—reinforce the book's underlying truths:

There is only where you are going, though you seem so still,
there is only that somehow we see each other
from two trains in the station, parting so slowly
we can't for the life of us say which of us is moving.

Robert Wrigley's *Beautiful Country* is a collection in search of consequence—but to give Wrigley credit, he knows that. In the face of what can be seen as today's shallow materialism, his is a quest for substance. But it's also a search for poetry, or for a place where a poem can matter.

One poem stands out, for me, as an almost-perfect answer to the poet's quandary. The first line of "Wait" strikes a somewhat inscrutable note, "He also finds the wood and steel beautiful," with the ending comma announcing to the reader that some kind of clarification will surely follow. But for the moment there's that "also" to contend with. As in, along with what other things? As in, along with who else? Or as in, remember that poem about war, the one called . . . I think it was . . . "Naming of Parts," with its contrasting images: "Japonica / Glistens like coral in all of the neighboring gardens"? Yes, Henry Reed. Only one line, and I'm already ahead of myself, to say nothing of the poem. But clearly that's where Wrigley wants me to be because his second line catches me up—"and the slickness with which all the moving parts"—and there they are, those parts, as yet unnamed. The sentence completes itself in six more lines that both advance the facts and hold back the denouement—serving to postpone any focus on the protagonist for as long as possible:

He also finds the wood and steel beautiful,
and the slickness with which all the moving parts
slide open and shut, lifting and lodging
into place the sleek, copper-clad,
steel-jacketed projectile, which, weighing less
than half an ounce, will cover, once

the trigger is pulled, the eighty yards to the doe
in the time it would take him to blink.

"He" has now become the speaker of the poem, using third person to distance himself from himself, from the act he is about to commit. And yet he finds the wood and steel beautiful, finds the neat mechanism and the language used to describe it beautiful—as surely beautiful as the light snow that has been falling. And beautiful, too, is the knowledge he carries, not only of how the gun works, but also of the "machinery / of her living"—the bladder, liver, and entrails he knows, in prospect, he will leave on the forest floor. Beautiful, too, the coyotes and birds that will pick his leavings clean, and the mountain fescue that has attracted the doe and that he has staked out for just this purpose. The seven six-line stanzas seem to wait (remember that title?) with him as he aligns the crosshairs and hopes for an easy kill. Time slows; the snow on the rifle barrel will (in future tense) fall away when the trigger is pulled, or melt and freeze again along the metal. The final line further fends off time, even as it acknowledges the future that is coming: "he knew all he'd have to do was wait long enough, as he has."

This moment was inevitable not only on the day in question but on the day "he" found the spot from which he would shoot. And probably on the many days before that, when experience gave him the knowledge he now brings to bear on this moment. Take one line as a unit of attention: "should such a clean kill be accomplished, still . . ." Here, the subjunctive thrusts the entire poem into the realm of the imagined future, while its internal rhyme and near iambic pentameter tug it back into the past and the traditional. The suspended adverb "still" almost acts as an adjective, incipient movement that gives way to stasis. In fact, after that one word, "still," a series of internal and slant rhymes carry the trajectory of emotions: still/will/will/stilled/full/all:

> he will mourn and be glad simultaneously and will
> for the next hour or more be bathed in her blood
>
> and intimate with the then-stilled machinery
> of her living—the yards of guts, the probably full
> bladder, the buttery liver, and more—nearly all
> of which he will leave on the forest floor . . .

These, in turn, give way to the low rumble of mourning—hour/more/more/floor—before they resume their fatalistic arc in the next stanzas: still/falling/fall away . . . day . . . day.

Time elongates, along with the hunter's breathing, which (he is aware) is synchronized with the breathing of the doe, whose mountain air "he also breathes." There it is again, that "also" of shared experience, though surely the deer does not love the wood and steel, so the circle of involvement is wider, more comprehensive, than the simple pairing of predator and prey. Without any overt statement, the nation's history is evoked and we are implicated. Wrigley completes the poem with the gun poised, breath held. There is no ambiguity. The shot will ring out; the doe will die; but the moment of the poem is the moment of waiting.

"Wait" in many ways feels like a flawless free-verse poem. Its stanzaic structure provides a kind of stave on which its music is orchestrated; the forward movement of its (non)action accelerates even as multiple commas hold the poem in check, imitating the fits and starts of a mind reeling with anticipated action, intimate knowledge, remembered specifics. Syntax is all. This is no simple noun/verb/object construction but a complex of mixed emotion and determined deliberation. The repeated "also" enlarges the arena. This poem faces itself squarely in the mirror. Its first line leads inevitably to its last, and still—yes, still—it subtly asks that we participate.

"Wait" is followed by three moose poems, each progressively more fanciful. In an odd way, they undermine Wrigley's achievement by going suddenly playful—and perhaps that was the intention. But why *not* own the mastery, and the depth of the moment?

Beautiful Country thrives on contradictions—love of country and despair for it, desire to praise and impulse to condemn. Wrigley examines contemporary American society and finds it sadly devoid of what you might call "character" even as it is full of "characters." Here you can find (however oblique the method) poems against war, poems against big oil companies, poems against mindless fear, poems against mindlessness. Although Wrigley does celebrate individual moments of love, compassion, generosity, and bravery, he sometimes chips away at these with his sense of irony, as in the title poem, where drugs and politics deliberately mix in a mash of stoned perceptions:

> . . . and before the rest of them
> pleaded not merely ordinary fear
> but conscientious objection. They said they meant it, in other words,
> even as they wondered how killing Nixon could be anything but right.
> When they could talk at all they had those kinds of conversations.
> They thought about what was wrong and more wrong.

Overall, Wrigley does not resolve his oppositions, but he does formulate a way to *enact* them. The poems to which I respond best turn out to be ones in which the persona (like the speaker of "Wait") seems closest to representing real, examined experience. For example, the opening of "I Like the Wind" sounds as though someone is speaking directly from the "here" it mentions:

> We are at or near that approximate line
> where a stiff breeze becomes
> or lapses from a considerable wind,
> and I like it here, the chimney-smokes
> right-angled from west to east but still

for those brief intact stretches
the plush animal tails of fires.
I like how the stiffness rouses the birds
right up until what's considerable sends them
to shelter.

The "I" here has been there, done that. And the second use of the word "considerable" gives a sense of wry self-awareness, a desire to play around with language just to see what it will offer up. On the other hand, "Memoir" is perhaps too lighthearted:

Then I came to a fork,
one of those top-end knockoff
stainless steel three-tine jobs,
a little meat-gaff bean shanking mashed potato trowel.
The duchess fed me with it, marshmallows

warmed in her décolletage. Therefore I volunteered.

You get the point. I got the point. But the point wears thin and the "fun" seems just a little too familiar.

In many ways, I think Robert Wrigley may have produced this new book too quickly, writing poems he felt needed to be written instead of waiting the requisite time it takes for new material to make itself known. A few poems remind me of the earlier, tougher-minded poet, who allowed his material to offer up its own incontrovertible meanings. The tensions generated by his restless lines give this new book its nervous energy, yet the collection does not quite cohere; it seems to be on the verge of something larger, waiting with held breath for the poet to find himself truly out far, and in deep.

Elizabeth Bradfield's second book, *Approaching Ice*, chronicles the history of, and the impulse toward, polar exploration. In a sequence of third-person "portraits," Bradfield manages not only to give an account of the well-known adventures of Robert Scott, Richard Byrd, Ernest Shackleton, and Admiral Peary, but also to probe the sensibilities of these men, searching out mindset and motivation, the human choices that led to ruin or to glory. In addition, she approaches such ice-bound history through the eyes of lesser-known explorers—who has heard of Carsten Borchgrevink, Jules d'Urville, Adrien de Gerlache, Louise Boyd?—and from the perspective of crew members, photographers, and the many spouses who waited at home (among whom she surreptitiously inserts her own name). These not-quite-narratives are offset and underscored by the poet's own familiarity with the polar tundra.

Bradford, always aware that her poems are speculative and that she knows she doesn't *know*, is amazed at the very act of setting off into the unknown. Along the way, the reader learns some little-known history and many fresh aspects of science, geography, and meteorology. Almost any first line in this collection could be chosen to give a sense of the wide white expanse of ice and of the precariousness of the venture. For example, "Why They Went" opens with "Frost bitten. Snow blind. Hungry. Craving"—and the three caesuras feel for all the world like solid footprints in the snow, while the last word in the line tilts toward uncertainty. Thus the reader is not surprised when the poem ends with "And they came home and longed again," turning the "craving" of its inception into the answer to the title's implicit question.

I'd like to inspect a more complex poem in order to note the similar implications of *its* opening line. "The Third Reich Claims Neu Schwabenland" describes how, in 1939, Germany determined to lay claim to Antarctica by sending airplanes to photograph its vast regions and drop huge swastika-marked darts onto the frozen expanse. The whole first section describes the details of the mission. It begins "Ice is not land, so how to claim it? How to mark it owned"; again, the line hovers on the brink of something unknown and, again, there is a characteristic caesura, a pause to contemplate, then enter into the interrogation. The second section makes a surprising departure into an italicized reverie as the poet (here dissolving into first person and speaking for herself) thinks of the various elusive claims she has made: mementos brought home from travels; a star she "bought" on the Internet and named Incognita; a dog; the lips of a potential lover before she knew the woman was married. How, she almost seems to be asking by implication, was the German project any different except in scale, and hubris? The poem's third section appears, at first, to act as a refrain—"Ice is not land. Is restless. And what was claimed"—but then the poet departs from description in favor of conjecture, and "what was claimed"

> has moved, is inching toward the sea,
> has maybe broken off,
> calved from the frozen edge, and now trails
> its dust and shit and egg shards and abandoned fuel tins,
> trails what stories it held
> through the ocean's haloclines
> and thermoclines, its pelagic and benthic layers,
> scattering them across its sea floor.

With the inevitable drifting of the ice, the speaker moves to speculation; "maybe," she repeats, as she imagines those darts—stripped of their markings—

sliding beneath miles of water, "declarative not of claim, but of time." The poem has made its own incremental shifts to demonstrate the tenuous relationship between claim and ownership, the force of time that frees the ice to its own silent devices. And I would go so far as to say there is a hint of that cold drifting in the white space surrounding those lines that stop midway before they move on into new territory.

The ice's very imperturbability becomes part of a history that encompasses bush pilot and umiak and the timelessness of "whalecall" or the "cries of flightless birds." The impact of this endless region, not exactly indifferent but nevertheless impassive, is echoed again and again in Bradfield's endings. A poem about Richard Byrd concludes with "not one green flicker in the emotive sky cared," and John Forbes Nash Jr., the self-declared Emperor of Antarctica, finds "a land to quiet his mind's static" while his brief forays to the region end in the visual spaces of a line without punctuation:

open   wild   white

The poems of *Approaching Ice* are meticulously researched, and as a result the book is filled with fascinating details, eerily precise descriptions, and captivating speculations. But none of these makes a poem on its own, so Elizabeth Bradfield has fashioned her lines to reinforce the more mysterious areas where there are gaps in knowledge. Her fitful unit of attention is focused on connective tissue (or its lack). She makes a poetry of not-knowing, "marrying what you know to what you see / and all it tells of knowing's impossibility," as she writes in "Vicarious." Articulating the powerful urge that drove these (mostly) men to negotiate uncharted terrain, she has found a way to contain their stories without appropriating them. Always careful to distinguish between her own experience and that of others, this poet is not afraid to ask the hard questions that help her perceive where and when and how event and understanding coincide.

Also, Bradfield has produced an effective mix of the scientific and the personal. This can best be seen in the scattering of seven separate pieces, each titled "Notes on Ice in *Bowditch*," in which she takes terms from the glossary in *The American Practical Navigator* by Nathaniel Bowditch and follows them with private commentary. In all, there are thirty such entries, and here are three:

> ***ice edge***. *The demarcation at any given time between open sea and sea ice of any kind, whether fast or drifting.*
>
> This is where you jump. This is the map-edge that can't be drawn or that must never cease being drawn, the edge that crumbles or that grows new boundaries. This is the demarcation of lovers.

ice jam. *An accumulation of broken river ice or sea ice caught in a narrow channel.*

Is that what you call the creaking, popping mass stuck in the thin throat of an argument? Hissing streams rapid around it? Slurry of dislodged bits thick along the banks, rounding sharp corners to rush out and be absorbed?

ice stream. *The part of an inland ice sheet in which the ice flows more rapidly and not necessarily in the same direction as the surrounding ice. The margins are sometimes clearly marked by a change in direction of the surface slope, but may be indistinct.*

Are you so sure of the difference between freeze and thaw? One is not necessarily moving toward the other. Always a place between that is flowing and hard to define. This is why apologies are difficult.

Interestingly, the "individual utterance" here comes not in the line but in these unlineated rejoinders. Call and response—the answering voice is intimate, providing a hint of the person who is navigating her own unmarked channels. This is a thought- provoking second book, and I look forward to seeing where this poet will take us next.

I always feel regret when I "discover" a poet whose work I should have read much earlier. *Walking with Ruskin* is Robert Cording's sixth collection, but I confess it is the first complete book I've read by this poet I've known only piecemeal in the pages of literary journals. I think of Cording as "the poet of birds," and there are a slew of birds in this gathering—but now I see how they serve as markers for one man's walking (waking) life. Oh, how those ubiquitous sparrows, "generic for any of the small brown birds / We find everywhere," suddenly become a religious reminder that we have the poor and needy among us. Or, comparing notes with an imagined Ruskin about the shades of blue on a kingfisher's back, the poet is reminded of the kind of attention that one must pay in order to love fact. And those flaring swallows, with their sprung syllables, demonstrate over and over in "Swallow Syllabics" one of nature's harder lessons, "undoing any thought / that they could be settled onto lines."

Walking with Ruskin pays religious attention to the world and, in doing so, becomes a form of religious experience all its own. Invoking the tenets of Judaism, Christianity, Buddhism, and others of the numerous ways humans have found to contemplate the meanings of existence, Cording takes us into the one lived life of a self-described ordinary family man. The poems chronicle days of tedious work, sunlit vacations, parties and meals and walks in all seasons—nothing monumental, yet everything immense.

Cording's lines vary more in length and intention than those of the other poets discussed in this review. This is partly because he works fluently both within and without form. Even if a poem is not traditionally formal, he sometimes imposes his own rhyme scheme or metric upon it, as in the short opening lines of "Rain, Snow, Rain":

> Without plot
> the day out-
>
> side my window
> slips from snow
>
> to rain, slips
> from little drips
>
> of water to silence—
> the rain's presence
>
> within the snow,
> and again the snow.

"Rain, snow, rain, / and, within, // without relief, / anger and grief"—but the tight rhymes cannot contain the enormity ("I can't sort / the sordid facts") of a neighbor's murder, so the sounds become a bit unruly, turning into disquieting pairs of near-rhymes: water/hour, up/stop, outruns/stubborn. The poem ends on the mind's stubborn "need to make sense / where no sense is."

In "Dangling," Cording skillfully uses enjambment to let his own lines, along with the monk on Mt. Athos, remind him to take stock:

> I suppose it's a way of restoring the grace
> of insignificance, hanging like that
>
> between the sky and the sea. I like to think
> my thinking is a form of spiritual exercise . . .

And Cording does like to think, and we like to think along with him—whether it's contemplating Czesław Miłosz's reading glasses, or George Herbert's God or Mozart's starling, or a single drop of rain, or three cows in a field, or the mortgaged life of a husband and father. All of these, it seems, are fodder for learning to read the "Book of Concealment." And none of these, it seems, prepares the poet for the thoughts he will have as he struggles with the import of this book's middle section, "Backward."

This central section of *Walking with Ruskin* comprises four poems that could not have been written without Cording's ongoing celebration of life—nor without his fertile imagination, his protective fear for his own children, his memory of a frantic search for a young Hasidic girl lost for two days in the woods, his sense of needing to make sense where no sense is. The thirteen-year-old son of friends has been killed in an accident. The mother mourns, and the four poems mourn with her; they are, perhaps, a definition of empathy, of the humble and inadequate attempt to inhabit another's grief, and of how words cannot do full justice to emotion. In these poems Cording most exemplifies Marvin Bell's observations about the complexity of syntax and Marianne Boruch's perceptions of the rebelliousness inherent to lineation choices.

Here is a sentence: *Now December is dying once again into the roosting dark: cold air, cold flame, the sky burning itself clean.* There are myriad possible ways to break this into lines, but see how Robert Cording, working within the syntax, orchestrates its nuances in the middle of "December Prayer," the fourth section of "Four Prayers":

> Now December is dying once again
> into the roosting dark: cold air, cold
> flame, the sky burning itself clean.

The slant rhymes of *again* and *clean* contain the cold—the doubled cold—the mother must bear. We cannot distinguish the trajectory here—does it veer toward *now/into/flame* or *again/cold/clean*?—but the lines that follow move deeper into this December knowledge:

> Lord I ask this much for her,
> who knows too well she will go on
> missing him until she dies: let rooms
> made small by the violence of grief
> be amplified by the wan light
> the sun hoists up over the inch
> of new winter snow.

Hardly a large word, except for "amplified," and yet the syntax provides a way to amplify the grief through the orchestration of the lines. Boruch's "rebel thing," the line that contains the "deeply personal," announces itself in "who knows too well she will go on," which on its own almost asks a question. But the speaker of the poem, in his incantation, is also one who knows too well, knows that the mother is the one who must go on while his words can only call down their sympathetic prayer.

Watch the way the lines highlight syntax in the second and third stanzas of "Kin":

> And if, despite all our prayers to *Help her,*
> *O Lord, to lay down her burden,* she lifts up
> her bundle of sadness and sorrow each day,
> then let her be comforted by its weight
> and the task of carrying it; and if one day,
> nearly a year after her son has died,
> there's another occasion for bells,
>
> though this time they chime for a wedding,
> and the day, though rain was predicted,
> has opened out into yellow and green dresses
> winking in the sun and a whirling breeze
> that blows open the blues and whites
> of suits and shirts and makes kites of ties,
> then let the day be joyous even for her.

The opening words generate the mind's movement with *And/ then/ there's/ though/ that/ then*, while the line ends create their own hint of story: *lifts up/ each day/ weight*; *one day/ bells/ wedding*; *dresses/ breeze/ kites/ joyous*. Even for her.

"Kin" contains the insight of a man who knows what it is to suffer loss, confirmed by two poems in the collection about a friend who has recently died of cancer. "The Chair" ends with the image of an empty one filling with snow: "Then my waking sense / of everything missed, and missing again." The book's final poem, "Gift," recounts this same friend's fierce hold on ordinary things, such as the odor of lilac or the cold of the window glass: "To all of it he said *yes*."

Walking with Ruskin also says "yes" to life's odd synchronicities and pervasive doubts. To walk with Ruskin is to walk the (figurative) line, embracing the details of the world with the hope that they might, in some sense, suffice. Ultimately, the affirmation comes from knowing that the poems, too, are "part of a world so hard to finish loving." The book's signature line may be the first of "Why I Live Here": "Because the view is always partial." Understanding that nothing reveals itself in all its facets, this poet lives to see through, and around, and within. The view may indeed be "partial," but Robert Cording's sure ear and eye let us appreciate the line at work, shaping a sensibility that can begin with "because" and, thirty-one lines later, end with "still surpasses understanding."

A Question Takes

On (interactively)[1] Marvin Bell's *Vertigo: The Living Dead Man Poems* and *Whiteout* (with photographs by Nathan Lyons); Jane Hirshfield's *Come, Thief*; Kevin Prufer's *In a Beautiful Country*; and Kevin Goodan's *Upper Level Disturbances.*

And controversy hence a question takes,
Whether the horse by him became his deed,
Or he his manage by the well-doing steed.

"A Lover's Complaint," attributed to William Shakespeare,
published by Thomas Thorpe as an appendix to the sonnets in 1609

RECENTLY THERE'S BEEN CONTROVERSY in the poetry world, sparked by Helen Vendler's hard-hitting review of Rita Dove's *Penguin Anthology of Twentieth-Century American Poetry* (2011) in the *New York Review of Books*. The follow-up exchange between Vendler and Dove has, in turn, generated articles, letters to the editors, blogs, Facebook posts—you name it. This has been fascinating, but it is only good if the ensuing discussion can tell us something about the state of the art.

I found myself first on one side of the argument and then the other—so much so that it occurred to me the argument itself was not very well defined. The problem, as I see it, lies to a large extent in the way Penguin elected to advertise

1. With thirteen covert references to or quotes from Frost, MacLeish, Plath, Stafford, Stevens, and W. C. Williams.

the anthology, claiming it is "an unparalleled survey of the best poems of the past century." If only with the omission (due to cost) of Sylvia Plath and Allen Ginsberg, the collection can hardly live up to that claim—and maybe if there had been less hype, the responses would have been more measured. But couple this overreaching assertion with the usual disputes with any anthology over which poets—and what poems—have been included under the label of "best" (and therefore which poets—and what poems—have been omitted/demoted), and you have a recipe for heated literary debate.

Anthologies, by their very nature, seem to imply "best" when they should probably, at most, be considered "representative." Dove's twenty-four-page introduction gives a lucid overview of the various movements in American poetry, along with the offshoots they spawned. With 176 poets represented, Dove makes it clear that she is trying for widespread inclusion. But American poetry exploded in the twentieth century, and any editor would need at least double this book's 570 pages to do justice to the many tentacles. Vendler's more scholarly approach, on the other hand, would require a more comprehensive overview of fewer poets. From the outset, Dove and Vendler were on different critical pages, and one could argue with each of them on her own terms: "best" is the issue around which Vendler mounted her quarrel; being "representative" is what Dove makes clear she wanted to accomplish as she made some radical shifts in what has, up to now, been widely considered the twentieth-century canon.

I think the reviewer's task—of assessment and prediction—is very like the job of an anthologist. Almost every worthwhile discussion involves a look at how the work under consideration fits into a tradition, a reflection on how it does or doesn't push at the boundaries of content and craft, and a guess at how it will make an impact on the future. Very early in the process, any committed reviewer begins to compile a life list of names that make up his or her "ghost" anthology.

So, I found it instructive to read the introduction to F. O. Matthiessen's *Oxford Book of American Verse*, published just before his death in 1950. With only fifty-one poets in 1,103 pages, Matthiessen might seem to favor Vendler's approach. But he managed to be remarkably inclusive, indicating the many ways that Americans had added their own brand of energy to the art. His introductory tone is leisurely and, at the same time, balanced and informative. He states that "Anne Bradstreet still remains our first American poet," and his lucid discussions of Emily Dickinson, Marianne Moore, and H.D. further demonstrate that he was not interested only in the work of dead white men. On his calibrated scales, and with some crucial critical distance, he was able to state that "Stevens has proved steadier than Pound" and "Frost is the poet of individualism," while Eliot shows the "need for the individual to find completion in something larger than himself."

Mathiessen uses a gentle humor as he establishes his working methods:

> There are so many different ways of making anthologies that any anthologist had better begin by stating the rules of the game as he accepts them. A generation ago the usual practice was to include as many poets as possible, represented by two or three poems apiece. That served to introduce you to all the talents, but had the same confusing effect as a party that is too big. So my first rule has been: fewer poets, with more space for each. . . .
>
> The second rule accepted here is to include nothing on merely historical grounds, and the third is similar, to include nothing that the anthologist does not really like, no matter what its reputation with others. These rules . . . grant that the pleasure of savoring and comparing different periods is one of the rewards of a lively interest in cultural history. . . .
>
> Rule four is: not too many sonnets. They may seem to provide the easiest and neatest way of filling your pages, but they will kill one another. . . .
>
> Rule five runs counter to all Golden Treasuries by holding that, whenever practicable, a poet should be represented by poems of some length. One of the effects of anthologies upon popular taste has been to overemphasize the lyric at the expense of all other genres. . . .
>
> The sixth and last rule is: no excerpts.

Even within his own restrictions, he admits that "the space allotted to the various poets is not always proportional to their relative importance" and acknowledges that "mere length is of course deceptive." He breaks his own rules by including excerpts from Pound's *Cantos* and Hart Crane's *The Bridge*. In closing, his astute analysis leads him to deduce that "If this poetry reveals violent contrasts and unresolved conflicts, it corresponds thereby to American life."

Matthiessen's selection reminds me that anthologies are about the past as much as the future. There will always be some poets in need of resurrection, and he finds ample room for those important, now-neglected southern poets John Crowe Ransom, Conrad Aiken, and Allen Tate. I find myself reading them again, in new contexts. Even more telling, I am faced with what I consider to be a problem for all anthologies that cover a set period of time (as opposed to a particular subject, or movement, or mode)—and that is how the most recent material (the stuff that is most often the province of the reviewer) is handled. It's relatively easy to sort through the past and see what work has stood the test of time; it's a bit more difficult to uncover work that has been overlooked or to resurrect work that has a personal attraction; and it is decidedly *not* easy to predict which contemporary works will speak to, and for, the future. Yet future relevance is where the difference of opinion has genuine critical ramifications. The predicament is that an anthology of any note may—no *will*—be used in the classroom as though it were the definitive arbiter for an entire period: a canon-maker of its own.

Imagine an anthology of nineteenth-century British poetry, printed in 1911. Such a collection almost certainly would trivialize someone like Yeats, who had yet to write his important later poems. It could not predict how Wilfred Owen would couple his elegant use of form with the stark realities of World War I, making him a potent addition for the twentieth century. Here is my question: how can any anthologist represent present-day poems when we do not yet know the subterranean forces at work and the way the future will likely see them playing out in poetry? Those forces include the political scene—not an upcoming election but the large-scale shifts in philosophy and outlook that characterize certain times, the kind that make us just now able to assess what was happening in the Germany of 1933 or the South Africa of 1970. But they also include linguistic experimentation (the kind that influenced the surrealists or today's Language poets) and quantum leaps in poetics (the kind that made for movements such as "imagism" or "the confessionals"). What, I wonder, would have happened if any of those movements had come in the last ten years of a century, before they had time to make their way into a more general consciousness?

F. O. Matthiessen deliberately skirted those issues, taking the route of "fewer poets." Of the seven under the age of fifty in his selection, six are still integral to American letters: Robert Penn Warren, W. H. Auden, Karl Shapiro, Delmore Schwartz, Randall Jarrell, and Robert Lowell. Only Howard Baker is not instantly recognizable. (Note: in 1950, Elizabeth Bishop's first book was four years old, Robert Hayden was still offstage, and Sylvia Plath was not yet on the horizon.) Although today we would probably allocate these poets' work in different proportions, this is an amazing track record—one with which any anthologist (or reviewer) would fear to compete.

Rita Dove has elected to include a larger percentage of younger poets—thirty-eight were under fifty (and ten of them were under forty) in the year 2000. These younger writers show a broadening base for poetry, yet, for all their numbers, they do not reveal a new aesthetic hovering in the wings, nor is there sufficient range to cover the experimental atmosphere presently at play. In order for them to be included, the full accomplishment of the previous generation seems to have been shortchanged, and several prominent poets born between 1935 and 1945 are mysteriously absent.

Maybe the solution is to be even more bold. If we can't predict what will prevail, we might at least put our fingers on the tenuous pulse of a nation, feel out its range of moods and its underlying diversities. Why not state the obvious—that it's too soon to do anything other than indicate the various, multiple directions and concerns of contemporary work—and then open the door with a proliferation of, say, fifty or more new poets, giving the reader a sense of the century opening out, rushing toward a future that will only later be measured and evaluated? This would entail some demarcation, maybe even a two-volume set, but it could empower future students by asking them to be the perceptive readers we hope they will become. The good teacher might open up the newer poems to examination—or offer up to debate the relevance of poetry itself. Penguin's ads might have to shift from "best" to "representative" in the most accurate sense of the latter. The tenor of the discussion would change—and the impassioned "complaint" might be seen for what it is: a lovers' quarrel.

In this light, I will examine some recent work for how it makes a transition from the old century to the new, and speculate on its eventual long-term effects.

Marvin Bell's *Dead Man* appeared at the tail end of the 1980s but didn't declare himself fully until 1994 when he asked that we follow him into brave new worlds. However, these things take time, so he returned in 1997; then, in 2004, the faint sound of his "resurrected footsteps" summoned us again. Now, in 2011, he is almost apocryphal and has emerged in two new books, asking—no *demanding*—more of us. The Dead Man is urgent; he has something to say, and he needs a response:

> He dares to wake the audience.
> He is of a mind to taunt and defy, to provoke and to goad.
> . . . .
> Tell him you know.
> Cover your mouth if you need to, but speak up.

Okay, just who *is* the Dead Man? He's not quite Bell, but he is the product of his mind. In fact, he's mostly mind, touching as the mind touches—a roving catchall for scraps of thought, observation, speculation, meditation, oddball coincidence, idiosyncratic cosmology, past, present, future, wit, worry, wisdom. He may have tried—and failed—to "cut a break in the Möbius strip of experience," but still he takes us on a dizzy ride along interconnection's scenic highway. The electronic world of the Internet is perhaps his métier; he is as fast, as random, as all-informed and underwhelmed as that. Here, let him speak for himself:

"The dead man is the ultimate camouflage. / He is everywhere, but where is he?" One might say, as Randall Jarrell said of William Carlos Williams, "There is no optimistic blindness in [him] though there is a fresh gaiety, a stubborn or invincible joyousness."

Vertigo: The Living Dead Man Poems is not just more of the same, however. The book announces itself in enigma with an epigraph: "The point of philosophy is to start with something so simple as not to seem worth stating, and to end with something so paradoxical that no one will believe it" (Bertrand Russell). Although Bell has retained the sentence as his working unit for the line, the poems of *Vertigo* are arranged alphabetically by title, as if to say there is no rhyme nor reason, no chronology or logic to it all. But remember the subtitle. He's "living" now—he does not "mean," but is—and that suggests that his thoughts are more connected, his sentences are more likely to follow one another in associative patterns we recognize. The haphazard becomes a method of coherence. If the Dead Man thinks about hats, for example, he sticks to his subject, even if it does take him as far as the desert, Astaire & Rogers, Prague, Havana, fedoras, helmets, hard hats, berets. "The dead man does not come to you hat in hand"—and you are challenged, again, to see that poetry does not beg, but proffers. If the Dead Man considers wartime, he does not let you off easy: "He has unpinned the grenade and cocked his arm like a pitcher with no target. / He has lobbed death into the distance without knowing where or why. . . . The dead man touches the horror day and night, why don't you?"

Taking in a few sentences of *Vertigo* at random, any reader would find it impossible to miss the sure ear that dominates this collection. The rhythms are those of speech, but speech raised to the *n*th power, speech infused with the vigor of aphorism and the echo of prosody. The music, though somewhat masked by the sheer energy of Bell's combinatorial method, is the river in which the ideas eddy, mix, and remix.

I have said before that I think the Dead Man challenges readers of poetry to think about what poetry really is, what it really *does*. He asks us to rethink the endeavor; the spaces he opens are new places. The Dead Man may take an ordinary walk, but his quotidian observations are never just simple insight, warmed-up nostalgia, or false epiphany. He shuns what's easy in favor of widely ranging topics and complex juxtapositions that leave the reader to fill in gaps and find new directions. In short, he involves us in the making of meaning.

In *Vertigo*, Bell makes this challenge overt by tackling the relationship between ideas and things. Two fifteen-sentence disquisitions ("About the Dead Man and 'The Red Wheelbarrow'" and "More About the Dead Man and 'The Red Wheelbarrow'") introduce a whole new form of literary criticism, and they belong alongside any critical study of William Carlos Williams' famous poem. The Dead Man's "take" demonstrates intimate knowledge of the good doctor's entire body of work:

> Not an actual wheelbarrow, not the thing itself.
> The dead man has been asked about the thought of the barrow.
> Not of a pushcart, not of the gardener, not of the farmer.
> This red wheelbarrow sits pristine after rain.
> The dead man can tell it is spring and all, it's the rain.

The reader is laughingly asked to participate. "Thus" did the Dead Man "peel the layers of claptrap." And further, thus did he talk, with reverence, about the poem:

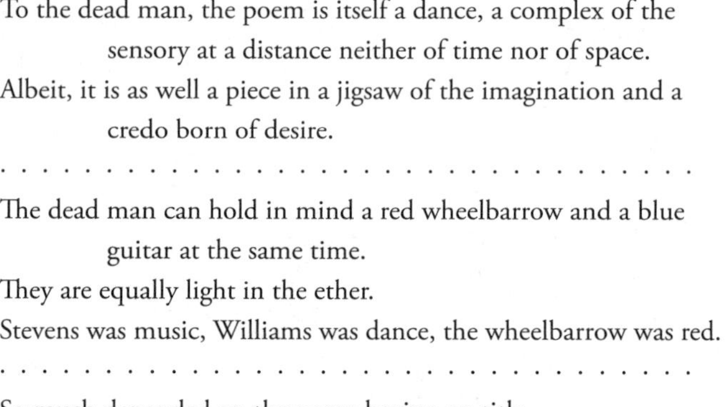

> To the dead man, the poem is itself a dance, a complex of the
> sensory at a distance neither of time nor of space.
> Albeit, it is as well a piece in a jigsaw of the imagination and a
> credo born of desire.
> . . . .
> The dead man can hold in mind a red wheelbarrow and a blue
> guitar at the same time.
> They are equally light in the ether.
> Stevens was music, Williams was dance, the wheelbarrow was red.
> . . . .
> So much depended on the poem having no title.

Marvin Bell treats us to his own wily mind making its own dancing connections and, at the same time, asks us to put even that activity into perspective. With his restless inventiveness, the dead man (now lower-case *d*) is equally light in the ether. The camera zooms out, and out, until the individual becomes a dark speck on the floor of the canyon below, while poetry itself . . . well, the wheelbarrow was red.

And then the camera zooms in again. *Whiteout* pairs four of the poems from *Vertigo* and twenty new Dead Man poems with photographs by Nathan Lyons, the founding director of the Visual Studies Workshop in Rochester, New York. In his introduction, Bell states that their desire was not to illustrate but to work so that "Each photograph would create a perimeter. Each poem would look over its shoulder." The resulting poems are neither description nor commentary, but accompaniment. *Whiteout* has been beautifully produced, and Lyons' astutely observant and imaginative eye reminds us just how real the Dead Man is: in image after image—masks, skulls, graffiti, statues, gargoyles, icons, windows, signs, and shadows—Lyons has uncovered the skeletal evidence of his presence in the world. The lost and the obsolete are his domain, and the corresponding poems play with idea more than image, forcing uncanny perception ("the spraycan is just a shortcut, like camera obscura") and uncomfortable recognition ("They come and go like the neutral stares of strangers"). The photograph engages the eye; the writer enlarges the image until what he says of it becomes a part of what it is.

So, with the added substance of these two books, I'll inch myself further out on my limb and restate that I believe Marvin Bell's Dead Man poems should close any anthology of the twentieth century and open any anthology of this new century's work. They change the game. They insist that we pay a new and different kind of attention. They ask for abstract thought about concrete event: Williams squared. And they persist—like the dead man who speaks them, like the poet who speaks him—as a testament to what it is to have lived in these turbulent times, to have loved this world with a clear, unclouded eye, reminding us in every possible way that "A poem is about what is happening as you read it."

In his several ways of looking, Wallace Stevens tried to distinguish between the idea of the thing and the thing itself, eschewing Kant's "thing in itself" in favor of Nietzsche's more subjective views of art. Marvin Bell finds common ground between Williams and the more cerebral Stevens by holding red wheelbarrow (object) and blue guitar (imagination) in his mind simultaneously. Jane Hirshfield bridges the same gaps, but with entirely different methods. The "things" of *Come, Thief* are multitudinous—the table of contents, with its characteristic emphasis on the noun, might suggest a hard examination of the tangible world: "French Horn," "The Pear," "Chapel," "Sweater," "Protractor," "Green-striped Melons," "Wild Plum," "Sheep," "Suitcase." But "idea" also proliferates, with titles such as "Critique of Pure Reason," "If Truth Is the Lure, Humans Are Fishes," and "When Your Life Looks Back." More telling are the titles using the conjunction "and"—the connective tissue that combines and recombines to spark the neurons: "Vinegar and Oil" with its unexpected reversal; "Building and Earthquake" with its flare of apprehension; "Heat and Desperation" to whet the appetite; "Stone and Knife" to solidify association. Even a glimpse at such titles jolts the reader into new terrain—a cloud chamber where particles collide and suggest new possibilities.

Like Shaker furniture, Hirshfield's work is more complex than its simple lines might suggest. Not content to let the idea simply reside in the "thing," and not satisfied with a purely theoretical approach, Hirshfield melds object, abstraction, and imagination in something more akin to collage. Her poems move so quickly—a Chinese painter's brushstroke—from thing to idea to thing that the two are, almost literally, inseparable. The shifts are mercurial, so much so that we apprehend them in the same instant of time. Consider the gap between the title of "The Decision" and its first two lines:

> There is a moment before a shape
> hardens, a color sets.

Via that white space, the reader is drawn into an emotional landscape where the nature of the decision is unknown, but the ephemeral quality of the experience is almost material. The letter that could be snatched back, the word still unsaid: "The thorax of an ant is not as narrow. / The green coat on old copper weighs more." So small, and yet something, even in potential, has changed, and "it cannot be after turned back from." The poem catches the ineffable moment when the mind, or heart, could go in any direction—the moment that, by its very existence, introduces alternative, option, choice. What is unspoken or unacted is, therefore, also *something*. Some thing, caught in the currents that hold the stillness exactly.

In many ways, Hirshfield demonstrates not so much the ideal "vortex" of Pound's imagism as the fusion of moment and insight found in the best haiku. Like haiku, where the juxtaposition hinges on a *kireji* that cuts the stream of thought and thus colors the way the ideas are related, her poems are anchored in the natural world yet make associative connections and quicksilver adjustments that let the mind do its subterranean work. Two small poems on opposing pages give a feel for the way the blend of external and internal worlds creates a new, and insistent, awareness:

> *The Dark Hour*
>
> The dark hour came
> in the night and purred by my ear.
> Outside, in rain,
> the plush of the mosses stood higher.
> Hour without end, without measure.
> It opens the window and calls its own name in.
>
> *
>
> *Everything Has Two Endings*
>
> Everything has two endings—
> a horse, a piece of string, a phone call.

Before a life, air.
And after.

As silence is not silence, but a limit of hearing.

Each of these poems captures a moment in time and then opens out, reaching for the infinite. The thing in itself is considered in its fuller context—its possibilities and limitations, its history and future as well as its palpable present. The poem is completed in the reader—it "happens" as you read it.

Yet Hirshfield's poems do not happen in a vacuum. She alerts us, again and again, to the moments that could otherwise be lost, the shimmer of possibility inherent in any situation. "There is something that waits inside us, / a nearness that fissures, that fishes," she writes in "Of Yield and Abandon," and in "A Thought" she senses the source of that something: "One word's almost / imperceptible shiver."

Come, Thief contains three dominant images: window, bell, and water. Sight, sound, and fluid life force. In each case, she complicates before she clarifies: "A lit window at night in the distance: / idea almost graspable, finally not" ("Big-Leaf Maple Standing over Its Own Reflection"). She asks in "Of Yield and Abandon," "But what is the point of preserving the bell / if to do so it must be filled with concrete or wax?"—yet in another instance (in "A Roomless Door") silence is made dynamic as the sound of weeping becomes "a piano's 89th key." And what of metaphor? "Too slow for rain, / too large for tears, / and grief / cannot be seen" ("It Must Be Leaves"). "A Blessing for Wedding" unites all three images in its litany:

Today when windows keep their promise to open
. . . .
Today when rain leaps to the waiting of roots in their dryness
. . . .
Let the vow of this day keep itself wildly and wholly
Spoken and silent, surprise you inside your ears
Sleeping and waking, unfold itself inside your eyes
Let its fierceness and tenderness hold you
Let its vastness be undisguised in all your days

Poems like these work their best magic when juxtaposition calls up an almost instantaneous recognition. Otherwise, the reader will struggle to force the perception and the resulting comprehension will be overly intellectual. For this reason, some of the poems are more successful than others, and many of those I most appreciate pay extra attention to sound—in the form of rhyme. The echoes come hard on each other's heels, deftly dodging expectation in favor of surprise. "Three-Legged Blues" plays with interior refrain as it goes through variations on "What almost happens, doesn't. / What might be lost, you'll lose." "My Luck" fools around with "up" and "down" until syntax itself becomes a driving force. "A Hand Is Shaped for What It Holds or Makes"* is an electrifying cross between terza rima and villanelle, then and now, memory and loss. It erases time even as it takes its measure. "Once we were one. Then what time did, and hands, erased / us from the future we had owned." The line break erases the "us" and propels the poem toward its final stanza, where the poet recognizes what poetry cannot do:

> Wasps leave their nest. Wind takes the papery case.
> Our wooden house, less easily undone,
> now houses others. A life is shaped by what it holds or makes.
> I make these words for what they can't replace.

And so I nominate that poem for inclusion in my own imagined anthology because it pulls the tradition into the next century, a tribute of the current to its source. And, if I could have a second entry, it would surely be the final poem of the book, "The Supple Deer," which opens with simple description of how a buck (antlers to hind hooves) "poured" through a gap in a fence without leaving behind even a tuft of belly hair. But Jane Hirshfield's felt longing elevates the description to insight: not self-knowledge, less fleeting than that . . . something more encompassing, more akin to the indefinable suddenly given expression:

> I don't know how a stag turns
> into a stream, an arc of water.
> I have never felt such accurate envy.
>
> Not of the deer:
>
> To be that porous, to have such largeness pass through me.

Over a decade ago, in 2001, I was reading thousands of individual poems nominated for another anthology—the Pushcart Prize. How would I choose only fifteen? Which fifteen? So many poets whose work I did not know, so many poets writing about so much, in so many ways. And then there was one poem—by Kevin Prufer—and I knew. Knew instantly that it was a poem

* Editor's note: Originally published in *The Georgia Review* (Winter 2007)

that spoke both of the past and to the future. The twenty-first century was underway, and here was one poet who had opened himself fully to its brutal beginnings.

Four books later, Prufer is still exploring our nation's most difficult issues—not in the docudrama style of much contemporary poetry but within a visionary landscape that acts as moral challenge. By evoking a state of post-apocalyptic trauma, Prufer plunges himself into imagined realms where perspective shifts and shimmers; he can concentrate on the microscopic and the infinite within the same poem; he can "look down" on his subject as if from a great height, can weigh, and grapple, and enter.

In a Beautiful Country is not very different in tone from Prufer's two preceding books, both of which also posit a fallen empire, something at the flute end of consequence—a battle-scarred landscape within which we see the world with a post-9/11, post-Iraq, post-the-next-war outlook. "Transparent Cities," a kind of futuristic fairy tale, reminds us not only of the recent past but of the potential future:

Terrible city many years from now
                                        and the burning paper
that sears the hair with embers—
. . . .
                                   I rocked with every step
the black horse took
                              and gasped to see transparent towers rise
like God's great hands unflexing from the snow banks,
. . . .
Such buildings and the dust
                                           that glittered over us.

The personal terrain is once again covered with snow; it sifts through cracks and colors the heart. In "The Ambassador" snow hides the corpse that takes its surprising indifference with it into another state of being:

    I am a worthless, unproductive thing,
far beneath the weeds:
                              jawbone split by roots, a useless finger bone,
while natives turn the earth above and, once or twice,
a piece of me turns with it,
                                   rising to catch the air,
then down again into the soil.

The narrator of the poems is often just such a generalized figure, an abstracted being who seems more spokesman than speaker, but even when the "I" plays a more conventional role, it retains the detached distance necessary to assess and comment, note anomaly and pinpoint irony. Much of the material of these poems is familiar: hospital, illness, war, conflagration, aftermath, aftermath, aftermath. But the speaker's remove gives it all a retrospective blush; his is the light of the mind, cold and planetary. In "Night Watch" even grief is softened and blurred by imagination:

> My father, as I implied, would die that night.
> That was thirty days ago.
>
> And the boy,
>
> he was far below, in a story I invented,
> sleeping in a car
>
> as daylight broke through clouds,
>
> and try as they might,
>
> they couldn't wake him.

In a very real way, it's true that the child does die with the parent's death, and the admittedly invented story unearths a universal.

As shown, Prufer's lines range across the page, and the stanzas are often set off by the use of intervening marks. Like gems, each facet is framed with white space, seeming to float a bit like the often-invoked snowflakes. Even more, these poems read easily out loud, unfolding their sense in sure cadences that lull you into a dreamscape, then startle you awake, face to face with what you'd hoped to guard against. In this manner, *In a Beautiful Country* forces you to peer into the cloudy mirror of incrimination that solidifies Prufer's reputation for walking the tightrope between the personal and the political, and rounds out his cautionary tale.

Of course, this now-familiar landscape—of burning buildings, falling people, myths that fail and failure turned to myth, obliterating snow and stars that glitter overhead in their great cold—could begin to seem redundant. So, to rekindle the reader's imagination Prufer will need to find new ways to augment and even alter his project as he continues to examine what he sees as the moral fissures in modern-day America.

One of Kevin Prufer's strengths is his ability to startle with the apt adjective, the unpredictable verb, or the eccentric perspective. The patriot missile has a "perfect, absent brain"; bombers "unzip" the sky; the "body / buried in the black char of branches" is "after all, not a man, but a woman, / that was, after all, / a pile of leaves—" And, oh, those "pills" of snow. But facility with words is not all that will be needed to intensify his now-established message.

In a Beautiful Country does contain hints of something new to come. The first is an increased attention to form and rhyme—often a rhyme that deliberately deteriorates as the material gets more and more problematic, going from true to slant to none as though to demonstrate that rhyme itself can be an obfuscation. Beginning with light humor, these poems often veer into unexpected places. Humor can trivialize, and some of Prufer's rhyming poems seem to want to show us how that happens by letting their subjects deteriorate right under our ears.

Those poems are complemented by the second new ingredient—a proliferation of the ars poetica, culminating in "Four Artes Poeticae." Within the larger context of the book's dark vision, they imply the perennial question: what is the meaning of poetry in such a world? The first stanza of "Ars Poetica" announces itself as a kind of nursery rhyme:

> A bomb undid the barn
> and blew the horse apart
> and charred the little lamb
> I loved with half my heart.
> (It made me think of art.)

In the following poem (also titled "Ars Poetica"), the speaker addresses the plight of a man who has just badly injured himself crashing through the glass patio doors:

> And where was I? There I was, on the other side of town, looking out
> the window at the snow,
>
> holding this brand new poem in one hand and my phone in the other.

The dialogue between the poems makes it obvious that, for Prufer, the answer to the larger question is less than clear. If a poem cannot save a person, then the poet cannot save the world (no matter how much he "thinks of art"). Finally, in the series of four "artes poeticae," the speaker discloses his fallback position: "Dear God of Art, / I was always talking to you." That the God of Art was not impressed is a given. He was not impressed when the poet dissected the butterfly and laid it out for all to see, nor was he moved when the speaker cut his finger watching "your hundred deer" devour plants in the garden. The lonely, solitary "I" is left to "the long night of the mind," and God's "million glass stars / keep falling / on the rooftop" ("In My Brain Is a Room; In That Room You Are Sleeping").

The big question remains: what *can* poetry do in a degraded world? At the end of this present century, an anthologist may provide the answer, but for now one can only predict that Prufer's unsettling prophecies will have staying power. There is no other contemporary voice quite like his, and I believe that, taken as a whole, Kevin Prufer's prognostic backward gaze may someday prove to have shown us where we were going before we got there. Maybe the God of Art will approve.

Every once in a while a writer emerges for whom language is ultimate. Not just Coleridge's "best words in the best order," but the Word. Kevin Goodan's third book, *Upper Level Disturbances*, establishes him as one of these. Anchored to history and place, rooted in personal experience and loss, the poems do not find closure but instead open out into question—and quest. Goodan knows that a question takes a long time to answer, and that maybe the answer cannot be found, so he moves in language as though to reach for the something he knows is not there—and in so doing to find, somehow, the something that is.

For Goodan, the "things" are, for the most part, of the land—but silo and corn-crib, thresher and kill-truck, are as much a part of the landscape as river and bluff, pine and hawk. Rain falls on them all in equal measure. The land, with its cycles of death and renewal, legends itself deep, the way it is. Goodan's focus here is on the work—the tools and the drudgery and the rare moments of providence. His poems display the vocabulary of hard use, not just *hay-rake* and *band-saw*, but words with which we are less familiar: *swale* and *stob* and *kerf* and *knurl*. In fact, at times sound is almost a substitute for language. Goodan gives voice to the machines, finding in them a "link" to understanding. "Thus I Am Called, Thresher to the Fields" begins where Frost's "The Tuft of Flowers" began, by following "the one who has come before," but Goodan blurs the "I," moving intimately into the gears so that driver and thresher are one:

> And I move with a hub on trunnions,
> A spring draw bar, a friction clutch—
> Its hinged arms beveling the flywheel
> For its sacred duty.

Frost's "questions that have no reply" become, in Goodan's hands, a laborer's prayer:

> That the tandem simple valves not seize,
> That the bedplate and guides be bored,
> And the automatic band cutters,

Automatic weighers,
Pneumatic stackers
Forget not the weight per bushel of grain
The state of heaven requires—
And grant me torque blocks
Against which to twist my life.

With its clatter of precise nouns, this poem might almost be an anti-pastoral, but Goodan is equally eloquent when it comes to description of the natural world:

I watch the air become
Si, si, si, si of a migrant bird unknowable.
Last night I glimpsed storm through slits between trees.
Whispered home to the lightning
Which came down and came down then vanished.

Goodan's work closely exemplifies Donald Hall's description of a poem as being "one man's inside talking to another man's inside." The poem completes itself inside the reader—not as a statement or story, but as a second voice simultaneously reaching for the unknowable. Goodan understands the difference between correlation and cause and effect, and so his poems refuse to "add up" so much as they "add to." They proceed with the quickened "logic" of instinct so that meaning is generated not by what they say but what they *do*—by their very method of coming into being.

Sentences end with missing subjects or predicates. Or sentences proceed with such radical enjambments that parts of lines become units of sense, to be read forward and backward with the shifting perspective of an Escher painting. Compound nouns turn lines gnarled and dense. Verbs disquiet them. Often, new words are coined—words that ought to exist, need to exist, in order to better approximate a feeling. Consonants crackle; vowels woo; phrases twist their recombinant DNA down through the vertical plane. Like stones in a creek bed, the capital letters that begin each line disrupt the horizontal flow, and sense is deflected, is cut through by wind, by fire, by memory's insistent claims. Often the gap between the extended title and the poem can only be bridged by intuition. "The Flame-Front I Maintain Is for This Tinder Only," with its one long sentence staking out an emotional meteorology, exhibits most of these attributes:

Smoke
And the scent of smoke
The yellowed curls rising,
Bramble knurled, thorn-riven,

A surge of scorn-briar across the brakes,
Poplar storm-torqued in the gaze,
Stone-boat keeled to the dead-furrow flooded,
A thrashing in the fire,
In the brindle gussets of the fire,
I stir, I stir, white oak, sugar maple sappy,
Flame-spits from the bark
Of every feral being,
My face a roiling seepage of code
Down into the fire,
A name for every wrongness,
The harsh, the true,
A brightness not the world,
A blinding, like voices surging through the keys
Trying to find home-notes
By the intercession, at the intersection
Of the crown-fire in the folds of the mind,
Poplar that are memory,
Briar about my face, the fire
Cresting the ridge of my words
In the dry, autumnal dark,
In the fields of the floodplain,
In my eyes, in our eyes
Where the fire feasts upon the patterns of other weathers.

Each poem in *Upper Level Disturbances* acts in a similar manner. Images coalesce, and the reader discerns meaning by piecing together scraps taken from the entire collection.

With its Plath-like intensity, the opening poem, "Come Take These Words from Me," establishes not the book's tone but its pitch:

And through the day we feed the fires
And transform the field-jumble into lines.
Far faces bleared by fire, who are you
That the bright mares of language stride forth
Their flames? I am never more than this.

Fire becomes the book's informing metaphor. If Kevin Prufer's conflagration serves a futuristic vision, Kevin Goodan's functions as reminder—and forge. His fires do not lick and fawn; they blaze up, searing the lungs. Goodan is no stranger to fire, having served as a firefighter with the U.S. Forest Service for ten years; in poem after poem, he uses its vocabulary (cauterize, smolder, cinder, ash, tempering, carbonized) and knows its predilections ("stobs and understory kilned by the radiants"). He understands how the tinder is fuel, the bellows is agent. Words are "rivets" of fire, and a dead starling gives off a "negative flame."

In many ways, each poem aspires to its vanishing point. "I write letters to the unseen," the speaker states. As with Goodan's first two books, there is an ever more elusive "you" so shrouded that it serves in turn as the poet, the reader, a loved one gone, and a cryptic god whose very shape is silence: "And I will live another year / Without you, but this rain / Makes the present and past / Almost marry." Here present and past coincide even as the poet moves into the future, knowing that the ever-expanding present will always include the loss. But "You do not come near me now as you did years ago" ("Last Moth Before Winter") and "Yours is a landscape where no past thrives" ("She Called Your Name Over and Over Then Died They Said").

In this new collection, Goodan seems haunted not so much by loss as by remembered violence. Again and again, he finds a kind of beauty in the knuckle and hock, the "band-saw arcing through bone." Using memory as a kind of back-fire—"flame to vanquish flame"—he conjures the slaughterhouse:

> In the dream I come back to slaughter—
> Gelid blood upon me, bone flecks, ingots of tallow
> Stacked in the cold-room, sawdust fresh and bloodless
> And fragrant in the chill beneath the halves of beasts—

"Listening to Arvo Part's *Fur Alina*," the final poem, is chilling in its self-recrimination—or, possibly, its stoic acceptance. Dedicated to Joe Grady, shot dead in Hungry Horse, Montana, 1997, this poem is set at the tail-end of the century ("Music, winter, the whites and bitumens / of winter"), and the "you" with "the small hole / I need not touch to know—" is

> . . . here now, within the music
> Within winter, you
> who called for me
> And I who chose not to save you.

The poet shows himself no mercy. In the face of such enormity, what is left but wonder? Who is he, that he could wield the sledge? What is death, that it so resembles sleep? Where is God, whose time zone has no clock?

Upper Level Disturbances distills the tradition of the psalm: "Let me shut mine eyes"—and the poems lift from the page, neither supplication nor praise. A cross between Hopkins and Merton, rapture and asceticism, Kevin Goodan's petitions reach into those places you can "see through, but not beyond." This is a young poet whose career I intend to follow. He approaches those instances "When the unsayable is lodged in the throat" and "Where every moment is a landscape / We enter, depart, at the same time"—and he does so with such lyric authenticity that we can chart the age-old course any vital question takes: "Who are you that I am left beneath the rumble of clouds with no way to answer?"

With a Little Help from My Friends

On Natasha Trethewey's *Thrall*; Kathleen Flenniken's *Plume*; John Hodgen's *In My Father's House*; Alice Derry's *Tremolo*; and Lola Haskins' *The Grace to Leave*

James Boswell: "Then, Sir, what is poetry?"
Samuel Johnson: "Why, Sir, it is much easier to say what it is not. We all know what light is, but it is not easy to tell what it is."

IN 1961, I BOARDED a Holland America Line passenger ship and set sail for England. I'm amazed, now, to realize it was cheaper then to spend a week at sea than to fly. I was heading for a year at the University of Edinburgh—and Edinburgh did not disappoint me. The October winds scoured the soot-covered alleys and stirred up the dust of centuries. Boswell's ghost walked the streets on rainy nights, Scots to the hilt with his fierce ambitions, and the cobbles threw back the sheen as he set out to discover—in Johnson's life—an answer to his prudent questions. In the waning light of mid-afternoon, I found it appropriate to imagine him whispering past the doorways of churches and pubs, filled with a sense of what he could not find the words for.

Go to any source and you will find controversy about Boswell's famous biography, *The Life of Samuel Johnson*. You will read that Boswell was too young, that he shortchanged the early years (or the later years), was obsequious, was devious, altered quotes, shaved the truth. But it's Boswell's Johnson whom we know, Boswell's Johnson who probes the very heart of literature, and when he suggests the elusive nature of the poem—its refusal to define itself—we find ourselves nodding in agreement. Taking my cue from him, I ask myself what I would say poetry is not:

Not politics, no matter how "political" it ultimately is.
Not theology, despite the fact that it aspires to the spiritual.
Not narrative, though it often rides on a sea of story.
Not beautiful sounds, for they can be deceptive.
Not sheer cadence, for Hitler's army marched to music.
Not beautiful thoughts, because they are often facile.
Not merely exotic, for that will soon pall.
Not easy pronouncement, which can be misguided.
Not sheer desire to change the world, even if some poems have done so.
Not what is known, but something that asks questions.

Ah . . . at last, a turning toward a definition, though if I question how poetry asks a question I find myself with multiple variations on the theme. And who, I end up interrogating myself, is doing the asking—the poet or the poem? And then I get caught up in the problem of how we can tell the dancer from the dance, and . . . well . . . you can see how this will end if I don't extricate myself. So I turn to others for help. Poets have "defined" poetry for centuries, and much of the litany is familiar:

Poetry . . . takes its origins from emotion recollected in tranquility.
William Wordsworth

Poetry: the best words in the best order.
Samuel Taylor Coleridge

If I feel physically as if the top of my head were taken off, I know that is poetry.
Emily Dickinson

Poetry is what gets lost in translation.
Robert Frost

Poetry is the art of creating imaginary gardens with real toads.
Marianne Moore

Poetry is not a turning loose of emotion, but an escape from emotion; it is not the expression of personality, but an escape from personality.
T. S. Eliot

These definitions, though, further attest to the difficulty of pinning down poetry's specific hold on us. They are sometimes abstract, sometimes fanciful—either all image or all idea. They strike me as being accurate without being practical. I still need something I can *use*.

This past summer, I was sitting in a large audience listening to two poets read their work. The introductions were enthusiastic; the poets dressed the part, but the work did not. Instead of poetry, I heard "stories." The stories were mildly interesting, but they never rose beyond their narratives. Since the poets already knew the outcome, the stories seemed to complete themselves ahead of time, and sometimes they did not even live up to the "story" the poets told of the poems' inceptions. Honestly, they were all prose. So, add this to the "not" list: not merely prose broken into lines.

> If it doesn't work horizontally as prose . . .
> it
> probably
> won't
> work
> any
> better
> vertically
> pretending
> to
> be
> poetry.
> —Robert Brault[1]

Never mind that if I could see the work on the page, the lines might break in interesting ways. The poems might even have some internal rhymes, might even bear the whiff of something metrical. I'm sure some of them had something we might call "poetic." (Certainly other people in the audience seemed to think so.) But they were not poems. They produced no emotions; no toads appeared; my head stayed implacably intact.

Afterwards, when others were gushing around me, I found myself at a loss for words. What do you say when you're expected to praise, and you simply can't bring yourself to do so? I opt for comments on delivery, or the one poem that left me with a question, or a line that seemed to me particularly engaging. In other words, by default, I comment on what is not there. Does this make me sound like the curmudgeon I feel myself to be at such a time? Partly. But it also makes me the critic I have become over the past quarter century. It makes me the reader in search of something subtle, even magical.

Here's all I know:

A poem completes itself in the reader. It does not know what it knows until the reader senses its presence. It has no agenda. It is full of wonder—and wondering. It listens for its own music. It complicates itself. It simplifies itself. It understands that it

1. www.rtbrault.blogspot.com

does not understand. It accepts the ineffable. It loves white space, wallowing in what is not said, what cannot be said, what will not be said. It says everything. It speaks across time, and space, and difference, and indifference. It insists itself. It insinuates itself.

And there I am, as abstract as anyone else, making my own generalizations. These characteristics define *how* poetry works on us. But still, they give no sense of how the poet works this magic, how the poem can be *recognized*. Which means, I guess, that what other people at that large reading identified as poetry might—maybe—have to be *called* poetry. I have to acknowledge that each reader comes with his or her own definition, his or her own taste, his or her individual requirements. But that would imply that I am comfortable with the idea that poetry can be whatever the reader claims for it—and I do not believe that, not for one second. As Whitman reminded us, "To have great poets there must be great audiences too."

Thus I am back where I started, weighing the poem against my personal inclinations. Measuring and judging by standards I've developed over years. So now I realize that Johnson's somewhat parsimonious outlook compels me to try to say a bit more than what poetry is not. Compels me to make an effort to describe the unbearable lightness of its being. To do so, I'll look at several contemporary collections, considering not only the whole, but also the individual poems for what they bring to the table. I won't be able to spend much time on the lines—the assonance or consonance or meters—but I will look at how the poem resounds, and I'll try to cover a wide range of styles, techniques, and—dare I say it?—intentions.

Where better to begin this exploration than with our new poet laureate, Natasha Trethewey? Her latest book, *Thrall*, expands her ongoing focus on what it has meant historically to be of mixed race. Looking at ancient myths, Mexican *casta* paintings (along with the precise nomenclature listed in the *Book of Castas*), medical histories, etc., Trethewey shifts perspectives, sometimes moving close by taking on the persona of one figure in a painting, sometimes using the tool of distance to examine multiple points of view. But always the material is infused with personal experience: white father, black mother. As in her acclaimed second book, *Bellocq's Ophelia* (2002), the angle of vision by which Trethewey looks at art or history has been influenced by her own struggle with identity, and this gives the poetry its distinctive charge—its *incentive*, if you will.

In *Thrall*, Trethewey sheds all masks as she moves seamlessly from her interpretations of history to her own experiences and back again—thus re-envisioning history through the lens of the present. For example, "Miracle of the Black

Leg" looks at several pictorial representations of the mythic transplantation of a leg by Saints Cosmas and Damian. Each of its four sections explores a different perspective, and the final lines of the poem fuse them in one overarching question:

> How not to see it—
> the men bound one to the other, symbiotic—
> one man rendered expendable, the other worthy
> of this sacrifice? In version after version, even
> when the *Ethiopian* isn't there, the leg is a stand-in,
> a black modifier against the white body,
> *a piece cut off*—as in the origin of the word *comma*:
> caesura in a story that's still being written.

Trethewey's poems force you to think, and to question. Is it true that, in Western society, we accept the sacrifice without thinking? There's certainly a tendency to say that this has been the norm—and yet we also know that, throughout history, there have been individuals who have called accepted practice into question. *Thrall* reminds us that the work is unfinished: the fact that history is being assessed even as it is still being forged is everywhere in this book. Aware that race is still at least partly a determinant in one's fate, Trethewey looks to her own life for ways that she has learned to look at the world. Never once does she embrace the role of "victim," but at the same time she does not avoid naming realities. If we are to take these poems on their own terms, her father mirrored the scientists dissecting a drowned woman in a charcoal sketch as he studied his "crossbreed" child, and her careful rendering of the black mothers in the various paintings is occasioned by her sense that her own mother was often the forgotten figure in the photograph. In "Kitchen Maid with Supper at Emmaus; or, The Mulata," the maid in the 1619 painting by Diego Velázquez is a stand-in for the poet four centuries later: "Listening, she leans / into what she knows. Light falls on half her face."

Natasha Trethewey leans with nuance into what she knows, exhibiting a delicate ear, a precision of language, a meticulous sense of craft—all in service of a subject that is complex, and inescapable. History haunts the pages of *Thrall*, trapping alternatives in its net. The poet's main focus is on the parents in the examined paintings—white fathers who dominate the canvas, black mothers who recede into "flat outline." Race trumps gender in these renditions; still, the reader can't help but wonder if, in today's society, divisions may begin to crop up along gender lines. In "Enlightenment," Trethewey's portrait of Jefferson is fraught with ambiguity: how "white" his mistress might have been to make her "worthy / of Jefferson's attentions," how to interpret her father's not-quite-suppressed attitudes.

> *Imagine stepping back into the past*
> our guide tells us then—and I can't resist
>
> whispering to my father: *This is where*
> *we split up. I'll head around to the back.*

His laughter at her joke becomes the fulcrum on which the poet can find comfort in "this history / that links us—white father, black daughter—/ even as it renders us other to each other." In naming herself "black daughter," she identifies with the tradition where "one drop" of blood is a stain, tainting the person in ways that can persist through generations.

Even the annotations Trethewey discovered in a secondhand book give rise to *Thrall*'s pivotal dualities. "Illumination" ends the collection, and its ending is provocative:

> Between
> the printed words   and the self-conscious scrawl
> between   what is said and not
> white space framing the story
> the way the past   unwritten
> eludes us   So much
> is implication   the afterimage
> of measured syntax   always there
> ghosting the margins that words
> their black-lined authority
> do not cross   Even
> as they rise up   to meet us
> the white page hovers beneath
> silent   incendiary   waiting

Poetry is an orphan of silence. The words never quite equal the experience behind them.
Charles Simic

In "Illumination," there are no punctuation marks to bring closure. Silence reigns. Meanings, neither black nor white, are lost in ghostlike implications; everything that is unsaid and unwritten waits for words that might equal the experience behind them. Waits for a poetry equal to the magnitude of the issue.

My assessment could stop at this point—deducing that, for the poet, poetry has not yet found that moment—were it not for the opening poem of the book. Remembering a day when she was fishing with her father, the narrator finds herself trying to mine the event in order to "fix" the moment for an eventual elegy she plans to write. "Elegy" is that rare poem that helps define poetry simply by honoring the metaphor that rises to the surface. The poet's job, then, is to get out of the way of metaphor, to make room for its subtle revelation. Understanding that she—the daughter of a poet—was self-consciously framing the present, Trethewey abandons an anticipated future in favor of what the moment actually evokes:

What does it matter

if I tell you I *learned* to be? You kept casting
your line, and when it did not come back

empty, it was tangled with mine. Some nights,
dreaming, I step again into the small boat

that carried us out and watch the bank receding—
my back to where I know we are headed.

Like a piece of ice on a hot stove the poem must ride on its own melting.
Robert Frost

"Elegy" is a perfect example of Frost's melting. The careful couplets fuse father and daughter, locked (before the fact) in the book's complicating issues, and locked as well in a series of near rhymes that underscore their differences. Intended to act as a foreshadowing, the poem begins as though it is sure of its "politics," but ends in the wisdom of uncertainty. Memory speaks its own predictive language as the poem, freed of its restraints, finds its source of heat. The poet reclaims her personal past by watching the bank instead of the river. The poem becomes an elegy for the moment of its central discovery—that emotion is to be recollected, not invented. The arc of the "invisible line" that sliced "the sky between us" remains hidden, even as the speaker knows the eventual death of the father will spawn a genuine elegy.

All the poems that follow hark back to the core insight that, even though we know where we're headed, we do not know what we'll find there. The weight of that insight—its unanticipated significance—helps define what poetry can do: it can conjugate the verb *to be*.

On 21 August 2012, newspapers reported that radioactive leaks had recently been discovered in a double-wall storage tank at the Hanford Nuclear Reservation in eastern Washington. A second leak was confirmed on 31 August. The leaks, found at the site of what was already the nation's costliest environmental cleanup project, further threaten at least 300 miles of the Columbia River as nuclear waste that will last thousands of years makes its way through the water table. This disclosure makes Kathleen Flenniken's *Plume*, published earlier in 2012, all the more relevant. Currently poet laureate of the state of Washington, Flenniken grew up in Richland, close by Hanford and a place where her father boarded a bus each morning and "disappeared to fuel the bomb." Many years after working there as a scientist herself, she began the research that resulted in the convergence of her own story with those of others, especially the father of her childhood friend who died of radiation exposure.

Plume examines the mindset of the Cold War, probes the growing doubts of scientists, and worries away at the "art" of censorship. The poems, for all their weight, do not impose a political stance so much as they explore a range of perspectives. No one style or point of view could contain the complexity of Flenniken's subject, and she employs an impressive array of personal lyrics, persona poems, songs, and fragments—along with "found" poems from documents and reports—to consider the origins and scope of this particular environmental disaster. The questioning mode leads the poet to imagine the lives of others—prominent scientists, workers, survivors—and consequently she grants herself sufficient latitude to investigate fully not only the government's subsequent indifference (and even cover-up), but the limits of scientific knowledge as well. For the most part, the poet reproduces the innocence of childhood, only allowing her present knowledge to intrude as subtle irony or self-interrogation. Thus she effectively reproduces the flavor of the times: the isolation of the landscape, the naïveté of the workers, the foreboding sense of external threat, the unswerving patriotism, the imminent potential. Yet a mature sensibility hovers over the whole, providing a retrospective angle: "This is the future. // Dad holds me up to see it coming."

A poem is true if it hangs together. Information points to something else.
A poem points to nothing but itself.
E. M. Forster

Luckily for us, these poems are not merely information. The "Notes" section at the back of the book reveals the shameful facts, but the poems are restrained, incorporating those facts in ways that convey a collective innocence and a budding apprehension. Flenniken amplifies her vision by using (or breaking away from) formal structures. Consider the careful tercets of "The Cold War" as it tumbles down the page, through bomb shelters and H-bombs and Khrushchev's shoes, to its ending:

> I remember the red phone, and missile codes,
> how every movie hinged
> on a clock ticking down.
>
> We called it the arms race
> and there were two sides.
> It was simple.

Or watch language itself break apart in the spare columns of the title poem:

> it migrates
> between grains
> down to
> saturated sediment
> manifestly down
> and when
> it descends
> as far as it can
> it will swim
> ride droplets
> like swanboats
> float
> spread
> diffuse
> distend
> trailing its
> delicate
> paisley scarf
> and like
> anything
> with a destiny
> a flock of birds
> sperm
> breath
> it will move
> downstream
> to the river
> yes the river
> will take it in

"Plume" slows the flow of words until they, too, "unfurl" and "fan" and "feather" and seep through permeable soil until the conclusion seems inevitable. This is not L=A=N=G=U=A=G=E poetry, but poetry that demonstrates the fluidity of language, taking meaning "as far as it can" as it moves downstream.

The lines in the two stanzas of "Afternoon's Wide Horizon" reverse themselves so that, technically, the poem reads the same forward and backward, but punctuation intrudes to shift the meanings of the lines in subtle ways. The couplets of "Bedroom Community" end with mild half-rhymes that keep the ear alert even as they disrupt any sense of certainty. Three separate poems, each titled "Redaction," force us to turn the book on its side to experience the effects of censorship. They begin with typescript from pamphlets, articles, and speeches of the times, then reproduce the typewritten quotes with huge sections blacked out, leaving only a few words and letters available. The second of these redactions quotes J. Robert Oppenheimer from 1947; it begins with "The whole point of science is . . . to invite the detection of error and to welcome it" and goes on to implore open examination of what was happening at the Hanford site. Through Flenniken's careful choice of which letters and words to leave intact, the censored version reads "science vetted in ignorance may incite chaos." The reader is compelled to read the documented assertion, the redacted version, and their juxtaposition as one complete experience; the resulting insight can be seen to apply to many contemporary issues.

> *Out of the quarrel with others we make rhetoric; out of the quarrel with ourselves we make poetry.*
> W. B. Yeats

Plume does make its quarrel with others, but it is also full of self-doubt. "Museum of Doubt," addressed to an unknown "you," demands that we look at photos of Nagasaki—the shadows that are like "interrupted sundials"—but the "you" at its ending seems, somehow, to have merged with the speaker:

> Meaning is lost
> between the vulnerable eye
> and well-defended mind.
>
> Who's on your side (you keep asking)?
> Not righteousness, not at this late hour?
>
> Look at you, unsure
> but sure underneath.

The quarrel is never more pronounced than in "Museum of a Lost America," where the country the speaker was taught to love (its cardinal directions: "orchard in bloom; / crickets at dark; / wheat up to the ridge; / fence line in snow") has betrayed her. And yet she loves it still—

> Oh Beautiful,
>
> I will not stop.

—and adds it to her "losses."

"Going Down," one of my favorite poems in the collection, begins its stanzas with a nursery-rhyme echo of "This is the house that Jack built" ("This is the guy in the white fastback Mustang . . . This is the woman with wooly blond hair . . . These are the thousands who rise before dawn . . . This is a pattern of acting out") to evoke the sameness of the mornings—the Mondays or Tuesdays or Wednesdays—as the hundreds of workers head off for the site. There's humor here, but a humor that utilizes metaphor as it turns serious by the final stanza:

> This is the landscape bleak and brown
> that can hold its secrets for only so long
> till they spill and spill, but for now and instead
> the woman goes down on the man driving fast,
> we cop our looks while they rocket past
> and the rest of us feel . . . not closer to death, but further
> from life as we slow at the gate for security check
> on another Wednesday morning.

The University of Washington Press has done a beautiful job with the production of this book: the space between lines makes for easy readability; the poems fit perfectly on the page, providing a visual sense of their methodology; and the elegant austerity of the design gives dignity to its subject. The overall effect is one of elegy—and urgency. Flenniken would like us to recognize what the future could hold. And still she loves the place itself. This might best be shown in the words she has put in the mouth of John A. Wheeler in "A Great Physicist Recalls the Manhattan Project": "Think of it—a *desert* in Washington State. Along the icy blue Columbia. . . . As for whether // I solved the poisoning riddle, let no man be his own judge. . . . I think of that place as a song not properly sung." In *Plume*, Kathleen Flenniken reminds us that a central definition for poetry is song, properly sung.

Discovering a previously unfamiliar voice can be exciting, and several presses now perform an important service by bringing back work that may have been missed the first time around. Published by Bluestem Press in 1993 and out of print since 1994, John Hodgen's first book has recently been reissued in paperback by Lynx House Press. Like Trethewey's collection, *In My Father's*

House opens with an elegy of sorts, and the loss of the parent quietly dominates the rest of the collection. "For Mr. Grimes Who Tried to Teach Me Physics after My Dad Died" makes the father loom large by relegating him to the title alone. The vocabulary and principles of physics become the language in which the adolescent begins to accept death:

> He spoke of ellipses,
> of things coming round again.
> He spoke of resistance,
> of the forces that act upon us.
> He spoke of gravity,
> of the earth that draws us to itself.
>
> He said the mass of the earth,
> the changes of state.
> He said that a body at rest
> would remain at rest.
> He said that a boy
> standing at the end of a moving train
> could toss the red ball of his life
> up into the heavy air
> and catch it again.

If you know what you are going to write when you're writing a poem, it's going to be average.
Derek Walcott

Hodgen's opening poem alerts the reader to the collection's underlying themes. Time and time again, the poet addresses untimely deaths—whether it be his cousin dying of AIDS or a stranger whose death is reported in the newspaper. Titles such as "For the Woman Whose Husband Fell Seven Stories to His Death Trying to Get in the Window of Their Locked Apartment," "For the Faceless Boy," and "Boy Struck by Lightning Survives" function almost as headlines, and the reader expects the story to follow. But Hodgen avoids the "average" because he almost always ends up surprising himself as well as the reader. The poems veer off in interesting directions. For example, here's what the boy struck by lightning sees:

> Slender lines alive in the light,
> the swirl of magician's wands,

the dance macabre in the veins
of an old woman's legs,
chiaroscuros of the blind,
eyesockets of snakes,
spun gyros, filaments,
the wrinkled skin of the air,
every jot and tittle,
the blue and red whirlygigs
pulsing on the walls of the placenta.

Some go intensely internal, as in "For One Whose Daughter Is Gone, and for Others":

If this were Solomon's world, all cut and halved,
I, two-daughtered, would offer him one,
or, if daughters were blossoms, I would harrow bouquets,
turn vendor for nothing at intersections, corner lots,
daughters curling like vines about my rusted van.

To imagine the lives of others is to reconnect with your own. Hodgen demonstrates how poetry so often is the fusion of two separate concerns, each one informing the other. He weaves fleeting references to his own losses throughout, and as he lightly touches down the reader experiences these events as almost tangential, part of the larger collective story—the "many mansions" that blaze in the daily headlines. As if to underscore the poet's desire to invent new variations on old themes, one pair of poems even looks at the same event from slightly different perspectives. "Flying Out of Charlottesville Fog on All Hallows Day" has as its focus the fog, the tedious wait, the final takeoff, and, from above, the sudden sight of a burning house. "Flying Out of Charlottesville and Seeing from the Air a House Engulfed in Flames: Variation" begins with the spectacle of the fire and moves to the passengers' helplessness, which leads to a contemplation of the nature of God:

Perhaps He sits there now like a handcuffed juggler,
        like one Hardy boy,
waiting for the Buick Dynaflow to come streaming, slowly,
around the corner of the world, His father getting out,
after driving all the way around Robin Hood's barn,
and now, with the help of the silent farmer next door,
rolling the stone away.

Since this is neither the first nor the last reference to the Buick, we realize how quickly Hodgen can personalize a situation, how readily his own father rises up to provide metaphor. By the final lines of the poem, Hodgen has extended his list of possible deities, and specific circumstances, to include his present situation, with all its shared vulnerability:

> Or those rows of TVs in Sears, and He the tired salesman,
> always wandering off, now in household, now in hardware.
> Or all the windows in an airplane when it breaks into the light,
> each one a little home, like the windows in a school bus,
> a face in each one, shining.

> *Everything one invents is true, you may be perfectly sure of that. Poetry is as precise as geometry.*
> Gustave Flaubert

Hodgen's geometry is meticulous. The poems of *In My Father's House* are full of details that seem, like that TV salesman, to be pulled from the poet's prolific imagination. Invention is necessity; the reader recognizes his method as a way to "read" the world—not measuring one thing against another so much as taking the measure of everything. Just below the surface of every poem is the suggestion that the poet understands the limits of human speech to make logic of the irrational:

> The words stand around unemployed in my throat, like shirts, frozen
> left out on a line, or dogs in a yard, the family gone away.
> I am the quick brown fox's lazy dog. I lift my head.
> I look the other way.

And what *can* be said in the face of death? What is it that pilots say most before they crash?

> *Oh shit*, we say, as if we've always been in it,
> this ground, this stink, this awful place,
> the earth coming up at us like the right hand of God,
> us seeing it coming. *Oh shit*, we say, *oh shit, oh shit, oh shit.*

For a poet, another form of invention is craft—the constant reworking to fit the syllables to the cadence of one's inner music, or the absorbed attention to sound or pattern, the echo of tradition even as the poem strives for eccentricity. So it is too bad that Lynx House did not do a better job of copyediting; often words or lines are run together, words are broken up, or lines don't break as they were clearly meant to. These problems stem from careless digital formatting, and they are understandable but inexcusable. For example, "bedroll" becomes "be / droll." There are enough of these instances to cast doubt on the lineation—and therefore on the perceptible rhythms. But there is no doubt that there is craft to be found; note how "For Grace and a Print by Bernand Khnoppf" fuses memory and art in a complex of unexpected rhyme (*abacdecfe dabafegg*) that pulls one stanza inextricably into the other. Via Hodgen's reversal of sound, as well as of the flow of time, the issue of whether the artist dreamed the future is transformed into the poet's resurrected past:

> Here in the brown and gray of this print, this face,
> as surely as I once believed there lived somewhere
> my twin, my lonely double, is my aunt, weary Grace,
> wide-jawed, glad-eyed, too ready, always, for death.
> She lay in a rosy bier in Dorchester in 1955
> while her ham-fisted husband who beat her by day
> and who called me Palooka, always, in his beery breath,
> coughed till he shook in the stains of his shirt
> and cried, punch drunk, when they took her away.
>
> Did he dream her, Bernand Khnoppf, in Germany, 1905,
> the way we make the canyoned moon our father's face,
> form safe heaven out of flimsy clouds and air?
> Did you walk before us in a pre-war place,
> lending beauty for nothing against the future's hurt,
> holding a glass up, lovely, to the trembling day?
> Or do you live again, if only for an hour,
> here, now, brown eyes, blue flower?

I would be tempted to caution the poet that the inventive can sometimes become a crutch, but then I remember that this is a first book from two decades ago, and I suspect that by now the poet must have already learned this lesson. The poems of *In My Father's House* have a young man's compulsive sense of morality—that things must be made right. They question God, even as they acknowledge Him. This fierce impulse seemingly still prevails, because during an interview in 2010 Hodgen said the following:

> Every poem has its own prism of morality, a single voice registering its sense of what is just and valuable. One of the reader's tasks is to sound out that voice,

> to align with or against it. If the poem isn't about something right or wrong, if it doesn't try to help or heal in some way, even in its anguish, humor, irony, or even rage, it doesn't really ever fully become a poem.
>
> —interview with Brian Brodeur on "How a Poem Happens"[2]

I'm not sure I agree that poems should help or heal, or even that we would recognize when they do, but at least John Hodgen adds to the ongoing discussion—and I look forward to new humor, irony, even anguish and rage, from this poet with whose work I have just recently become acquainted.

Alice Derry uses musical terms as titles for the five sections of her fourth full collection, *Tremolo*. These terms, along with their definitions, help to orchestrate and shape the emotions that fuel this book. Derry moves easily in and out of history, pondering the presence of the Quilleute Indians of her native Northwest as her family camps or walks along the Pacific. She also looks at the forces at work on individuals as she delves into the bombing of Dresden as well as the cost of the Holocaust, the documented diary of Anne Frank and the imagined time when a young woman overheard her husband planning a new Nazi sweep and warned her doctor to leave—that night. Recognizing the personal in the political, Derry extends her equations to encompass contemporary events, characteristically interweaving family stories (her mother's death, her father's dementia, her daughter's upcoming departure from home) with those of others around the world. These are narrative poems, simply told—but music is their scaffolding, and Derry's stories are almost always accompanied by the grace notes of the past.

These poems have no "speaker" other than Derry herself; she owns them from the outset, using the words "I" and "my" in several titles, inserting such descriptive phrases as *talking to my daughter* and *on our visit to Europe, 2007* between title and text—and thus ensuring, by specifics of time and place, that the experience recounted is solely hers. "Deposition," one of my favorites, is preceded by an admonition that the natural process of building narrative will not be adequate: *It's not a storytelling process, my attorney reminds me*. Under questioning, nothing is quite what it seems: "The knowledge rises in me / I have lost my side / of what happened forever." "Deposition" comes early in the book, and all the poems that follow seem to struggle with the sense that words will not suffice.

"What My Student Discovers" recounts a conversation after the student has visited a cemetery in Austria that contains graves embellished with swastikas along with a memorial to the Holocaust. Two histories are contained in one

2. howapoemhappens.blogspot.com/2010/09/john-hodgen.html

small plot of ground to which the bodies of the soldiers had been sent home for burial. The final stanza reveals a growing comprehension by student and teacher, and offers the same to the reader as well:

> The living soldiers struggled on
> toward Stalingrad, leaving behind them—
> in ditches they covered over
> after they had done the shooting
> and the bodies had tumbled in—
> the Jews of Russia.

Derry's poems do not rely on chronology to tell their story, but on juxtapositions that allow things to collide and activate emotion. So it is, for example, that her daughter can one moment be a young woman and the next a child in school. In "On the Radio, Mozart's Piano Trio #7 in G Major," the poet finds herself sitting in stalled traffic listening to notes that seem like beads on a necklace; she slips into a reverie that ticks off the Twin Towers, an earthquake, a bomb at Passover Seder, child abuse—until she shakes herself into the present: "And still Mozart's notes pass over your tight-stretched / eardrum, sound wave after wave translated to vibration." The poem could end there, but it doesn't. The poet knows she cannot shake the "scalding necklace," knows that that suffering has inserted itself into her sheltered life. Still, there's that music . . . and later, "Through the open window, frogs' bright insistent chorus / announces the complications of hope." The poem could end *there*, but it doesn't. The emotions are far too complex—for how does one weigh beauty against atrocity? Therefore it ends with Shakespeare's Desdemona singing, and the gesture is not so much resolution as recognition:

> The notes of the song flood the night
> no less than dread.

Poetry is Emotion put into measure.
Thomas Hardy

In the case of *Tremolo*, the measures are syncopated. Derry does not give us meter so much as the vestiges of meter, yet the combinations of vowels and consonants, along with the mixture of rising and falling rhythms, make them eminently "singable." But never singsong. The first stanza of "I Mean *Beach, Fir, Yellow*" describes a hike, but the description also illustrates her working method:

A ridge isn't what you'd think,
level on top while all the struggle
falls to either side. It's a steady rise
and fall and rise through fir and pine,
then meadows, then up into the scree,
the last steep scramble for the view.

Husband, wife, daughter—the family's camping trip is fraught with understated emotion. This is no idyll. Tension seems to fill the air. If the speaker looks closely, flowers become yellow stars that "burn / their little wells of growing space / into the melting snow"; her too-tight boots become "boots marching across a continent." Everything is seen in terms of something else. "All I have now is my own story." She piles up words and scenes, but there is no song for refugees who unravel image after image of what has been lost: "words bring back the ache / without the things themselves."

Poetry provides the one permissible way of saying one thing and meaning another.
Robert Frost

Derry's poems do not say one thing and mean another so much as they mean both things at once. She is not as deliberate as Frost, possibly because she is not so sure of what she means. Always probing, she proceeds through seemingly spontaneous association to blend threads of narrative in such a way that they play with—and against—each other. Aware of the various alternative paths inherent in any one moment, Derry looks at the forces of history as they lead up to and away from events that impinge on ordinary lives. At times she gives just a tiny bit too much exposition; some of her final lines or sentences could be omitted, allowing the poems to end with less resolution, and thereby compelling us to follow them out into the world, or to look inward, interrogating the self.

Derry, who has been a teacher of German as well as writing, uses the German language (its "tight syntax") as a portal through which she examines warring emotions. Weaving both the words and their translations throughout, she gives voice to many points of view. The word *raps* (rape)—with its English connotations—takes an innocent crop and turns it into a killing field, and the "beech forest" that is *Buchenwald* provokes its own disturbing commentary:

A word can be tied by torment
to so many things opposite of tree and leaf,

. . . .

> that to say it
> is to break a certain kind of faith
> with those who heard it as death.

In the end, Derry gives the two connotations equal measure, but her final stanza seems to opt for restoration:

> Say *Buchenwald.* Without its sound,
> we might forget this forest.
> Trees don't need to speak. We do.

Emotion suffuses these poems through understatement, implication, and allusion. That's not to say they are offhand or casual. They are intense, but often the intensity is deflected so that its focus is elsewhere, letting the emotion quietly claim its place. Alice Derry shows us *how* to gain perspective. Staring at the paintings of Morris Graves, the poet sees through another's eye and alleges she has entered "another dimension." Still, she needs sound to clarify: the "unlikely tones" of his paint lift from the canvas and his bird flies; the snow outside her window is background to the thrush, whose "high clear solos / break into the cold, each bird, one note, / drawn out until it fades, as it has to." Expression reveals its counterpart in wordless music, and we become attuned to what she is not saying. Meaning becomes implicit. The fifth section's epigraph alerts us to what Derry is striving for as she digs deep, then deeper: "*At that specific point [of music], emotion has staggered into inarticulacy beyond the boundaries of language* . . ." —Brian Friel.

Tremolo is an act of discovery—no, not discovery so much as detection. It is as though the poet understands that if she sifts through the fragments of her own life, she will solve—or at least resolve—some of its many mysteries.

Genuine poetry can communicate before it is understood.
T. S. Eliot

Eliot's statement is more complex than it first appears. I would contend that his assertion is more true for lyric than for narrative poetry; after all, a story has shape, needs to unfold to be understood, but the lyric—with its quality of interiority—only needs to convey its urgency in order to communicate. The reader instantly "understands" its psychology. This is certainly true for the poems of Lola Haskins' newest collection, *The Grace to Leave*. Haskins trusts that her emotions will speak in their own language, and that, in time, we will discern both source and consequence.

The Grace to Leave is orchestrated in four sections, each of which moves fluidly within time. The effect is that of taking stock, in no particular order, of what it has meant to be daughter, wife, mother, grandmother; what it has meant to be single, married, divorced, single; what it has meant to know—and love—a place, a person, a way of being; what it means, in the present, to look back to the past; and what it means, in the present, to look to a future in which you will no longer exist. The book opens with a singular poem, "Seven Turtles," where, while paddling on the Withlacoochee, the speaker notes first the "routine" turtles on a log, then wood storks "hunched like priests in a tree," on her way to remembering a woman in Cairo who grasped her hand and said "in the only language / we both understood: *Pass this on.*" And that is what Haskins is doing—in short, lyrical bursts, she is passing on her idiosyncratic experience of the world, encapsulating the emotional highlights, the moments that matter in a life spent noticing.

The first section looks hard at the body. With titles like "Brows," "The Considerations of My Teeth," "Nostrils," "Pavan for the Little Finger of the Right Hand," "Ode to My Small Hair," "The Great Toe," "Knuckles," "Footsoles," etc., Haskins makes *us* alter our way of seeing; over and over the lines, or sentences, find a natural simile or metaphor—as in "Capillaries":

> I love that my body has many tributaries like these, fine as hairs lit
> by oxygen.

and in "Moles":

> Constellations   Archipelagos   The heads of swimming animals
> Umlauts   Ellipses   Dust on a tabletop   Speckles on a shell

But these poems do not settle for mere figurative language. They move inevitably to images that enlarge the poem, force it into significance. "Of the True Ankle Joint" advances from the literal to the associative in three short segments. The final one reveals how rapidly Haskins can shift into implication:

> Consider love, consider fine china:
> One hairline, almost invisible, fracture,
> and the tea will steep unstoppably into your hand.

> *A poet is a man who manages, in a lifetime of standing out in thunderstorms, to be struck by lightning five or six times.*
> Randall Jarrell

Suddenly the poems of this section pivot to the moors of England, and we find ourselves bodily walking the Roman road between Skipton and Addington in North Yorkshire. Flanked by blueberries, harebells, dock, gorse, the poet has to look down in order to see up, noting the clouds that "still swim in the standing water." The final sentence speaks volumes: "How casually they let the centuries fall." Time recedes; we have entered the silent eternity of nature.

At this point, lightning strikes. "The Ballad of Foot and Mouth" is one of those five or six poems a poet waits a lifetime to produce. How does this happen? Luck, confluence, insight, being in the right place at the right time, patience, recognition. In this case, Haskins was able to use ancient counting rhymes to accentuate the loss as local farmers were forced to incinerate their sheep to prevent the spread of the disease. Through the repetition of words and lines, even the present becomes a kind of rhyme, keeping time with the past in an ageless lament:

One-ery, Two-ery, Ziccary, Zeven
Hollow-bone, Crack-a-bone, Ten-or-eleven
Spin, Spun, It-must-be-done

So they push them up—the ewes,
the wethers, the lambs, the tupps—
With their yellow dozers like flowers o

and so on until, stanzas later, what is happening is internalized:

And what is motherhood now o
as the ash smoulders in the backs of our throats
of the ewes, the wethers, the half-grown lambs

And the moors all empty but for the wind
that moans as it licks at the dry stone walls
And that's your motherhood now o

Spin, Spun, It-must-be-done
Twiddledum, Twaddledum, Twenty-one.

The wind moans. It knows nothing of loss, but the language of grief is universal.

And, if it is possible to be struck by lightning twice in quick succession, the next poem further memorializes place. "Moor" opens with a question: "And what survives? Only the voracious / gorse, with its dark green prickles . . ." and the heather, the bracken, each trying to choke the rest. This is a place where "no map, no piece of paper at all, no page from / the psalms, no verse from the Quran, not even James Joyce / can hold back the mist." It is outside of religion, or literature. It is of itself. So the third part of the poem becomes an italicized, ecstatic "day spent staring"—which is as close as Haskins comes to defining how a poem comes into being. The poet emerges, in first person, with a kind of faith:

even the unstarred night
would not matter

. . . .

I was not dying
but ascending another scale,
like the curlew for whom flight is not
enough   but she must sing too.

"The Return" imagines a mother and son coming back to a cottage where they had once lived. Everything is in ruins, but the poem rebuilds field, walls, home as the speaker remembers the feel of her baby's head under her hands, and the boy remembers his mother as a bird. These longer "moor poems" are so strong they tend to overpower the other poems, especially so early in the book. They probably deserve a section all their own. For an ideal sense of balance, they might be situated in the middle, and then the lyrics could revolve, like planets, around them.

The Grace to Leave is, essentially, a coming to terms. Sometimes the poems are infused with the questioning voice of the child, and sometimes they carry the wisdom of the sage, but always they speak with refreshing candor and with surprising combinatorial power. Haskins launches herself into the world, wanting to remove all barriers, "to lift away without touching, any cloth that lies between you and my skin." The images worm their way inside; the voices take on various tenors; things are presented in terms of other things; generations fuse; time becomes fluid; the alchemy of ideas can appear to be almost surreal. The range and variety—from formal structures to prose poems to tangential meditations—show not only versatility in style and technique, but also a brand of generous receptivity.

Poetry and Hums aren't things which you get, they're things which get you.
And all you can do is go where they can find you.
A. A. Milne, *Winnie-the-Pooh*

Haskins places herself firmly where poetry can find her, and she hums its various tunes in remarkable synchronicity with the world. At times, the poems approach the impressionistic, each brushstroke infused with a concentrated energy that suggests an equal force within the writer: "If only we could always live on the verge // of shivering, on the cliff-edge of too much." But the mind knows better, understands that "what we must love instead is zero." More than most contemporary poets, she has mastered the art of white space. Refusing to be haiku, "Enlightenment" is simply suggestive:

As the heron lifts it free,
the fish suddenly
understands.

Lola Haskins understands that we all must learn how to relinquish what holds us. However, the closing poem exposes some crucial ambiguity. "The Sandhill Cranes" captures the ephemeral. Coupled with the title of the book, its final stanza is wonderfully contradictory:

The long bones of sandhill cranes
know their next pond. Not us.
When something is too beautiful,
we do not have the grace to leave.

I like to imagine Johnson and Boswell sitting in a coffee house. It's raining, and they have come in to get warm. Their woolen coats steam before the fire, and in my fantasy they resume their former conversation:

Boswell: "But Sir, one cannot prove the negative. I'd like to know what poetry positively is."
Johnson: "Perhaps I should reiterate, Sir, that it can't be defined so much as experienced."

I like to imagine their contemporary counterparts. It's a beautiful autumn afternoon, but they have sequestered themselves in a dark corner, each alone at a table with his laptop open before him. Two men are looking for answers. They are not talking to each other, but are asking a question of someone out there, somewhere. They have forgotten that outside the leaves are burnished and clouds skid across the sky. They do not notice the clock on the wall, or the intricate design on their lattés, or even the coffee's somewhat bitter taste, as each of them clicks on Google and types in the phrase "definition of poetry." Silently, each begins to quarrel with what he finds. The definitions on their screens are clever, but they always stop short. They do not really take into account the flicker of doubt that lies at the heart of most good poems. Or the fleeting music of the mind as it makes inspired connections.

It's a rainy winter morning and I have failed in my quest for a comprehensive definition. My friends seem to have deserted me, lost in their abstract—if original—characterizations. Outside my window, there is no sky—only a pervasive cloud cover the color of the sea. The pyrrhic drumming on the skylight taunts me with Hart Crane's words: "And the rain continues on the roof / With such a sound of gently pitying laughter." I laugh at myself. Maybe it would be easier to tell the poet from the elusive poem . . .

To be a poet is a condition, not a profession.
Robert Frost

The poet is the priest of the invisible.
Wallace Stevens

A poet must leave traces of his passage, not proof.
René Char

Da Capo al Coda

On Michael Mlekoday's *The Dead Eat Every Thing*; Kerrin McCadden's *Landscape with Plywood Silhouettes*; David Koehn's *Twine*; Laura Donnelly's *Watershed*; and Kasey Jueds's *Keeper*.

From the beginning, I knew there could be trouble: a box of cheeky new books on my doorstep, all dressed in their shiny covers, waiting to be read. All week I had been ranting about the contemporary world—its lack of tradition, its misuse of grammar, its insidious technologies. One television ad talked about the motel's recent "refresh." I was certain those brash new books would be full of such travesties, and my trusty old dictionary had been published in 1976. The newer dictionary is heavier, taller, three times the volume, and that means I can hardly lift it from the only shelf it fits on. So I stick with the flimsy pages that, for thirty-eight years, have given me most of the words I will ever need.

Oh, I'm aware that technology has outpaced my old red companion, and that I could just as easily consult online dictionaries. But that would feel strange. When it comes to technology, it's nice to be able to revise with a simple "cut" and "paste" (I can remember retyping whole pages because of one mistake, usually making another in the process). It's not so nice to read everyone's private life spilled out on Facebook as though they were next-door neighbors and we were talking over now-nonexistent clotheslines. *Well, then, don't go on Facebook*, you say, and I retort *All well and good*, but I've also encountered some interesting discussions and/or opportunities there. So change is . . . well, change: something we might be cautious of, but also something we need to open ourselves to.

Some people court the new, but for most of us, change requires adjusting over time. For example, in trying to protect its players from injury the NFL has come up with new rules that result in more penalties, more stopping of the game, more frustration for the fans. They'll probably work out new ways both to protect players and let them play, but that hasn't happened yet. In soccer, however, using a simple can of foam shaving cream to mark the line where players must stand during a direct free kick has made the game faster and less confrontational. All that jostling, the encroachments, the whistling, the stopping and starting—gone the way of the fast-fading foam. The only problem seems to be where the referees should store the can, and I'm sure that pretty soon their uniforms will sprout a convenient pocket.

And what does all of this have to do with poetry, aside from the way Ray Hudson, my favorite sportscaster, can say, "There's been an almighty monkey thrown into the wrench" or "He could make an onion cry"?

When I spread out the contents of the box, I wondered what organizing principle my editor had used. The answer: they were all by people whose names he did not recognize. A quick glance told me I recognized only a couple—so, did that mean both of us had been settling for the familiar? That it was time to shake us up? Further inspection revealed at least a partial answer. Many of the collections were first books, and all the rest were second ones. We could let ourselves off the hook; how could we be expected to recognize those names?

Not so fast . . . weren't we keeping up by reading all the various traditional and online journals that were publishing these poets? No, we weren't, or not as assiduously as we used to. There are so many people now doing it for us—prominently displaying the daily poem culled from somewhere else, throwing up the hasty review on blogs, proclaiming, propounding, proliferating.

It was clearly time for me to look at work about which I had no preconceptions. I decided to limit myself to first books, and I determined to document the process. What basic observations could I make? To begin with, I was surprised to discover that most of the poets were not as young as I had expected them to be. For years now the seminal age of forty set by Yale has been creeping lower and lower. Maybe that trend is reversing. Next, I found no direct correlation between how much I liked the work and how much I liked the work of the poets who wrote blurbs for the cover jackets. In fact, the opposite almost held true. Blurbs, I've decided, mean almost nothing—and their vocabulary is so similar that my old dictionary developed a healthy sneer over the lack of variety.

In general, first books have more individually published poems than subsequent books, and there did seem to be a correlation between the books I selected and prior publication. For the most part, the poems had appeared in good, substantial magazines. I was heartened to see a long list of regulars—*Kenyon Review*, *Gettysburg Review*, *Missouri Review*, *AGNI*, *American Poetry Review*, *Rattle*, *Alaska Quarterly Review*, *New England Review*, *Crab Creek Review*, *Beloit Poetry Journal*, *Barrow Street*, *Poet Lore*, and *CutBank*, to name only a few—along with now-established online journals such as the *Cortland Review* and the ever-present *Verse* and *Poetry Daily*. But does noting external validation say more about me than it does about the poets and their publications? Since I came to that question after the fact, I suspected this was due to my preferences, not my selection process. There's little I can do beyond trying to keep a semi-open mind.

With relative ease I divided the tall pile in half—those I needed to look at again and those I found nearly unbearable. Just what is "unbearable"? It turns out that I expect poetry to be more than prose with line breaks. More than a "story" with some vague insight tacked on in the final two lines. More than fragment, or odd combinations of words I must struggle to make sense of, and certainly more than trauma—however well dissected—for sensation's sake. When I cannot hear any "echo" of meter, when there's no pattern of sound, when the lines clunk along or make me roll my eyes, then I end up shutting the book.

What other tendencies did I see? Aside from what I somewhat generously think of as an overall "innocence" concerning forms, throughout my original boxful, I encountered an epidemic of surrealism that even now perplexes me. Often, these poets seemed to be trying a bit too hard to see things slant . . . even deformed. In their hands, things do not work the way I expect them to. The world does not fall into place, slightly altered, the way it does in the hands of someone for whom even the surreal image is instinctive. Their gestures feel gratuitous, even learned, and I am left with the impression that many of today's graduates are trying to *manufacture* mystery.

As I began to whittle, I eventually narrowed my pile to the five books (just 12.5 percent of the total) that spoke to me in some way—probably my old ways, but with a new voice. For what it's worth, I noticed that four of my "top five" books contained three sections (with the occasional prologue or epilogue poem thrown in), and all but one had a section of follow-up "Notes" to explain the sources or references for some of the poems. (The one that didn't seemed to contain all that information in the poems themselves.)

I also realized that all of my selections were winners of contests, most for first books. Three had been chosen by a distinguished judge and the other two by a group of editors. I usually take no notice of contests, but I have to admit the judges were successful in discovering exciting new work and I applaud the presses that are willing to promote the accomplishments of previously unknown writers. I considered cutting another book to save space, but instead I determined to write shorter, snappier assessments with a focus on aspects of craft that might distinguish these new voices for the future.

Then, because I hoped to develop an informed discussion, I tried to think of a favorite older poem that combined the real world with its actual mysteries.

James Wright's "To the Muse" came instantly to mind, and serves as an excellent prototype. It opens with simple, declarative sentences:

> It is all right. All they do
> Is go in by dividing
> One rib from another.

Yet the poem undercuts any feeling of assurance. The rest of the first stanza increases the discomfort but does, in the end, reveal that the poet is speaking to an intimate—someone named Jenny the speaker has known over years. By the time Wright says "I lead you back to the world," the reader is aware that Jenny has drowned. "Three lady doctors in Wheeling open / Their offices at night." Rhythm—those three iambic ladies—carries the mystery forward. What follows (complete with wire, contraption, needle, tube) is an accurate and detailed description for medically treating a collapsed lung. There is also the mounting sense that this poem *matters*:

> I wish to God I had made this world, this scurvy
> And disastrous place. I
> Didn't, I can't bear it
> Either, I don't blame you, sleeping down there
> Face down in the unbelievable silk of spring.

Mutating from "I wouldn't / Lie to you" to "I would lie to you / If I could," the poem pivots on contradiction. Of course one suspects suicide ("didn't" and "either" act as qualifiers). Now the line breaks disrupt the flow of sense; a string of commas replicates the flow of less-rational emotion; internal rhymes ("place" and "face") catch at the ear; repetitions ("down there" / "face down") push her further away as the "suckhole" of the second stanza is transformed into the "silk of spring." Resurrection is only possible in the imagination.

"How can I live without you?" This plea is surely neither surreal nor symbolic. It's a cry from the heart, but it's not maudlin, not when it's followed by "Come up to me, love / Out of the river / Or I will come down to you." There's that word "down" again. Because of the poem's title, we realize that this is actually a subtle statement—that poetry tugs us under, connects us to the past and to each other, reveals the "scurvy" world as something to be wrestled with. By drawing on the world's intrinsic images, Wright's poem is an attempt at clarification, not obfuscation. My question becomes rhetorical. Why not strive for such an eloquent, intuitive mystery?

"This is poetry, not just words thrown together, not just ideology and hot button stuff," says Dorianne Laux of Michael Mlekoday's *The Dead Eat*

Every Thing, her selection for Kent State's Stan and Tom Wick Poetry Prize. The unexpected declares itself early—"you write poems / like they brass knuckles"—but it takes only a second glance at "Self-Portrait with Gunshot Vernacular" to realize that such language is how the poet denotes the raw realities of his old neighborhood, full of the actual juxtapositions that depict life on that side of the tracks. We step into the surprising and nuanced ghetto world of Polish immigrants, a superstitious grandmother, churches and curses and physical violence.

A progression of other "Self-Portraits" (with subtitles such as "Wearing Bear Skull as Mask," "July," "Downtown," "with Pollination," "Fat Tuesday," "with Blight," "from the Other Side," "with Power Outage," "with Big City Religion," "Wherein Everything Whirrs with the Spirit," "after Drive-By," and "Kneeling") highlights or underscores the sense of then and now as the speaker explores his own background in light of a deliberate "otherness." Under the mask of a bear, the human body goes through a series of imaginative transformations. "You are . . . you are . . ." on down the page, looking out through strange eyes. The poem ends by bringing a remembered boy back to reality:

> but you are still just skull and imagined claw
> to the world, just the dumb perfect body
> of death. You stopped speaking long ago.
> You haven't eaten yet today,
> and the world looks bright as winter.

The world wakes from hibernation. By skirting the perimeters of surrealism, Mlekoday preserves the visual even as he renews language. His cadences provide active energy, so it's not surprising to discover that he is a Slam champion. So often, the vocal poems of Slam work only on the stage; they fail to persist as poetry on the page. Here, however, the poems incorporate the spoken word rather than rely on it. The long sixteen-section central self-portrait ("with Blight") rollicks and repeats its way toward its final "Amen." The *s* and *r* richness of one short segment demonstrates how written words might be doubly effective as they "flash" in performance:

> When I was growing up, I thought
> it was normal for police searchlights
> to shine into apartment windows
> every once in a while. A natural
> cycle of nights. The way the moon
> reflects in every river, makes itself big
> before recoiling. They snaked across walls,
> reshaped the shadows. Never any news

of what they were looking for, what they found.
Just the lights and then dark. Lights and then dark.
Lights and then dark.

If sound dominates this book, it is sound less in service of elegy than of reincarnation. In the third section, the dead materialize to make a claim on the past. Dogs still roam, the father still lies dying, *Baba* is "still bootlegging white lightning / nightly," gunshots make their brushfire noises—such references haunt the old streets even as they define the meaning of "home." Everything—every thing—is brought to bear on retrieving identity. Follow the intricate vestiges of device and craft into the tunnel of self: "Become the bridge / falling into the water." "I, river, everything becomes me," the speaker asserts in "Flood," and then reiterates

        I, river, I,
I, I, I.
        My name
floods
        away from me.
I raise my feet to the table.
I listen to traffic and rain
and my pulse is both.

Michael Mlekoday has that rare voice that crosses the boundaries between public and private performance, and in "Maker" he explores the physical nature of those borders:

Without mouth, the body is
a closed circuit. Without
meat, I eat only microphone
& make
        only sad boom bap
-less sex.

The third, and final, section of *The Dead Eat Every Thing* begins to sound like an extended prayer, but its language is as lively as imprecation. Even as it is having fun with oddball adjectives and crazy combinations, it insists on being taken seriously. I believe this poet when he declares, "The halo is more / hard hat than headrest. Do not tell me / to rest in peace."

"Thaumaturgy" records, "I've never / seen the ocean" and Mlekoday's online academic biography states, "He has never seen the ocean," yet I take in the fact that this poet has seen "a bloodstain shaped like a wave." Without skipping a beat, his ocean and mine are one. I predict that we'll hear much more from Michael Mlekoday as he finds his way through the maze of possible directions his work could take. I hope he will not stray too far from this passionate spirit that engages ear, eye, mind, and heart.

If my perception is correct that recent first books are now less the province of the very young writer, then I should not be surprised that the content of first books has shifted to reflect the various concerns of adulthood: marriage, children, divorce, aging, etc. Kerrin McCadden's *Landscape with Plywood Silhouettes* was selected for the New Issues Poetry Prize by David St. John, who calls the book "mature and tender." The ubiquitous black plywood silhouettes found throughout New England might well be stand-ins for true-life experience, and are certainly substitutes for the various town characters McCadden includes in her register, giving them voice and/or finding insight into their circumstance and outlook. The silhouettes have been courting for years, he leaning against the trailer and she under the apple tree. They look sidelong at each other, carrying on their imaginary conversations. Aside from the fun the poet is having, there's a basic human lesson built into their condition:

They dream and dream, notwithstanding
the way the layers of plywood have gapped in the weather
over the years since they began trying to bridge the void
inside their outlines, which is all we are ever able to do.

McCadden divulges her core concerns in a series of titles: "How to Miss a Man," "How to Say Goodbye," "Love Poem Not for a Husband," "Once, I Was Not Lonely," and "Apology, Its Absence." The list almost tells its own story, but each of these poems contains more surprise than confirmation. Throughout, the speaker measures emotion in units of geography: "This is the kind of island I was," and "Here is the acre after the string of words and before / the reply." "The Death of the Reader" unfolds with a variety of reasons the speaker can no longer read, mostly due to the demise of "the forty / open acres of marriage." We do not need long to recognize the landscape of loss, but in McCadden's hands loss is less primary focus than background, woven through daily sights and sounds, children and chores and choices. In "What I Said to the Night," the speaker delineates the lonely plight of the single mother:

I walked upstairs, downstairs. I made myself

busy with Christmas, with a nap. I made
overtures to the night. I stood on the back
deck & threw my palms up in the cold.

Line breaks emphasize meaning here. "I made myself," she announces; i.e., this is my doing. "Made / back / cold." Winter creeps everywhere in the periphery.

Repetition belongs to McCadden as much as to Mlekoday, but hers is more a tangle of sentiment. "Here . . . here . . . here . . . or . . . or . . . or . . ."—the variations play themselves out against each other as the poet tries on alternatives, dresses up in different lives, thinks her way into might-haves and might-bes. In "How to Miss a Man," the poet fashions an intricate scaffolding for argument: "Breathing is just a rhythm. Tell yourself this. . . ." Then, later, "Also, breathe. It is a rhythm. Walk / around the block. . . ." And later: "Your feet will take you. They can. If you listen / / they are a rhythm also. . . ." Even later: "Hold. Breathe. / / Hold. Breathe. Like that, like you are swimming . . ."—right up to her finale:

> You can draw two
> lines on a graph that can never touch. This is what you are building.

"Ante Up" raises issues of parallel lives, of what she would give up: books, but not letters; the farm, but "not the paths / / worn into the fields." More:

> I would give up all the lakesides, but not the late afternoons.
> The dusk sky, even, but not the swallows. The front and back door,
> but not the neighbors. The map, but not the way here.

Here is an emotional terrain that McCadden mines with facility. The material may be fraught, but these poems are shaped and refined. A quibble: more than once, I felt as though the poem had ended only to find another line or two. McCadden's strength is the stanza; she finds novel ways to organize and orchestrate so that we are not privy to spontaneous personal anguish but to the *idea* of anguish and how it can be added to the vocabulary. This is most evident in the middle section of "Insomnia," where words themselves soothe and console:

> When the body is sleeping, there is sift, shuttle, meter. Shift,
> treadle, metronome. Lift, settle, measure.

Sift/shift/lift combines with the voluble movement of the loom (shuttle/treadle/settle), and those sounds, in turn, remind us that poetry—meter/metronome/measure—offers a way to make sense through music and craft. I prefer this subtle suggestion to her more overt poems about poetry. I look forward to following Kerrin McCadden into new territory. We can rely on her for more than a rendition of life experience; we can count on her to create a reflective world for us to enter.

David Koehn's *Twine*, selected by Jeff Friedman, won the May Sarton Poetry Prize, and Bauhan Publishing has done a beautiful production which highlights the more formal poems in the collection. Sestina, villanelle, sonnet, terza rima—Koehn has mastered them all, and then he's concocted unique variations that provide a charge of energy. It's almost as if he had taken a guide to poetic terms and experimented with every entry. He also finds ways to incorporate words that my poor dictionary has held its tongue over. "Camphorous," "mycelium," "globuliformis," "hemimetabolous," "scuppernong," "thalassic," "mirroneurons," "pantagruelists," "dithyrambic": these spicy tongue-twisters add vim and vigor as they force the reader to "Jam / tongue into syllables." There is no doubt in my mind that Koehn could take on any poetic task—anyone who employs the backward rhyme of "risen" and "resin" has my admiration—so my only question is . . . what is *his* underlying question?

It's abundantly clear that David Koehn is fascinated by scientific phenomena. In addition, he loves detail: stanzas filled with movie lore, including names, dates, every other kind of specific; lines full of statistics; a plethora of *things* such as Red Man tobacco, Royal Crown Cola, hula-hoops, cisterns, raspberries, mannequins, mayflies, the Delta flight from Cincinnati. A glance at some of the titles—"The Taxi Driver," "Swimming Laps at High Altitude," "The Attempted Assassination of Jules Verne," "The Graffiti Artist Settles in the Eskimo Village," "Shopping at Williams-Sonoma," and "Communications in Accordance with Article 5, Paragraph 1 of the Agreement on the Rescue of Astronauts, the Return of Astronauts, and the Return of Objects Launched into Outer Space Partial Pantoum"—shows such a wide range of subject matter that diversity itself seems to be the glue holding the book together. The contemporary "ringtone" is as endangered as the nearly-extinct lunch tins, clothespin bags, and VHF antennae. Often a moment is "defined by what it is not." We are forced to look at each poem individually; each plays out on its own terms, and so often the terms are illuminated—and complicated—by invention.

Koehn repeatedly distills the particulars of some moment. For example, "Cottage at Red Bluff" locates itself in the title, then locks in detail through intricate slant rhyme:

> A picket fence, a white border, its shale steeps
> Wind-whipped with mosquito husks. Askew, stairs step
>
> Down to a beach of layered scales, the revenge
> Of wave-packed shale, its beveled rock avenged
>
> By mendicant winds thwacking the cottage's shutters
> A lopsided shipwreck of picnic, fire, and weather.
>
> The rain's squall line, a distant ghost net. Clank
> Go the close-enough horseshoes. "Close enough," we say,

"That is close enough." Against the wave-worn veneer,
Parched on the edge of the water's memory,

The abandoned plow on the beach, figurehead, prow,
Grandfather's wake, spinning in the undertow.

Internal rhyme—shale/scales; whipped/ship; packed/thwacking/wreck/wake—is further reinforced by alliteration and assonance. Somehow this poem becomes all the more personal as we watch the poet at play, working his words. "Parched" suggests "perched" (probably because of the word "edge") even as it harks back to water; water's memory (and we do believe it has one) thus holds thirst along with the sense of several generations who have loved this place.

The opening of "The Windmills of Altamont Pass" generates the whirling blades of repetition. The cyclical internal markers give the poem intellectual force:

The hills are the hulls of upside-down boats;
The rotations sprinkler the vineyard:

Herb garden, wine press, fishbones.
Canary date palms spread like an idea of

The rotations: Sprinkler. The vineyard's
Tractor tires, now gardens, now sandboxes.

After thirteen such couplets, the poem again situates itself with its title for a closing tercet, reminiscent of the way a sestina gathers its end words or a villanelle marshals its potent lines:

The hills are the hulls of upside-down boats:
The windmills of Altamont Pass.
Herb garden, wine press, fishbones.

Poem after poem provides this kind of ingenious pleasure. We cross the threshold of a finely drawn personal world, colored by intense observation, and often underscored through levity. Endings allow Koehn to leave us shaking our heads: of a girl in white skates, "The strings of crystal lace, the thread of & and &"; of a suitcase with thirty-five cubic feet of space, "enough for any life."

Twine is an extremely accomplished first book. The ending of "The Aquarium at the Potluck" could serve as an *ars poetica*:

A shadow of light passes through the room like a shark.
What is it that brings us together, and keeps us apart?
What holds us in our frame, suspended? What art?"

I have to admit to being more smitten with the formal distances of the book's first section. In the absence of a strong narrative thread, and in the presence of such density, I suspect the collection is probably just a little bit too long, maybe too much of a good thing. Shaping the whole as meticulously as the individual poems would have resulted in something even more impressive, but if David Koehn continues to give us this blend of the formal and the idiosyncratic, it won't be long before readers of poetry easily recognize his name.

Winner of the *Cider Press Review*'s Editors' Prize, Laura Donnelly's *Watershed* quickly establishes itself as proficient. Craft, here, is more often than not found in its rhythms. I use the plural because there are two *types* of rhythm here. One is meter—the poetry flows with subtly accentuated beats. The other is the interrupted rhythm of thought—each poem builds its separate trajectory in order to follow its own deliberative process. Each is thus "personalized" by an interior voice as the two rhythms combine to establish what might be termed its "individuality." The cadences of the spoken word leap off the page, and reading them becomes a kind of conversation.

Watershed begins with "Anamnesis," a litany of what the speaker is "not forgetting": swing set, fireflies, dance, fireworks, junior high—right up to "Not forgetting even our not-knowing." From the outset, imperfect knowledge becomes an issue, and the speaker questions not only her own experiences but those of others as well. So much needs to be qualified; she retracts or corrects, equivocates, pauses to change direction, comments on her very hesitations—and all of this is in pursuit of a delicate precision, not of detail but of distinction. For Donnelly, nuance *is* accuracy. In "Letter from Stonington," it matters whether a boat is called *Hermitage* or *Heritage*; it is important to know, even if one is not willing to say:

> We fought on our way to the island.
> I don't recall why, or I do
>
> now, something about motorcycles
> and death, but it doesn't
>
> bear repeating.

This same tendency toward exactitude can be seen in the proliferation of qualifying phrases ("of course," "but that isn't it," "as if"), and it's also the source of self-interrogation in the form of clarifying questions. The reader is taken into the mind at work so that any observation about music, or painting, or even family, is really an exploration of the self.

The concept of "flickering" becomes a guiding principle. Thinking about Malevich's painting of the knife-grinder, Donnelly applies his theories of movement to all of life. Everything is in motion, even the still life that can be animated, a bit like a flip-book cartoon. Even the human relationships that made Bonnard turn his wife's head to allow her some privacy. Even the music—Casals playing Bach—where the notes "wait always / for someone to touch them again, for that / / same, not-quite-same-again flight—." (This unexpected insight may be the best definition of "interpretation" I have ever encountered.) Later in the book, Donnelly returns to music, realizing that "scale after skeleton scale" can only approximate the "flesh" of the piece and might actually get in the way of what was heard.

Endings may be Donnelly's strength. If so, it's because she earns them by building an intricate edifice of reflection that leads to their surprising truths. Sometimes the "I" at the end is an accumulated personality; sometimes the "I" is introduced to underscore the fact that there is an exterior sensibility paying its own attention to the poem's underlying meanings. To quote endings might imply her way of "wrapping up," but really her closures confirm and reconnect. They also surprise:

> World no longer flat, I've seen how the wind blowing
> one direction comes back to haunt from another.
> ("Saint Reparata")

And confront:

> Irresponsible want.
> Irresistible spring that cares
> nothing for what we have done,
> what it does in return.
> ("Watershed")

And extend:

> *It will shatter*
> *if you walk through*, someone warns.
> It would shatter if I didn't.
> ("Once, in the door of")

If anything, *Watershed* may be too short. Family members "flicker" in and out of the poems; even the works that are ostensibly about art or music often have familial underpinnings. Lost father, estranged brother, scientific mother, the lover who helps shape the speaker's thoughts: they hover at the edges, broken into stilled components like the paintings Donnelly describes. They whet the appetite.

There are other issues left mostly to the reader's imagination: childlessness, anger, absence, the singular poetic "O" of longing. Often, we are granted only the "meanwhiles"—the interstices that give the poems their latent energy. Laura Donnelly has such a sure way with orchestration that I believe she might well pursue the "nots" at the center of her work. Further exploration might satisfy some of the reader's natural curiosity without destroying the elusive quality that lends tact and grace to this endeavor—and beyond grace, honesty. In "Possum," Donnelly's correctness in describing late spring in upstate New York makes her description of the animal that will come pressing its nose at the sliding glass door all the more convincing. Her realistic conclusion is yet another dimension in her inventory of negative capabilities:

> But we take it
> for what it is—not omen.

Watershed just may serve as a watershed. Or as a genuine omen. Laura Donnelly has waited long enough for this first collection that it has arrived with all the accomplishment of a later book. Her voice feels instantly necessary, even compulsory.

Keeper, by Kasey Jueds, opens with a poem that deserves to be seen in its entirety:

> First dark, then more dark
> smoothed down over it.
>
> First sleep, then eyes
> open to the ceiling
> where something circles. For a moment
> you can't name it. And for a moment
>
> you're not afraid. Remember
>
> Blake's angels, how they leaned
> toward each other, and balanced
> by touching only the tips of their wings?
> Between their bodies, a space
>
> like the one just after rain begins, when rain
> isn't rain, but the smell
> of dust lifted, something silent and clean.

Spare and elegant, a bit like a Zen garden, the lines circle and balance as the poem proceeds to open the world—that distinct smell that *is* rain, that knowledge of what rain can sometimes be. So it comes as no surprise to me that the University of Pittsburgh Press selected this book for the prestigious Agnes Lynch Starrett Award. This debut collection is nearly perfect—measured, never pretending to ask more than it can deliver, and yet producing poem after proportional poem with a satisfying precision. "Balance" might be the exact word to express what Jueds is striving for. Typically her poems advance by association, then take a small sidestep (often over an enjambed stanza break) and go on, creating a sense of the inevitable.

Enjambment may be Kasey Jueds's most effective tool. In her hands, words blink on, assert their multiple meanings, thrust the poem forward, twist back on themselves, hold the poem hostage to nuance. Oddly, though enjambment usually allows for a kind of syncopation, here it seems to smooth the rhythms in such a way that meaning is elucidated and intensified. Along with varied lines, each adjective, each simile, is—and this is the best word I can find—fitting. And yet each adjective, each simile, seems unique, even matchless: the "train's brief scribble of smoke"; the "winter-polished" fields of Wisconsin; even the mine pit's "extravagant black."

In fact, Jueds explores darkness—its condition—from more angles than would seem possible. For example, in "A Kind of Vanishing" the inside of a tin mailbox is compared to the total darkness of an abandoned silver mine, but all of this is in service of an imagined envelope: "How perfect the things / we are not meant to see." But the poet also touches on the things meant to be seen, as in "The Sleeping Gypsy" where she looks hard at the dark night of Rousseau's painting, noting the wind in the lion's mane, the lack of wind on the sleeper's robe. At this point, she eschews description in favor of poetry's other upshot: "Let him be touched. / Let him sense breath, wind, / another, wilder body's tide."

Kasey Jueds has an uncanny sense of the way things are of a piece—even the absences: those hollow birds' bones with an "emptiness at the center that lets them fly." Uncanny, too, the places where *Keeper* intersects with Laura Donnelly's *Watershed.* There's the same focus on music, art, and swimming, the same basic images (swings, parallel tracks, even the same painting by Bonnard, though Jueds has her focus on the model, not the painter). Scattered throughout the book, related poems on the names of flowers, the habits of birds, cave paintings, the human/seal selkies of Scots and Irish lore, dead animals, shark and skin and blood—all do double duty, reinforcing each other even as they launch ideas in new directions.

Knitting, for example, becomes a central metaphor; Jueds not only looks at the "wrong" side of a Fair Isles sweater or the particular cable pattern that allows the body of a drowned fisherman to be identified, she also thinks about the ball of yarn, the raw material. "You start / to see how it's made," the speaker notes, and yes, you begin to see the poem's inner workings. The opening lines of "Secondhand Dress" demonstrate one of Jueds's devices; the writing is lucid and lively as, letting one word or idea slip into (or inside) the next, she creates a seamless knit and purl of her own:

Somewhere between
blue and silver
color that asks
nothing in return
that returns
nothing you know
not river not windows not swallows'
tilting flight

Over and over, Jueds creates the circumstance of waiting, body and mind on alert as the poem hovers in the conditional. This poet is searching for *sources*. Origin. Root cause. Foundation. The opening lines of "The Selkie Returns to the Sea" articulate both impetus and method:

I used to think my longing had an end.
I dreamed the sea so many years, the sea
became a dream.

To this end, Jueds tackles everything with a strong, sure intelligence, unravelling the "reverse sides" in order to see how the world works. There's more to it, though, as the speaker interacts with the very world she has laid bare. Near the end of the title poem, she gives voice to her ambivalence, and its accompanying conflict:

. . . everything is something
I tried to keep, and
couldn't, and can't,
and won't, and won't
stop trying

You can almost hear the catch in the throat, the desire to hold on to the "everything" of experience. But, the speaker in "Mackerel Sky" insists, "Seems we can only look / a little at a time." This outstanding collection is the result of that careful, microscopic looking, and from the attention this poet has paid to her sinuous craft. Kasey Jueds is a keeper.

Coda:

I took a look at some online commentary on Wright's "To the Muse" and found myself appalled. So many assumptions. Such glib assertions. If we are going to expect our poets to have some sense of tradition and ask that they bring their own form of music to their task, then we must demand something of readers as well.

To my knowledge, Wright never had a wife named Jenny, no wife who died of breast cancer; the procedure described in the poem is certainly *not* an abortion; this poem is *no*t about Adam and Eve; James Wright did *not* commit suicide; there were nine muses, not three; and the doctors can remain doctors. Even the myth of Orpheus does not really apply (though it may hover as a kind of "ghost").

Where do all these "critical" assertions come from? Most of these "readings" would (I hope, even today) never be accepted by any creditable journal—and this is important to note if we are going to maintain anything that even resembles critical standards. Those standards get lost, too, as many journals print criticism so full of theory that the poems vanish in the process. My recommendation: a good dollop of common sense—and, if we want to toss around "facts," a bit of fact-checking.

Simple use of the web would have provided those self-proclaimed critics with some accurate information. Yes, the poem mentions ribs, breast, snake, doctors, river, night—but they have a context that needs to be considered. "To the Muse" adds itself to a long list of works Wright wrote for or about the disenfranchised, the forgotten, the poor and unwanted. It is not about him, except in his ability to identify and empathize and grieve. The grief is both personal and general—and that is an important distinction.

Readers do not have to know Wright's biography, but they cannot—should not—simply reach into their meager bags of personal associations. They need to know some basic facts of the world, need to note the emotional tenor of the poem, and . . . something else: they need to see how poetic craft shapes meaning, need to pay attention to stanzaic structure, to line breaks, to periods and commas and repetitions—and to sound. The unmistakably emphasized "do" and "you" of Wright's earlier stanzas gives over to the long *o* of "alone" and "know" before the poem returns to a final "you" (the "muse"—whose vowel sound makes for further connection). The word “alone” appears twice—once at the end of a line, once on a line by itself—reinforcing the finality of death, its singularity. Poet and subject: each is alone, and the divide cannot be bridged except by the poem.

So, readers and would-be reviewers—please, oh please, honor what a poet has actually accomplished. Honor the mysteries uncovered and explored. Speak a little tentatively. Do not indulge in easy conclusions that are merely surreal in their own right. Let language lead you by going where it has to go.

Appendix

NOTES ON THE OTHER TWENTY-EIGHT ESSAYS not included in this collection, with short excerpts (selected by the author) from the introductions plus a list of books and authors discussed.

Summer 2014: "When the River Is Ice"

"Each of the four poets discussed here veers away from the intense self-questioning of the original Confessionals and . . . begins with the premise that the self does not take center stage, but exists within a larger context. . . . It may just be that judicious distance actually makes the poem *more* personal."

On Andrea Hollander's *Landscape with Female Figure: New and Selected Poems, 1982–2012*; Sophie Cabot Black's *The Exchange*; Sean Hill's *Dangerous Goods*; and Linda Bierds's *Roget's Illusion*.

Fall 2013: "Register, Resonate, Ring"

"With [Joseph] Epstein's printed words ('the poetry game is over, kaput, fini, time, gentlemen, time') now rattling around in *my* head, I've decided to look for poetry that still lives and breathes. I want to see how, despite the death knells, . . . poets can find ways to 'register, resonate, ring.'"

On Bruce Beasley's *Theophobia*; Annette Spaulding-Convy's *In Broken Latin*; Bill Neumire's *Estrus*; and Stanley Plumly's *Orphan Hours*.

Winter 2011: "Tradecraft"

"[Spies] are like writer and reader, shadowing each other, playing cat and mouse, slinking down dark cobblestone streets with collars pulled up around their ears, each trying to outthink the other while waiting for some move that will reveal what was always suspected. "

On Adam Foulds's *The Broken Word*; Melissa Range's *Horse and Rider*; Nick Lantz's *We Don't Know We Don't Know*; and Alice Friman's *Vinculum*.

Spring 2010: "Great Expectations"

"We keep asking our writers to "grow" when it's not clear what we mean, yet I find myself examining books with precisely this request hovering in the back of my mind. In other words, I often compare an author to his or her earlier self, and I look for thematic or technical progressions—something to show me which directions the work is going to take, and what is of new concern to the writer."

On Colum McCann's *Let the Great World Spin*; Graham Swift's *Making an Elephant: Writing from Within*; Heather McHugh's *Upgraded to Serious*; David Baker's *Never-ending Birds*; Fred Chappell's *Shadow Box*; and Jess Walter's *The Financial Lives of the Poets*.

Fall 2009: "Seconds"

"Second books are difficult. Unless the poet achieves a complete departure from the first (thus, effectively, writing two first books), he or she needs to establish a widening range and a deepening understanding to differentiate the new poems from the earlier work. Yet surely something must also link the two books, remind the reader that these poems are the beginning of something that promises to grow larger."

On Sharon Olds's *One Secret Thing*; *The Dream We Carry: Selected and Last Poems of Olav V. Hauge*, translated by Robert Bly and Robert Hedin; Kevin Goodan's *Winter Tenor*; Richard Kenny's *The One-Strand River*; and Carl Phillips' *Speak Low*.

Winter 2008: "Keeping Company"

"Fascinating how, in one or two sentences, so much can be said about poetry—its ways of 'being,' its resistance to 'meaning,' its value, and its values. Juxtapose one person's few sentences with another's pithy remark, and a lively dialogue ensues."

On *Quote Poet Unquote*, edited by Dennis O'Driscoll; Lars Gustaffson's *A Time in Xanadu*; Todd Boss's *Yellowrocket*; Paisley Rekdal's *The Invention of the Kaleidoscope*; M. R. Peacocke's *In Praise of Aunts*; Kevin Prufer's *National Anthem*; Rick Barot's *Want*; and David Huddle's *Glory River*.

Fall/Winter 2006: "The Letter of the Life"

"The voices I encountered in these books [of letters] are clearly distinctive—and separate from the poems. They are at once more intimate, more candid, more easily emotional. Or less formally rigorous, less universal, less linguistically complex. I can only conclude that the difference resides in the fact that letters have an intended reader. Their means of expression is that of presence. When one speaks to the void (or the world), the speech is far more isolated and inimitable; the poem is breathed into that netherworld where language moves beyond personality. The letter wants to connect, so much so that it often fails to do so. The poem assumes no connections, and therefore makes them possible."

On Renée and Theodore Weiss's *The Always Present Present: Letters-Poems*; *The Letters of Robert Lowell*, edited by Saskia Hamilton; *A Wild Perfection: The Selected Letters of James Wright*, edited by Anne Wright and Saundra Rose Maley; and *Love, Amy: The Selected Letters of Amy Clampitt*, edited by Willard Spiegelman.

Spring 2006: "Grouching toward Bethlehem: A Look at First Books"

"What I sensed in most of these first books, however, was an external world—one where the internal is essentially covert and the poem plays out on an imaginative screen where anything might happen, and does, as long as the poet can fend off self-confrontation and/or turn it into something cleverly shrouded in irony."

On Christian Hawkey's *The Book of Funnels*; Elizabeth Edwards' *The Chronic Liar Buys a Canary*; Gina Franco's *The Keepsake Storm*; John Brehm's *Sea of Faith*; Amy Fleury's *Beautiful Trouble*; and Kevin Goodan's *In the Ghost-House Acquainted.*

Spring 2005: "The Properties of Rain"

"Only the rain is tame—gauzy and indistinct, a bit like memory itself, a presence in the air, something felt but not quite seen. There's a sheen on the pavement, a damp chill at the back. Yet I am drenched in speculation. What if I took one image—rain—and charted its course in the hands of several poets? What would it tell me about the landscape of metaphor?"

On Linda Allardt's *Accused of Wisdom*; Chris Forhan's *The Actual Moon, The Actual Stars*; Pattiann Rogers' *Generations*; Ted Kooser's *Delight and Shadows*; Sherod Santos' *The Perishing*; and Carl Phillips' *The Rest of Love.*

Summer 2004: "RowRow"

"Who first discovered that the three ascending stressed syllables of "gently down the stream" could be paired with the four descending dactyls of "merrily merrily merrily merrily" and they would be harmonious? That the body could adjust its timing so perfectly? But when we read, we do not so much *adjust to* as *listen for*. That is, we wait for a comparable ear, and then we chime in, singing."

On Robert Wrigley's *Lives of the Animals*; Heather McHugh's *Eyeshot*; Edward Hirsch's *Lay Back the Darkness*; and Marvin Bell's *Rampant*.

Spring 2004: "Second Thoughts: On Re-Reading Robert Lowell"

"I've missed him. Crazy, because he's been sitting on my shelves, twenty-eight books . . . some of them first editions, some "extras," (just in case), the collected prose, Hamilton's biography, Jonathan Raban's selections, and four critical studies. He takes up half a shelf . . . but I've missed him."

On Robert Lowell's *Collected Poems*, edited by Frank Bidart and David Gewanter.

Winter 2003: "Anthologizing—The Good, The Bad, and the Indifferent"

"To anthologize is to compromise, so the reader of any anthology needs to know the work well enough to recognize omissions—and their implications. Yet anthologies are aimed at precisely the other kind of reader—one who is relying on the anthology for some guidance, or worse (as in the classroom), relying on it to be definitive."

On *Word of Mouth: Poems Featured on NPR's "All Things Considered,"* edited by Catherine Bowman; *Poetry 180: A Turning Back to Poetry*, edited by Billy Collins; *Stand Up Poetry: An Expanded Anthology*, edited by Charles Harper Webb; *Hammer and Blaze: A Gathering of Contemporary American Poets*, edited by Ellen Bryant Voigt and Heather McHugh; *The Norton Anthology of Modern and Contemporary Poetry*, 3rd ed., edited by Jahan Ramazani, Richard Ellmann, and Robert O'Clair; *Good Poems*, edited by Garrison Keillor; and *Poems to Read: A New Favorite Poem Project Anthology*, edited by Robert Pinsky and Maggie Dietz.

Summer 2003: "In Trouble"

"[Poets] act as though they might be able to change people's minds, or at least cause them to consider the issues. In doing so, they also take on the responsibility of what they say—and how they say it. If they present something as "fact," then that fact is subject to scrutiny. If they present something as imagined, then the nature and direction of their imagination is subject to scrutiny. And their silences, too, are subject to scrutiny."

On Kevin Prufer's *The Finger Bone*; William Olsen's *Trouble Lights*; Sam Hamill's *Dumb Luck*; Deborah Cummins' *Beyond the Reach*; and Eamon Grennan's *Still Life with Waterfall.*

Summer 2002: "Thinking About Love"

"Most love poems are not about love at all. 'Christ, that my love were in my arms'—but already there is loss, and absence. Lost love, it seems, lasts longer than its opposite."

On Gregory Orr's *Orpheus and Eurydice*; Eavan Boland's *Against Love Poetry*; Andrea Hollander Budy's *The Other Life*; Carl Phillips' *The Tether*; Louise Gluck's *The Seven Ages*; Jane Hirshfield's *Given Sugar, Given Salt*; and James Richardson's *Vectors: Aphorisms and Ten-Second Essays.*

Summer 2001: "Q & A"

"[S]ong alone is not sufficient to establish a "voice." It seems to me that there is something else, a psychology, if you will, or an outlook (maybe an *in*look) that establishes the relationship of the poet to the world. . . . It's the old nature vs. nurture question in another guise: is "voice" something you are born with, or something you acquire?"

On Conor O'Callaghan's *Seatown and Earlier Poems*; Lia Purpura's *Stone Sky Lifting*; Ralph Black's *Turning Over the Earth*; and Marvin Bell's *Nightworks: Poems, 1962–2000.*

Summer 2000: "The Subjective Correlative"

"Assuming that all poems are subjective in some sense of the word, I find it interesting to note the relative proportions of the public and the private, the ways that individual poets move into and out of the public sphere. I'm increasingly interested in how a poem achieves its degree of subjectivity or objectivity, and whether these change in some fashion as history relegates the poem to its particular era or circumstance."

On Marcia Southwick's *A Saturday Night at the Flying Dog and Other Poems*; Lynn Emanuel's *Then, Suddenly*; Dana Levin's *In the Surgical Theatre*; Jorie Graham's *Swarm*; and Philip Booth's *Lifelines: Selected Poems, 1950–1999.*

Winter 1999: "A Flash and an Hour"

"I read too many poems that fail to recognize what might be their genuine emotion. They do not struggle with the ineffable; rather, they avoid the struggle altogether, settling for what *can* be said, for what can be told and then made something of: reportorial, strangely unimaginative poems. . . . There is no flash, no hour, in which I re-inhabit myself and realize just what it is to have been alive in the rarefied light of the mind of another."

On Ida Affleck Grave's *The Calfbearer*; Laura Kasischke's *Fire & Flower*; Tony Hoagland's *Donkey Gospel*; Robert Hedin's *The Old Liberators: New and Selected Poems and Translations*; and Lola Haskins' *Extranjera*.

Summer 1998: "Simplicities"

"That there will be more than one simplicity, or that simplicity will be achieved in a number of ways, is a natural postulation. But to probe the core of a poem is to search, like the physicists, for the Big Bang. To examine the structure is to build, brick by brick, the framework of the poet's world. And to attempt to articulate the complexity that necessarily surrounds clarity is the biggest challenge of all."

On Jo McDougall's *From Darkening Porches*; Kinereth Gensler's *Journey Fruit: Poems and a Memoir*; Marie Howe's *What the Living Do*; Joan Aleshire's *The Yellow Transparents*; and Brendan Galvin's *Sky and Island Light*.

Winter 1997: "I Gotta Use Words"

"Maybe we demand too much, flit through poetry as if we were surfing the Net, impatient with the hard work it takes to discern subtle changes. And new voices—what do we expect from them? Usually we want to be startled into new vision, to be seduced by a voice so compelling that it won't leave us alone."

On Elizabeth Holmes' *The Patience of the Cloud Photographer*; Sandy Solomon's *Pears, Lake, Sun*; Laure-Anne Bosselaar's *The Hour Between Dog and Wolf*; Annie Finch's *Eve*; Cal Bedient's *Candy Necklace*; Marilyn Nelson's *The Fields of Praise: New and Selected Poems;* and Marvin Bell's *Ardor: The Book of the Dead Man, Volume 2*.

Winter 1996: "A Convention of Things"

"The writer trusts something inherent in the image and, at the same time, trusts the reader to understand its significance. . . . The miracle is how often the poem is able to cross its own Continental Divide. . . . Emotional geography is the terrain we enter when we read poetry, and its real value disappears if we lose sight of this fact."

On Christianne Balk's *Desiring Flight*; Allison Funk's *Living at the Epicenter*; Anita Feng's *Internal Strategies*; Stephen Dunn's *Loosestrife*; and Sharon Bryan's *Flying Blind*.

Winter 1995: "A Terrible Beauty: The Politics in Poetry"

"To the extent that a poet's overriding concerns are personal, the poem can expand with each successive reading. Or shrink to nothing. To the extent that those concerns are public, the poet runs the risk of immediate impact followed by rapid obsolescence, but the poem also has the chance of becoming a shaping force. A terrible beauty may burn for all time."

A review of Nadine Gordimer's *Writing and Being*; Carolyn Forché's *The Angel of History*; Charles Simic's *A Wedding in Hell*; Dionisio D. Martinez's *Bad Alchemy*; Donna Masini's *That Kind of Danger*; Paul Muldoon's *The Prince of the Quotidian* and *The Annals of Chile*.

Summer 1995: "Fourteen Ways of Looking at Selecteds"

"Furthermore, because selecteds have the feel of the posthumous, they invite an assessment; the reader can note the way the poet has expanded on early themes or has shifted focus, the way certain poems have gained or lost importance in a larger context."

On *The Darkness Around Us Is Deep: Selected Poems of William Stafford*, edited by Robert Bly; Heather McHugh's *Hinge & Sign: Poems, 1968–1993*; Stephen Dobyns' *Velocities: New and Selected Poems, 1966–1992*; Stephen Dunn's *New and Selected Poems, 1974–1994*; David St. John's *Study for the World's Body: New and Selected Poems*; Pattiann Rogers' *Firekeeper: New and Selected Poems*; John Engels' *Walking to Cootehill: New and Selected Poems, 1958–1992*; and Marvin Bell's *A Marvin Bell Reader: Selected Poetry and Prose*.

Fall 1994: "Inner Worlds"

"[Rita} Dove is a woman who, like Bishop, prizes her privacy . . . This is the sort of poetry—intensely felt and affirming the significance of individual experience—that can find a broader audience . . . not written for political ends or merely to an occasion, they arise naturally from the imagination of someone whose inner life is the source of her poetry."

A review of Fleda Brown's *Do Not Peel the Birches*; Janet Holmes's *The Physicist at the Mall*; Lawrence Joseph's *Before Our Eyes*; Sherod Santos' *The City of Women: A Sequence of Poems and Prose*; and Marianne Boruch's *Moss Burning*.

Spring 1994: "A Mind of Winter"

"But these are poems *of* winter, not poems *for* winter. Opening a book in such weather, one longs for the tropical, for words that spill from the page with the high heat of noon. Surely there is a poetry for this season—something to fill abandoned spaces, to dance the fandango."

A review of Albert Goldbarth's *Across the Layers: Poems Old and New*; Susan Howe's *The Nonconformist's Memorial*; Kelly Cherry's *God's Loud Hand*; John Hollander's *Tesserae and Other Poems*; Walid Bitar's *2 Guys on Holy Land*; Martha Collins's *A History of Small Love on a Windy Planet*; and Susan Ludvigson's *Everything Winged Must Be Dreaming*.

Spring 1993: "The Woods Around It"

"How does nature function in contemporary poetry? Have contemporary poets resituated the self in nature with an intimacy as "natural" (note how this common adjective is itself a metaphor) as that which sustained Frost? Conversely, are we inevitably the heirs to Stevens' modernist dualism? Or have we gone past both into something new?"

A review of Kathryn Stripling Byer's *Wildwood Flower*; Mary Oliver's *New and Selected Poems*; Dennis Hinrichsen's *The Rain That Falls This Far*; James Richardson's *As If*; and Louise Glück's *The Wild Iris*.

Fall 1992: "For the Moment: Essential Disguises"

"Poems are made objects. The person who makes the poem is the same person who washes the dishes. But the writer differs from the washer, mainly in his or her conscious *sense* of self, the way the writer becomes (however briefly) "other"—these aspects of a book make up the identity of its temporal (and temporary) human speaker."

A review of William Stafford's *Passwords*; Tess Gallagher's *Moon Crossing Bridge*; Gerald Stern's *Bread Without Sugar*; Agha Shahid Ali's *The Nostalgist's Map of America*; David Baker's *Sweet Home, Saturday Night*; and Nancy Eimers' *Destroying Angel*.

Fall 1991: "Under the Umbrella"

"It is easy to wonder why poetry doesn't count more for us, especially when we have the vivid recent image of Yevgeny Yevtushenko standing next to Boris Yeltsin on the balcony of the Russian "White House," reading a poem to commemorate the day Soviet-style communism began to crumble. There, we feel, is poetry that surely *does* matter. Yet I would caution that the *act* of poetry was what mattered—not the particular poem. . . . His poem, so moving in its context, must still withstand the test of time."

A review of Stephen Dunn's *Landscape at the End of the Century*; Dan Masterson's *World without End*; John Skoyles' *Permanent Change*; Renate Wood's *Raised Underground*; and Anne Douglas' *After*.

Spring/Summer 1990: "A Want Ad"

"While reading books of poetry by women for this review, I found myself questioning, over and over again, whether the poems felt as though they needed to be written, or whether they were somehow "fashioned" in order to create a writing self. . . . The books I've chosen to discuss appealed to me because they went against the current grain in one way or another. And because they held out a variety of directions for women's poetry that might shed some light on women's particular way of knowing."

A review of Elizabeth Seydel Morgan's *Parties*; Janet Kauffman's *Where the World Is*; Emily Hiestand's *Green the Witch-Hazel Wood*; Lisel Mueller's *Waving from Shore*; Rita Dove's *Grace Notes*; and with commentary on *No Man's Land* by Sandra Gilbert and Susan Gubar.